Christianity
through
Non-Christian Eyes

FAITH MEETS FAITH

An Orbis Series in Interreligious Dialogue

Paul F. Knitter, General Editor

In our contemporary world, the many religions and spiritualities stand in need of greater intercommunication and cooperation. More than ever before, they must speak to, learn from, and work with each other, in order to maintain their own identity and vitality and so to contribute to fashioning a better world.

FAITH MEETS FAITH seeks to promote interreligious dialogue by providing an open forum for the exchanges between and among followers of different religious paths. While the series wants to encourage creative and bold responses to the new questions of pluralism confronting religious persons today, it also recognizes the present plurality of perspectives concerning the methods and content of interreligious dialogue.

This series, therefore, does not want to endorse any one school of thought. By making available to both the scholarly community and the general public works that represent a variety of religious and methodological viewpoints, FAITH MEETS FAITH hopes to foster and focus the emerging encounter among the religions of the world.

Already published:

Toward a Universal Theology of Religion, Leonard Swidler, Editor
The Myth of Christian Uniqueness, John Hick and Paul F. Knitter, Editors
An Asian Theology of Liberation, Aloysius Pieris, S.J.
The Dialogical Imperative, David Lochhead
Love Meets Wisdom, Aloysius Pieris, S.J.
Many Paths, Eugene Hillman
The Silence of God, Raimundo Panikkar
The Challenge of the Scriptures, Groupe de Recherches
  Islamo-Chrétien
The Meaning of Christ, John P. Keenan
Hindu-Christian Dialogue, Harold Coward, Editor
The Self-Emptying God, John B. Cobb, Jr. and Christopher Ives, Editors

FAITH MEETS FAITH SERIES

Christianity through Non-Christian Eyes

Paul J. Griffiths, Editor

ORBIS BOOKS

Maryknoll, New York 10545

The Catholic Foreign Mission Society of America (Maryknoll) recruits and trains people for overseas missionary service. Through Orbis Books, Maryknoll aims to foster the international dialogue that is essential to mission. The books published, however, reflect the opinions of their authors and are not meant to represent the official position of the society.

Published by Orbis Books, Maryknoll, NY 10545
Printed in the United States of America

Library of Congress Cataloging-in-Publication Data

Christianity through non-Christian eyes / Paul J. Griffiths, editor.
    p. cm. — (Faith meets faith series)
    Includes bibliographical references.
    ISBN 0-88344-662-6. — ISBN 0-88344-661-8 (pbk.)
    1. Christianity and other religions.   I. Griffiths, Paul J.
  II. Series: Faith meets faith.
BR127.C47428 1990
261.2 — dc20   89-77870
                                                   CIP

This book is for Judith

89444

Contents

Preface

This book originated in an undergraduate theology course I have been teaching at the University of Notre Dame since 1986. The course is entitled "Pluralism and Christian Faith," and one of its goals is to show a largely Roman Catholic undergraduate audience how the problem of religious pluralism appears from beyond the bounds of Christianity. By so doing I have hoped to further understanding of the difficulties involved in a faithful member of one religious community making judgments of any kind about the beliefs and practices of faithful members of religious communities in traditions quite other than his or her own.

I have, I think, learned more from the students who have taken these courses than they have from me; and I would like to make special mention here of Chenoa Seaboy, Philip Lau, Brian McCarthy, Javed Aslam, Juliet Bradley, and Omar al-Farisi.

The University of Notre Dame has been hospitable and supportive during the time I have been thinking about and working on this book. I have benefited especially from conversations with David Burrell, Joseph Wawrykow, Patrick Gaffney, and Roger Brooks. Charles Hallisey has been extremely helpful in suggesting sources, providing addresses, and roundly criticizing the whole enterprise. While I have ignored many of his criticisms, this book would be much worse than it is without his help. Finally, I have learned a great deal from Francis X. Clooney about the problems involved in thinking about adherents of religious communities other than one's own.

Finally, I am delighted that this book appears in the *Faith Meets Faith* series sponsored by Orbis Books. I am grateful to Paul Knitter, the general editor of that series, for his interest in and support of the project, and to Robert Ellsberg and Eve Drogin at Orbis for their help and patience.

Acknowledgments

I am grateful for the following permissions to reprint the pieces found in this volume: to the editors of the *Union Seminary Quarterly Review* (Union Theological Seminary, 3041 Broadway at Reinhold Niebuhr Place, New York, NY 10027), and to Mrs. A. Heschel, for Abraham J. Heschel's "No Religion Is an Island"; to Hippocrene Books (171 Madison Avenue, New York, NY 10016), for Stuart E. Rosenberg's "Christianity and the Holocaust"; to Baker Book House (PO Box 6287, Grand Rapids, MI 49516–6287), for Michael Wyschogrod's "Judaism and Evangelical Christianity"; to the Pontifico Instituto di Studi Arabi e d'Islamica, and to Mohamed Talbi, for Mohamed Talbi's "Islam and Dialogue"; to the Bibliotheca Islamica (PO Box 14474, University Station, Minneapolis, MN 55414) for Fazlur Rahman's "The People of the Book and the 'Diversity of Religions' "; to Mansell Publishing Limited (Artillery House, Artillery Row, London SW1P 1RT, England), for extracts from Syed Muhammad Naquib al-Attas's *Islam, Secularism and the Philosophy of the Future*; to *Concilium* (Pr. Bernhardstr. 2, 6521 AB Nijmegen, Holland), for Seyyed Hossein Nasr's "The Islamic View of Christianity," and for Bithika Mukerji's "Christianity in the Reflection of Hinduism"; to the Buddhist Publication Society (54 Sangharaja Mawatha, PO Box 61, Kandy, Sri Lanka), for extracts from K. N. Jayatilleke's "The Buddhist Attitude to Other Religions"; to Golden Leaves Publishing Company (2190 Wilbur Avenue, Antioch, CA 94509), for extracts from Gunapala Dharmasiri's *A Buddhist Critique of the Christian Concept of God*; to Snow Lion Press (PO Box 6483, Ithaca, NY 14851), for H. H. the XIVth Dalai Lama's "Religious Harmony," and extracts from *The Bodhgaya Interviews*; to the University of Hawaii Press (2840 Kolowalu Street, Honolulu, HI 96822), for Masao Abe's "Self-Awakening and Faith — Zen and Christianity" [this material is © Masao Abe and William R. Lafleur]; to the Soka Gakkai (32 Shinano-machi, Shinjuku-ku, Tokyo 160, Japan), for Ikeda Daisaku's "Scholastic Philosophy and Modern Civilization"; to the Sarvadeshik Arya Pratinidhi Sabha (Dayanand Bhawan, 3/5 Asaf Ali Road, New Delhi 110002, India), for extracts from Dayananda Sarasvati's *The Light of Truth*; to the Advaita Ashrama (5 Dehi Entally Road, Calcutta - 700 014, India), for Swami Vivekananda's "Christ, the Messenger"; to the Navajivan Trust (P.O. Navajivan, Ahmedabad-14, India) for extracts from Mohandas K. Gandhi's *The Story of My Experiments with Truth*; and to Bibhuti S. Yadav for extracts from "Vaishnavism on Hans Küng: A Hindu

Theology of Religious Pluralism," *Religion and Society* 27/2 (1980): 31–44. Extracts from the letter of Franz Rosenzweig to Eugen Rosenstock are reprinted by permission of Kluwer Academic Publishers.

Every effort has been made to contact copyright holders. Our apologies to any who may have been inadvertently omitted.

Christianity
through
Non-Christian Eyes

Introduction

THE CONTENT AND PURPOSE OF THIS BOOK

Content

The main part of the book is divided into four sections: one on Judaism, one on Islam, one on Buddhism, and one on Hinduism. Each section contains a number of essays on Christians and Christianity by representatives of these traditions. Each of these essays is prefaced by some brief biographical comments on its author and, where necessary and relevant, some interpretive comments upon the content of the essay.

Each of the essays is also provided with a certain amount of annotation: notes marked with an asterisk (*) are those given by the author of the piece; these are sometimes supplemented by editorial comments in brackets. Notes without an asterisk are supplied by the editor of this volume. I have, where necessary, altered the bibliographic forms used by the original authors to accord with the usage of this volume.

While I have usually given each writer's work in full, without omissions, I have on several occasions omitted a passage or two. Such omissions are noted. I have also generally reproduced the authors' idiosyncrasies in matters of style, spelling, and punctuation; the reader should recall that several of these pieces were translated into English by translators not entirely familiar with English idiom, and that some were composed in English by those who do not have it as a mother tongue. I have, however, silently corrected obvious typographical errors.

Each of the book's four sections begins with an introduction to the historical and systematic constraints that have influenced faithful Jews, Muslims, Buddhists, and Hindus in their thinking about Christians, Christianity, and other religions. Some suggestions for additional reading are appended to each of these introductory essays.

Purpose

Christian theologians have always been interested in non-Christian religious communities. This interest has usually been motivated by a desire to turn faithful non-Christians into Christians; sometimes by a desire to defend Christianity against attacks by non-Christians; and, most rarely, by a simple scholarly interest in the history, practices, or doctrines of some non-Christian community. In the decades since the final decay of the European colonial empires and the end of Europe's most recent attempts at self-destruction, this interest has flourished, grown and, in some respects, changed.

Both the World Council of Churches, an association of the mainstream Protestant churches, and the Roman Catholic Church have devoted a good deal of energy to a reconsideration of the theological presuppositions underlying traditional missionary activity and have encouraged and supported individual theologians in their work on the conceptual problem of religious pluralism. The Vatican, since the promulgation of its "Declaration on the Relation of the Church to Non-Christian Religions" (*Nostra Aetate*) at the Second Vatican Council in 1965, has pursued the suggestions implicit in that document by creating a Commission for Religious Relations with the Jews and a Secretariat for Non-Christians. Both of these bodies have issued numerous consultative documents. The latter, in a change indicative of alterations in Roman Catholic thinking about non-Christian religious communities, has, since 28 June 1988, been known as the Pontifical Council for Interreligious Dialogue.[1]

Protestant churches also, partly through the World Council of Churches and partly in other ways, have shown increasing interest in this question and have produced much literature on it. The World Council of Churches created a body called the Sub-Unit on Dialogue with the Peoples of Living Faiths and Ideologies in 1971, and this has sponsored a number of meetings and consultations and produced some important statements on interreligious dialogue and the significance, from a Christian perspective, of meeting with and possibly learning from representatives of non-Christian religions.[2]

The volume of published Christian theological work on non-Christian religious communities has, therefore, increased enormously since the Second World War. In some respects the thinking underlying this work has also become more sophisticated. Perhaps the single most striking change is that many Christian theologians are now prepared to acknowledge that interreligious dialogue—frank and open discussion among members of different religious communities with overt evangelization far from the immediate agenda—has an inherent value and should be encouraged.

But if such dialogue is to be successful it is surely important that the participants in it know as much as possible about the ways in which they and their communities have interacted with one another in the past. Most religious communities think about each other in stereotyped images. These range from the demonic to the ridiculous; they are very rarely based upon accurate knowledge. They are also much more influential than the sophisticated intellectuals who write about the value of interreligious dialogue, and who sometimes also engage in it, are usually prepared to admit. Stereotypes govern perceptions; they have great historical weight. The fact that a significant proportion of contemporary Muslims have, and are encouraged to have, a stereotyped vision of Jews as barbaric blood-drinking demons intent upon world conquest is not irrelevant to the future of Jewish-Muslim dialogue. Similarly, the fact that both Buddhists and Hindus have a tendency to think of Christians as aggressive beef-eating monsters incorrigibly addicted to dualism in both theology and ethics is bound to have an effect upon the possibilities inherent in Buddhist-Christian and Hindu-Christian dialogue.

Most interreligious dialogue has until now been initiated by Christians. This may change; there are some signs that it already is changing. But there is little doubt that one of the things that Christians—both theologians and ordinary non-intellectual Christians—need to understand better is the images of Christ, Christians, and Christianity that non-Christians have and use. Christians have said a great deal about how they see Buddhists, Hindus, Jews, and Muslims, and about what place they are prepared to allot the members of these communities in God's plan for human salvation; they have as yet not learned to listen very carefully to what members of these communities have said and are saying about them.

This volume is intended partly to supply this need by making available, in a format capable of being used in an undergraduate classroom as well as of being read by an interested but non-expert layperson, some texts that will help Christians to see how they appear to others.[3] The criteria for selection are simple: I have chosen only texts written during the last hundred years by individuals with some significant connection to one of the four great complexes of events that we label Judaism, Islam, Buddhism, and Hinduism. Each of the authors chosen is concerned to interpret and apply his tradition as he sees it to one of two questions (or sometimes to both): the question of how to think about Christians, and/or the question of how to think about other religions in general.

I have tried also to represent different views from within each tradition, for there are, naturally, many different views of Christianity within the Hindu tradition, just as there are within each of the others, and to allow roughly equal space to representatives from each of the four traditions. I have also made an effort to use fairly lengthy pieces in the belief that it is important to allow the thinkers represented space enough to develop an argument. It should be emphasized that there is no such thing as *the* Jewish, Buddhist, Islamic, or Hindu position on Christianity, just as there is no single Christian position on the significance of any non-Christian religious community. Instead there is an enormous variety of positions and attitudes; the constraints acting upon a member of any religious community in the formation of his or her views about other religious communities are not generally specific enough to determine the outcome, even when the same constraints are acknowledged to exist and allowed to operate. Thus, within the section on Islamic perceptions of Christianity, for example, opinions range from the irenic openness of Seyyed Hossein Nasr to the polemical violence of Sayyid Qutb.

Also, there is no single sense in which the authors of these pieces belong to or represent the religious communities that have given them life. Some hold or have held positions of recognized power and authority—they are rabbis, or (in at least two cases in the section on Buddhism) acknowledged heads of large religious communities. But others are more or less marginal, gadflies and activists rather than public spokespersons. This diversity has its value; it illustrates the fact that there is tremendous variety within each of those multicultural, polyglot, semifictional entities that we commonly call world religions, and this realization is itself important for the furtherance of responsible interreligious dialogue.

This book as a whole, then, is intended as an educational tool for Christians and as an instrument to further discussion of one of the most pressing and difficult theological questions now facing all Christian communities. Christians must learn, if they are to reappropriate and give new voice to their gospel in such a way that it can be heard by faithful members of non-Christian religious communities, to think about these faithful in ways that are not corrupted by ethnocentricity and which are sensitive to the complex realities of interreligious communication. If the essays included in this book do nothing else, they should make Christians aware of how lamentably and profoundly they have failed to do this during the present century.

THE THEORETICAL DIMENSIONS OF THE PROBLEM OF RELIGIOUS PLURALISM

The issue of how Christians are perceived by non-Christians is a specific and historical question of interest, I assume, largely to Christians. But there is, underlying this specific issue (with which this book largely deals), an important set of broader theoretical and practical questions. Some grasp of these will be useful for a full understanding of the essays that make up the body of this book, for although they tacitly inform most of the contributions, they are adverted to openly only rarely. I offer here, then, some necessarily sketchy comments on the theoretical problems of religious pluralism.

The Problem of Truth

DOCTRINE-EXPRESSING SENTENCES

Let's assume that truth is a property capable of possession by sentences in natural languages (such as English or Chinese). This is not an uncontroversial assumption among philosophers, especially when it is connected with a propositional view of how it is that natural-language sentences can come to possess this odd property.[4] But these controversies need not, I think, detain us for long here. It is certainly still a common way of talking in English to say that such-and-such a claim (or doctrine, or sentence, or utterance) is true, and that others are false; and, as I shall go on to suggest, many religious communities are prepared to assert that their doctrines (expressed, inevitably, in natural-language sentences) are true. To say that truth is a property capable of possession by natural-language sentences is therefore a claim that will be of some use in what follows, though it should not be taken as an exhaustive definition of truth.

Religious communities, then, tend to have doctrines and tend to express them in natural-language sentences. Some religious communities, it is true (for example, Zen Buddhists), appear to deny that they have any doctrines; but such a denial is itself a doctrine, so it seems fair, or at least useful, to say that religious communities have doctrine-expressing sentences. By this I mean, rather formally, sentences in some natural language (whatever the language of the community happens to be), which are taken by the community either to make or to entail claims about the nature of things or about the value of certain courses of action; these sentences must also be regarded by the community as of some significance for its religious life and/ or for the salvation of its members. I assume that most religious communities engage in the production of such sentences, and that even those that do not nevertheless demonstrate their implicit assent to some set of doctrine-expressing sentences by what they say and do.

To illustrate: the sacred texts of the Theravada Buddhist communities contain a large number of sentences in Pali, a natural language, even though it is no longer anyone's mother tongue. What is explicitly said in these sentences (and, therefore, what is entailed by what is explicitly said) is taken by the representative intellectuals of those communities to be both true and of great salvific significance. Further, the sentences formulated by contemporary intellectuals representing the Theravada Buddhist communities, often in expounding and commenting upon those contained in the sacred texts, are also, though in somewhat different ways, taken to be authoritative for such communities. So it is possible to find without too much difficulty sentences, formulated by the representative intellectuals of these Buddhist communities, that make claims about the nature of things.

It is frequently said, for instance, that every existent is transient; sometimes, with more precision, that every existent is strictly momentary; often that there is a set of necessary and sufficient conditions for the occurrence of any event whatever. It is also often claimed that personal proper names, such as Devadatta (the Indian equivalent of John Doe), while certainly capable of being used in all the usual conventional ways, refer to nothing. They label, that is to say, no substance, no possessor of properties, which can properly be designated by such linguistic items as *Devadatta*. And so forth.

This Buddhist example illustrates splendidly a convenient way of classifying doctrine-expressing sentences: I shall assume that these are either descriptive claims about the nature of things or assertions of value. Of the former kind are such doctrine-expressing sentences as the Qur'anic *There is no God but God and Muhammad is his prophet*; of the latter kind are such Christian doctrine-expressing sentences as *You should love the Lord your God with all your heart, all your mind, and all your soul.* The former makes a claim about what exists and the nature of what exists; the latter recommends, or even demands, that a certain course of action be undertaken, with the suggestion (sometimes explicit but usually implicit) that the course of action in question is valuable — perhaps supremely valuable. I do not claim that this way of classifying doctrine-expressing sentences is the only way, or even that it will account for all of them (though I rather suspect that it will). I make use of this classification and analysis for heuristic purposes only.

I also assume that doctrine-expressing sentences of both kinds are capable of being true or false, which is not the same thing as claiming that knowledge of their truth or falsity is available to me, or to anyone. This is perhaps more obvious for descriptive claims about the nature of things than for assertions of value; but even in the latter case, in which doctrine-expressing sentences are often sentences framed in the optative or imperative moods, it should not be difficult to see that the assertions of value that necessarily underlie such commands or pious hopes can be true or false. If, for example, I tell you to engage in ceaseless recollection of the Buddha, and if I further claim this as a doctrine-expressing sentence of my religious community, this is presumably because I judge the sentence *It is desirable that you engage in ceaseless recollection of the Buddha*, or perhaps even the sentence *It is desirable that everyone should engage in ceaseless recollection of the Buddha*, to be true. So, the same would apply, making the appropriate changes, for claims such as *Sell all you have and give to the poor.*

Before I leave the topic of doctrine-expressing sentences, another relatively minor issue needs to be mentioned. For any religious community, the set of its doctrine-expressing sentences will not be coextensive with the set of sentences to which its members give assent. This is for obvious reasons: presumably most American members of religious communities would assent to the sentence *Magic Johnson was one of the ten best players in the NBA in 1988*, but few (save for those for whom the Los Angeles Lakers are of ultimate significance) would want to claim this sentence as a doctrine-expressing sentence of the community, simply because it is of no salvific significance and has no clear functions within the religious life of any religious community.

I reiterate, then, that a doctrine-expressing sentence is one that is taken by a specific religious community to be of some salvific importance or (not always the same thing) to be of some importance for the religious life of the community. Doctrine-expressing sentences, then, are objects available for empirical study. It's relatively easy to find them out and to analyze them, though rather less easy to be sure that one knows what the community that formulated them means by them if one is not a member of that community (and sometimes even if one is). If one wants to know what the doctrine-expressing sentences of a given religious community are, one simply has to go to the representative intellectuals of that community and ask. Many religious communities take the trouble to set down their doctrine-expressing sentences in books for the delectation of the casual reader, some enshrine them in credal formulae, chant them in ritual settings, and otherwise scatter them abroad.

ALIEN CLAIMS

To understand more fully the problem of truth we need at this point a new notion: that of the alien religious claim.[5] What, then, is an alien religious claim? Briefly, a particular claim is an alien religious claim with respect to some religious community if and only if it is a doctrine-expressing sentence of another religious community which does not express a proposition also expressed by any doctrine-expressing sentence of the religious community with respect to which it is alien.

For example: the Roman Catholic doctrine-expressing sentence *One should attend Mass frequently* is an alien religious claim with respect, among many other examples, to the community of Rissho Koseikai (one of Japan's so-called new religions) members. The Buddhist doctrine-expressing sentence *passionate attachment is to be avoided as detrimental to the practice of the religious life* is an alien religious claim with respect to the community of Shi'ite Muslims. And so forth. It is important to notice that the fact of a particular doctrine-expressing sentence being an alien claim with respect to some community does not by itself mean that it is unacceptable to that community or incompatible with any of its own doctrine-expressing sentences. It is at least conceivable, even if not very likely, that a group of representative Rissho Koseikai intellectuals might come to accept and promulgate the Roman Catholic doctrine-expressing sentence mentioned (in which case, of course, it would cease to be an alien claim with respect to the Rissho Koseikai), and yet not thereby dissolve themselves into the Catholic Church. The fact that a given religious claim is alien to a specific religious community says only that what is expressed by that claim is not also a doctrine of that religious community; it is neutral with regard to acceptability. It may turn out, upon examination, that the alien claim can become a doctrine-expressing sentence of the community with respect to which it was once alien. Or this may turn out not to be possible, in which case the claim remains alien.

The nature and scope of the problem of truth, as one of the theoretical problems of religious pluralism, should now be evident. It consists, above all else, in some of the members of some religious community coming to realize that the members of other religious communities believe in and propound doctrine-expressing sentences that are not obviously or easily compatible with their own, and so realizing that some judgment must be made about such alien claims.

It is possible — indeed, I should say, inevitable — that the representative intellectuals of a religious community might judge some alien claim to be incompatible with some one (or several) of their own doctrine-expressing sentences. What forms might such incompatibility take? There are two basic types correlated with the twofold classification of doctrine-expressing sentences already given. The first kind of incompatibility is strictly logical and might occur between two descriptive doctrine-expressing sentences. If one doctrine-expressing sentence is true, the other cannot be. For example: suppose one (Christian) religious community asserts the doctrine-expressing sentence *Jesus Christ is the same yesterday, today, and forever*, and another (Buddhist) religious community the doctrine-expressing sentence *Everything that exists does so momentarily*. The prima facie incompatibility is clear enough to need little comment. Of course, the appearance of incompatibility of this direct and irreconcilable kind is not the same as its reality; it is often the case that two assertions that appear to be incompatible when considered in isolation turn out not to be so when considered in the broader context of the conceptual system that gives them meaning. But there seems to be no pressing reason to assume that such direct incompatibility never occurs or cannot occur.

The second kind of incompatibility that I have in mind is practical and is related to those doctrine-expressing sentences that prescribe (or proscribe) a certain course of action, and thus express a value. Suppose one religious community enshrines among its doctrine-expressing sentences the recommendation that one should be ceaselessly mindful of God; and suppose a member of that religious community learns that there is an alien religious claim that recommends the ceaseless chanting of an invocation to the Buddha. Such a person might well conclude, not unreasonably, that these two injunctions are practically incompatible because it is not possible for one and the same individual to carry them both out. The chain of reasoning that might lead to such a conclusion would presumably include the judgments that being mindful of God and chanting an invocation to the Buddha are not the same thing, and that one cannot do both at once. Anyone who came to such a conclusion might justifiably be accused of excessive literal-mindedness, of not being sensitive to the hyperbole so often employed in doctrine-expressing sentences. Such might indeed turn out to be the case, but it is, at least, not obviously so.

The recognition of incompatibility between the doctrine-expressing sentences of one's own religious community and some alien claim(s) is not the only possibility. Another is the recognition of compatibility and truth in alien claims. Suppose, for example, that I am a faithful Anglican Christian, assenting to all of the doctrines enshrined in the thirty-nine articles of the church; suppose, further, that I come to realize, on the basis of some exposure to Buddhism, that there are Buddhist doctrines not found among those I assent to as an Anglican Christian, and that at least some of these appear to contain truths not found in my own tradition. I might come to this conclusion, for example, about some Buddhist claims as to the desirability and effects of certain kinds of meditational practice; these practices are not part of my own tradition and my community has no doctrines about them. I might nonetheless come to regard the practices as desirable and the doctrines as true.

The problem of truth, then, is one that faces all religious communities when they become aware of the fact that their own doctrine-expressing sentences are not the only ones in the field. Many responses are possible. Most radical, perhaps, is the exclusivist response, which judges that all the central doctrine-expressing sentences of the home religious community are true and that all those of other religious communities are false. Perhaps some sectarian groups approach this kind of exclusivism on the question of truth, but it is not a widely held view and has some obvious difficulties. Most pressing is the fact that it does not allow that any doctrine-expressing sentence of the home religious community might also be a doctrine-expressing sentence of another religious community.

Less extreme is the inclusivist position, which is that all the central doctrine-expressing sentences of the home religious community are true; and that while there may be true doctrine-expressing sentences belonging to other religious communities, all these are already numbered among the doctrine-expressing sentences of the home community. This, perhaps, is close to the standard position of the Roman Catholic Church. A still more moderate version would allow for the presence of true doctrine-expressing sentences outside the home religious community not already known to that community.

At the other extreme, some communities might answer the question of truth in a pluralistic way. They might say, that is, that the central doctrine-expressing sentences of all religious communities are true; and that each religious community may possess doctrine-expressing sentences belonging to none of the others. This pluralistic answer has difficulties in dealing with the presence of contradictions among the doctrine-expressing sentences of different religious communities—consider, for example, the Islamic doctrine-expressing sentence *Jesus of Nazareth was a prophet, created by God*, and the Christian doctrine-expressing sentence *Jesus of Nazareth is uncreated and consubstantial with God*. Varieties of relativism or perspectivalism might be introduced to deal with this kind of problem.

But my purpose here is not to explore the merits and demerits of these answers to the question of truth. I wish simply to note that the question of truth is an unavoidable issue for religious communities that have become aware of the facts of religious pluralism; it is therefore also an issue implicitly—and sometimes explicitly—for all of the essays reprinted in this volume.

The Question of Salvation

Another issue, at least theoretically separable from the question of truth, is the question of salvation. Religious communities typically have some idea as to what the ultimate goal of the religious life is and how it should be pursued; they typically also think that belonging to them, assenting to their doctrines and engaging in the practices entailed by such assent, is relevant to, perhaps even directly productive of, this ultimate goal.

Such views have influenced the traditional exclusivism of many religious communities, perhaps especially that of Christians. If one believes, as many Christians do, that salvation is available only to those who avow explicit allegiance to Christ, then no matter what one thinks about the availability of truth outside the Christian community, one will have difficulty in judging that any non-Christian can be saved. A similar position might be reached by some Muslims on the ground, perhaps, of the necessity of assent to the status of the Qur'an as divinely inspired; or by some Buddhists on the ground of the necessity of comprehending and assenting to the four truths for the attainment of Nirvana. And so forth.

An extreme version of this exclusivist answer to the problem of salvation would be simply that only membership in the home religious community is sufficient to bring about salvation. Other answers are possible. At the extreme liberal end of the spectrum it is possible to imagine a radical pluralist's answer to the question of salvation: that membership in any religious community is sufficient to effect salvation. An intermediate position would be the view that, all other things being equal, membership in the home religious community is more likely to effect salvation than is membership in any other religious community; but that, in special circumstances, membership in other religious communities might suffice for salvation.

Once again, the point of offering this sketchy analysis of possible answers to the question of salvation is not to judge any one of these positions superior to any other. Neither is it to recommend the adoption of one to any particular religious community. The constraints that membership in a religious community place upon those who wish to develop a position on religious pluralism from within that community are very varied; no single answer is likely to be appropriate for all religious communities. The analysis is given only to serve as an aid in the analysis of the essays that are presented in this volume. It will often be of great heuristic value to try and assess the position taken by the contributors to this volume on the questions of truth and salvation, as well as the possible relations between answers given to these questions.

The Question of Attitude

Answers to the purely theoretical questions of truth and salvation necessarily spill over into the behavioral and practical realms. This is most obvious in connection with what Christians would call evangelism and mission. Exclusivist answers to the questions of truth and salvation often go hand in hand with a more or less aggressive interest in mission. If you are a member of a religious community that believes all non-members are damned and, moreover, that all non-members have nothing but false religious beliefs, then it will be entirely natural (assuming a certain level of interest in the well-being of one's fellow humans) to try hard to make non-members into members. Alternatively, if one thinks of all members of all religious communities as necessarily saved, interest in missionary activity will be minimal.

The attitudes of the members of one religious community to those of another are not, though, determined solely by the answers given by that community to the questions of salvation and truth. They are also intimately linked with the relations of power that obtain between the members of the home religious community and those of another community. So, for example, when Christians represented a dominant colonial power vis-à-vis Buddhists, it is not surprising that Christian thinking about Buddhists tended to be fairly uncritical in its assumptions of superiority and the desirability of converting Buddhists to Christianity. And now, with the reassertion of national, ethnic, and religious identity that has followed upon the independence of Asian countries, the position is often reversed: Christian theologians suffer from post-colonialist guilt, while Buddhist, Hindu, and Islamic assertions of superiority are intimately connected with quasi-nationalistic resurgence.

In considering the implications of the pieces that follow, then, it will be important to pay attention not only to the purely conceptual influences upon the positions taken, but also to the historical and political situations that shaped the thinking of their authors. Some brief comments are offered upon these also in the materials that follow.

PART I

Jewish Perceptions
of Christianity
in the Twentieth Century

INTRODUCTION TO PART ONE

Most Christians, throughout most of Christian history, have been pro-foundly anti-Semitic.[1] Anti-Jewish prejudice and the hatred and violence that it spawns are very deeply rooted in Christian history. As early as the second century the Christian rejection of the people of Israel was evident in Marcion's (85–165) suggestion that Christians should no longer consider the Hebrew Bible as canonical scripture. And while Marcion's views were later declared heretical by the church, there have been and remain many Marcionite tendencies among Christians.[2]

Along with this Christian tendency to reject the people of Israel as God's chosen, God's elect, has gone a Christian interpretation of the New Testament accounts of the trial and crucifixion of Jesus as reports of Jewish guilt, Jewish responsibility for the crime of deicide. These things together have warped Christian perceptions of and responses to Jews and Judaism from the beginning of Christian history until now; they have also, inevitably, shaped Jewish perceptions of and responses to Christians and Christianity. It is difficult to feel anything other than hatred and fear for those who are your persecutors, and almost impossible to engage in serious religious dialogue with them.

Bearing this background in mind, it should be easy for Christians to understand why most twentieth-century Jewish discussions of Christianity focus upon the state of Israel and the Holocaust. It is through a consideration of Christian attitudes to the foundation of the state of Israel and its continued existence, and to the slaughter of six million or so Jews by the Nazis in the 1940s, that Jews can try to show Christians where they have gone wrong in developing theological views on Judaism in the past, and thus to define their own views on Christianity. Christianity and Christians have been a threat to the very survival of Jews and the people of Israel. It is therefore quite proper that Jewish discussions of Christianity should focus upon this and should try to redefine the relationship between the communities through such discussion.

The Theological Basis for Jewish Perceptions of Christianity

The Jews regard themselves as a chosen people, a people given both special promises and special duties by God. The duties are enshrined in the Torah, in God's law; the promises in the assurance that Israel's election cannot fail and that God's mercy will ultimately prevail. The fundamental theological idea here is that of covenant: the relationship between God and God's people is one in which both covenanter and covenanted have rights, duties, and obligations. The paradigmatic event in the history of the Jewish people and the constitution of this covenant is the exodus from slavery in Egypt and the giving of the law to Moses on Sinai.

The Jews are, therefore, marked out, separated from all other peoples. They have a special relationship with God. But this is not to say that only the Jews have a covenant relation with God or that only the Jews are recipients of God's promises and God's mercy. Traditionally, most Jews have asserted that all peoples are in relationship with God through the covenant made with Noah,[3] and that all peoples therefore have rights and duties in their relationship with God and may have their part in God's plan for the salvation of humankind through their proper fulfilment of these duties. It is thus open to Jews to allot Christians a covenant relationship with God, for Christians are Gentiles and all Gentiles may have such a relationship.[4]

The theological ideas of covenant and election, fundamental though they are for Jewish self-understanding, have not led to exclusivism. They have not led Jews to consign all Gentiles to God's wrath; neither have they led them to think it desirable to make all Gentiles into Jews. These ideas have, though, fostered a certain self-conscious separatism on the part of Jewish thinkers. The impulse to interreligious dialogue has not been deeply felt, and Jewish intellectuals and theologians have not, typically, been leaders in developing it. Christians have, for most of Jewish history, been of interest to Jews in practical and political ways, but only rarely in theological ones.[5]

Christians, then, may very well be regarded by Jews as a covenanted people, and this is evident in several of the essays reprinted in this volume. For most Jews, however, they must also be regarded as a people in possession of some quite fundamental theological misconceptions. I shall mention only two of these, both centering upon the person and work of Jesus of Nazareth. The first is the question of whether or not it is proper to call Jesus the Messiah, the anointed one of the Jews and the fulfilment of God's promises to the people of Israel. The answer here, for almost all Jews, has always been an emphatic negative. Jesus was not and could not have been the Messiah, and to think that the Hebrew Bible in any way refers to or points to him is a fundamental misreading of the text. Jesus did not fulfil the traditional Messianic expectations of the Jews, and it is ludicrous to think that he did.

An associated but even more profound disagreement between Jews and Christians is more strictly theological. Setting aside the question of Jesus of Nazareth's status as the Messiah, Jews have always rejected the Christian claim that Jesus was God incarnate, the second person of the Trinity, because this seems to most Jews to be an absurdly idolatrous claim. God is not an idol, not a physical object, and most certainly not a flesh-and-blood human being. To think that God could be such is, strictly, idolatrous. There are many analogies here between the Jewish perception of Christianity and Christ and the Islamic (see Part 2 of this volume).

These theological disagreements about the identity and significance of Jesus of Nazareth only rarely surface in the essays contained in this volume. But they are implicitly present, and it is important to have them in mind as the discussion proceeds.[6]

The State of Israel and the Holocaust

The state of Israel was effectively established as an independent political entity in 1947–48, following upon Nazi Germany's attempt to rid Europe of all Jews. Meditation upon and participation in this complex of events has been at the center of most Jewish attempts to develop a Jewish view of Christianity since then. Even before the second world war and the Holocaust—and this is evident in the extract from Franz Rosenzweig's letters to Eugen Rosenstock-Huessy (Chapter 1), the only document written before 1939 included in this volume—Jewish responses to Christianity were heavily influenced by perceptions of the "Christian dogma" of the stubbornness of the Jews, as Rosenzweig put it, and of the anti-semitism that went with it. After 1947 it became effectively impossible for any Jewish thinker to write about Christianity without adverting to these events; this is true even of the most detached and intellectual of the essays included here, that by Michael Wyschogrod (Chapter 4).

The reasons are clear: the Christian churches were (and are) perceived by Jews as partly responsible for the Holocaust. Neither the Vatican nor the Protestant churches in Europe made a concerted effort to resist fascism, even when they knew of Hitler's "final solution" to the Jewish problem. Both England and the United States failed to direct military efforts to bring the operation of the death camps to an end, even when they could easily have done so. And the roots of Nazi anti-Semitism in traditional Christian anti-Semitism are very evident.

It is beyond dispute that there is a good deal of truth in these Jewish perceptions. Such perceptions, and the distress and anger that goes with them, have not been markedly altered by the slowness of the major Protestant churches and of the Vatican to publicly acknowledge past mistakes and to recognize and support the state of Israel. Such omissions are almost always construed by Jews as yet further evidence of Christian anti-Semitism at work.

To oversimplify matters somewhat: since the 1950s, two kinds of Jewish perception of and response to Christians and Christianity on the issues of the Holocaust and the state of Israel have developed. The first is vituperative and confrontational. Rabbi Rosenberg's essay in this volume (Chapter 3) represents this strand. Christianity is seen as the major contributor to anti-Semitism, and anti-Semitism in turn is seen as evidence of a fundamental problem with Christianity. A recurring theme is that Christians are pagan, not truly religious. Those Jews who take this line tend to demand of Christians radical repentance, a new self-definition that is constituted entirely by a proper response to the Holocaust and to the state of Israel. Only if Christians can transform their traditional anti-Semitism, can re-Judaize themselves and learn to reconstitute their faith in terms of its relation to Judaism, is there hope for Christians as a people of God. Jews already know what Christians have to learn, according to this model.

The second strand is more irenic and more liberal, though it too takes its point of departure from the Holocaust. It is represented in this volume by Rabbi Heschel (Chapter 2). Here, although Christian complicity in the events of the Holocaust is acknowledged and deplored, there is also an attempt to appreciate Christianity in its own terms and for its own virtues, independently of its relationship to Judaism. Here, typically, there is an appeal to the common scriptural heritage, to the worship of the same one God, and to the possibility of Christian-Jewish cooperation in the future. So Heschel says:

> What is urgently needed are ways of helping one another in the terrible predicament of here and now by the courage to believe that the word of the Lord endures for ever as well as here and now; to cooperate in trying to bring about a resurrection of sensitivity, a revival of conscience; to keep alive the divine sparks in our souls, to nurture openness to the spirit of the Psalms, reverence for the words of the prophets, and faithfulness to the Living God.

In this view Christianity is not only a dialogue-partner but also an active helper. Christians can be a mirror for Jews, representing one aspect of God's intentions,[7] just as Jews can be for Christians.

A theme that connects these two kinds of response to Christians and Christianity is a desire to call into question traditional Christian theological attempts to show that Judaism has been superseded and has no continuing theological relevance. If Christ fulfilled the law and the prophets and abrogated the requirements of the law, then, so runs this traditional position, the community of Jews is a community of those who have not recognized God's saving actions: its continued existence is a mistake. Christians have often read their own sacred texts in just this way, and from a Jewish point of view such a reading contributed indirectly to the occurrence of the Holocaust. Such a reading makes conceptual space for an attempt to eliminate Judaism, whether by conversion or annihilation, for such elimination is then theologically grounded.

Jews have therefore often been concerned to argue that Christians misunderstand their own scripture and tradition in coming to such a conclusion. And it is in this context that Michael Wyschogrod's carefully argued essay (Chapter 4) is best understood. Even the apostle Paul, whose rhetoric can most easily be taken to support such a supersessionist interpretation, should be read with care: other readings are possible, and, from a Jewish perspective at least, much to be preferred.

In conclusion: twentieth-century Jewish perceptions of Christianity focus upon Christian attitudes to the Holocaust and to the foundation and continued existence of the state of Israel. They tend to see Christians as fundamentally anti-Semitic, as significantly theologically mistaken about the nature and significance of Jesus of Nazareth, and as having an inappropriately supersessionist view of the relations between Judaism and Christianity. There are many signs that these Jewish challenges are being met by at least some Christian theologians, and that Christian perceptions of Judaism are at present being changed more drastically than at any time since the first century of the common era. It remains to be seen whether, and how, Jewish perceptions of Christianity will change in the future.

SUGGESTIONS FOR FURTHER READING

There is now an enormous body of literature on Jewish-Christian relations and the perceptions of each community by the other. The bulk of this literature focuses upon Christian perceptions of and theological thinking about Jews and Judaism, and so is of only indirect relevance to the approach taken in this volume. Useful bibliographical guides may be found in two recent publications by Michael Shermis: *Jewish-Christian Relations: An Annotated Bibliography and Resource Guide* (Bloomington, IN: Indiana University Press, 1988); "Recent Publications in the Jewish-Christian Dialogue: An Annotated Bibliography," *American Journal of Theology and Philosophy* 9/1–2 (1988): 137–42.

Recently a number of anthologies on the topic of Jewish-Christian relations have appeared with significant contributions by both Jews and Christians. Among the most useful of these are: Marc H. Tanenbaum, Marvin R. Wilson, and A. James Rudin, eds., *Evangelicals and Jews in Conversation on Scripture, Theology, and History* (Grand Rapids, MI: Baker Book House, 1978); Richard W. Rousseau, ed., *Christianity and Judaism: The Deepening Dialogue* (Scranton, PA: Ridge Row Press, 1983); Eugene J. Fisher, A. James Rudin, and Marc H. Tanenbaum, eds., *Twenty Years of Jewish-Catholic Relations* (New York, NY: Paulist Press, 1986); Roger Brooks, ed.,

Unanswered Questions: Theological Views of Jewish-Catholic Relations (Notre Dame, IN: University of Notre Dame Press, 1988).

Useful historical background may be found in: Frank Ephraim Talmage, ed., *Disputation and Dialogue: Readings in the Jewish-Christian Encounter* (New York, NY: Ktav, 1975); J. Van den Berg and Ernestine G. E. Van der Wall, eds., *Jewish-Christian Relations in the Seventeenth Century: Studies and Documents* (International Archives of the History of Ideas #119; Dordrecht/Boston/London: Kluwer, 1988); George L. Berlin, *Defending the Faith: Nineteenth-Century American Jewish Writing on Christianity and Jesus* (Albany, NY: State University of New York Press, 1989).

1

Extracts from the Eleventh Letter to Eugen Rosenstock-Huessy[1]

FRANZ ROSENZWEIG

INTRODUCTION

Franz Rosenzweig (1886–1929) was a pupil of Hermann Cohen, a Jewish neo-Kantian philosopher. He grew up with only a marginal connection to Judaism, became convinced that greater commitment was required of him shortly before the outbreak of World War I, and thereafter devoted most of his intellectual energies to reinterpreting the Jewish tradition, to working with Martin Buber on a new German translation of the Hebrew Bible, and to many other intellectual projects. Perhaps his most influential work was The Star of Redemption, *in which he offered an attempt at a systematic reinterpretation of the entire Jewish tradition from the viewpoint of human existence as dominated and defined by the inevitability of death. Rosenzweig was in reaction against the dominant Hegelianism of his time, and so stressed individual experience rather than abstract ideals and historical process. His experiences in the trenches in World War I had great influence upon the development of his thought.[2]*

In his letters to Rosenstock-Huessy, a Christian and a philosopher, Rosenzweig attempts to define and delimit Judaism using Christianity as a foil. In the letter from Rosenstock-Huessy to which the extracts reprinted here respond, Rosenstock-Huessy had said that the Church "needs its Jews" and that "the stubbornness of the Jews is, so to speak, a Christian dogma." He also emphasized the capacity of the Jews for suffering. Rosenzweig replies that the stubbornness of the Jews is indeed a Christian dogma, and that it is from this dogma and others associated with it that anti-Semitism springs. The Christian attempt to take Jewishness away from Jews by converting them is, to Rosenzweig, an attempt to remove the identity of Jews as human persons. As he puts it, the "galley" of Judaism is his galley; he has been chosen for it; how then can he abandon it to be converted?

Rosenzweig also outlines the Jewish dogmatic view of Christianity: Christianity is seen as an impoverished, artificial, excessively ceremonious preparer-of-the-way for Judaism. Christians have to learn what Jews automatically know: that God is their father. The Jew is, simply, closer to God. The demand that Rosenzweig places upon Rosenstock-Huessy, and by extension upon all Christians, is that Jews be allowed the freedom to be what they are, to row their galley wherever they like. Only then will a free meeting between Judaism and Christianity — or better, between Jews and Christians — "on the open sea" be possible.

EXTRACTS FROM THE ELEVENTH LETTER TO EUGEN ROSENSTOCK-HUESSY

I want to begin to answer you at once ... our present correspondence is suffering from the fact that on the one hand we could not put it off, while on the other hand it is still too soon for it. I can see that very clearly, because I am the one who was responsible for the long gap (of the winter of 1913–14).[3] I could not write to you then, though you were continually sounding me and were offended because of my silence. I could not, because I thought I had done with you as you were up to then, and as I had dug you out at the end of our time in Leipzig, up to certain undiscoverable fragments (I won't say which parts of your body), put you together, and exhibited you in my museum in a gallery on a revolving pedestal, with a piece of dark blue stuff, which made a good background to you. That you were walking about alive despite this statue was almost an insult to me. I had to ignore it, and to appease my pangs of conscience with the idea that I had "put the matter off." That you were in fact walking about very much alive I realized, of course, when you were in Berlin in the spring, but I didn't feel myself strong enough, not indeed physically, but spiritually, to challenge you all over again (since it would only have been done as a challenge, and will so be done again); to my mind I was not actual enough, not tested enough, not enough on the spot, and to me there would have been no point in a merely theoretical controversy. Formerly, I had confronted you as a point of view, as an objective fact, and you were the first to summon me to an analysis of myself, and thereby cast me down. I would have liked to wait until I could again confront you as a fait accompli. Till then we could have kept our guest rooms ready for each other, and put some little cheap flowers in them as a token of our feeling for one another. That does, and would have done.[4]

"Then the War came." And with it came a time of waiting against one's will, a chasm that one does not make artificially for oneself, but that was opened blindly in every life; and now it is no longer any good to wait deliberately; fate is now so calmly patient with individuals (from indifference towards them, because it has its hands full with nations) that we individuals ought just now to be impatient, unless we want simply to go to sleep (for fate certainly won't wake us up now). So now we are talking to each other theoretically, *faute de mieux*.[5] But for that reason everything that we say to each other is incomplete, not incomplete like the flow of life that completes itself anew in every moment, but full of static incompletenesses, full of distortions.

You "leave me alone." You "don't know why." You "stop at me." Nevertheless, I reply, and give you an answer that is theoretically correct, interesting, and I'm sure you will agree with it. You want to know what business I have on that galley[6] — but it were better you did not agree, did not know, but *just saw me set sail on that galley* without knowing what business I had on it, rather than that *my galley should now be lying idle in a neutral port since the beginning of the war*, and that I should incur your intellectual sympathy, since the *vis major*[7] of the war prevents me from acquiring your active hatred; for there is in the delay the danger of indifference, which lies beyond love and hate, and that would be the worst of all.

Now to the point. You could have formulated your objection still more strongly; I should like perhaps later to do it for you. But first let's stick to your formulation. Yes, the stubbornness of the Jews is a Christian dogma. So much so that the Church, after she had built up a substantial part of her particular dogma — the part having to do with God and Man — in the first century, during the whole of the second century turned aside to lay down the "second dogma" (the formal part of her dogma, i.e., her historical consciousness of herself). And in its aftereffects this process continued through the third and fourth centuries and beyond; and Augustine applied himself to it personally, though the Church had already for some time been moving away from it. That is, it had been becoming a Church of writings or rather of tradition, instead of spirit; in other words it was becoming exactly the Church that history knows. Paul's theory concerning the relation of the Gospels to the Law could have remained a "personal opinion"; the Hellenizing "spiritual" Church (of John's Gospel) of the first century, in the marvellous naiveté of her "spiritual believers," had scarcely worried about it. Then came gnosticism, which laid its finger on Paul and sought to weed out the personal element from his theory and to develop its objective aspects in distinction from the personal in it. (Paul said: "The Jews are spurned, but Christ came from them." Marcion[8] said: "Therefore the Jews belong to the devil, Christ to God.") Then the Church, which hitherto had been quite naive in its own gnosticism (in St. John we read that salvation comes from the Jews), suddenly seeing this, pushed the spirit [*pneuma*] to one side in favor of tradition, and through a great *ritornar al segno*[9] fixed this tradition by returning to its cardinal point, to its founder Paul; that is, she deliberately established as dogma what previously had been considered Paul's personal opinion. The Church established the identity of the Creator (and the God revealed at Sinai) with the Father of Jesus Christ on the one hand, and the perfect manhood of Christ on the other hand, as a definite, correlated Shibboleth against all heresy—and thereby the Church established herself as a power in human history. You know the rest better than I do.[10]

Thus, in the firm establishment of the Old Testament in the Canon, and in the building of the Church on this double scripture (Old Testament and New Testament) the stubbornness of the Jews is in fact brought out as the other half of the Christian dogma (its formal consciousness of itself—the dogma of the Church—if we may point to the creed as the dogma of Christianity).

But could this same idea (that of the stubbornness of the Jews) also be a Jewish dogma? Yes, it could be, and in fact it is. But this Jewish consciousness of being rejected has quite a different place in our dogmatic system, and would correspond to a Christian consciousness of being chosen to rule, a consciousness that is in fact present beyond any doubt. The whole religious interpretation of the significance of the year 70[11] is tuned to this note. But the parallel that you are looking for is something entirely different. A dogma of Judaism about its relation to the Church must correspond to the dogma of the Church about its relation to Judaism. And this you know only in the modern liberal-Jewish theory of the "daughter religion" that gradually educates the world for Judaism.[12] But this theory actually springs from the classical period in the formation of Jewish dogma—from the Jewish high scholasticism which, in point of time and in content, forms a mean between Christian and Arabian scholasticism (al-Ghazzali—Maimonides—Thomas Aquinas).[13] For it was only then that we had a fixing of dogma, and that corresponds with the different positions that intellectual conceptions of faith hold with us and with you. In the period when you were developing dogma, we were creating our canon law, and vice versa. There is a subtle connection running all through. For instance, when you were systematizing dogma, we were systematizing law; with you the mystical view of dogma followed its definition, while with us the mystical view preceded definition, etc. This relation is rooted throughout in the final distinction between the two faiths. Indeed with us, too, this theory is not part of the substance of our dogma; with us, too, it was not formed from the content of the religious consciousness, but belongs only to a second stratum, a stratum of learning concerning dogma. The theory of the daughter religion is found in the clearest form in both of the great scholastics. Beyond this, it is found, not as dogma but as a mystical idea (see above), in the literature of the old Synagogue, and likewise in the Talmudic period. To find it is no easy task, however. For whereas the substantial dogma in our scholasticism was based on trials, the connection between the old mysticism and medieval philosophy is brought about by the free religious spirit of the people, not by a fettered relationship to the past. But I should like to quote you one such legend. The Messiah was born exactly at the moment when the Temple was destroyed, but when he was born, the winds blew him forth from the bosom of his mother. And now he wanders unknown among the peoples, and when he has wandered through them all, then the time of our redemption will have come.

So that Christianity is like a power that fills the world (according to the saying of one of the two scholastics, Yehuda ha-Levi:[14] it is the tree that grows from the seed of Judaism and casts its shadows over the earth; but its fruit must contain the seed again, the seed that nobody who saw the tree noticed). This is a Jewish dogma, just as Judaism as both the stubborn origin and last convert is a Christian dogma.

But what does all that mean for me, apart from the fact that I know it? What does this Jewish dogma mean for the Jew? Granted that it may not belong to the dogmas of the substantial group, which like the corresponding Christian dogmas can be won from an analysis of the religious consciousness. It is rather like the corresponding Christian one, a theological idea. But theological ideas must also mean something for religion. What, then, does it mean?

What does the Christian theological idea of Judaism mean for the Christian? If I am to believe E[ugen] R[osenstock-Huessy]'s letter before last (or before the one before the last?): Nothing! For there he wrote that nowadays König[15] and he are the only people who still take Judaism seriously. The answer is already on the point of my pen—that it was not here a question of theoretical awareness, but whether there was a continual realization of this theological idea by its being taken seriously in actual practice. This practical way in which the theological idea of the stubbornness of the Jews works itself out, is *hatred of the Jews*. You know as well as I do that all its realistic arguments are only fashionable cloaks to hide the single true metaphysical ground: that we will not make common cause with the world-conquering fiction of Christian dogma, because (however much a fact) it *is* a fiction (and *fiat veritas, pereat realis*,[16] since "Thou God art truth") and, putting it in a learned way (from Goethe in *Wilhelm Meister*): that we deny the foundation of contemporary culture (and *fiat regnum Dei, pereat mundus*,[17] for "ye shall be to me a kingdom of priests and a holy people"); and putting it in a popular way: that we have crucified Christ and, believe me, would do it again every time, we alone in the whole world (and *fiat nomen Dei Unius, pereat homo*,[18] for "to whom will you liken me, that I am like?").

And so the corresponding Jewish outcome of the theological idea of Christianity as a preparer-of-the-way is the *pride of the Jews*. This is hard to describe to a stranger. What you see of it appears to you silly and petty, just as it is almost impossible for the Jew to see and judge anti-Semitism by anything but its vulgar and stupid expressions. But (I must say again, *believe me*) its metaphysical basis is, as I have said, the three articles: (1) that we have the truth, (2) that we are at the goal, and (3) that any and every Jew feels in the depth of his soul that the Christian relation to God, and so in a sense their religion, is particularly and extremely pitiful, poverty-stricken, and ceremonious; namely, that as a Christian one has to learn from someone else, whoever he may be, to call God "our Father." To the Jew, that God is our Father is the first and most self-evident fact—and what need is there for a third person between me and my father in Heaven? That is no discovery of modern apologetics but the simplest Jewish instinct, a mixture of failure to understand and pitying contempt.

These are the two points of view, both narrow and limited just as points of view, and so in theory both can be surpassed; one can understand why the Jew can afford his unmediated closeness to God and why the Christian may not; and one can also understand how the Jew must pay for this blessing. I can elaborate this argument in extreme detail. It can be intellectualized through and through, for it springs in the last resort from that great victorious breaking in of the spirit into what is not spirit that one calls "Revelation."

But now I want to formulate your question in a way that seems profitable to me—but is not such intellectualizing, as an activity of knowing, preparing, acting on the future, like every cultural activity, a Christian affair, not a Jewish affair? Are you still a Jew in that you do it? Is not part of the price that the Synagogue must pay for the blessing in the enjoyment of which she anticipates the whole world, namely, of being already in the Father's presence, that she must wear the bandages of unconsciousness over her eyes? Is it sufficient if you carry the broken staff in your hand, as you do— I am willing to believe it—and yet take the bandages away from your eyes?

Here the polished clarity of antitheses ends; here begins the world of more and less, of compromise, of reality, or, as the Jewish mysticism of the late Middle Ages very finely said for "World of Reality, of Thinghood," [substitute] "World of Activity, of Matter of Fact"; and as I should prefer to say, the "World of Action." Action alone can here decide for me, but even if it has decided for me, I still always need indulgence? Not as if thought is here entirely left behind; but it no longer goes as before along a proud, sure king's highway, with vanguard, flanks, and countless trains of attendants; it goes lonely along the footpath in pilgrim dress. Something like this:

You recollect the passage in the Gospel of John where Christ explains to his disciples that they should not leave the world, but should remain within it. Even so, the people of Israel—who indeed could use all the sayings of this Gospel—could speak to its members in such a way, and as a matter of fact it does so: "to hallow the name of God in the world," is a phrase that is often used. From this follows all the ambiguity of Jewish life (just as all the dynamic character of the Christian life follows from it). The Jew, insofar as he is "in the world," stands under these laws and no one can tell him that he is permitted to go just so far and no farther, or that there is a line that he may not cross. Such a simple "as little as possible" would be a bad standard, because if I wished to govern all of my actions by the standard "as little as possible from outside Judaism" it would mean, in the circumstances, a diminution of my inner Jewish achievement. So I say to myself as a rule: "as much as possible of the inner Jewish life" — though I well know that in the particular case I cannot anxiously avoid a degree of life outside Judaism. I also know that thereby, in your eyes, I open the way to a charge of soullessness. I can only answer fully at the center and source of my activity; at the periphery it escapes me. But should I then let the citadel fall in order to strengthen those precarious outworks? Should I "be converted" when I have been "chosen" from birth? Is that a real alternative for me? Have I only been thrown into the galley? Is it not *my* ship? You became acquainted with me on land, but you have scarcely noticed that my ship lies in harbor and that I spend more time than is necessary in sailors' taverns, and therefore you could well ask what business I have on the ship. And for you really to believe that it is my ship, and that I therefore belong to it (*pour faire quoi? y vivre et y mourir*)[19] — for you really to believe me will only be possible if the voyage is once more free and I launch out. Or only when we meet out on the open sea?

2

"No Religion Is an Island"[1]

ABRAHAM JOSHUA HESCHEL

INTRODUCTION

Abraham Heschel was born in 1907 in Warsaw, received a Ph.D. from the University of Berlin, and taught there and in Warsaw until the rise of Nazism made it necessary for him to leave Europe. In 1940 he came to the United States after a stay in England, and taught rabbinics and Jewish philosophy at Hebrew Union College in Cincinnati and at the Jewish Theological Seminary in New York City. He died in 1972.

Rabbi Heschel wrote more than two dozen books, including works on medieval Jewish thought, on the Old Testament prophets, and on the philosophy of religion. In the essay reprinted here Heschel argues for an association of religions after the model of the United Nations, an association within which both autonomy and difference would be acknowledged and respected, but within which no threat to the continued existence of any participant would be allowed. Heschel is thus guardedly optimistic in his Jewish perspective on Christianity: profound and irreconcilable differences are recognized, but the possibility of fruitful coexistence and dialogue is also stressed.

He argues especially for a recognition on the part of Christians of their Jewish roots, and for a recognition on the part of Jews that a debt of gratitude is owed to Christians for their success in spreading the knowledge of the God of Abraham throughout the world. Christians and Jews worship the same God and acknowledge a body of sacred texts that is in large part held in common; each, according to Heschel, has much to teach the other.

Heschel's thought in this area is important not only for its intrinsic interest — of which it has much — but also for its historical influence upon the development of Christian (especially Roman Catholic) thinking about Jews. Heschel was a consultant to those who formulated the Catholic Church's "Declaration on the

Relationship of the Church to Non-Christian Religions" at the Second Vatican Council.

"NO RELIGION IS AN ISLAND"

I speak as a member of a congregation whose founder was Abraham, and the name of my rabbi is Moses.

I speak as a person who was able to leave Warsaw, the city in which I was born, just six weeks before the disaster began. My destination was New York, it would have been Auschwitz or Treblinka. I am a brand plucked from the fire, in which my people was burned to death. I am a brand plucked from the fire of an altar of Satan on which millions of human lives were exterminated to evil's greater glory, and on which so much else was consumed: the divine image of so many human beings, many people's faith in the God of justice and compassion, and much of the secret and power of attachment to the Bible bred and cherished in the hearts of men for nearly two thousand years.

I speak as a person who is often afraid and terribly alarmed lest God has turned away from us in disgust and even deprived us of the power to understand His word. In the words Isaiah perceived in his vision (6:9–10):

Then I said, "Here I am! Send me." And he said, "Go, and say to this people: Hear and hear, but do not understand; see and see, but do not perceive. Make the heart of this people fat, and their ears heavy, and shut their eyes; lest they see with their eyes and hear with their ears, and understand with their hearts, and turn and be healed."

Some of us are like patients in the state of final agony—who scream in delirium: the doctor is dead, the doctor is dead.

I speak as a person who is convinced that the fate of the Jewish people and the fate of the Hebrew Bible are intertwined. The recognition of our status as Jews, the legitimacy of our survival, is only possible in a world in which the God of Abraham is revered.

Nazism in its very roots was a rebellion against the Bible, against the God of Abraham. Realizing that it was Christianity that implanted attachment to the God of Abraham and involvement with the Hebrew Bible in the hearts of Western man, Nazism resolved that it must both exterminate the Jews and eliminate Christianity, and bring about instead a revival of Teutonic paganism.

Nazism has suffered a defeat, but the process of eliminating the Bible from the consciousness of the Western world goes on. It is on the issue of saving the radiance of the Hebrew Bible in the minds of man that Jews and Christians are called upon to work together. *None of us can do it alone.* Both of us must realize that in our age anti-Semitism is anti-Christianity and that anti-Christianity is anti-Semitism. Man is never as open to fellowship as he is in moments of misery and distress. The people of New York City have never experienced such fellowship, such awareness of being one, as they did last night in the midst of darkness.

Indeed, there is a light in the midst of the darkness of this hour. But, alas, most of us have no eyes.

Is Judaism, is Christianity, ready to face the challenge? When I speak about the radiance of the Bible in the minds of man, I do not mean its being a theme for "Information, please" but rather an openness to *God's presence in the Bible*, the continuous ongoing effort for a breakthrough in the soul of man, the guarding of the precarious position of being human, even a little higher than human, despite defiance and in face of despair.

The supreme issue is today not the *halacha*[2] for the Jew or the Church for the Christian—but the premise underlying both religions, namely, whether there is a *pathos*, a divine reality concerned with the destiny of man which mysteriously impinges upon history; the supreme issue is whether we are alive or dead to the challenge and the expectation of the living God. The crisis engulfs all of us. The misery and fear of alienation from God make Jew and Christian cry together.

Jews must realize that the spokesmen of the Enlightenment who attacked Christianity were no less negative in their attitude toward Judaism. They often blamed Judaism for the misdeeds of the daughter religion. The casualties of the devastation caused by the continuous onslaughts on biblical religion in modern times are to be found among Jews as well as among Christians.

On the other hand, the Community of Israel must always be mindful of the mystery of aloneness and uniqueness of its own being. "There is a people that dwells apart, not reckoned among the nations" (Numbers 23:9), says the Gentile prophet Balaam. Is it not safer for us to remain in isolation and to refrain from sharing perplexities and certainties with Christians?

Our era marks the end of complacency, the end of evasion, the end of self-reliance. Jews and Christians share the perils and the fears; we stand on the brink of the abyss together. Interdependence of political and economic conditions all over the world is a basic fact of our situation. Disorder in a small obscure country in any part of the world evokes anxiety in people all over the world.

Parochialism has become untenable. There was a time when you could not pry out of a Boston man that the Boston state-house is not the hub of the solar system or that one's own denomination has not the monopoly of the holy spirit. Today we know that even the solar system is not the hub of the universe.

The religions of the world are no more self-sufficient, no more independent, no more isolated than individuals or nations. Energies, experiences and ideas that come to life outside the boundaries of a particular religion or all religions continue to challenge and to affect every religion.

Horizons are wider, dangers are greater. *No religion is an island.* We are all involved with one another. Spiritual betrayal on the part of one of us affects the faith of all of us. Views adopted in one community have an impact on other communities. Today religious isolationism is a myth. For all the profound differences in perspective and substance, Judaism is sooner or later affected by the intellectual, moral and spiritual events within Christian society, and vice versa.

We fail to realize that while different exponents of faith in the world of religion continue to be wary of the ecumenical movement, there is another ecumenical movement, world-wide in extent and influence: nihilism. We must choose between interfaith and inter-nihilism. Cynicism is not parochial. Should religions insist upon the illusion of complete isolation? Should we refuse to be on speaking terms with one another and hope for each other's failure? Or should we pray for each other's health, and help one another in preserving one's respective legacy, in preserving a common legacy?

The Jewish diaspora today, almost completely to be found in the Western world, is certainly not immune to the spiritual climate and the state of religious faith in the general society. We do not live in isolation, and the way in which non-Jews either relate or bid defiance to God has a profound impact on the minds and souls of the Jews. Even in the Middle Ages, when most Jews lived in relative isolation, such impact was acknowledged. To quote, "The usage of the Jews is in accordance with that of the non-Jews. If the non-Jews of a certain town are moral, the Jews born there will be so as well." Rabbi Joseph Yaabez, a victim of the Spanish Inquisition, in the midst of the Inquisition was able to say that "the Christians believe in Creation, the excellence of the Patriarchs, revelation, retribution and resurrection. Blessed is the Lord, God of Israel, who left this remnant after the destruction of the second Temple. But for these Christian nations we might ourselves become infirm in our faith."

We are heirs to a long history of mutual contempt among religions and religious denominations, of religious coercion, strife and persecution. Even in periods of peace, the relationship that obtains between representatives of different religions is not just reciprocity of ignorance; it is an abyss, a source of detraction and distrust, casting suspicion and undoing efforts of many an honest and noble expression of good will.

The Psalmist's great joy is in proclaiming: "Truth and mercy have met together" (Psalm 85:10). Yet so frequently faith and the lack of mercy enter a union, out of which bigotry is born, the presumption that my faith, my motivation, is pure and holy, while the faith of those who differ in creed — even those in my own community — is impure and unholy. How can we be cured of bigotry, presumption, and the foolishness of believing that we have been triumphant while we have all been defeated?

Is it not clear that in spite of fundamental disagreements there is a convergence of some of our commitments, of some of our views, tasks we have in common, evils we must fight together, goals we share, a predicament afflicting us all?

On what basis do we people of different religious commitments meet one another?

First and foremost we meet as human beings who have so much in common: a heart, a face, a voice, the presence of a soul, fears, hope, the ability to trust, a capacity for compassion and understanding, the kinship of being human. My first task in every encounter is to comprehend the personhood of the human being I face, to sense the kinship of being human, solidarity of being.

To meet a human being is a major challenge to mind and heart. I must recall what I normally forget. A person is not just a specimen of the species called homo sapiens. He is all of humanity in one, and whenever one man is hurt we are all injured. The human is a disclosure of the divine, and all men are one in God's care for man. Many things on earth are precious, some are holy, humanity is holy of holies.

To meet a human being is an opportunity to sense the image of God, *the presence* of God. According to a rabbinical interpretation, the Lord said to Moses: "Wherever you see the trace of man there I stand before you."

When engaged in a conversation with a person of different religious commitment I discover that we disagree in matters sacred to us, does the image of God I face disappear? Does the difference in commitment destroy the kinship of being human? Does the fact that we differ in our conceptions of God cancel what we have in common: the image of God?

> For this reason was man created single (whereas of every other species many were created) ... that there should be peace among human beings: one cannot say to his neighbor, my ancestor was nobler than thine (Sanhedrin 37a).

The primary aim of these reflections is to inquire how a Jew out of his commitment and a Christian out of his commitment can find a religious basis for communication and cooperation on matters relevant to their moral and spiritual concern in spite of disagreement.

There are four dimensions of religious existence, four necessary components of man's relationship to God: a) the teaching, the essentials of which are summarized in the form of a creed, which serve as guiding principles in our thinking about matters temporal or eternal, the dimension of the doctrine; b) faith, inwardness, the direction of one's heart, the intimacy of religion, the dimension of privacy; c) the law, or the sacred act to be carried out in the sanctuary in society or at home, the dimension of the deed; d) the context in which creed, faith and ritual come to pass, such as the community or the covenant, history, tradition, the dimension of transcendence. In the dimension of the deed there are obviously vast areas for cooperation among men of different commitments in terms of intellectual communication, of sharing concern and knowledge in applied religion, particularly as they relate to social action.

In the dimension of faith, the encounter proceeds in terms of personal witness and example, sharing insights, confessing inadequacy. On the level of doctrine we seek to convey the content of what we believe in, on the level of faith we experience in one another the presence of a person radiant with reflections of a greater presence.

I suggest that the most significant basis for meeting of men of different religious traditions is the level of fear and trembling, of humility and contrition, where our individual moments of faith are mere waves in the endless ocean of mankind's reaching out for God, where all formulations and articulations appear as understatements, where our souls are swept away by the awareness of the urgency of answering God's commandment, while stripped of pretension and conceit we sense the tragic insufficiency of human faith.

What divides us? What unites us? We disagree in law and creed, in commitments which lie at the very heart of our religious existence. We say "No" to one another in some doctrines essential and sacred to us. What unites us? Our being accountable to God, our being objects of God's concern, precious in His eyes. Our conceptions of what ails us may be different; but the anxiety is the same. The language, the imagination, the concretization of our hopes are different, but the embarrassment is the same, and so is the sigh, the sorrow, and the necessity to obey.

We may disagree about the ways of achieving fear and trembling, but the fear and trembling are the same. The demands are different but the conscience is the same, and so is arrogance, iniquity. The proclamations are different, the callousness is the same, and so is the challenge we face in many moments of spiritual agony.

Above all, while dogmas and forms of worship are divergent, God is the same. What unites us? A commitment to the Hebrew Bible as Holy Scripture. Faith in the Creator, the God of Abraham, commitment to many of His commandments, to justice and mercy, a sense of contrition, sensitivity to the sanctity of life and to the involvement of God in history, the conviction that without the holy the good will be defeated, prayer that history may not end before the end of days, and so much more.

There are moments when we all stand together and see our faces in the mirror: the anguish of humanity and its helplessness; the perplexity of the individual and the need of divine guidance; being called to praise and to do what is required.

In conversations with Protestant and Catholic theologians I have more than once come upon an attitude of condescension to Judaism, a sort of pity for those who have not yet seen the light; tolerance instead of reverence. On the other hand, I cannot forget that when Paul Tillich, Gustave Weigel and myself were invited by the Ford Foundation to speak from the same platform on the religious situation in America,[3] we not only found ourselves in deep accord in disclosing what ails us, but above all without prior consultation, the three of us confessed that our guides in this critical age are the prophets of Israel, not Aristotle, not Karl Marx, but Amos and Isaiah.

The theme of these reflections is not a doctrine or an institution called Christianity, but human beings all over the world, both present and past, who worship God as followers of Jesus, and my problem is how I should relate myself to them spiritually. The issue I am called upon to respond to is not the truth of dogma but the faith and the spiritual power of the commitment of Christians. In facing the claim and the dogma of the Church, Jews and Christians are strangers and stand in disagreement with one another. Yet there are levels of existence where Jews and Christians meet as sons and brothers. "Alas, in heaven's name, are we not your brothers, are we not the sons of one father and are we not the sons of one mother?"

To be sure all men are sons of one father, but they have also the power to forfeit their birthright, to turn rebels, voluntary bastards, "children with no faithfulness in them" (Deuteronomy 32:20). It is not flesh and blood but honor and obedience that save the right of sonship. We claim brotherhood by being subject to His commandments. We are sons when we hearken to the Father, when we praise and honor Him.

The recognition that we are sons in obeying God and praising Him is the starting-point of my reflection. "I am a companion of all who fear Thee, of those who keep Thy precepts" (Psalm 119:63). I rejoice wherever His name is praised, His presence sensed, His commandment done.

The first and most important *prerequisite of interfaith is faith*. It is only out of the depth of involvement in the unending drama that began with Abraham that we can help one another toward an understanding of our situation. Interfaith must come out of depth, not out of a void absence of faith. It is not an enterprise for those who are half learned or spiritually immature. If it is not to lead to the confusion of the many, it must remain a prerogative of the few.

Faith and the power of insight and devotion can only grow in privacy. Exposing one's inner life may engender the danger of desecration, distortion and confusion. Syncretism is a perpetual possibility. Moreover, at a time of paucity of faith, interfaith may become a substitute for faith, suppressing authenticity for the sake of compromise. In a world of conformity, religions can easily be levelled down to the lowest common denominator.

Both communication and separation are necessary. We must preserve our individuality as well as foster care for one another, reverence, understanding cooperation. In the world of economics, science and technology, cooperation exists and continues to grow. Even political states, though different in culture and competing with one another, maintain diplomatic relations and strive for coexistence. Only religions are not on speaking terms. Over a hundred countries are willing to be part of the United Nations; yet no religion is ready to be part of a movement for United Religions. Or should I say, not yet ready? Ignorance, distrust, and disdain often characterize their relations to one another. Is disdain for the opposition indigenous to the religious position? Granted that Judaism and Christianity are committed to contradictory claims, is it impossible to carry on a controversy without acrimony, criticism without loss of respect, disagreement without disrespect? The problem to be faced is: how to combine loyalty to one's own tradition with reverence for different traditions? How is mutual esteem between Christian and Jew possible?

A Christian ought to ponder seriously the tremendous implications of a process begun in early Christian history. I mean the conscious or unconscious dejudaization of Christianity, affecting the Church's way of thinking, its inner life as well as its relationship to the past and present reality of Israel—the father and mother of the very being of Christianity. The children did not arise to call the mother blessed; instead, they called the mother blind. Some theologians continue to act as if they did not know the meaning of "honor your father and your mother"; others, anxious to prove the superiority of the Church, speak as if they suffered from a spiritual Oedipus complex.

A Christian ought to realize that a world without Israel will be a world without the God of Israel. A Jew, on the other hand, ought to acknowledge the eminent role and part of Christianity in God's design for the redemption of all men.

Modern Jews who have come out of the state of political seclusion and are involved in the historic process of Western mankind cannot afford to be indifferent to the religious situation of our fellow-men. Opposition to Christianity must be challenged by the question: What religious alternative do we envisage for the Christian world? Did we not refrain for almost two thousand years from preaching Judaism to the Nations?

A Jew ought to ponder seriously the responsibility involved in Jewish history for having been the mother of two world religions. Does not the failure of children reflect upon their mother? Do not the sharp deviations from Jewish tradition on the part of early Christians who were Jews indicate some failure of communication within the spiritual climate of first-century Palestine?

Judaism is the mother of the Christian faith. It has a stake in the destiny of Christianity. Should a mother ignore her child, even a wayward, rebellious one? On the other hand, the Church should acknowledge that we Jews in loyalty to our tradition have a stake in its faith, recognize our vocation to preserve and to teach the legacy of the Hebrew Scripture, accept our aid in fighting Marcionite trends as an act of love.[4]

Is it not our duty to help one another in trying to overcome hardness of heart, in cultivating a sense of wonder and mystery, in unlocking doors to holiness in time, in opening minds to the challenge of the Hebrew Bible, in seeking to respond to the voice of the prophets?

No honest religious person can fail to admire the outpouring of the love of man and the love of God, the marvels of worship, the magnificence of spiritual insight, the piety, charity and sanctity in the lives of countless men and women, manifested in the history of Christianity. Have not Pascal, Kierkegaard, Immanuel Kant or Reinhold Niebuhr been a source of inspiration to many Jews?

Over and above mutual respect we must acknowledge indebtedness to one another. It is our duty to remember that it was the Church that brought the knowledge of the God of Abraham to the Gentiles. It was the Church that made Hebrew Scripture available to mankind. This we Jews must acknowledge with a grateful heart.

The Septuagint, the works of Philo, Josephus, as well as the Apocrypha and Pseudepigrapha, and the *Fons vitae* by Ibn Gabirol[5] would have been lost had they not been preserved in monasteries. Credit for major achievements in modern scholarship in the field of Bible, in biblical as well as hellenistic Jewish history, goes primarily to Protestant scholars.

The purpose of religious communication among human beings of different commitments is mutual enrichment and enhancement of respect and appreciation rather than the hope that the person spoken to will prove to be wrong in what he regards as sacred.

Dialogue must not degenerate into a dispute, into an effort on the part of each to get the upper hand. There is an unfortunate history of Jewish-Christian disputations, motivated by the desire to prove how blind the Jews are and carried on in a spirit of opposition, which eventually degenerated into enmity. Thus any conversation between Christian and Jew in which abandonment of the other partner's faith is a silent hope must be regarded as offensive to one's religious and human dignity.

Let there be an end to disputation and polemic, an end to disparagement. We honestly and profoundly disagree in matters of creed and dogma. Indeed, there is a deep chasm between Christians and Jews concerning, e.g., the divinity and Messiahship of Jesus. But across the chasm we can extend our hands to one another.

Religion is a means, not the end. It becomes idolatrous when regarded as an end in itself. Over and above all being stands the Creator and Lord of history, He who transcends all. To equate religion and God is idolatry.

Does not the all-inclusiveness of God contradict the exclusiveness of any particular religion? The prospect of all men embracing one form of religion remains an eschatological hope. What about here and now? Is it not blasphemous to say: I alone have all the truth and the grace, and all those who differ live in darkness, and are abandoned by the grace of God?

Is it really our desire to build a monolithic society: one party, one view, one leader, and no opposition? Is religious uniformity desirable or even possible? Has it really proved to be a blessing for a country when all its citizens belonged to one denomination? Or has any denomination attained a spiritual climax when it had the adherence of the entire population? Does not the task of preparing the kingdom of God require a diversity of talents, a variety of rituals, soul-searching as well as opposition?

Perhaps it is the will of God that in this aeon there should be diversity in our forms of devotion and commitment to Him. In this aeon diversity of religions is the will of God.

In the story of the building of the Tower of Babel we read: "The Lord said: They are one people, and they have all one language, and this is what they begin to do" (Genesis 11:6). These words are interpreted by an ancient Rabbi to mean: What has caused them to rebel against me? The fact that they are one people and they have all one language.

> For from the rising of the sun to its setting My name is great among the nations, and in every place incense is offered to My name, and a pure offering; for My name is great among the nations, says the Lord of hosts (Malachi 1:11).

This statement refers undoubtedly to the contemporaries of the prophet. But who were these worshippers of One God? At the time of Malachi there was hardly a large number of proselytes. Yet the statement declares: All those who worship their gods do not know it, but they are really worshipping Me.

It seems that the prophet proclaims that men all over the world, though they confess different conceptions of God, are really worshipping One God, the Father of all men, though they may not be aware of it.

Religions, I repeat, true to their own convictions, disagree profoundly and are in opposition to one another on matters of doctrine. However, if we accept the prophet's thesis that they all worship one God, even without knowing it, if we accept the principle that the majesty of God transcends the dignity of religion, should we not regard a divergent religion as His Majesty's loyal opposition? However, does not every religion maintain the claim to be true, and is not truth exclusive?

The ultimate truth is not capable of being fully and adequately expressed in concepts and words. The ultimate truth is about the situation that pertains between God and man. "The Torah speaks in the language of man." Revelation is always an accommodation to the capacity of man. No two minds are alike, just as no two faces are alike. The voice of God reaches the spirit of man in a variety of ways, in a multiplicity of languages. One truth comes to expression in many ways of understanding.

A major factor in our religious predicament is due to self-righteousness and to the assumption that faith is found only in him who has arrived, while absent in him who is on the way. Religion is often inherently guilty of the sin of pride and presumption. To paraphrase the prophet's words, the exultant religion dwelt secure and said in her heart: "I am, and there is no one besides me."

Humility and contrition seem to be absent where most required—in theology. But humility is the beginning and end of religious thinking, the secret test of faith. There is no truth without humility, no certainty without contrition.

Ezra the Scribe, the great renovator of Judaism, of whom the rabbis said that he was worthy of receiving the Torah had it not been already given through Moses, confessed his lack of perfect faith. He tells us that after he had received a royal *firman* from King Artaxerxes granting him permission to lead a group of exiles from Babylonia: "I proclaimed a fast there at the river Ahava, that we might afflict ourselves before our God, to seek of Him a right way for us, and for our little ones, and for all substance. For I was ashamed to require of the King a band of soldiers and horsemen to help us against the enemy in the way: because we had spoken unto the King, saying, the hand of God is upon all them for good that seek Him" (Ezra 8:21–22).

Human faith is never final, never an arrival, but rather an endless pilgrimage, a being on the way. We have no answers to all problems. Even some of our sacred answers are both emphatic and qualified, final and tentative; final within our own position in history, tentative—because we can only speak in the tentative language of man.

Heresy is often a roundabout expression of faith, and sojourning in the wilderness is a preparation for entering the promised land.

Is the failure, the impotence of all religions, due exclusively to human transgression? Or perhaps to the mystery of God's withholding His grace, of His concealing even while revealing? Disclosing the fullness of His glory would be an impact that would surpass the power of human endurance.

His thoughts are not our thoughts. Whatever is revealed is abundance compared with our soul and a pittance compared with His treasures. No word is God's last word, no word is God's ultimate word.

Following the revelation at Sinai, the people said to Moses: "You speak to us, and we will hear; let not God speak to us, lest we die" (Exodus 20:19).

The Torah as given to Moses, an ancient rabbi maintains, is but an unripened fruit of the heavenly tree of wisdom. At the end of days, much that is concealed will be revealed.

The mission to the Jews is a call to the individual Jews to betray the fellowship, the dignity, the sacred history of their people. Very few Christians seem to comprehend what is morally and spiritually involved in supporting such activities. We are Jews as we are men. The alternative to our existence as Jews is spiritual suicide, extinction. It is not a change into something else. Judaism has allies but no substitutes. The wonder of Israel, the marvel of Jewish existence, the survival of holiness in the history of the Jews, is a continuous verification of the marvel of the Bible. Revelation to Israel continues as a revelation through Israel.

The Protestant pastor, Christian Furchgetott Gellert, was asked by Frederick the Great, "Herr Professor, give me proof of the Bible, but briefly, for I have little time." Gellert answered, "Your Majesty, the Jews."

Indeed, is not the existence of the Jews a witness to the God of Abraham? Is not our loyalty to the law of Moses a light that continues to illumine the lives of those who observe it as well as the lives of those who are aware of it?

Gustave Weigel spent the last evening of his life in my study at the Jewish Theological Seminary. We opened our hearts to one another in prayer and contrition and spoke of our own deficiencies, failures, hopes. At one moment I posed the question: Is it really the will of God that there be no more Judaism in the world? Would it really be the triumph of God if the scrolls of the Torah would no more be taken out of the Ark and the Torah no more read in the Synagogue, our ancient Hebrew prayers in which Jesus himself worshipped no more recited, the Passover Seder no more celebrated in our lives, the law of Moses no more observed in our homes? Would it really be *ad Majorem Dei gloriam*[6] to have a world without Jews?

My life is shaped by many loyalties — to my family, to my friends, to my people, to the U.S. constitution, etc. Each of my loyalties has its ultimate root in one ultimate relationship: loyalty to God, the loyalty of all my loyalties. That relationship is the covenant of Sinai. All we are we owe to Him. He has enriched us with gifts of insight, with the joy of moments full of blessing. He has also suffered with us in years of agony and distress.

None of us pretends to be God's accountant, and His design for history and redemption remains a mystery before which we must stand in awe. It is arrogant to maintain that the Jews' refusal to accept Jesus as the Messiah is due to their stubbornness or blindness as it would be presumptuous for the Jews not to acknowledge the glory and holiness in the lives of countless Christians. "The Lord is near to all who call upon Him, to all who call upon Him in truth" (Psalm 145:18).

Fortunately there are some important Christian voices who expressed themselves to the effect that the missionary activities to the Jews be given up. Reinhold Niebuhr[7] may have been the first Christian theologian who at a joint meeting of the faculties of the Union Theological Seminary and the Jewish Theological Seminary declared that the missionary

> activities are wrong not only because they are futile and have little fruit to boast for their exertions. They are wrong because the two faiths despite differences are sufficiently alike for the Jew to find God more easily in terms of his own religious heritage than by subjecting himself to the hazards of his guilt feelings involved in conversion to a faith which, whatever its excellencies, must appear to him as a symbol of an oppressive majority culture, ... Practically nothing can purify the symbol of Christ as the image of God in the imagination of the Jew from the taint with which ages of Christian oppression in the name of Christ have tainted it.*[8]

Tillich has said:

Many Christians feel that it is a questionable thing, for instance, to try to convert Jews. They have lived and spoken with their Jewish friends for decades. They have not converted them, but they have created a community of conversation which has changed both sides of the dialogue.*⁹

And a statement on "relations with the Roman Catholic Church" adopted by the Central Committee of the World Council of Churches in its meeting in Rochester, New York, in August, 1963, mentions proselytism as a "cause of offence," an issue "which must be frankly faced if true dialogue is to be possible."*¹⁰

The ancient Rabbis proclaim: "Pious men of all nations have a share in the life to come."

"I call heaven and earth to witness that the Holy Spirit rests upon each person, Jew or Gentile, man or woman, master or slave, in consonance with his deeds."

Holiness is not the monopoly of any particular religion or tradition. Wherever a deed is done in accordance with the will of God, wherever a thought of man is directed toward Him, there is the holy.

The Jews do not maintain that the way of the Torah is the only way of serving God. "Let all the peoples walk each one in the name of its god, but we will walk in the name of the Lord our God for ever and ever" (Micah 4:5).

"God loves the Saint" (Psalms 146:8) — "They love Me, and I love them. ... If a person wishes to be a Levite or a priest, he cannot become a saint, even if he is a gentile, he may become one. For saints do not derive their saintliness from their ancestry; they become saints because they dedicate themselves to God and love Him." Conversion to Judaism is no prerequisite for sanctity. In his Code Maimonides[11] asserts:

Not only is the tribe of Levi (God's portion) sanctified in the highest degree, but any man among all the dwellers on earth whose heart prompts him and whose mind instructs him to dedicate himself to the services of God and to walk uprightly as God intended him to, and who disencumbers himself of the load of the many pursuits which men invent for themselves. ... God asks for the heart, everything depends upon the intention of the heart. ... All men have a share in eternal life if they attain according to their ability knowledge of the Creator and have ennobled themselves by noble qualities. There is no doubt that he who has thus trained himself morally and intellectually to acquire faith in the Creator will certainly have a share in the life to come. This is why our Rabbis taught: a gentile who studies the Torah of Moses is (spiritually) equal to the High Priest at the Temple in Jerusalem.

Leading Jewish authorities, such as Jehuda Halevi[12] and Maimonides, acknowledge Christianity to be *preparatio messianica*,[13] while the Church regarded ancient Judaism to have been *preparatio evangelica*.[14] Thus, whereas the Christian doctrine has often regarded Judaism as having outlived its usefulness and the Jews as candidates for conversion, the Jewish attitude enables us to acknowledge the presence of a divine plan in the role of Christianity within the history of redemption. Jehuda Halevi, though criticizing Christianity and Islam for retaining relics of ancient idolatry and feast days, "they also revere places sacred to idols," compares Christians and Mohammedans to proselytes who adopted the roots but not all the branches (or the logical conclusions of the divine commandments).

The wise providence of God towards Israel may be compared to the planting of a seed of corn. It is placed in the earth, where it seems to be changed into soil, and water, and rottenness, and the seed can no longer be recognized. But in very truth it is the seed that has changed the earth and water into its own nature, and then the seed raises itself from one stage to another, transforms the elements, and throws out shoots and leaves. . . . Thus it is with Christians and Moslems. The Law of Moses has changed them that come into contact with it, even though they seem to have cast the Law aside. These religions are the preparation and the preface to the Messiah we expect, who is the fruit himself of the seed originally sown, and all men, too, will be fruit of God's seed when they acknowledge Him, and all become one mighty tree.

A similar view is set forth by Maimonides in his authoritative Code:

It is beyond the human mind to fathom the designs of the Creator; for our ways are not His ways, neither are our thoughts His thoughts. All these matters relating to Jesus of Nazareth and the Ishmaelite (Mohammed) who came after him served to clear the way for King Messiah, to prepare the whole world to worship God with one accord, as it is written, *For then will I turn to the peoples a pure language, that they may all call upon the name of the Lord to serve Him with one consent* (Zephaniah 3:9). Thus the Messianic hope, the Torah, and the commandments have become familiar topics — topics of conversation (among the inhabitants) of the far isles and many peoples.

Christianity and Islam, far from being accidents of history or purely human phenomena, are regarded as part of God's design for the redemption of all men. Christianity is accorded ultimate significance by acknowledging that "all these matters relative to Jesus of Nazareth and Mohammed . . . served to clear the way for King Messiah." In addition to the role of these religions in the plan of redemption, their achievements within history are explicitly affirmed: Through them "the Messianic hope, the Torah, and the commandments have become familiar topics ... (among the inhabitants) of the far isles and many peoples." Elsewhere Maimonides acknowledges that "the Christians believe and profess that the Torah is God's revelation (*torah min hashamaiim*) and given to Moses in the form in which it has been preserved; they have it completely written down, though they frequently interpret it differently."

Rabbi Johanan Ha-Sandelar, a disciple of Rabbi Akiba,[15] says: "Every community which is established for the sake of heaven will in the end endure; but one which is not for the sake of heaven will not endure in the end."

Rabbi Jacob Emden maintains that heretical Jewish sects such as the Karaites and the Sabbatians belong to the second category whereas Christianity and Islam are in the category of "a community which is for the sake of heaven" and which will "in the end endure." They have emerged out of Judaism and accepted "the fundamentals of our divine religion ... to make known God among the nations ... , to proclaim that there is a Master on heaven and in earth, divine providence, reward and punishment ... , Who bestows the gift of prophecy ... and communicates through the prophets laws and statutes to live by. ... This is why their community endures. ... Since their intention is for the sake of heaven, reward will not be withheld from them." He also praises many Christian scholars who have come to the rescue of Jews and their literature.

Rabbi Israel Lifschutz of Danzig (1782–1860) speaks of the Christians, "our brethren, the gentiles, who acknowledge the one God and revere his Torah which they deem divine and observe, as is required of them, the seven commandments of Noah."

What, then, is the purpose of interreligious cooperation?

It is neither to flatter nor to refute one another, but to help one another; to share insight and learning, to cooperate in academic ventures on the highest scholarly level, and what is even more important to search in the wilderness for well-springs of devotion, for treasures of stillness, for the power of love and care for man. What is urgently needed are ways of helping one another in the terrible predicament of here and now by the courage to believe that the word of the Lord endures for ever as well as here and now; to cooperate in trying to bring about a resurrection of sensitivity, a revival of conscience; to keep alive the divine sparks in our souls, to nurture openness to the spirit of the Psalms, reverence for the words of the prophets, and faithfulness to the Living God.

3

"Christianity and the Holocaust"[1]

STUART E. ROSENBERG

INTRODUCTION

Stuart Rosenberg was born in 1922 in New York City and has served as rabbi both there and in Toronto. He has written extensively, and often polemically, on Jewish-Christian relations, and on the perception of Jews by non-Jews in the United States and Canada.

The essay reprinted here is one chapter of a larger work entitled The Christian Problem. *In it Rabbi Rosenberg explores in depth and from a number of different perspectives the problem of Christian anti-Semitism. He presents this as a problem for Christians just as much as for Jews. Dealing with anti-Semitism is a test for the survival of Christianity just as much as it is a test for the survival of Judaism: "After Auschwitz, the central moral test and religious question for Christianity is the survival of the Jews in a Christian world."*

In the chapter given here Rosenberg draws out the roots of the Holocaust in the history and doctrines of Christianity and represents the events of the 1930s and 1940s in Europe as a direct and natural outgrowth of Christian doctrine. He denies that Nazism was an anti-Christian aberration, but rather describes it as a perfectly natural development of traditional Christian anti-Semitism. In order to show this he draws parallels between the medieval anti-Jewish practices of the church and the measures adopted by Hitler's Germany. Rosenberg also points, with highly flavored rhetoric, to the "three silences" of Christians: the silence of collusion with Hitler's anti-Semitism; the silence about the Christian roots of Nazi anti-Semitism in the years immediately following the end of World War II; and the silence in the face of Arab threats to destroy the state of Israel in 1967 and after.

Rabbi Rosenberg's work is polemical and passionate, and shows very clearly important dimensions of the ways in which post-1945 Jewish views of Christianity are colored by, almost defined by, the events of the Holocaust. For Jews

42   *Stuart E. Rosenberg*

who hold this view, the Holocaust is not only the most important event ever to have shaped how Jews think about themselves, but ought also to play the same role for Christians. This is largely because it shows — or should show — Christians how close they always are to paganism and to the idolatry and blasphemy that goes with it. There are analogues in what Rosenberg says, even if an enormous difference in style and intellectual background, to Rosenzweig's emphasis on Christian ignorance of what Jews naturally know (see Chapter 1).

It is difficult for the Christian reading this essay — or Rosenberg's other work — not to feel himself or herself in the presence of a man with an idée fixe and an extremely restricted view of what is important in history. Most Christians — and many Jews — would disagree with the thesis that the Holocaust is the single definitive event in the history of both Judaism and Christianity (what about the exodus? the resurrection? the Bar Kochba revolt?), or even that it is the most striking and important example of human evil and suffering in history. But one-sided views can have great heuristic value, and it is important for Christians to know that there are Jewish perceptions of Christianity like Rabbi Rosenberg's.

"CHRISTIANITY AND THE HOLOCAUST"

"There are some things that weary of speech; they welcome silence."[*2] Surely the murder of six million Jews, among them one million children, causes words to die on one's lips. For almost two decades after those numbing, genocidal events, Christians barely spoke of them. Church councils scarcely considered them, only faintly remembering. Jews, too, though hardly forgetful, kept their wounds and memories largely to themselves, and they slowly began the painful work of rebuilding the shattered lives of those who had somehow survived. In those days, too, they rarely spoke of or described the horrors, and when some few did, their voices were muted, almost inaudible to others.

"Death brings to Jewish lips a prayer of glorification that speaks not of death (the doxology called the *Kaddish*), so let these six million dead rest in peace undisturbed by words of reproach that cannot touch them or regenerate the living who killed them. Silence is the aftermath; *words only in the anticipation of new disaster.*"[*3] Until the 1960s even the most sensitive Jews felt this way. Not until the very eve of that decade would the word "Holocaust" be "invented" to refer specifically to the death of six million Jews.[*4] No clear language or vocabulary was yet at hand that would, in an instant — in a single, unmistakable, and penetrating locution — say what should have been said. Not words, but silence was virtually everywhere.

But the silence of the Jews then was of a far different order from the silence of the Christians. Jews know this, but many Christians still do not and that problem remains as an obstacle even now in our new "age of dialogue," when the word "Holocaust" comes more easily and quickly to the lips of many.

It will be helpful to understand how it was that what was barely mentioned mere decades ago—regarded almost as taboo—has now become part of the common realm in television programs, magazine articles, books—even Christian theological books—and on the interfaith lecture platforms of churches and synagogues. Even now, however, when *some* Christians and most Jews are "silent" no longer, the "Holocaust" means different things to each group. Before we explore this phenomenon, we need first to examine both of those older, yet vastly different silences, to see what they may still teach. To do so in proper perspective, we must note with reverence that there were indeed *some* Christians who did set a different example for their own co-religionists. They had refused to stand idly by.

"Righteous Gentiles"—Christians Who Saved Jews

It cannot be forgotten that there were Christian martyrs who willingly endangered, or even sacrificed themselves, in the hope that they could save their Jewish neighbors. Jews have especially remembered. In Jerusalem at Yad Vashem—the national shrine memorializing the six million Jewish victims of the Holocaust—an honored place is reserved for those "righteous Gentiles," as the Jewish tradition refers to them, who served the cause of justice and mercy in their own godly ways. Overlooking the capital city of the Jewish state, high atop a once barren, rocky hill, is a quiet avenue known as *l'Avenue des Justes*. Here trees have been planted by Jews, each dedicated to the memory of every European Gentile known to have saved the life of even a single Jew during the Holocaust. The street is now verdant with evergreens and carob trees. Further, as a dramatic sign of the love and reverent esteem in which these people are held by Jews, in May, 1985, on the occasion of the fortieth anniversary of VE Day commemorating the close of World War II in Europe, the Israeli government conferred honorary citizenship upon all known "righteous Gentiles"—living or dead. These people must have numbered in the thousands. Some worked clandestinely, and as a result have remained unknown. Others considered their efforts a "religious duty" for which they would accept no public acknowledgment or publicity after the war. Still others, fearing reprisals from antisemitic neighbors or groups, cloaked their life-saving work in anonymity. Then, as in Denmark and Greece, there were also whole populations who rallied to the Jewish cause. In October, 1943, when the Danes learned of the German plan to deport their fellow Jewish citizens, rescue committees sprang up overnight and went into action. At great risk to their own lives, they transported the entire Danish Jewish community—some six or seven thousand souls—under cover of darkness across the Sea of Malmo to safety in Sweden.[*5] Many hundreds of Greek Jews were also transported from the Greek islands to Turkey by their Christian neighbors. In Holland, a Nazi attempt in 1941 to effect the mass deportation of Jews was met with a general strike by Amsterdam workers. And in Finland and Bulgaria, the strong and openly expressed antipathies of local populations prevented the deportation of Jews which had already been ordered by the Nazis. There are others, too, whom Jews remember with feelings of awe and reverence. Among the most notable are Raoul Wallenberg, who served as a plenipotentiary of the king of Sweden, and Charles Lutz, a Swiss Consul, who persistently intervened against the edicts of the Nazis, and whose efforts helped to save tens of thousands of Hungarian Jews from imminent death.*6 Not to be forgotten is Jean-Marie Mussy, once president of the Swiss Confederation, whose careful and skillful negotiations with the Nazis helped virtually at the eleventh hour to snatch several thousand doomed Jews from the Theresienstadt and Bergen-Belsen death camps.

Not many churchmen, however, risked their reputations to defy the authorities in favor of the Jews. When they did, it was usually a personal choice, not an official one. One Jewish scholar notes:

> How important the individual feelings were for the rescue operations of Jews can be proven by the different attitudes of two bishops in Lithuania in 1941. When a delegation of Jews from Kovno approached Bishop Brizgys to ask for help, he answered, "I can only cry and pray myself; the Church cannot help you." On the other hand, Bishop Rainis of Vilna preached to the monasteries that help be given to Jews. He also refused to bestow his blessing on a Ukrainian auxiliary battalion attached to the German army, because the battalion participated in actions against the Jews.*7

An American Catholic priest, at the conclusion of his careful study of *Vatican Diplomacy and the Jews During the Holocaust, 1939–43* reminds us that Pope Pius XII did not instruct his diplomats or priests to denounce the racial laws or the deportations. Instead, he "chose reserve, prudence, and a diplomatic presence in all the capitals over any other goal or needs. Vatican diplomacy failed the Jews during the Holocaust by not doing all that it was possible for it to do on their behalf." It pursued "a goal of reserve rather than humanitarian concern . . . it betrayed the ideals it had set for itself. The nuncios, the secretary of state, and most of all, the Pope, share the responsibility for this dual failure."*8

All of which makes more poignant the quiet but searing testimony of one unforgettable Christian who died a martyr at Nazi hands. He saw things quite differently from Pius XII. This man from Holland, a devout member of the Plymouth Brethren, explained why he had to oppose the Nazis: "Anybody who takes part in the persecution of the Jews, whether voluntarily or against his will, is looking for an excuse for himself. Some cannot give up a business deal, others are doing it for the sake of their families; and the Jewish professors must disappear for the sake of the university. I have to go through these difficult days without breaking, but in the end my fate will be decided and I shall go like a man."*9

How do we explain these widely differing Christian choices? While diffident about generalizing regarding the varying attitudes of Christians to Jews, a leading Holocaust historian, Yehuda Bauer, does throw some light on the question. He writes:

> In Poland, Lithuania, Latvia, and the Ukraine, in Croatia and Romania, the attitude of the overwhelming majority of the local population, including that of the majority churches, and excepting the left-wing political parties, ranged from hostile indifference to active hostility . . . Minority churches tended to protect Jewish minorities . . . On the whole, the tragic situation of the Jew in a Gentile environment was one in which the Jew could only appeal to mercy, compassion, and loving kindness. In some places he met people who had these qualities; *in most places he did not.* . . . The Jew was powerless, and the *European background of antisemitism* did not permit for more than a partial reassertion of humanism in the attitude toward him.*[10]

The Second Christian Silence

The exceptions—the relatively few and notable "righteous Gentiles"—help prove the rule. During the twelve years of Hitler's "kingdom of night" which culminated in 1945, most Christian churches distanced themselves from the Holocaust, whose destructive force was moving inexorably toward the fulfilment of Hitler's "final solution to the Jewish problem": the wholesale slaughter and destruction of that people, for no other reason than that they were Jews. But even after the war, when the work of reconstruction and reconciliation should have begun—even then, few Christian leaders or their church councils reached out to assist the remnants of European Jewry. Worse still, few, if any, actively sought to address their own crucial religious question: the meaning of the Holocaust for believing and practicing Christians.

The second silence of the churches must surely be related to their first—their almost total acquiescence to, and acceptance of, Hitler's anti-Jewish measures in the 1930s and 1940s. The so-called "European background of antisemitism" was in fact little more than its own Christian history.[11]

Why, then, in the years immediately following World War II, did so few churches or their leaders fail to see that there was a relationship between the long and continuous history of Christian anti-Judaism and the end product of Nazism—the calculated murder of one-third of the Jewish people? Many of their communicants still hid their faces, or, even worse, placidly accepted the doom of the six million in Hitler's Europe as a divine judgment for the "Jewish rejection of Jesus."

Sensitive souls among them are now inquiring: how could we have failed to see that the Holocaust was a judgment upon us as Christians, and not upon the Jews as Jews?*[12] How could we not have understood that the six million unredeemed crucifixions have left us with blood on our own hands? As a Jew, I draw strength from the growing number of devoted Christians who are now willing to state, without hesitation or equivocation, that *after Auschwitz, the central moral test and religious question for Christianity is the survival of the Jews in a Christian world.* Indeed, all of those earlier issues relating to this question which I have called "the Christian problem" – are now beginning to be re-examined, reviewed, and in some quarters courageously acted upon.

Yet I am convinced that Jews still have a crucial role to play in this process. Without Jews to raise these questions, to remind the churches repeatedly and tirelessly to confront Christian conscience with the moral and religious implications of these spiritual shortfalls, there are strong signs that new silences will again prevent them from coming to terms with their "Christian problem."

This is what makes a thorough understanding of the Holocaust and its implications for Christianity so crucial for the outcome of any religious dialogue between Jews and Christians. To suppress a serious discussion and analysis of the Holocaust out of "genteel" concerns for personal sensitivities, or out of fear of erecting barriers to ongoing and continuing encounters, is to miss the point, if not the ultimate purpose of these dialogues altogether. In the language of Robert McAfee Brown, a leading Christian ecumenist, "each partner [to the dialogue] must accept responsibility in humility and penitence for what his group has done, and is doing, to foster and perpetuate division; each partner must forthrightly face the issues that cause separation as well as those that create solidarity."*13

These words, originally addressed to the Catholic-Protestant encounter are probably of even more force when applied to the meeting of Christians and Jews. It is especially in light of earlier Christian silences that Jewish partners to the dialogue have a special role to play: to help "sear into memory" what many Christians may have forgotten.

I have borrowed the phrase "sear into memory" from a high prelate of the Catholic Church. When, in May 1985, President Reagan decided to visit the cemetery at Bitburg, Germany, where many S.S. troops were buried (Reagan proceeded with this trip despite agonized pleas of many Americans and the Jewish community in particular urging him to cancel his plan), Cardinal John J. O'Connor, Archbishop of the Roman Catholic Archdiocese of New York, joined in the protest. He said that he was not prepared ever to forget those who perpetrated the horrors of World War II. He declared: "I cannot forget it as a Christian and I am grateful that it is our Jewish brothers and sisters who keep reminding us. It must be seared into our memories."*14

The "new Jews" of the 1980s are prepared to serve as untiring prods to Christian conscience. Beginning in the late 1960s, they began to opt for a different posture than the one taken by their parents or friends two decades before. The latter, as already indicated, had been "Jews of silence." They rarely invoked the Holocaust; they hardly ever spoke publicly about those dreaded events. The "new Jews" of our time, however, lose no opportunity to remind the world that "silence" is a mortal sin; it is the mother of future catastrophes.[15]

The Third Christian Silence

I have said that Vatican Council II was a source of some reassurance to Jews.[16] Yet one cannot overlook some of the disquiet and confusion it also deposited in Jewish hearts. In his search for "church renewal"—*aggiornia-mento*—Pope John XXIII convened the Second Vatican Council, in 1962. It could not have been foreseen that he would stretch the "new ecumenism" beyond his fellow Christians, the Protestants, and reach out to Jews as well. By 1965, however, the Vatican had issued a major decree, part of its final "Declaration on the Relationship of the Church to Non-Christian Religions"—known as *Nostra Aetate*—that dealt with the Jews alone, and it has since been known as "The Jewish Declaration."

The "Declaration" did take into account "the bond that spiritually ties the people of the New Covenant to Abraham's stock," and did state that the Church should not "forget that she draws sustenance from the root of that well-cultivated olive tree on to which have been grafted the wild shoots, the Gentiles." But there had been great and often ugly wrangling within the Council—led by the conservative forces within the Curia, and heavily abetted by Catholic bishops from Arab and Middle Eastern countries and their supporters. The final version passed in 1965 after the death of Pope John and during the new reign of Pope Paul—and even then only after several years of sharp controversy—was greatly watered-down from what had originally been proposed by the preparatory secretariat.

What had been intended as a statement to foster friendship and mark a new accord became severely blunted in its effect, and many North American Catholics were themselves deeply disappointed. In the words of one of them, John Cogley, then religion editor of the *New York Times*, the Declaration became "a reason for shame and anguish on the part of many Catholics, and of suspicion and rancor on the part of many Jews."*[17] The unwillingness of the Council to deal in any fundamental way with the persistence of anti-Judaism and antisemitism; its amazing silence concerning the events of the Holocaust; and its refusal to recognize the special relationship of the Jewish people to the land of Israel, became all the more prominent, because in one way or another these issues had been thoroughly discussed at the Council sessions and were then overwhelmingly rejected in the showdown of the final vote. The recorded vote which approved the Declaration was 2,221 to 88. In hindsight, this would be later regarded as an ominous foreboding of what soon lay ahead.

Not many months would pass before there appeared on the horizon the spectre and portent of possible new Jewish dooms. In April and May of

1967, prominent leaders in the Arab world openly began to call for the destruction of the Jewish state and vowed that they would soon "drive all Israelis into the Sea." I can never forget the fear that clutched at the hearts of even those Jews who had wandered from the organized community, as Israel's total annihilation seemed imminent. And then, again, the world held its tongue. Even many Jews who were assimilated began streaming back to their own people as the days were ticking quickly away and no nation on earth was either willing to stand in the way of Arab threats or to defend Israel. Indeed the United Nations even assisted President Nasser of Egypt in his plans to be rid of Israel by allowing the Straits of Tiran to be blockaded by Egypt. When these straits were no longer protected as an international waterway under U.N. surveillance, the Egyptians and their allies could attack Israel by sea at will. On May 16, 1967, the official voice of the Egyptian Government, Radio Cairo, openly declared: "The existence of Israel has continued too long ... the great hour has come. The battle has come in which we shall destroy Israel." One historian has written: "Even as Israel mobilized its forces to defend its life against that threat of destruction, Israeli Rabbis were consecrating extensive burial grounds for expected Jewish losses."*18 The vision of a new nightmare descended upon the Jewish community, not only in Israel but all over the world. No Jew then living will ever forget. The spectre of two holocausts within a single generation became too much to bear. No one moved to help Israel; no voices were raised to give it hope.

Incredibly, in six lightning days in early June, 1967, the Israelis won a "miraculous" victory, one which not only made military history, but which also fundamentally changed Jewish self-perceptions thereafter. The Six Day War, I believe, was chiefly responsible for creating a new Jewish identity in North America and elsewhere in the free world. Before that time, many Jews could only think silently and inwardly of the Holocaust and then only with lamentation and tears that were enshrined in their earlier recollections of the slain six million. Before that time they seemed to repress these painful memories — as Jews of Silence — but ever since, the Holocaust was itself turned into a challenge to survive. To remember the helpless martyred dead was now also to vow that it would never happen again. A strong Israel, most Jews came to feel, was the only guarantor of that.

In a strange way it was this third Christian silence that contributed to these repossessed feelings of Jewish solidarity, in which Holocaust memories now played a crucial role.[19] ... If, as claimed, the causes for these crucial Christian silences "lie deep in the Christian soul," what, indeed, lies even deeper? What is at the roots — at the bottom of it all? I believe that if Christians would willingly and unflinchingly face up to these silences, which, jointly and severally, hark back to their reluctance to see the Holocaust as a problem for Christianity — they may themselves discover what lies at the roots. They should then find the ineluctable culprit: the clinging pagan elements that still adhere to a Gentile Christianity shorn of its Jewish lifelines. Paganism can perhaps finally be expunged from their midst when Christians seek to fathom what the Holocaust should mean for them *as Christians*. The task is arduous and demanding; it requires hard choices. Indeed, as one Christian scholar, Franklin H. Littell, who himself has made these choices, reminds us: "A Jew has to choose to be a pagan, while a Gentile has to choose not to be."*20

Choosing Not To Be Pagans

If, from the thousands of stories that have reached us out of the depths of the Holocaust experience, only a single tale were permitted to be told, there is one which fully epitomizes the moral questions facing Christianity and its leaders in these post-Auschwitz days:

> As the German *Einsatzgruppen* (mobile killing units) were about to execute the Jewish population in a small Ukrainian town, a Hasidic Jew walked over to the young German officer in charge and told him that it was customary in civilized countries to grant a last request to those condemned to death. The young German assured the Jew that he would observe that civilized tradition and asked the Jew what his last wish was. "A short prayer," replied the Jew. "Granted," snapped the German. The Jew placed his hand on his bare head to cover it and recited the following blessing, first in its original Hebrew, then in its German translation: "Blessed art thou, O Lord our God, King of the Universe, who hath not made me heathen!" Upon completion of the blessing, he looked directly into the eyes of the German and, with his head held high, walked to the edge of the pit and said: "I have finished. You may begin." The young German's bullet struck him in the back of the head at the edge of the huge grave filled with bodies.*21

Every day of the year, as part of their morning prayers before food may be partaken, traditional Jews pronounce that benediction: praise to the God of Israel for not having been born into a pagan community. But things are very different for Christians. Littell has again clarified this issue by reminding us that "the 'Christian' Gentile can take on again the protective coloration of the dominant society, that is the heathen world; the Jew cannot. When the Jews suffer from antisemitic attacks they suffer for that which Christians would also suffer if they stayed Christians. But the 'Christians' can homogenize and become mere Gentiles again, while the Jews, believing or secularized, remain representatives of another history, another providence."*22 In their dialogue with Jews, the Holocaust issue becomes crucial for Christians: they can see how important it is for them to cut their pagan ties by returning to their Jewish sources.

The Jewish world view, as we have already seen, regards idolatry and paganism as the root of all moral evil. Pagan idolatry, of course, is not merely the worship of things—of sticks, stones, or nature itself—as some simple minds might surmise from the ancient stories narrated in the Hebrew Bible. Idolatry occurs whenever we absolutize the relative: when we worship the part as if it were the whole, and confuse the means with the ends; or when we trivialize morality by not holding human life as God-given and sacred.*[23] The Nazi cult worshipped "blood and soil," and in narcissistic fashion deified their own so-called "Aryan race." In the process, they harnessed their false "gods of science," which many German scientists had made into objects of adoration. As a product of their own pagan mythologies and fictions, the Nazi-Germans and their collaborators saw themselves as *übermenschen*, a superhuman people whose scientific knowledge could be used with impunity to engage in "scientific" barbarities, to be applied to all sub-human types—the *untermenschen*—as a matter of "absolute" right. Inevitably, it was the Jews, arch-enemies of these and all other forms of paganism, who were their prime targets. But it was not Nazism alone that served pagan gods.

When some contemporary Christian theologians remind us that Christians must choose *not* to be pagans, they use as their prime model and object lesson the virtual apostasy of many European Christians during the Holocaust. One such historian writes as follows:

> It has become popular among some churchmen and general historians to deal with Nazism as a "pagan" irruption—essentially atavistic, tribal, anti-Christian. There is much to be said for this argument. . . . The trouble with this line of argument [however] is that it relieves the Christians and their leaders of their guilt for what happened. . . . If the churches had used the means of spiritual government at their disposal to call the Nazi leaders to repentance, to return to minimal Christian standards, if the Nazi elite had been excommunicated for failure to respond, then today the churches could say truthfully, "They were pagans. They left our fellowship in the covenant. They were not of us." But the churches did not do this. Instead they retained in their membership and accorded signal honors to traitors to human liberty, mass murderers, apostate Christians. Adolf Hitler died a Roman Catholic, and an annual mass is celebrated in his memory in Madrid. Hermann Goering died a Lutheran. We Christians cannot come back today and claim no responsibility for what they did in the name of law and order and anti-Bolshevism, claiming to protect "religion."*[24]

Even now, more than four decades after the Holocaust, there is a growing attempt on the part of some to push those barbaric events far from the concerns of Christendom. Unless these current "revisionist" efforts at downplaying and falsifying the Holocaust are met with a firm Christian response that denies them any standing, the "new Jews" of our time will find it impossible to respond affirmatively to invitations to "dialogue" and "meeting."

"Stealing" the Holocaust

Edward Alexander reminds us that one of the earliest and best-remembered attempts "to steal from the Jewish victims of the Holocaust precisely that for which they were victimized" was the dramatization for the American stage of the book, *The Diary of Anne Frank*. He explains that the playwrights had

> expunged from the stage version all of Anne's (diary) references to hopes for survival in a Jewish homeland and changed Anne's particular allusions to her Jewish identity and Jewish hopes to a blurred amorphous universalism. One example should suffice to illustrate the general pattern. In the *Diary* Anne writes: "Who has made the Jews different from all other people? Who has allowed us to suffer so terribly up until now? . . . If we bear all this suffering and if there are still Jews left, when it is over, then Jews instead of being doomed, will be held up as an example. . . . We can never become just Netherlanders, or just English, or just representatives of any country for that matter, we will always remain Jews." In the stage version this is reduced to the following: "We are not the only people that've had to suffer . . . sometimes one race, sometimes another."*[25]

The lessons to be learned from this single example are many. Morally insensitive persons often relate to the awful particularity of Jewish suffering in clearly amoral fashion, for when they insist on universalizing the unique Jewish condition they succeed in trivializing it. Thus today virtually all urban slums are called "ghettos," and even neighborhood fires are referred to as "holocausts" by the print and electronic media. When the unique Jewish deprivations and degradations are made into universal metaphors for disabilities of all kinds—large or small—not only is the currency of language devalued, but other difficulties, even if not immediately obvious, also ensue. From the point of view of improved Jewish-Christian understanding, for example, this word-play has become a "new game" that helps to obliterate the history of Jewish suffering from Christian memory. As a result, some Christians can be prevented from seeing and learning what they *must* see and learn: both Christianity and Nazism singled Jews out as special and perennial targets for their hostilities. Yet, as Cardinal John O'Connor has cautioned: Christians need Jews to help sear into their memories what they might otherwise forget. Religious dialogue can play an important role in helping Christians listen to the testimony of an important "witness"—the Jewish remembrancer.[26]

If true dialogue and reconciliation are to occur, these "memories" must be openly faced and fully probed. The Holocaust must continue to remind both parties of a fundamental and abiding truth: Both need each other; both must be able to rely on each other.

Together, Christians and Jews should be able to stand. And standing together, both will find it possible to join their voices in unison, speaking these words from the most ancient and majestic of Hebrew prayers—words of rousing hope that still serve as the concluding signature to the prayers traditional Jews recite three times every day, every day of the year:

> We therefore hope in You, O Lord our God, that we may soon behold the glory of Your power, as You remove the abominations from the earth and heathendom is abolished. We hope for the day when the world will be mended as a kingdom of the Almighty, and all flesh will call out Your name; when You will turn unto Yourself all of the earth's wicked ones. May all the earth perceive and understand that only unto You should every knee bend, and only unto You every tongue vow loyalty. Before You, O Lord our God, may they bow in reverence, giving honor only unto You. May they all accept the yoke of Your sovereignty. Rule over them speedily and forever more. For dominion is Yours and to all eternity will You reign in glory; as it is written in Your Torah: The Lord shall reign for ever and ever. And it has also been foretold: The Lord shall be King over the whole earth; on that day the Lord shall be known as One, and only One.

4

"Judaism and Evangelical Christianity"[1]

MICHAEL WYSCHOGROD

INTRODUCTION

Michael Wyschogrod (1928–) is professor of philosophy at Baruch College, City University of New York. He has written on Kierkegaard and Heidegger, as well as on Jewish-Christian dialogue.

In the piece reprinted here Wyschogrod speaks as a Jew to evangelical Christians.[2] Evangelical Christians in the United States have been less active in interreligious dialogue than any other Christian group. This stems largely from their tendencies toward biblical literalism, if not fundamentalism, and their radical exclusivism in regard to salvation. Such views make dialogue of little value, unless it is seen as a prelude to conversion of the partner in dialogue. Wyschogrod, without entering into any discussion of the systematic problems inherent in the evangelical position, tries to show that there are special problems for the evangelical in accounting for Jews and Judaism, even if all the evangelical presuppositions are allowed.

He begins by pointing to the similarly high evaluation acccorded to the Pentateuch, the Torah as the Jews would call it, or the first five books of the Old Testament as the Christians would prefer, by both Jews and evangelical Christians. Taking the Pentateuch seriously, he suggests, as evangelicals say they wish to, requires that God's promises to the people of Israel also be taken seriously. The Jews are God's chosen people, and Wyschogrod goes on, in a lengthy discussion of the attitudes of Paul and the early church, to suggest that there is no rejection of the idea of Jewish election among early Christians, and that even Paul's most apparently negative statements about the law are best taken as warnings to Gentiles not to place themselves under it if they can avoid doing so.

It follows, then, that God's election of the Jews remains a fact, and should be recognized as such by evangelical Christians upon their own presuppositions. Acknowledgment of this by evangelicals should, in Wyschogrod's view, bring them to see that, as he puts it in a striking phrase, "Christianity becomes the Judaism of the Gentiles," and conversion of Jews to Christianity cannot properly be the aim of even the most evangelical of Christians. Jews already have what Christians gain through allegiance to Christ, runs the argument, and therefore Christians would do well to realize that the promise of salvation that they have through Christ's atoning death simply promises to Christians what the Jews have already been promised.

The principle value of Wyschogrod's piece for Christians is that it goes a long way toward breaking down Christian stereotypes of Judaism as a religion of law and merciless justice, and that it does so by taking seriously presuppositions about God's action that are held in common by both Jews and Christians. Scriptural seriousness requires seriousness on the part of Christians about their Jewishness.

"JUDAISM AND EVANGELICAL CHRISTIANITY"

A Jewish assessment of evangelical Christianity is no easy task. First and foremost, evangelical Christianity is Christianity, and a Jewish assessment of evangelical Christianity can easily become an assessment of Christianity rather than specifically of evangelical Christianity. Secondly, evangelical Christianity is Reformation Christianity, so that a Jewish assessment of evangelical Christianity requires, at least to some degree, an assessment of some issues raised by Luther, Calvin, and the other Reformers in their dispute with the Catholic Church. The matter is further complicated by the diverse interpretations of Judaism currently extant, each of which might respond quite differently to one or another aspect of evangelical Christianity. Should these complications prove insufficient, there is still another. The Jewish response to evangelical Christianity must necessarily be an external one, the response of one faith to another which is distinct from it and which it can address only from the outside. To some extent this is indeed the situation that obtains between Judaism and evangelical Christianity. But there is also the respect in which Judaism and evangelical Christianity speak to each other from within a common frame of reference provided by the Hebrew Bible (the Old Testament, in Christian parlance) and, as I hope to show, the Jewish dimensions of the New Testament. There is therefore a subtle interplay between fixing the differences between us and the tendency of each side to summon the other to a better understanding of its own tradition from within the common premises of the two faiths. A thorough separation of all the strands mentioned will not be possible within the confines of a short paper. While not overlooking these complications entirely, the focus will be on some basic responses of a Jewish observer of evangelical Christianity in the context of the two-thousand-year-old dialogue between Judaism and Christianity.

The single most important contact between Judaism and evangelical Christianity is the centrality of the Bible in the two faiths. Before proceeding to qualify this point of contact—and qualify it we must—we must first pause to appreciate the significance of this point as a point of contact. Both Judaism and evangelical Christianity would be inconceivable without a Book which is the center of the two faiths. The sacred space of the synagogue centers on the Ark in which the Torah, the parchment on which the Pentateuch is handwritten, is kept and from which it is removed to be read to the congregation during worship. In spite of the significance Judaism attaches to the rabbinic interpretation of the Bible, the reading of the Pentateuch and prophetic portion in the synagogue is not accompanied by the reading of any rabbinic interpretation, though many texts exist whose public reading as an accompaniment to the biblical lection could have been ordained. Instead, the biblical text is read in Hebrew to be heard by the congregation as the Word of God. The study of the Hebrew Bible is the foundation of Jewish education. As the child grows older he is introduced to the study of rabbinic texts to which great weight is attached. But the biblical text always remains in a class unto itself, unapproachable by any other writings, ancient or modern.

The centrality of a text would be a point of contact between Judaism and evangelical Christianity even if the texts central to the two faiths were entirely different texts. But, of course, they are not entirely different texts. To a very large extent they are the same text, the Hebrew Bible. But there is also the New Testament which is sacred to Christians but not to Jews. Reduced to its simplest terms, this is the crux of the difference between Judaism and evangelical Christianity. The evangelical Christian hears the New Testament as the Word of God and it is this basic fact which becomes a foundation of his beliefs. Since Judaism does not hear the New Testament as the Word of God, a deep division between the two faiths becomes apparent. But why does the Christian hear both the Old and the New Testaments as the Word of God while the Jew hears only the Hebrew Bible? Each side can attempt to justify its obedience to its Scripture by appealing to external validating criteria designed to demonstrate the divine inspiration of its canon. A debate is then conceivable in which each side attempts to demonstrate that its canon is more adequately validated by the criteria which have been agreed upon. The reason that this procedure is not promising in the context of the dialogue between Judaism and evangelical Christianity is that neither Judaism nor evangelical Christianity is prepared to submit its sacred books to any validation other than self-validation. To validate a biblical work by demonstrating that its teachings are in conformity with some preconceived ethical norms (to give one example of the kind of external validation that has been attempted) is to raise the validating criteria, rather than the work being validated, to the status of the ultimate authority.

Validated in this way, a sacred text would cease to be what it is supposed to be because it would no longer be the source of all judgment but itself subject to judgment. The difference between those who believe that a given text is of God and those who do not believe that it is, is therefore not easily bridged because it is the mystery of faith that confronts us in such a situation.

But in spite of this difference there is, as we have seen, an important area of agreement. Both Judaism and evangelical Christianity hear the Hebrew Bible as the Word of God. This is surely a matter of decisive significance. The Hebrew Bible is approximately 80% (in words) of the Christian canon. It might therefore be thought that Judaism and Christianity agree 80% of the time and disagree only 20%, but such a conclusion would, of course, be simplistic in the extreme. Because the Christian canon includes the New Testament, the Christian reads the other 80% of his canon differently than does the Jew. For the Christian the content of the New Testament sheds a totally new light on the content of the Old Testament and he therefore reads the Old Testament from the vantage point of the New. The events of the Old Testament are taken to foreshadow those of the New; moreover, the significance of the Old Testament events would remain shrouded without the vantage point of faith in Jesus as Christ and God. Jews, of course, have traditionally resisted such a reading of the Jewish canon as a retroactive revision of the true meaning of the text, while Christians have accused the Jews of misunderstanding (wilfully or otherwise) their own Scriptures. There has therefore grown up an extensive Jewish-Christian polemical literature, much of it focused on certain well-known Old Testament passages which are read Christologically by Christians and otherwise by Jews. It might be pointed out that in connection with this particular issue modern scholarship has generally sided with the Jews simply because the historical scholar will not accept that a text written four or five hundred years before the birth of Jesus is in fact referring to him. Lest this support gladden Jewish hearts excessively, it must also be pointed out that the modern historical scholar does not read the biblical text from the standpoint of faith and that his methodology cannot be the ultimate arbiter of meaning for either the Jewish or Christian believer.

What is the Jewish response to the evangelical reading of Scripture? Let us for the moment examine simply the evangelical method of interpretation. I realize that it is not easy to characterize that method and to distinguish it from the fundamentalist and the Barthian,[3] the approaches to the Bible most closely related to it. Without attempting any very fine characterization of the evangelical approach to Scripture, I feel rather safe in defining it as a method that takes Scripture seriously. It is not prepared to allegorize or spiritualize the text nor is it prepared, with Bultmann,[4] to demythologize it to make it palatable to modern man. It does not attempt to penetrate below or above the text, but it assumes that God speaks straightforwardly in the Bible and that he means what he says. The evangelical theologian is aware that the Bible includes various literary forms and that these must be taken into account in properly interpreting the sacred text. He fears above all imposing on the text his own philosophy as an interpreter and then proceeding to extract from the Bible, not what he actually found there, but what he injected into it in the first place. The Catholic doctrine of tradition as a parallel and equal source of authority has little support in evangelical circles because — to the evangelical mind — it amounts to deifying something human, the tradition of the church, instead of what is truly of God, his word in the Bible. How does all this sound to Jewish ears?

In one sense, the Jewish position is closer to that of Catholicism and its doctrine of tradition than to the purer biblicism of evangelical theology. Judaism speaks of the two Torahs, the written Torah which consists of the words of Scripture, and the oral Torah which accompanies and elaborates the meaning of the written Torah. Both of these Torahs were, according to Judaism, revealed by God to Moses. Scripture, for example, teaches the law of an eye for an eye. But the oral law, which was revealed to Moses concurrently with the written, interprets this to mean that one who injures his neighbor's eye must pay monetary damages. The verse is interpreted as demanding the value of an eye for an eye. From the point of view of Jewish tradition, we have here not an act of rabbinic legislation but the transmission of the proper meaning of the verse through the oral tradition which, as I have already pointed out, is as divine in its source as is the written law.

Nevertheless, it would be false, I think, to identify the Jewish point of view with the Catholic view of tradition. The essential difference is that tradition in Judaism is a tradition of biblical hermeneutics. The oral law interprets and clarifies the meaning of the biblical text. It is not, as such, an independent Torah. Nor would Judaism apply the term *Word of God* to rabbinic texts. The Vatican II Statement on Revelation asserts that "the task of authentically interpreting the word of God, whether written or handed on, has been entrusted exclusively to the living teaching office of the Church."[5] This makes the expression *Word of God* apply equally to Scripture and tradition. I do not believe it would be proper, from the Jewish point of view, to apply the term *Word of God* to rabbinic texts. After the weekly reading of the prophetic portion in the synagogue, the reader concludes with a blessing that praises God "all of whose words are true and just" and "who is faithful to all of his words." In so doing, the reader expresses the conviction that the text he has just read is the Word of God. No such blessing is conceivable over a rabbinic text. From the halakhic (legal) point of view, a Jew who recites a rabbinic text without understanding its meaning has achieved nothing, while one who recites a biblical text without understanding its meaning has performed a mitzvah (commanded act), though it is, of course, preferable to understand the meaning of the biblical text. The biblical text is unique as the Word of God. The oral law elaborates and interprets the scriptural text in such a way that in spite of all the importance Judaism attaches to the oral law, it does not eclipse the primacy of the Bible as the Word of God.

Having established this much common ground in the attitudes of Judaism and evangelical Christianity toward the Bible as the Word of God, we must now turn to the evangelical Christian reading of the Old Testament from the vantage point of the New Testament. That the New Testament is for the Christian the Word of God, while it is not for the Jew, is a point, as we have already said, of primary significance. Nevertheless, this does not solve the question as to how exactly the Christian is to interpret the Old Testament. For the Catholic, it seems to me, this is less of a problem. He interprets both the Old Testament and the New Testament in the light of the tradition of his church and is therefore not under great pressure to take seriously the text in its simple and direct meaning. But presumably this is not so of the evangelical Christian. Nothing intervenes between him and the text of the New Testament. He is not given to allegorizing or spiritualizing the text or to the many other strategies that human beings have invented to escape coming to grips with the demand that the biblical text makes on man. And yet, while he may firmly reject these hermeneutic maneuvers when it comes to the New Testament, he might slip into them when he deals with the Old Testament. The problem is this: if the Christian is capable of extracting the spiritual kernel of the Old Testament, while rejecting the material dross that surrounds it, is it not to be expected that others will do the same to the New Testament by extracting some sort of spiritual (ethical?) kernel from it and rejecting the Christological incarnation in which these spiritual teachings appear? If the latter is unacceptable, so is the former. No spiritual essence can be extracted from the biblical truth, because biblical truth, as the Word of God, is clothed in the form in which God wishes it to be clothed and it is not for man to improve it by separating the essential from the nonessential. But if the Word of God must not be read selectively, then the canonicity of the Old Testament should put a stamp on evangelical Christianity of considerable interest to Judaism.

Let us take as an example the bond between the Jewish people and the land of Israel. It is quite clear that from the initial election of Israel in Abraham the bond with the land is an essential part of the divine promise to Abraham and his descendants. It is equally clear that Israel's disobedience places possession of the land in jeopardy because possession of the land is contingent on the people's adherence to their side of the covenant. And it is further clear that Israel's loss of the land as the result of their disobedience is not a permanent loss but that, because God's promises are not in vain and because man's disobedience cannot cancel God's purpose, it is God's promise that Israel will be restored to their land and will dwell in it in safety. It seems to me that the position I have outlined summarizes the simple meaning of a large number of Old Testament texts strewn over almost the whole of the New Testament. Yet this simple meaning can be undercut by various less-than-straightforward readings of the text. The promised land can be spiritualized and made to refer to a spiritual state which is the reward of all righteous men. Israel can be interpreted to mean the church. The church can be and has been designated the new Israel and the promises made to the old Israel can be and have been transferred to the church. If at the same time the land of Israel retains its geographic reference, the church finds itself promised a territory in which, except perhaps during the crusades, it has expressed relatively little interest. But these less-than-straightforward readings of the text do not recommend themselves to the evangelical mind and, therefore, unless I am badly misinformed, evangelical Christianity has been quite sympathetic to the recent Jewish return to the land of Israel precisely because evangelical ears hear the biblical promises to the people of Israel, the concreteness of which is not dissipated in sophisticated if not sophistical demythologizations but connected with the real world in which the people and land of Israel are existing entities. If this is the result of the evangelical understanding of the authority of the Bible, then, from the Jewish point of view, there must be something profoundly right with that method of understanding.

How about the law? Much of the Pentateuch consists of legislation which Judaism, particularly orthodox Judaism, considers normative to this day. The commandments in the Pentateuch address themselves to the most diverse aspects of human existence, from the commercial to the sexual, from the ethical to the dietary. Judaism hears these commandments and attempts to obey them. While it is true that in a sense the rabbinic interpretation is interposed between the direct biblical command and its execution, this interposition, except perhaps in the most unusual cases, does not annul the biblical commandments but elaborates and applies them. If the Bible forbids the seething of a kid in its mother's milk, rabbinic law develops and extends this prohibition and so, to this day, meat and milk are separated in the Orthodox Jewish home in accordance with the biblical prohibition. And the same is true of Jewish religious life in general. Fundamentally, Orthodox Jews attempt to be obedient to the Torah, the commandments and prohibitions of the Pentateuch.

The Jewish observer of the Christian scene, particularly of the evangelical Christian scene, finds it difficult to understand why the legislation of the Pentateuch plays such a relatively small part in the evangelical consciousness. These commandments are there in the Pentateuch, in black and white, for everyone to read. Why does Christianity, including evangelical Christianity, not pay more attention to the Mosaic law? The Jewish observer is, of course, aware that the Christian attitude to the law is conditioned by the New Testament. But it is precisely here that Jewish-Christian dialogue is necessary. Jesus and the apostles were Jews. The New Testament is a book that comes out of the Jewish world and largely presupposes the rabbinic universe of discourse without which much of it is easily misunderstood. Let us focus on the question of the law as one example.

The interpretation that is commonly accepted by Christians is that while it is indeed true that the Mosaic law was of divine origin, its relevance was superseded by the coming of Jesus as the Christ. The justification of the Christian is by faith and not by works of the law. There is no denying that the writings of Paul, particularly in Galatians, can easily be read this way. Yet the Jewish reader of the New Testament finds this reading incorrect. A good example of this is David Flusser's *Jesus* which portrays the founder of Christianity as a Torah-observant Jew whose disagreements with the Pharisees are very much in the spirit of the perennial intra-Jewish debates so characteristic of rabbinic literature. Evangelical Christians ought not to overlook Matthew 5:17–20:

Do not suppose that I have come to abolish the Law and the prophets; I did not come to abolish but to complete. I tell you this: so long as heaven and earth endure, not a letter, not a stroke, will disappear from the Law until all that must happen has happened. If any man therefore sets aside even the least of the Law's demands, and teaches others to do the same, he will have the lowest place in the kingdom of Heaven, whereas anyone who keeps the Law, and teaches others so, will stand high in the kingdom of Heaven. I tell you, unless you show yourselves far better men than the Pharisees and the doctors of the law, you can never enter the kingdom of Heaven.

And again Matthew 23:2, 3:

The doctors of the law and the Pharisees sit in the chair of Moses; therefore do what they tell you; pay attention to their words. But do not follow their practice; for they say one thing and do another.

The Jewish reader cannot help but notice such passages and they confirm his conviction that the continuity between the teaching of Jesus and rabbinic Judaism is considerable.

There are those who, while granting a considerable degree of continuity between rabbinic Judaism and particularly the synoptic gospels, draw the line at Paul. He, it is maintained, broke the bonds that tied Christianity to Judaism. Did not Paul forbid newly converted Christians to undergo circumcision and to live in accordance with the Mosaic law? The commonly accepted interpretation is that Paul believed the Mosaic law to have been merely a preparation (Galatians 3:24) for the coming of Jesus as the Christ and therefore to continue obeying the law after the coming of Jesus is to deny the event that was central to Paul's theology. And yet, there is something that does not ring true, at least to this Jewish reader. Let us take Acts 15 as our focus. Here we are told that, after Paul had converted certain Gentiles to faith in Jesus as the Christ, some Jewish Christians from Judea presented themselves to the new converts and informed them that "those who were not circumcised in accordance with Mosaic practice could not be saved" (v. 1). This information undoubtedly upset the new converts who had been informed by Paul that no such circumcision was necessary or perhaps even permissible for new Christians. The dissension reached such proportions that Paul decided to submit the matter to the judgment of the Jerusalem church whose leadership consisted of those who, unlike Paul, had known Jesus during his sojourn on earth. In any case, the problem was submitted to the Jerusalem church and "after a long debate" (v. 7) judgment was rendered in favor of Paul. The church in Antioch was so informed in a written communication which demanded of the new Christians not circumcision and acceptance of the whole Torah, but abstinence "from things polluted by contact with idols, from fornication, from anything that has been strangled, and from blood" (v. 20). Paul's position was thus vindicated and the principle was established that Gentile converts to Christianity do not require circumcision and the law.

The Jewish reader, however, is struck by two important points. The first is explicit and the other implicit but nevertheless persuasive. The demands made of the Gentile converts in Acts 15:20 have to be understood in light of the rabbinic view of the obligation that devolves on non-Jews. Because of the covenant made at Sinai with Israel, Jews are obligated to obey the commandments of the Torah. Non-Jews, however, are under no such obligation. Instead, they are obligated to obey the so-called Noachide commandments which the rabbis inferred from Genesis 9. These Noachide commandments, usually said to be seven in number, consist, broadly speaking, of the fundamental moral law and the commandment not to worship idols. From the rabbinic point of view, a Gentile who fulfills these commandments has a place in the world to come. Full conversion of a Gentile to Judaism remains possible. The full convert is circumcised, thus becoming a Jew under full obligation to the whole of the Torah. The predominant rabbinic attitude, however, is to discourage such full conversion because of the dangers involved. Israel has often failed to obey the commandments of the Torah and when it has done so, it has been severely punished by God. Why should a Gentile, reasoned the rabbis, put himself in this danger if he can attain his place in the world to come by adhering to the Noachide commandments? The decision of the first Jerusalem council is to demand the Noachide commandments of the Gentile converts and no more. In so deciding, the Jerusalem church is acting in accordance with the predominant rabbinic thinking of the day.

The second point, as I have said, is rather more implicit but nevertheless persuasive. When the problem presented by Paul—whether or not Gentile converts to Christianity require circumcision and the law—was brought to the Jerusalem church, the decision in favor of Paul ensued only after "long debate" (Acts 15:7). Now—and this is the point—if the Jewish members of the Jerusalem church had been of the opinion that with the coming of Jesus as the Messiah, circumcision and obedience to the Torah were no longer necessary for Jewish Christians, there could hardly have arisen any controversy as to whether circumcision and obedience to the Torah were demanded of Gentile converts. This could have become a debatable issue whose determination required long debate only if it had been generally assumed in Jerusalem that Jews who had come to accept Jesus as the Messiah retained their obligation to the Torah. The debatable question then was whether Gentiles who entered the fellowship of Jesus had to live as the Jewish followers of Jesus did (circumcision and obedience to the Torah) or whether it was sufficient for them to couple their faith in Jesus with obedience to the Noachide law.

The early church, I believe, envisaged itself as being made up of two segments, the Jewish and the Gentile. What they would have in common is what was most important—the faith in Jesus as the Messiah. The difference between them would be that the Jewish portion of the church, the original cultivated olive tree of Romans 11:24, would remain subject to the Torah, while the Gentile branch, the branch that "against all nature" was grafted onto the original tree, would obey the Noachide commandments and not the full Mosaic law. Should this appear strange in view of Paul's repeated assertions that in Christ there is neither Jew nor Gentile (e.g., Colossians 3:11), we must remember that while on the one hand Paul teaches that in Christ there is neither man nor woman, he does not hesitate to instruct women to remain silent in the church. In the ultimate sense, before God, men and women are alike in that they have immortal souls and their sins are forgiven in Christ, but in the penultimate sense the role of men and women is not identical. The same is true of Jew and Gentile. Through the coming of Jesus as the Messiah, his death and resurrection, the ultimate difference between Jews and Gentiles has been erased. But just as Paul's teaching about men and women is not to be taken to mean that men and women must begin acting identically, so in the case of Jews and Gentiles a difference remains: Jews are obligated to obey the Torah while Gentiles are not.

Before leaving the topic of the law, we must look at what Paul says about the law, particularly in Galatians. Much of the anti-Jewish tone of some aspects of Christianity can be traced to the Pauline polemic against the law. He speaks of the curse of the law by which no man is justified since justification is only by faith and never by works of the law (Galatians 3:10–12). Such statements have been widely interpreted as expressing the deepest possible rejection of that which is most holy to Judaism—the Torah and its teaching. But as a Jew who proclaimed himself faithful to the traditions of his people, Paul could not have thought of the law as a curse. The truth is that there is something entirely different at stake here. The question is whether Gentiles who wish to enter the church need circumcision and obedience to the law (all those who have been circumcised must obey the law; see Galatians 5:3). Paul's answer to this, as we have seen, is in the negative. Once this is granted, it becomes Paul's duty, in accordance with rabbinic thinking, to discourage Gentiles from circumcision and observing the law. The curse of the law about which Paul speaks refers to the curse (Deuteronomy 27:26) associated with violation of the law. Paul is not saying that the law is a curse. He is saying that the Jews have a promise and a threat—the promise of reward if they obey the law of God and the threat of a curse if they disobey it. Because Paul's purpose is to discourage Gentiles from circumcision and observation of the law, he speaks only of the curse and remains silent about the blessing. This is how any rabbi, past or present, proceeds in discouraging Gentile conversion. The potential convert is told of the dangers of becoming subject to the law. Only after he persists and insists on conversion is he told of the blessings which flow from the Torah. It is therefore a profound misunderstanding to read Paul's comments in Galatians as his full understanding of the law. It is a presentation of the law from one point of view, intended to cool Gentile passions for circumcision and the law. Were Paul writing to Jews, his discussion of the advantages of the law would not be omitted. But, as apostle to the Gentiles, Paul's purpose is to preach Christ crucified and risen to Gentiles and, in view of contrary opinions emanating from Jewish Christian circles in Jerusalem, to dissuade Gentile circumcision and acceptance of the yoke of the Torah.

When Paul says that man is justified by faith and not by works of the law, he is saying nothing that is strange to Judaism. A Jew who believes that man is justified by works of the law would hold the belief that man can demand only strict justice from God, nothing more. Such a man would say to God: "Give me what I deserve, neither more nor less; I do not need your mercy, only your strict justice." If there are Jews who approach God in this spirit, I have never met nor heard of them. In the morning liturgy that Jews recite daily, we find the following: "Master of all worlds: It is not on account of our own righteousness that we offer our supplications before thee, but on account of thy great compassion. What are we? What is our life? What is our goodness? What is our virtue? What is our help? What our strength? What our might?" The believing Jew is fully aware that if he were to be judged strictly according to his deeds by the standards of justice and without mercy, he would be doomed. He realizes that without the mercy of God there is no hope for him and that he is therefore justified—if by "justified" we mean that he avoids the direst of divine punishments—not by the merit of his works as commanded in the Torah, but by the gratuitous mercy of God who saves man in spite of the fact that man does not deserve it. From this it does not follow that obedience to the commandments of the Torah has ceased to be obligatory for the Jew, just as it does not follow from the Pauline teaching of justification by faith and not by works of the law that the Christian may become a libertine and do as he wishes as long as he retains his faith. It is imperative for the Jew to do everything in his power to live in accordance with the commandments. At the same time, he is aware that he will not succeed fully and that he is therefore in need of divine mercy. It is, then, quite incorrect to distinguish between Judaism and Christianity as if the former puts its emphasis on works while the latter its emphasis on faith. Both, it seems to me, emphasize works while realizing that the mercy of God is nevertheless essential.

We now come to probably the most difficult point, the question of Jesus. The thinking of Paul and of evangelical Christianity centers on Jesus as the Messiah, the only begotten Son of God in whose death and resurrection man's sins are forgiven and eternal life assured. Here we come to the mystery of the division between Israel and the church. Judaism did not accept Jesus either as the Messiah or as one of the persons in the triune God. For Judaism the Messiah was and is thought of as the legitimate Davidic monarch who will restore Jewish sovereignty and free the people from foreign domination. Since Jesus did not achieve this visible political goal, Judaism continued to hope for the coming of the Messiah. But even if Judaism had accepted Jesus as the Messiah—as Rabbi Akiba later thought of Bar Kochba[6] as the Messiah—it would not have thought of him as God or as an incarnation of God. It is important to recognize that from the Jewish point of view the question whether Jesus was the Messiah is a far less crucial matter than the orthodox Christian teaching concerning the divinity of Jesus. In view of the condemnation of those who worship the works of their hands, Judaism has come to be extremely sensitive about divinization of any material object, animate or otherwise. But we would be misunderstanding the issue if we rested the matter here. Apart from the question of who Jesus was, an equally important question is what he does for man and in this regard several simple points must be made.

In Judaism, God has two attributes—justice and mercy. At times, he acts as the judge dispensing justice to his creatures. At other times he acts mercifully by forgiving man's transgressions and witholding deserved punishment. There is no discernible rule that determines when mercy displaces justice. If there were such a rule, the application of mercy itself would be ruled by law and it would then cease to be mercy. The point, however, is that in Judaism it is the same God who is sometimes just and sometimes merciful. In Christianity, these two aspects of God are personified by two persons—the Father and the Son. God the Father is the God of justice while God the Son is the principle of mercy. The appearance of Jesus, it seems, assures the triumph of mercy for those who believe in him. In Pauline thinking there is a deeply rooted terror of the justice of God based on Paul's assessment of Jewish experience which he finds to have been an almost unbroken chain of acts of disobedience to the commands of God and the punishment resulting from them. The focus on Jesus is therefore the proclamation of the good news that the rigors of divine justice can be avoided. Through Jesus the mercy of God has triumphed over his justice. Judaism remains under the dialectic of justice and mercy. It is true that in the final analysis the mercy of God prevails over his justice. Israel has been told that it will be redeemed, that its election will never be withdrawn, and that while the anger of God is a passing phenomenon, his love and mercy endure forever. The Jewish people feel themselves so loved by God that they can endure his anger. They know the infinitely deeper love that is only slightly below the surface of the anger. But this requires a great sense of intimacy with God. As the children of adoption, the Gentile Christians are more frightened by the prospect of divine anger than is the Jew, and therefore the total guarantee of mercy in Jesus becomes central to the Christian relationship with the God of Israel. The Jewish relationship is with God the Father, who does for Israel everything that God as Jesus does for the Christian.

It seems to me important both for Jews and Christians to avoid arguing that God could have done what he has done only in the way he has done it. To do so is to convert both faiths into philosophic doctrines which lose sight of the fact that God's freedom is not compromised by restraints of necessity. Each side ought to concede that God could have done what the other faith claims he has done, even as each faith maintains its own belief as to what God has done and how he has done it.

Speaking of Israel, Karl Barth writes:

For it is incontestable that this people as such is the holy people of God: the people with whom God has dealt in His grace and in His wrath; in the midst of whom He has blessed and judged, enlightened and hardened, accepted and rejected; whose cause either way He has made His own, and has not ceased to make His own, and will not cease to make His own. They are all of them by nature sanctified by Him, sanctified as ancestors and kinsmen of the Holy One of Israel, in a sense Gentiles are not by nature, not even the best of Gentiles, not even the Gentile Christians, not even the best of Gentile Christians, in spite of their membership in the Church, in spite of the fact that they too are now sanctified by the Holy One of Israel and have become Israel.[*7]

"They too are now sanctified," writes Karl Barth. This, it seems to me, is the challenge to Christianity, particularly evangelical Christianity. Christianity thinks of itself as the new Israel, heir to the election which the old Israel lost because it did not recognize its Messiah in Jesus. If this is so, then, after Jesus there is no longer any theological significance to the existence of the Jewish people. It is still necessary, of course, to bring individual Jews to Jesus because all men need Jesus, but the existence of the Jewish people as such is displaced by the existence of the church.

This has been the view widely prevalent in much of Christianity. The alternative is to see the church as inconceivable without Israel. In this view, Israel remains the people of election; Israel is the nucleus of the cell while the church is the substance that clusters around the nucleus. In this second definition, the church can be understood only as that body of Gentiles that has joined itself to the body of Israel and whose destiny is therefore irrevocably intertwined with the destiny of the people of Israel. Jesus is not, then, severed from his special relationship with the people of Israel but, instead, the people of Israel is seen as the people chosen by God to carry his presence in the world. Since the election of Israel is intended as a blessing for all peoples of the earth, those who are addressed by the God of Israel can join their destinies to that of Israel as adopted sons in the household of Israel. In this interpretation, Christianity becomes the Judaism of the Gentiles.

In view of these considerations, the Jewish reader of the literature of evangelical Christianity finds himself somewhat puzzled by the extent to which Jews and Judaism go unmentioned. For example, the index to Bernard L. Ramm's excellent study, *The Evangelical Heritage*,[8] contains no references to Jews, Judaism, or Israel. And this is not untypical. A recent movie made under evangelical auspices, *The Hiding Place*, focuses with great sympathy on the Holocaust of European Jewry during the Nazi period. It depicts the heroic efforts of an evangelical Christian family to save as many Jews as possible from the Nazi murderers and the dreadful price that family had to pay for their effort. The film puts its primary emphasis on the heroism of the Christian family whose faith is the source of their strength; some critics have been puzzled by the failure of the film to point to the strength provided by the Jewish faith to the victims of this historic crime. At an early point in the film, as the elderly gentleman who is the head of the heroic Christian family walks the streets of his Dutch city, wearing the star of David which the Nazis had made compulsory for all Jews and which he had adopted voluntarily, he observes a roundup of Jews and exclaims: "They have touched the apple of God's eye." Here recognition of the election of Israel is implicit. Yet the film never connects Jewish suffering with the fact that God elected this people precisely because they are more precious to him than all other families of the earth. The average moviegoer can easily leave with the impression that persecution of the Jews is just another example of man's inhumanity to man rather than an event that can be understood only in biblical categories and in the context of Jewish election. While the suggestion that Jewish suffering is punishment for their rejection of Jesus as the Messiah is tossed out, not much of a parallel is drawn between the crucifixion of Jesus and the historic crucifixion of his people. My purpose is not to be critical of the film, but to voice my impression that the makers of the film were to some degree aware of the election of Israel and the significance of this election for Christianity, but not to the degree required. This may be evidence of one reason why dialogue between Jews and evangelical Christians is desirable.

PART II

Islamic Perceptions
of Christianity
in the Twentieth Century

INTRODUCTION TO PART TWO

The Theological Basis for Islamic Perceptions of Christianity

Muslims, unlike Jews, Hindus, or Buddhists, are restricted in what they can say about Christians and Christianity by the fact that the Qur'an, their sacred book, says much about these phenomena. The presence of statements about Jesus, Mary, the Gospels, and Christians in the Qur'an has always constrained Muslims in the development of their views on these matters. This does not mean that complete uniformity is to be found; sacred texts can always be interpreted differently, even when they appear to be explicit, and Islamic views of Christianity have, of course, changed in accordance with changes in social, economic, and political relations between Christians and Muslims. But the presence of Qur'anic material on Christians does mean both that the Qur'an is the point of first refuge for all Muslims who want to say something about Christianity—just as, until relatively recent times, the New Testament was the point of first refuge for Christians who wanted to say something about Jews and Judaism—and that Islamic debates about the Christian question tend usually to circle around questions of Qur'anic interpretation. This is very evident in almost all of the essays reprinted in this book.

It would be superfluous to go over once again the Qur'anic material covered in so much depth and with such a variety of interpretation by the writers whose work is reprinted here. It must suffice to say that in the Qur'an Jesus is regarded as a prophet, and a very great one; that the gospel he proclaimed is seen as a key part of "the book," of the history of God's revelatory speech to the human race; that his mother, Mary, is spoken of frequently and with great reverence; and that the community he founded is also spoken of with respect, even when some of its doctrines are rejected as misunderstandings or travesties of God's true intentions.

The nineteenth chapter (Surah) of the Qur'an is entitled "Mary," and is mainly devoted to the retelling of stories about Mary and Jesus. A brief quotation will suffice to give a sense of the tone of much of what the Qur'an says in this connection:

> Whereupon he [Jesus] spoke and said: "I am the servant of Allah. He has given me the Gospel and ordained me a prophet. His blessing is upon me wherever I go, and He has commanded me to be steadfast in prayer and to give alms to the poor as long as I shall live. He has exhorted me to honour my mother and has purged me of vanity and wickedness. I was blessed on the day I was born, and blessed I shall be on the day of my death; and may peace be upon me on the day when I shall be raised to life." Such was Jesus, the son of Mary (Qur'an 19:30–34, Dawood's translation).

Given this reverential tone, why is it that most Islamic perspectives upon Christianity are so negative? Syed Muhammad Naquib al-Attas (Chapter 8) puts the matter very clearly: "There were, and still are, from the Muslim point of view, two Christianities: the original and true one and the Western version of it." Though not all Muslims would express the position quite as starkly as this, almost all hold to some version of it. The need is then to provide some account, both historical and theological, of how original, true Christianity became corrupted, and of what a proper contemporary Islamic attitude to Christians and Christianity might look like.

The conceptual and theological differences between normative Islam and normative Christianity run very deep. Islam stresses, above all else, the unity and transcendence of Allah. From this emphasis on unity and transcendence flows a condemnation of all idolatry, of treating as God that which is not God. From it also flows an attempt to place every dimension of human life — political, social, economic, sexual, intellectual, "religious" — within its context as one aspect of the way in which human beings should be related to God. Here too there is an emphasis on unity, for it is not proper to separate some aspects of human life (say, the ritual and theological) from all others and label the former "religious" while relegating all the rest of human life to the non-religious or secular sphere. Every dimension of human life is "religious" if by that is meant that it operates, or should operate, within the context of God's all-embracing will and that it should be properly expressive of that will.

The Islamic rejection of idolatry involves, necessarily, a rejection of the Christian doctrine of the incarnation. There is no God but God, and so Jesus Christ cannot be God. To call him God is to associate him improperly with God, and this is simply a way of being idolatrous.[1] The rejection of the doctrine of the incarnation involves also the rejection of the trinity, for if Jesus Christ is not God then the trinity has no second person. In addition, of course, standard Christian trinitarianism offends, in Islamic eyes, against the unity of God; it looks like tritheism. The three persons of the Christian trinity look, very simply, like three gods.

This Islamic attempt to place every dimension of human life under the explicit direction of God's will leads to a radical rejection of what Muslims tend to perceive as Christian dualism. The dualism between flesh and spirit, between state and church, between human society and the natural order — all these are perceived by Muslims as improper attempts to separate some aspects of human life from the embrace of God's will and to permit them to function autonomously. Attempts to describe the historical processes that have brought these dualisms into being, and to show what is wrong with them theologically, are especially clear in the work of Sayyid Qutb (Chapter 5) and Syed Muhammad Naquib al-Attas (Chapter 8). Qutb's phrase "that hideous schizophrenia" captures the main thrust of this position splendidly. If "religion" is separated from the rest of life, it will inevitably cease to be what God intended it to be. It will become compartmentalized and corrupt and its practitioners schizophrenic, because sexuality, politics, economic systems, and the intellectual life will try to operate independently of God and independently of the practitioner's relationship with God.

Social and Political Influences upon Twentieth-Century Islamic Perceptions of Christianity

The Islamic attempt to show Christians how and why their religion has become corrupted and degraded is deeply rooted in Islamic tradition. It is probably fair to say, though, that it has become more strident in the last four decades than was the case for most of Islamic history. Again, the works of both Qutb and al-Attas illustrate this stridency. This trend is connected with the rise of Islamic fundamentalism since the 1950s, an attempt to reassert Islamic identity and dignity over against the cultural dominance of the West and Christianity. Sometimes this reassertion of identity has taken on explicitly political and revolutionary forms, as most obviously in the Iranian revolution in 1979. Sometimes it has been the driving force behind a slower process of "re-Islamization," as in countries like Egypt and Pakistan during the last two decades. But it has almost always produced an increasingly harsh anti-Christian rhetoric, a presupposition of which is that Western culture — initially European culture but more recently that of the United States — is self-evidently politically and militarily expansionist, morally corrupt, and religiously decadent, and that all of these things are more or less directly traceable to the influence of Christianity.

There can be little doubt that these negative Islamic perceptions of Christianity have been heavily influenced by the experience that most

Islamic countries had of being colonized by Western powers in the eighteenth and nineteenth centuries. As is also the case for Buddhist and Hindu perceptions of Christians and Christianity, the connection between Christianity and oppressive colonialism is so deeply rooted in Islamic thinking on this subject that it is effectively impossible for Christianity to be separated from Western political and military culture.

But it would be misleading to identify twentieth-century Islamic perceptions of Christianity with those of the extreme conservatives. Islamic modernism, a movement that began in the nineteenth century with such men as Jamal al-Din al-Afghani and Muhammad 'Abduh in Egypt,[2] and was reflected in the thought of the Indian reformers Sayyid Ahmad Khan and Amir 'Ali,[3] has also influenced twentieth century Islamic perceptions of Christianity, and it is much more favorable toward both Christianity and Western culture than are the conservatives. The modernists responded to the nineteenth-century Western and Christian hegemony over the Islamic world by arguing not that Islam should reject Western institutions and thought completely, but rather that Islamic reform could be stimulated by learning from the West.[4]

Those Muslims influenced by this attitude tend, in developing their views on Christianity, to look for points of agreement rather than points of disagreement and to emphasize those elements within the Qur'anic witness that make it possible to see Christianity as a religious community with its own gift and message rather than as a hopelessly corrupt tradition. Both Fazlur Rahman (Chapter 7) and Seyyed Hossein Nasr (Chapter 9) do this, though from somewhat different angles. They show that it is possible for Muslims to have a positive appreciation for Christianity, even if some of the theological disagreements already adverted to remain of importance.

In summary: Muslims traditionally recognize Jesus as a prophet and Christians as a people of the book, a people with at least the vestiges of a proper relationship to God. The Islamic tradition possesses the conceptual resources to develop a theology of religions that is neither fundamentalist nor radically exclusivist, and some of these resources are drawn upon in Chapters 7 and 8 of this volume. But the burden of a long history of sociopolitical and theological conflict between Muslims and Christians rests very heavily upon contemporary Islamic perceptions of Christianity, as also upon contemporary Christian perceptions of Islam.

SUGGESTIONS FOR FURTHER READING

Much of what is available, either by Muslims about Christianity or by others about Islamic views of Christians and Christianity, is in either French or Arabic. I shall restrict myself here to sources that are relatively easy to find in English.

Journals in which useful material is frequently found include the *Newsletter* published by The Centre for the Study of Islam and Christian-Muslim Relations at the Selly Oak Colleges in Birmingham, England; *IslamoChristiana*, published by the

Pontifical Institute for the Study of Arabs and Islam in Rome, which contains many useful resources in English, French, and Arabic; and the Roman Catholic Church's Pontifical Council on Interreligious Dialogue's (called the Secretariat for Non-Christians until June 1988) quarterly *Bulletin*, mostly useful for Christian perspectives on non-Christian religions (including Islam), but containing occasional pieces by representatives of non-Christian religions.

Jacques Waardenburg has published a great deal on Islam and the history of religions and is one of the few scholars to have taken seriously the attempt to explore how Muslims think and have thought about non-Muslims. Especially useful is his "World Religions as Seen in the Light of Islam," in *Islam: Past Influence and Present Challenge*, edited by A. Welch and P. Cachia (Edinburgh: Edinburgh University Press, 1979). Mohamed Talbi, one of whose essays is included in this volume (Chapter 6), has devoted a good deal of energy to the development of an Islamic view of Christianity. One of his recent essays is especially valuable, in part because of its extensive bibliography: "Possibilities and Conditions for a Better Understanding Between Islam and the West," *Journal of Ecumenical Studies* 25/2 (1988):161–93.

Other useful works include Stanley J. Samartha and John B. Taylor, eds., *Christian-Muslim Dialogue: Papers Presented at the Broumana Consultation, 12–18 July 1972* (Geneva: World Council of Churches, 1973); David A. Kerr, "The Problem of Christianity in Muslim Perspective: Implications for Christian Mission," *International Bulletin of Missionary Research* (1981):152–62; Richard W. Rousseau, ed., *Christianity and Islam: The Struggling Dialogue* (Scranton, PA: Ridge Row Press, 1985); The World Council of Churches, *Christians Meeting Muslims: WCC Papers on 10 Years of Christian-Muslim Dialogue* (Geneva: World Council of Churches, 1977); Zafar Ishaq Ansari, "Some Reflections on Islamic Bases for Dialogue with Jews and Christians," *Journal of Ecumenical Studies* 14 (1977):433–47; Mahmoud Ayoub, "Muslim Views of Christianity: Some Modern Examples" *Islamo-Christiana* 10 (1984):49–70.

5

"That Hideous Schizophrenia"[1]

SAYYID QUTB

INTRODUCTION

Sayyid Qutb (1906–66) was born in Upper Egypt. He visited the United States from 1949–51, and there became confirmed in his deeply anti-Western and anti-Christian views. Upon his return to Egypt he became a leading figure in the Muslim Brothers, a militantly conservative Islamic activist group. He was imprisoned in Egypt for seditious activities in 1954; released in 1964; rearrested in 1966, and condemned to death and executed that same year.

The essay reprinted here is a polemical piece in which Qutb traces the historical process by which the message of Jesus Christ — which Qutb, like all Muslims, regards as a prophetic message from God — became corrupted and in the end contributed directly to the current profoundly divided condition of Western culture. A deep dislike of all dualism pervades what Qutb has to say. He rejects what he sees as the Christian tendency toward a dualism of flesh and spirit, manifest in the importance of monasticism in the West, in the elevation of the celibate life that goes with it, and in the sexual promiscuity that is the inevitable result of any attempt to reject sexuality. He opposes also a separation of reason from faith, which leads to the unbridled exercise of human reason apart from or even in direct conflict with God's intentions for human beings. And he criticizes also the separation of religion from the public and social sphere, the turning of it into a matter of individual choice. His conclusion is that Christianity is no longer capable of mediating God's will to Western culture. Its corruption is irremediable.

Qutb's essay is part of a larger work entitled Islam: The Religion of the Future, *in which he connects his theological and historical reading of the history of the West with his political hopes for the future of Islam. For him, it is both inevitable and desirable that the West should be "Islamized." Qutb's work is important because in its view of Christianity it bears strong similarities to much* of what is now the common rhetoric of resurgent Islam. It can be considered, in part, as a precursor of the work of more sophisticated intellectuals like al-Attas (see Chapter 8 in this volume) and as an influence upon revolutionary Islam.

"THAT HIDEOUS SCHIZOPHRENIA"

It is not natural for religion to be segregated from life in this world, nor is it natural for the Divine system to be confined to conscientious feelings, ethical rules and ritualistic worship. Nor is it in its nature to be immured in a restricted corner of human life and labelled "a personal affair."

A revealed religion can never single out a narrow sector of human life and subject it to God, or be content with negativity, while other sectors and positive actions are subjected to other gods to administer, either individually or collectively, enforcing such laws, doctrines, institutions and organizations as they may deem fit.

It is not in the nature of revealed religion to initiate a road to the Afterlife, a road which leads people to Paradise, except that recognized path of active labor and toil for the purpose of developing life in accordance with the system approved by God.

It is not in the nature of revealed religion to become an irrelevant plaything, a disfigured, hideous and insignificant phantom, or a conglomerate of conventional functions completely inconsistent with rules for practical living.

It is not in the nature of religion, even those not revealed by God, to accept such a deformed and bleak outlook. Where, then, has this malaise of negativity come to contaminate religion? How has this deplorable distinction between religion and life come about?

This hideous schizophrenia took place under lamentable circumstances, leaving its destructive traces in Europe, and from there to the whole world wherever Western views, institutions and ways of life have conquered other human societies. Once people deviated from God's system, they had to continue following the fatuous ideologies of their own invention, leading predictably to their present miserable state wherein individuals suffer the terrible consequences of their ideological shortcomings, moaning from the pain inflicted upon them by their fellow men. Still worse is their ineffectiveness in ridding themselves of their abominable man-made Hell. But we shall leave this unhappy misery to later chapters and discuss here the circumstances leading to the Hideous Schizophrenia.

Judaism sought to establish a viable Divine system of life and was succeeded by Christianity, which pursued the same system after effecting some modifications. Nevertheless, the Jews reacted unfavourably to the message of Jesus (peace be upon him) and renounced the Atonement he introduced as commanded by Allah, though he said to them, as related in the Qur'an:

I have come to you to attest Law which was before me, and to make lawful to you part of what was before forbidden to you. I have come to you with a sign from your Lord. So fear God and obey me (Qur'an 3:50).

The Jews resisted Jesus and his message inviting people to gentleness, peace, spiritual purification and renouncement of ritual formalities which do not bear on faith. Finally, they induced Pontius Pilate, the Roman Governor over Palestine at the time, to attempt the murder of Jesus by crucifixion. But God alone ordained the time of his death and raised Jesus to Himself. (We do not know the manner of Jesus' death, as there is no definite injunction in our Qur'an or Traditions regarding this.)

Whatever the case may be, the relation between the Jews and the followers of Jesus took a deplorable course. The later converts, coming in great numbers from a Gentile cultural environment, had no love for the Jews, whereas the Jews developed even more enmity towards those converts. Consequently, each group stood apart in its isolated camp, resulting in the acrimonious detachment of Christianity from Judaism, despite the fact that the first Christians sought merely to renovate Judaism through a slight modification of its laws. As is so evident from the teachings of Jesus, Christianity sought to imbue an elevated spiritual consciousness to the moral ethics of the older faith. Consequent with this unpleasant separation of the two parties, the Christian Bible was also practically separated from the "Old Testament" though the latter continued to be respected as Holy Scripture. But the Christian legalism became independent from the Law of Moses (the mainstay of Judaism) and as a result of this alienation, Christianity lost the Divine legislative principles which administered the secular affairs of life.

Nevertheless, if the Christian ideological ideal had remained as sound as that expounded by Jesus Christ (peace be upon him), it could have presented still the right interpretation of the universe, of the situation of man therein and of his primary objectives in this world. It could have brought the Christians back to the Law of Moses, as clarified by Jesus to ease some of the Jewish restrictions on worship and human relations.

But what happened was that the followers of Jesus were subjected to atrocious persecution by both the faithless Jews and the pagan Romans who were their temporal rulers. This led the Disciples (the students of Jesus) and their followers to hide themselves and to move and act in secrecy for long periods of time. Amidst such circumstances they altered the text of their Scriptures, transmitting the history of Jesus and the events in his life in a haphazard fashion, being unable to verify freely the authenticity of those narratives. As a result, the Gospel (*Injil*) as inspired by God to Jesus, was interpolated among those legends and narratives about the life of Christ—stories which came from different and conflicting sources. These hybrid compositions have been called "Gospels" but they are for the most part the words of these students and their own versions about the biography of Jesus, with quotations here and there from what was originally The Gospel. The most ancient of these "Gospels" was written a full generation after Christ, and Christian historians greatly differ in fixing its date, estimating it between 40 A.D. and 64 A.D. They differ as well about the language it was originally written in, as they have found but one single translation.[2]

It was Paul who was considered the principal propagator of the Christian faith to the Gentiles, himself being a Roman heathen converted to Christianity.[3] Paul's conception of Christianity was adulterated by the residues of Roman mythology and Greek philosophy. That was a catastrophe which infected Christianity since its early days in Europe, over and above its disfiguration during the early period of persecution when the prevailing circumstances did not allow for examining and authenticating its religious textual bases.

Paul wrote his epistles after the first century A.D.[4] and such writings attest the blending of religious assimilations with philosophical mythology — especially that part concerning incarnation. He used to say: "the Christ is sitting on the right hand of God, praying for those to whom he beseeches the good so that His Word may abide in them." Or again "He begs Him forgiveness for them, declaring to them that they will attain glory once he comes back to earth." From his sayings, it seems that he expected a quick resurrection of Christ, and he often reckoned to him as ". . . our God, Jesus the Messiah." He even called himself "the messenger of Jesus the Messiah in accordance with the ordinance of God, our Saviour and Creator, Jesus the Messiah."*[5]

But the greatest calamity was the subsequent event which was considered, at face value, the triumph of Christianity. It happened when the Roman Emperor Constantine embraced the new religion and enabled the Christians to become the ruling party in 355 A.D. The American writer Draper describes this event and its deplorable results in his book *Science and Religion*, indicating that idolatry and polytheism entered Christianity by means of hypocrites who assumed high posts in the Roman Empire. They pretended to be Christians, though they did not heed the dictates of religion in the least, nor were they ever faithful to it. The nominal Christian Constantine was himself one of these. He spent his life in suppression and debauchery, never observing the rites of his church but for the last few days of his life, being baptized only on his deathbed.

The Christian community, while powerful enough to keep Constantine king, could not crush or eradicate idolatry. Christianity's principles became muddled and transmuted as a result of its struggles and conflicts, leading to formation of a new synthetic religion displaying conspicuously equal elements of both Christianity and paganism. In this respect Islam differs from Christianity. It completely exterminated its rival (idolatry) and propagated its principles pure and without opacity. But this Emperor, Constantine, was a slave to his lusts and had no genuine religious convictions and he deemed it in his interest and the interest of the two competing ideologies (idolatry and Christianity) to have unity and reconciliation. Paradoxically, the Christians did not object to the idea! It seems that they believed the new faith would prosper if mingled with the popular pagan creeds, but would eventually rid itself of the absurdity of idolatry.

However, the religion never did rid itself of the impurities of paganism, as devoted Christians had hoped for, but continued its course polluted with heathen myths and conceptions. Still worse, it was so encumbered with political and racial differences that it used to alter and modify its basic principles in accordance with its political aims. In this respect Alfred Butler in his book *Arab Conquest of Egypt*, says that these two centuries (fifth and sixth centuries A.D.) were an era of continuous strife between the Egyptians and the Romans, stimulated by differences of race and religion. The religious differences were more acute than the racial ones, since the main trouble at that time was the enmity between the Royalists and the Monophysites. The first faction, as the title indicates, was the party supporting the imperialist State and the king. They believed in the traditional dual nature of Christ, while the latter, which was the party of the Egyptian Copts, completely denied that belief and opposed it with such vehemence and fanaticism that we would hardly expect to find in any reasonable nation, let alone in a nation professing belief in the Bible.[6]

Again, T. W. Arnold, in his book *The Call of Islam*, commenting on these sectarian, political and racial differences and their effects on the innovations, additions and alterations in Christianity, stated that Justinian succeeded in giving the Empire an appearance of unity one hundred years before the Islamic conquest. But soon after his death the unity cracked and the Empire was in dire need of a strong, mutual feeling to tie the provinces to the capital of the State.

As for Heraclius,[7] he exerted many efforts to reunite Syria with the central government, yet achieved no success. Unfortunately, the measures he took for reconciliation led to the accentuation of the differences instead of their removal. There was no other substitute for patriotism but religious emotion. So, by interpreting the faith in such a manner that enabled him to pacify the people, he attempted to put an end to the disputes between the conflicting parties and to bring about conciliation between the Orthodox Church and those who denounced religion, and between the central Government and those who were at odds with it.

In 451 A.D., the Council of Chalcedon declared that Christ should be recognized in both his divine and human natures. These cannot be distinguished, they postulated, because of their unity. Thus, they viewed Christ as "true God" and "true Man," though united in one entity and in one body, not two divisible or separable bodies—but consolidated in one entity which is Son, God, and Word.

Arnold continues his analysis, stating that the sect of Jacobites[8] rejected that declaration and never admitted to but one nature of Christ. They claimed that he is the compound of entities, having all the Divine and human qualifications. Yet, the personality possessing such characteristics ceased to be dual and became one single compound of entities.

The unfortunate circumstances which influenced Christianity at its very inception, then its political success as shown above, added to the subsequent political and racial contentions, disfigurations and modifications in the creed. As a result, the ideological ideal was burdened with the elements of so-called "mysteries" quite alien to its nature as a Divine religion. Accordingly, the Christian conception, as modulated by successive graftings at the outset, and as edited by the general and private religious Councils later on, became unable to give authoritative Divine interpretation to the nature of existence and its genuine relation to the Creator. Nor could it elucidate the nature and attributes of the Creator, or the nature of human existence and the proper goals of mankind. These elements must be correctly assessed so that the social order deriving from and dependent upon them will be sound and correct as well.

Matters did not stop at undermining the vitality of the ideological ideal, but more unfortunate eventualities worsened the situation still further. The Church wanted to check the trend of extravagant Roman living and the voluptuous indulgence, which had become extreme just prior to the advent of Christianity. Draper describes the degeneration in an elaborate passage from *Science and Religion*. He stated that as the Roman Empire had reached the acme of military and political power, and as its civilization reached its zenith, it suffered an extreme setback in its morality, religious belief and social behaviour. Romans became lascivious and wanton, believing that this life is the chance for lustful enjoyment and that the individual should rejoice in luxury and sensual pleasures. Their casual abstinence and fasting acted on them as stimulants to greed and lust. Their tables were glittering with gold and silver utensils enamelled with gems. They were surrounded by servants in decorated attire and by half-naked girls who disclosed their lusts. They enjoyed their luxurious baths, their vast arenas for pleasure and wrestling, whether with each other or with lions, where they fought till they soaked in their own blood.

Somehow, those heroes who conquered the world believed that if anything were worthy of worship, it was Power. Power could bring man the wealth which others collected by their sweat and toil, and if one could win his battle, he would be entitled to confiscate monies and property, and to impose taxes and tributes on the defeated. They believed that the head of their Roman Empire was the symbol of this invisible power, and therefore the Roman life reflected pompous and glamorous royal ways of living. But all that was a superfluous illusion similar to those we perceive in the Greek civilization during its decline.

Though the Church well desired to curb this refractory canine appetite and to stop the prevailing degeneration, yet it did not tackle the problem from the right angle, nor did it possess any remnants of the genuine righteous Christian ideological ideal with which to establish justice among men and to strike a balance between the extremes of human behaviour.

In reaction to this malignant mode of life, a trend of rigorous monasticism pushed forth so ruthlessly that it brought more disaster to humanity upon the heels of the savagery of Roman atheism. Asceticism and abstinence (with the vows of poverty and celibacy) became a part of the welfare in life. The inventiveness of those natural potentialities which are necessary for human survival and civilization on the one hand, and for the performance of man's functions as vicegerent to God on the other, was suppressed and obliterated. This sharp deviation from man's nature was held up as the emblem of human perfection, piety and virtue, though such asceticism and abstinence were not sanctioned by God, and were not necessary for any normal life.

Monasticism did not remedy the degeneration; on the contrary, it gave vent to the struggle between two extreme parties, both of which were far from the right way and ignorant of the needs of humanity. W. Lecky, in his book *History of European Morals from Augustus to Charlemagne*, depicted the conditions of the Christian world in this historical era, where monasticism and debauchery prevailed side by side, stating that the outstanding characteristics of the social life at that time were gross immorality and debasement of character. Prostitution, lasciviousness, favoritism toward kings, princes, and the rich; competition in luxurious fashions and ornaments and counterfeit values such as these, were in full swing. The whole of life was oscillating between extreme profligacy and extreme monasticism. Indeed, the very cities that produced the greatest number of monks were the same cities that fostered the most flagrant prostitution!

Therefore monasticism, stemming from ecclesiastical conceptions which deviated from the original Divine Christian one, fell short of being even a moral code for the Christian world. In fact, it left a certain apathy against religion, even though religion was not to blame for monasticism, and feelings of revolt were incited against this system alien to human nature. That explains why monasticism was an unfortunate element in the formation of the eventual Hideous Schizophrenia.

It was a catastrophic event when people who underwent such strict deprivation lest they would not be admitted to paradise, discovered that the private lives of the clergymen were saturated with luxurious enjoyment and full of the most perverted debauchery.

Indulgences (dispensation certificates) were initially issued by the Church according to a resolution giving it that right in one of its numerous "ecumenical councils." These councils assumed the authority to change, add or omit whatever they wanted of the Christian creed. The Twelfth Ecumenical Council[9] resolved unanimously that, since Jesus Christ had conferred upon his Church the authority to grant forgiveness of sins, and since the Church had been exercising this right since the early days, the Church would reserve to itself the practice of this procedure for the salvation of the Christian peoples. The Council resolved as well to excommunicate anyone who alleged that these certificates were useless or who denied the Church its right to grant them. However, it was decided to use this right in moderation and with precaution, tradition says, so that this ecclesiastical instruction might not be misused or become unduly lenient.

When we add these certificates to the strictness of the Church regarding asceticism and abstinence in the name of religion and to the moral laxity of the clergymen and the perfidy of their private lives, we can realize the unfortunate circumstances which eventually led to the hideous schizophrenia which afflicted Europe in its dark history.

But the story did not end there either. The Church initiated acrimonious litigation against the emperors and kings not merely in the sphere of religion and morality, but also relative to political influence and sovereignty.[10] ... The Church, taking advantage of its disputes with emperors and kings over political power, exploited the people in the worst of ways by imposing exorbitant taxes which it collected directly. People began to grumble and suffer from these levies and the dissatisfied rulers manipulated the people's ordeal to insinuate revolts against the Church by every means possible. They resorted mainly to unveiling the scandals of the clergymen, exposing their clandestine perfidy and personal debauchery, which had been disguised behind priestly robes and ecclesiastical ritual.

Then came the final blow that established the hideous schizophrenia that put to an end any working relationship between religion and practical life in Europe, finally separating the religious ideal from the social order. It was the greatest crime committed by the Western Church against itself, the Christian religion and against all the religions of the world up to this time. How did the criminal act unfold?

First, the Church monopolized the right of understanding and interpreting the Bible by prohibiting any thinker from outside its own clannish cadre from trying to understand or interpret it.

Then followed the introduction into the creed of abstract dogmas that were absolutely incomprehensible, inconceivable and incredible. Some examples of these abstractions we have already quoted from Arnold's book on the truth about Jesus. The Church converted these vague doctrines into "divine mysteries" or rituals of worship, the most striking of which was its dogma about the Eucharist (Lord's Supper), against which Martin Luther, John Calvin and Ulrich Zwingli revolted in the establishment of what was called Protestantism.[11]

The issue of Eucharist was a novelty without foundation in the Holy Book, early Christian history or the ecumenical councils.

What happened was that Christians customarily ate bread and drank wine during Easter, and called this The Lord's Supper. Later on, the Church alleged that the bread and wine were "transubstantiated" into the actual body and blood of Christ. Whoever ate that bread and drank that wine when converted would find Grace through the flesh and blood of Jesus.

The Church had imposed this allegation upon its readers and forbade rational discussion of it in pain of excommunication!

Over and above these abstract fallacies inserted in the creed and rites, concurrent with prohibiting people to verify them in the Scriptures (which they were barred from trying to interpret), the Church followed suit with absurd theories about life and the universe. It gave intellectual sanction to certain geographical, historical and physical views and postulates which prevailed at that time and which were full of mistakes and fabulous imagination, declaring them exempt from discussion, correction, refutation or even replacement.

This was the final blow, because these unscientific dogmas represented sheer falsehood, susceptible to refutation by simple experimentation. Furthermore, seeking and verifying knowledge was an activity which God has exhorted the human mind to explore objectively with all its endowed qualifications, without any specified views pre-imposed by God. . . . [12] These, in general, are the most important events that caused the hideous schizophrenia from which Europe and the whole modern world now suffer. Europe revolted against an irrational brand of ecclesiasticism that passed for religion. Her example was followed by many others all over the world, without discriminating between one religion and another. Europe revolted against a Christianity that had been disfigured from its beginning, and whose Divine characteristics and conceptions, values and foundations had been dramatically forged and grafted. Europe revolted against the arbitrariness of the churchmen who committed this crime against themselves, against religion and against the whole ill-fated world, and who incurred upon themselves a universal enmity led by a West full of spite on account of this foisted religion and its daft priests. All these circumstances are (thanks to God) purely European and not universal. They are related to a particular sort of religious dogma, but not to the essence of religious Faith, and are rather confined to a particular historical span of time. It is certain that humanity can always dispense with the sad repercussions of these circumstances once it realizes the historical facts leading up to this struggle.

But salvation cannot be achieved through the European mentality. The soul of Europe is tightly enveloped in the web of its own historical aberrations and the consequential mental and emotional trauma. It has become schizophrenic by the unfortunate struggle between reason and religion, a pathology which is reflected in European literature, art, politics, economics and the very quality of life.

6

"Islam and Dialogue—Some Reflections on a Current Topic"[1]

MOHAMED TALBI

INTRODUCTION

Mohamed Talbi (1921–) is professor emeritus at the University of Tunis. From 1973–77 he directed the history department at the Centre d'Études et de Récherches Economiques et Sociales in Tunis. He holds a doctorate in history from the Sorbonne and is author of numerous articles on the history of medieval Islam, on Islamology, and on the possibilities of Muslim-Christian dialogue.

The essay reprinted here is a generous, irenic, open-minded piece on the need of Islam for serious dialogue with Christians. Talbi points to the difficulties of the enterprise, stressing that Islamic intellectuals have as yet shown little interest in the process while Christians have shown a good deal. Talbi does not minimize the difficulties of the process; he realizes that the central doctrinal differences between Islam and Christianity—specifically, on the person and nature of Jesus Christ—are important and may in the end turn out to be irreducible. He realizes also that the history of interactions between Muslims and Christians has left a legacy of bitterness and suspicion on both sides. But he points to the intellectual and theological resources present within Islam that not only allow but require interreligious dialogue, and he sketches a modus operandi which might make it fruitful.

"ISLAM AND DIALOGUE—SOME REFLECTIONS ON A CURRENT TOPIC"

Our century has seen the splitting of the atom, and it has also witnessed the disintegration of all forms of monolithic ideologies. Pluralism of cultures would appear to be undeniable, a movement that cannot be reversed. This fact, however, makes it indispensable that various intellectual disciplines should encounter one another, and that there should be constant dialogue between systems. In this line of thought, the last Council inaugurated in September 1962[2] opened up encouraging perspectives for reconciliation and for exchange of ideas, not only between Christians, but also between all the human families, whatever their spiritual and ideological attachment.

Islam, no more than any other system of thought, cannot afford to remain a mere spectator of this movement without risking a condemnation, which this time could be final and without appeal. Indeed what is at stake today is far more important (and attractive) than any issue which arose in the dark ages of Muslim civilization, a period of decadence whose after effects, in spite of a laborious *Nahda* (Renaissance), are still very much with us.

Revelation and Dialogue

Thus dialogue for Islam is first and foremost a necessary and vital re-establishment of contact with the world at large. This is still more urgent and beneficial for Islam than for other religions, such as Christianity, which have never really lost such contact, something which puts Christianity in a relatively privileged position today. It is also, in a certain sense, a revival of an old tradition. In fact the whole of Revelation invites us to do just this, and there is no sign of opposition to it. To be convinced of this point, one has only to meditate upon the following verses:

> Call thou to the way of thy Lord with wisdom (*bi-l-hikma*) and good admonition (*wa-l-maw'izat al-hasana*), and dispute with them in the better way (*wa jadilhum bi-l-lati hiya ahsan*). Surely thy Lord knows very well those who have gone astray from His way (*inna rabbaka huwa a'lamu biman dalla an sabilihi*), and He knows very well those who are guided (*wa huwa a'lamu bi-l-muhtadin*) (Qur'an 16:125).
>
> Dispute not with the People of the Book save in the fairer manner (*wa la tujadilu ahl al-kitab illa bi-l-lati hiya ashan*), except for those of them that do wrong (*zalamu*): and say, "We believe in what has been sent down to us, and what has been sent down to you (*amanna bi-l-ladhi unzila ilayna wa unzila ilaykum*); our God and your God is one (*wa ilahuna wa ilahukum wahidun*), and to Him we have surrendered (*muslimun*)" (Qur'an 29:46).

Thus the Revelation invites the Prophet and the Muslim to discuss and to enter into dialogue with men in general, and especially with the faithful of the biblical religions. We notice also that the duty of apostolate, which is implicitly referred to here and which is something we must not try to avoid but which we shall have to discuss further, harmonizes well with respect for other people and other beliefs, for it belongs to God and to God alone in the final instance to acknowledge His own: "Surely thy Lord knows very well those who have gone astray from His way, and He knows very well those who are guided."

The Handicap of Past History

Why then, someone may say, did things happen in the way they did? Why are we so badly handicapped by our past? Why has there been so much opposition, such misrepresentation, so many insults and so much abuse? Why in fact has force prevailed over courtesy?

The answer is that nothing is simple in the lives of men, and we have to examine carefully the sad past we have inherited so as to avoid making the same mistakes in the future. It is a fact that today people think of Islam as a religion of violence, not as one of dialogue. So we need to explain this point briefly. In the first place, let me emphasize that although certain countries were opened (*fath*) by force, it is practically unheard of that Islam was anywhere imposed upon people. It is also right that we should examine the world situation at the time of Islam's entry on the stage. The two super powers of the time, the empires of Byzantium and Ctesiphon, were striving to impose their supremacy over the other existing nations. Nobody thought it wrong to expand the empire by force. You either had to persecute the others or suffer persecution yourself. We have since learned too that all wars are just or can be justified. The martial spirit was—and alas perhaps still is—the noblest road to glory. And what are we to think of modern revolutionary movements which are supposed to win happiness for various races, and to sweep aside anything that might hinder progress? Islam then, having been revealed at a given time and in a specific country, enters into history, is lived by men and becomes subject to the law of contingency. Whether it liked it or not, Islam could not help but fit into its own period. The train was already moving; Islam had only to catch it.

And so it is a fact that more than one verse of the Qur'an incites to combat and promises the palm of martyrdom and paradise to whoever falls while striving in God's way. Such combat, however, is always put forward as second best, a last resort, which must conform to all sorts of material and moral restrictions in order to be acceptable. It is above all important to bring out clearly that the verses which incite to war have an essentially circumstantial application, connected with specific contingencies which today, we would hope, are definitely something of the past. They do not present us with the deep, permanent spirit of the Message, which is that of a hand respectfully and courteously held out to our neighbor, as we have already emphasized. It is this deep and permanent spirit that we must rediscover today in order to clear the path to dialogue of all misunderstandings which have blocked it in the past and which are in danger of blocking it again today in combination with other difficulties of the present time.

Present-Day Difficulties

Even when the mortgage of the past has been paid off, there still remain problems to be solved. Other difficulties continue to exist even after good will can be counted on.

DISPARITY BETWEEN THOSE TAKING PART IN DIALOGUE

We must begin by emphasizing the major difficulty: the enormous difference between those taking part in dialogue as well as the different level of studies within the respective traditions. There can be no doubt that this obstacle is the hardest to overcome in the immediate future as, even with the finest dispositions and the best will in the world, one cannot just instantaneously produce, as if by enchantment, people fully qualified and capable of taking part in dialogue. Now, it goes almost without saying that most of modern Islam belongs to the disinherited zone of under-development, an under-development which is not only material but perhaps above all intellectual. The fact that one can call to mind the names of one or two eminent thinkers does not affect the situation as a whole: the exception only goes to prove the rule. So we can say (with apologies to Corneille) that there is not only a risk of dialogue coming to an end, but of it never really beginning for lack of "dialoguers." It is this fact, far more than any difficulties over principles or methods of approach, which explains the hesitation, the reticence, the lack of trust even, and generally speaking the present sterility, despite several efforts made, as only to be expected, on the initiative of Christians.[*3]

UNEQUAL THEOLOGICAL DEVELOPMENT

There is also the fact of unequal theological development. Christian theology has been able to profit by its confrontation with other intellectual systems. The most dangerous of these have finally been the most salutary for its development, by subjecting it, under the pressure of contestation and criticism, to a fruitful tension. It has thus been able to understand its own values, work out answers, undertake at times agonizing revisions, in the course of which it has also, and perhaps most importantly, been enriched by elements which have proved to be compatible with its own internal dynamism. Christian thought has thus been constantly vitalized and, while safeguarding and even reinforcing its attachment to what is purest and most authentic in its Tradition, it has adapted itself to each age and continues daily to progress in this direction. This effort, noticeable from the 19th century onwards, resulted in the break-through of the recent Council. This of course did not take place without a certain amount of drama, of heartbreak, and even of crisis.[*4] But after it all the Church feels more committed, better armed and more ready for dialogue.

In every domain and in every scientific discipline the Church can produce people qualified to enter into dialogue, many of them real experts. Quite recently, for example, the book by Jacques Monod, *Le hasard et la nécessité*,[5] was almost immediately answered by that of Marc Oraison, the title of whose book, *Le hasard et la vie*,[6] shows an evident desire for dialogue, such as really did take place between the two authors, and to which the television assured the widest possible audience. Within the special framework which interests us, that of Islamology, there is a tremendous choice among clerics who are specialists, such as G. C. Anwati, L. Gardet, Fr. Hayek, Fr. Jomier, Canon Ledit, Kenneth Morgan, Y. Moubarac, Fr. Pareja, Dr. Hermann Stieglecker, Wilfred Cantwell Smith, W. Montgomery Watt, and many others, without mentioning numerous lay Islamologists, to one of whom I owe a special mention, my eminent master Louis Massignon[7] whose whole life was a living dialogue. Some younger men, such as M. Allard and Fr. Caspar, are beginning to make a name for themselves and there are many others still who are preparing to take the place of the older men.

And what is Islam doing in face of such an unprecedented effort by the Church? It offers us a theology whose evolution practically came to an end in the 12th century. Muslim theology thus progressively lost contact with the world. For centuries, no new problems arose to challenge it and force it to investigate more closely the mystery of the world and of God. It is thus seen as something congealed, something often merely of historical interest. It is true that there was the *nahda*, the renaissance of the 19th century, but this, while far from being something negative, has not yet succeeded in reinstating Islam in the movement of history. The distance covered may well seem slight in comparison with the journey which still lies ahead. Islam is far from possessing experts in all domains. In particular, as far as I know we cannot mention one real Muslim Christologist[8] to set beside the numerous Christian lay people and clerics who are Islamologists. One can understand how Muhamed Arkoun could ask in disillusionment: "How can we possibly get people to enter into useful dialogue, when their very conscience is divorced from its true tradition, and when they struggle on in economic and political misery, while the other side is fully conscious of its past as well as of its present condition?"*[9] In other words, how is an earthenware pot to argue with an iron one? If we wish to overcome this difficulty, which gives birth to mental reservations and distrust, we must expose it in public in all frankness and serenity. As long as one side suffers from a superiority complex and the other from an inferiority complex, no useful purpose can be served in trying to open dialogue.

ISLAM MUST OVERCOME ITS DIFFICULTIES

In order to avoid any misunderstanding let us say first of all that if at the present moment Christians and Muslims are unequally prepared for dialogue, as we have just stressed forcefully, Islam in itself has no need to maintain any sort of complex with regard to Christianity.

It still remains that at every level there is an unequal development of the followers of the two beliefs. And so we turn towards the Muslims who are liable, in such circumstances, to give way to the temptation to isolate themselves in a spirit of self-preservation, to become more rigid and to retire within their own camp and proudly reply with a resounding "No"! We would like to ask them whether this is the right solution. There is no doubt that in this way they can preserve the things they value and they will survive. But for how long? Frontiers today are full of gaps: they fail to stop human contacts, the seductive attraction of example, books, films, and still less radio transmissions, to be followed soon by television broadcasts. Isolation becomes more and more a pipe dream in a world in tumult and plunged in contestation. It is just as if humanity today is going through a new crisis of adolescence.

There is no way of escaping the upheaval. The democratization of teaching, the possibility of going to school and even to the university, the raising of the standard of life and thought, with all the demands this creates, all these changes which take place sometimes without any transition, could prove fatal to Muslims who have never been exposed to such infection nor vaccinated against it. Religions are becoming less and less a social factor and more and more a personal and conscious commitment. So then if present-day Islam does not succeed, through dialogue with all systems of thought with no exception or exclusion, in renewing the spirituality of its followers and in assimilating, as in the past, all values which are not opposed to its Witness, it will certainly be on the way to failing in its mission on earth. Such de-Islamization can already be detected in the universities, among the youth in general and among the members of the more developed classes who often, at best, keep a certain vague affection for Islam as a venerable cultural heirloom. Finally, then, the adventure of dialogue with both believers and unbelievers, whatever the differences and the inequalities of formation at the present moment, and taking all things into consideration, is less perilous than becoming more rigid in one's attitudes and fighting to defend frontiers in a world where frontiers are becoming more and more an anachronism. Unless one is to suppose that the Muslims, by some sort of despair or avowal of impotence, are to finish up by discharging on others—if such a thing were possible—the deposit (*amana*) which Heaven has confided to their care.[*10] For how else can one explain, other than by despair which torments some of our most lucid thinkers, the solution proposed by M. Arkoun in his *Supplique d'Un Musulman aux Chrétiens*[11] where he is reduced to saying:

> Under these conditions Christians could take over and assure the religious future of Islam with the same determination, total commitment and the same depth of conviction with which they serve Christianity. It seems to us that this is the best way of preparing for future dialogue, since when one strives to set others free one frees oneself at the same time.[*12]

May I be allowed to be less pessimistic? Thank God, things are not as bad as all that! In spite of all sorts of inequalities which we have not in any way tried to hide, we think that dialogue, with certain precautions, is still possible between partners who make no secret of their own convictions. One should never await passively to be liberated by others, but one should set about freeing oneself.

Preliminary Conditions for Dialogue

Of course it is evident that however possible dialogue may be it is not easy to realize. So we must establish clearly the conditions required in order to allow it the maximum possibility to succeed and to be equally fruitful for all taking part. The hidden obstacles are indeed numerous, and so we must discover them in some way in advance, so as to avoid them more surely and to make sure also that once we do begin we are not stopped in our tracks. For this purpose we must avoid two attitudes both of which could prove to be fertile sources of misunderstanding, disappointments and bitterness. These are the spirit of controversy and that of compromise and complacency.

WE MUST AVOID CONTROVERSY

A polemical spirit caused untold harm in the Middle Ages, not only in the material, but also in the moral and intellectual spheres, by giving rise to caricatures and falsifications and by spreading lies in the name of truth. It is rare, in fact, that disputes do not lead to a set-back and an abdication of the mind. In spite of the evolution of mentalities—which in any case is perhaps only relative—the temptation remains strong for all religions to find themselves, little by little, forced into a blind alley. Let us say clearly to anyone who is tempted by a spirit of adventure that the clashes between the great universal religions of today have no more chance of producing conclusive victories than they had in the past. W. Montgomery Watt is absolutely right when he says: "If a Christian and a Muslim are merely seeking arguments against one another, they will easily find many, but this will not lead to dialogue."*[13]

We must be very careful then to exterminate the hydra of polemics. The surest means of making it impossible for it ever to renew the immense damage done in the past and the sins committed against reason, is to renounce any idea of using dialogue, either openly or in one's own mind, as a means of converting the person we are talking to. If, in fact, dialogue is conceived as a new form of proselytism, a means of undermining convictions and bringing about defeat or surrender, sooner or later we shall find ourselves back in the same old situation as in the Middle Ages. It will merely have been a change in tactics. To address Muslims as, for example, Henri Nusslé does in his *Dialogue avec l'Islam* with such words as: "The West can offer you not only its culture, not only its genius for invention, but still more it can offer you the Kingdom of Christ,"*[14] is to use unsuitable language in spite of the sincerity of the author and the undoubted nobility of his sentiments.

FRONTIERS HAVE CHANGED

To take that tone does not even offer the advantage of a tactical success. It just puts the backs up of people who are more inclined to connect Western technical superiority with the fact of its emancipation from the religious yoke and its cult of material progress. The only really important mass conversions taking place today are from faith to atheism or agnosticism, considered as the new religions of efficiency and progress. All believers then, abstraction made of any sectarian divisions, must grasp the fact that the world has greatly changed since the Middle Ages. The dividing lines between different faiths no longer run in the same direction as before. The opposition today is not so much between different concepts of God and of the way in which to serve him. A far deeper division has taken place between those who are striving to attain to man's destiny without God, and those who can only conceive of man's future in God and through God; between those who consign indiscriminately to the rag-bag of myths all forms of religion, and those who continue to believe in their fathomless infinite truth. Thus Gennie Luccioni remarks with evident satisfaction in a review, which was in fact of Christian inspiration to begin with, and in a recent issue entitled "Le mythe aujourd'hui," that there is:

a strange lack of anyone who remarks on, if only to deny it, the collapse of our religious myths. No doubt silence under the circumstances is more eloquent than speech; so that we have been tempted to underline this by leaving an empty page. If the Christian myths are passing away one may suppose that they are disappearing just as others have done before them and in the way indicated by Lévi-Strauss in the same series. It should therefore be possible to rediscover traces of them in literature or in political, historical or philosophical writings. However the vault of heaven is disintegrating and the celestial map no longer means anything except to "mythomaniacs."*[15]

Surely there is no question of calling on those who believe to pledge themselves to some anachronistic and sterile Holy Alliance to engage in some queer new crusade. But they should understand all the same that polemics used to forward some doubtful sort of proselytism only falsifies and obscures the truth instead of illuminating it. It can only confuse sincere souls, cause them to lose their faith, and so add to the number of those to whom "the celestial map no longer means anything."

CONVERSIONS ARE NO LONGER BROUGHT ABOUT BY ARGUMENT

Besides, in the case of the great religions which have evolved to an equal degree, conversions are no longer obtained through proselytism and polemics. Neither that of Carlo Coccioli, the author of *Tourment de Dieu*, who went from Christianity to Judaism, nor that of Edith Stein who took the opposite road but was nevertheless sent to the furnaces at Auschwitz for being fundamentally a Jewess, nor that of Isabelle Eberhardt who took refuge in *L'Ombre chaude de l'Islam*, were brought about in this way. They were the final destination of a more demanding and more complex spiritual odyssey, the fruit of an intense individual psychological drama, whereby they acquired a higher value and a greater depth.

THE DUTY OF THE APOSTOLATE

But then, for a religion to renounce as one of its objectives the conversion of those who have not yet come under its sway, is that not the equivalent of abandoning its universalist vocation, denying its past, and failing to carry out its duty of the apostolate?

This is precisely the moment when we must get rid of any equivocation and point out, in order to be completely sincere and totally successful, the second peril to be avoided, that of excessive complacency and compromise. Nobody, whether believer or atheist, should ever compromise with his convictions or his ideas. This is the unquestionable law of progress and of the asymptotic progress towards Truth. Besides, true convictions that have become part of one's life are not negotiable. And so it is not a question of going from one extreme to the other and seeking at all cost, in a pure spirit of conciliation and without a real change of heart, accommodating solutions which only result in syncretism and confusion of thought. The sort of dialogue in which we are interested is not a question of policy, an exercise of the art of compromise. It is something much more important. It supposes total sincerity and, to be fruitful, it requires everyone to be completely himself, without aggressiveness or compromise.

Thus we get back to the full requirements of the apostolate, but this time purified from the slag of polemics and of a proselytism which leads to blindness. Seen from this point of view the apostolate becomes essentially an attentive openness towards our neighbor, an incessant seeking for truth through a continuous deepening and assimilation of the values of faith, and, in the final analysis, pure witness. This sort of apostolate is called, in Arabic, *jihad*. This statement may well surprise all those for whom this word recalls the clash of holy wars past and present. Let me explain to them that *jihad* both etymologically and fundamentally has nothing to do with war. Arabic has no lack of words to describe all kinds of warfare. If the Qur'an had really wanted to talk of war there would have been an embarassing choice of words to be found in the rich and colorful vocabulary of pre-Islamic poetry, which is entirely given over to exalting the "great days" of the Arab race (*ayyam al-'Arab*) when this people engaged in their favorite pastime of disembowelling one another. *Jihad* must therefore be something different. Essentially and radically it is an extreme, total effort in the Way of God (*fi sabil Allah*). Tradition makes it clear that the purest, most dramatic and most fruitful form of it is *al-jihad al-akbar*, the combat which takes place in the secrecy of one's conscience. This means that the finest form of apostolate is the witness of a life in which the struggle for moral perfection has succeeded. This form of apostolate through witness is the only one which gives results and is, moreover, in agreement with modern thought. It has no need of proselytism. Did not the Qur'an itself remind the Prophet personally that he could not guide men towards God just as he liked, but that it is really God who guides toward Himself those whom He chooses? (*innaka la tahdi man ahbabta wa lakinna Allaha yahdi man yasha u wa huwa a'lamu bi-l-muhtadin* – "Thou guidest not whom thou likest, but God guides whom He will, and knows very well those that are guided," Qur'an 28:56). In fact, as far as the apostolate is concerned, our duty is to give witness, and it is for God to convert people. "Thus we appointed you a midmost nation that you might be witness to the people, and that the Messenger might be a witness to you" (*wa kadhalika ja'alnakum ummatan wasatan li-takunu shuhada 'a cala al-nas wa yakuna al-rasulu 'alaykum shahidan*, Qur'an 2:143). So it is quite possible to develop a Muslim theology of the apostolate which scrupulously respects the rights of others. It is evident of course that this is just as possible for Christianity – a religion of witness through martyrdom – as well as for all other religions. Consequently, co-existence, or better still co-operation, without any denial of self or renunciation of one's own convictions, is not only possible but very fruitful. So when both extremes of political proselytism and complaisant compromise have been avoided the duty of the apostolate is not done away with. Rather it takes on its most noble and difficult form, that of an interior *jihad*, and opens the way to a healthy spirit of emulation in the pursuit of Good. However, this interior *jihad* should not deteriorate into a selfish mystical, or rather static, concentration on self, or into an all too easy form of self-satisfaction, or even tranquil indifference. It must remain at the same time witness, and bear evidence of a questing spirit marked by openness and a sense of disquiet. It is at this level that dialogue can be decisive. By creating a healthy climate of mutual exchange and of intellectual and spiritual tension, it can help towards a continuous and reciprocally deeper understanding of the values of faith. Movement will replace inertia.

PLURALITY OF WAYS OF SALVATION

This attitude implies, however, if ambiguity is to be avoided, that we admit that there are several ways to salvation. Now this problem is not the easiest one to resolve. The influence of the past makes itself felt here more than anywhere else.

With very few exceptions the theological systems of all religious confessions have been based on the axiom, expressed in different ways, that "outside the Church there is no salvation." Within each faith the group of faithful to benefit by salvation has been still more restricted by the rejection of various heresies whose followers have been consigned to eternal damnation. This leads to the conclusion that apart from certain chosen ones, the vast majority of human beings are destined for perdition. And yet all faiths proclaim that God is Justice, Mercy and Love! It is precisely in this area that we need a real theological renewal and a radical change of mentality. For what chance is there of an open-minded dialogue free of distrust if, from the very beginning, we lay down the absolute principle that those of the other side will inevitably be condemned to hell solely on account of their convictions?

On the part of the Church there has been a very evident evolution since Vatican II, which in particular addressed Muslims in these terms:

> Upon the Muslims too the Church looks with esteem. They adore one God, living and enduring, merciful and all-powerful. Maker of heaven and earth . . whose decrees are sometimes hidden, but to which one must submit wholeheartedly, just as Abraham submitted to God, Abraham with whom the Islamic faith is pleased to associate itself. Though they do not acknowledge Jesus as God, they revere him as a prophet. They also honor Mary, his virgin mother; at times they call upon her too with devotion. . . . Consequently they give worship to God especially through prayer, almsgiving and fasting. They strive to live a moral life in obedience to God at the individual, family and social level.
>
> Although in the course of centuries many quarrels and hostilities have arisen between Christians and Muslims, the council urges all to forget the past and to strive sincerely for mutual understanding. On behalf of all mankind, let them make common cause of safeguarding and fostering social justice, moral values, peace and freedom.[16]

In the same spirit G. C. Anawati states that where salvation is concerned "it has long been admitted that the two requisites for faith laid down by St. Paul exist in Islam." And he adds:

> This means that when I wish to engage in dialogue with a Muslim, I do not have to begin by placing him in hell merely because he is a Muslim. On the contrary I can assure him that under certain conditions, which are quite realizable, he can find salvation while still remaining a Muslim. Can one think of any better way of beginning a fruitful dialogue?*[17]

On the Islamic side, contrary to what one might think, the same attitude of mind already existed in the Middle Ages. One finds it expressed by a completely orthodox theologian whom all Sunnites without exception consider to be the authentic spokesman for Islam (*Hujjat al-islam*), namely Ghazali (1058–1111) who in his book *faysat al-tafriqa* admits that under certain conditions, particularly those of sincerity and an honest life, non-

Muslims can be saved.*[18] Nearer to our times a theologian of the *nahda*, Muhammed 'Abduh (1849–1905) expresses a similar opinion in his commentary on the following verse of the Qur'an:

> Surely they that believe (in Islam), and those of Jewry, and the Christians, and those Sabaeans, who so believes in God and the Last Day, and works righteousness – their wage awaits them with their Lord, and no fear shall be upon them, neither shall they sorrow (Qur'an 2:62).

Confirmation of this verse is found, with some slight variation, a little further on (cf. Qur'an 5:69; see also 2:111–112).*[19]

It is not impossible therefore, neither for Islam nor for Christianity, nor indeed for the other main religions, on the basis of their texts and with the support even of a certain ancient theological tradition, to elaborate a theology which would allow for a certain degree of plurality in the ways of salvation, were it only because one cannot forbid Divine Goodness from overflowing, in a gesture of justice, of mercy and of love, beyond the strict limits of any given Church in order to embrace all men of good will who live exemplary lives. In the end God remains entirely and freely the one who judges, and we must abandon ourselves confidently to His Wisdom. In any case we must abstain from passing judgment in His place.

This does not necessarily lead to a comfortable quietism or to a fading away of Truth seen as something vague and interchangeable. The danger which all religions face from this pluralistic outlook on the ways of salvation is that of becoming something relative. I trust that my readers will have understood that in my way of seeing things such a danger exists only for one who is not a true believer. For the true believer continues to be the epicentre of the Absolute of the faith he professes and to which he gives witness. Within the precise limits of the question with which we are concerned we must in fact stress, in order to keep our perspectives as clear as possible, that the Qur'an, by a multiplicity of arguments and warnings, forcefully and insistently calls people to Islam as to the final message from God which confirms and completes all the Scriptures which preceded it. It makes it crystal clear that if anyone, while being naturally convinced in his heart of the veracity of the Qur'anic message, wants to practice another religion for opportunist or other reasons, this will not be accepted from him: "in the next world he shall be among the losers" (Qur'an 3:85).

In a word, there is only one truth: it is our powers of understanding that vary. And what complicates the matter still more is that such powers are given to us by another. For if in fact we are not entirely passive and exclusively receptive, if we are indeed responsible for what we do and if we must work to fulfil our own destiny, tragically seeking our way through the shoals, it is also true that finally it is God who pilots our boat and keeps it from shipwreck. Our situation as men is an ambiguous one. Is it surprising then that we follow divergent paths to salvation? Under these circumstances complete good faith and sincerity are the only absolute requisites and the imperatives which allow for no exception. And so we set sail, trusting in God's grace. The fact, then, of admitting a variety of roads leading to salvation does not imply that we abdicate our faith, nor that we give up holding as true what we believe to be exact. Quite the contrary, the need to adhere to our faith becomes more imperative as it becomes more lucid. Then our faith ceases to be simply membership of a sociological group and a form of subordination. It becomes a real communion and a binding commitment. And so we come back to the duty of the apostolate through witness, which is as much a question of self-respect as of respect for others. For nobody has the right to water down his own convictions or to lose all consistency through bending over backwards trying to understand others and thus, in fact, refusing to face up to his own reality.

Object and Purpose of Dialogue

Perhaps someone will formulate the following objection: once the difficulties mentioned have been overcome, and the conditions postulated have been realized, does a dialogue still make sense or have any object?

Of course it does! Basically it becomes a disinterested and unqualified collaboration in the service of God, that is to say in the service of Goodness and Truth. In such a straightforward, relaxed and serene atmosphere, everyone without exception can profitably engage in dialogue. For let us have no illusion on this point: if dialogue is not equally fruitful for all, it will either not take place at all or it will get nowhere. Any community which feels itself in danger will raise customs barriers and will take refuge in a sort of intellectual protectionism, which, though it has no more chance of success than its economic counterpart, will nevertheless become firmly established. This is because, when in grave peril, people do not consider what they stand to lose by isolating themselves. In such cases the primitive instinct of self-preservation takes over.

On the contrary, in an atmosphere of confidence ideas circulate more freely, and if they are capitalized on and invested in they pay dividends to all. So the primary objective we must fix ourselves in any dialogue is to remove barriers and to increase the amount of good in the world by a free exchange of ideas. On all the great problems which confront us and which sometimes challenge the very meaning of our existence, all human families, whether their outlook is materialistic or spiritual, have something to gain from comparing their own solutions and coordinating their solutions wherever this is possible. Across the heights that divide us it is not all that difficult to hold out our hands to one another, even when we draw our inspiration from divergent or even discordant sources. Growing cultural unification, which is perhaps the most striking phenomenon of our time, is daily drawing men closer to one another and placing them on the same level. Concerning the crucial problems of our time, believers and unbelievers, whatever their opinions, often hold useful discussions together which bring enrichment through the confrontation of different points of view.

It should therefore be still easier for all believers, united in a unanimous service of God, to discuss matters between them and to discover, when the right atmosphere has been created in the manner indicated, a common language. For example, there is absolutely no reason at all why we should not consider together what answers should be given to the questions asked in the conciliar document *Nostra Aetate*. It may be useful to recall to mind these questions:

What is man? What is the meaning and purpose of life? What is goodness and what is sin? What gives rise to our sorrows and to what intent? Where lies the path to true happiness? What is the truth about death, judgment and retribution beyond the grave? What finally is that ultimate and unutterable mystery which engulfs our being, and whence we take our rise, and whither our journey leads us?[20]

Each one of these questions could serve as the theme for one or more meetings. Why not organize these meetings and invite representatives from all religions, whether they have their Scriptures or not? In order to avoid any appearance of confrontation it is very useful indeed that such meetings include people with outlooks as diversified as possible. Already historians, philosophers and doctors from all over the world, meet in their regular congresses. Why should not the same thing happen with believers of all shades of opinion who could thus bring their various sources of light to bear on the problems which face us all? Such meetings would be extremely useful if only because they would accustom, not merely the odd intellectual, but the officials in charge of different churches to meeting one another. Thus they would get to know one another and learn to communicate. In the world of contestation in which we live for any religion to close in on itself would be like taking an overdose of morphia in order to die peacefully.

Naturally one must be careful not to tread on any banana skins, and one must be on the watch for wolf traps in the forest! For example, one should be very careful to avoid inserting in the program of such meetings the sort of questions put by Y. Moubarac to his correspondents. This is a form of interrogation, not dialogue. Besides the replies given to these questions prove beyond doubt that the whole area is mined and to wander about without taking due precautions is always likely to produce unfortunate explosions. The "dialogue" in writing organized by Moubarac has thus at least served the useful purpose of showing us how not to go about it.

So we must be very careful and prudent in choosing, with the agreement of both sides and unilaterally, subjects which are capable of giving rise to fruitful comunications from all sides. Thank God, there are sufficient such projects to provide matter for research and deliberation now and for a long time to come. Gradually the way will be prepared for greater progress and more ambitious plans. One must not be in too much of a hurry.

For example, one could study together in greater depth the legacy of spiritual values which belong to all religions that follow a Biblical tradition. On 31 March 1965 Cardinal Franz Koenig of Vienna spoke about monotheism to two thousand students and professors in the most representative Muslim university of theology, that of Al-Azhar in Cairo. There can be no doubt that his talk helped to foster better feelings and dissipate various misunderstandings. And in fact his conference met with a really enthusiastic reception which was very revealing.*21 Shaykh Hasan Ma'mun, in concluding his vote of thanks, could not refrain from quoting the following passage from the Qur'an: "And thou wilt surely find that the nearest of them in love to the believers are those who say 'We are Christians'; that because some of them are priests and monks, and they wax not proud" (Qur'an 5:82).

So there are real possibilities of communicating and exchanging ideas. The chief thing is to discover them and make the most of them. The elaboration of a theology of religions, which has still to be done, of a moral theology as well as a social theology directly concerned with the problems of today, can only gain from the collaboration of those who are convinced that man's destiny is a part of God's plan, in reply to those who would make man the ephemeral yardstick of everything in a world closed-in on itself and without anything to follow, someone produced not by a conscious creative act of God, but someone evolved by sheer necessity and pure chance. If then we purge dialogue of anything which might lead it astray into useless argument, we shall find that it is far from being an empty and useless exercise. It is more likely to become more profound and more meaningful. In our drifting world of today, which is seeking new social structures and a new scale of values, the vast domain of ethics would supply alone a safe and practically unlimited basis for dialogue. What has the Message of God to offer to all the dispossessed people of the world, to all those without distinction who are alienated, to those who either cringe, beg and supplicate or who revolt and fight back and blaspheme? Here lies the most urgent need for dialogue because, in all religions, on the answer to these questions will depend the presence of God in men's hearts. For:

> If heaven (leaves) us alone like a still-born world,
> The just man will oppose disdain to absence,
> And his only response will be a loveless silence
> In answer to the eternal silence of the divinity.

One can see from this that Vigny had already experienced this crisis, and well before his time one could mention the case of Ma'arri.

Does this mean that one must always remain on the heights? Is it indispensable to lay down as an absolute and strict law that one should never tackle some precise point of doctrine concerning one or other religion in particular? Of course not. But here vigilance will be all the more necessary, and one should not try to go ahead too quickly. In the case of Islam and Christianity the general lines of a compared theology have already been traced out, which should make it all the easier for both sides to travel more freely along this road. Certain questions should be relatively easy to discuss together, such as the general economy of salvation that we have already referred to in these pages. But would it not be possible to work out something on these lines by making use of the Qur'anic ideas of *hidaye* (guidance), *lutf* (protection-help), *tawfiq* (assistance-direction), *dalal* (the trial of going astray), etc.? And if Islam and Christianity were to study together these respectively similar values, would it not lead to a better understanding of them, and a deepening of our appreciation which would benefit all concerned? There are plenty of other examples one could mention. For instance there is the extremely difficult problem of how to reconcile human liberty with the existence of a transcendent and almighty God. Would not the Christian and Muslim solutions stand to gain by being confronted, and would it not be possible to go beyond them both in the light of recent advances in human science, from genetics to metaphysics through the various discoveries and theories of social psychology? An immense field of investigation in common is available to us, and with a little imagination one should be able to find several points of contact. The only real limits to such an investigation come not from the objective but the subjective point of view, namely whether or not those taking part are properly prepared for dialogue. This brings us back to the difficulties we have already mentioned.

At the same time we must not expect too much. However prepared both sides may be for dialogue there are certain subjects which, for a long time yet, will be difficult to discuss together. It is far better not to touch them at all so as not to get bogged down in discussions in which neither side listens to the other and where the only results are bitter polemics. The Qur'an does indeed speak with respect and veneration about Jesus, the son of the Virgin Mary, and the Word of God. The same veneration is found in works about Jesus by al-'Aqqad, Kamil Husayn, Khalid Muhammad Khalid, 'Abd al-Hamid Juda al-Sahhar, Fathi 'Uthman, and 'Abd al-Karim al Khatib.[22] However, in spite of all the good will that inspired these writings, a Christian would not recognize in them the Christ God of the mystery of the incarnation and of the redemption. In the same way it is difficult for a Muslim to find in the numerous lives of Muhammad written in the West, often with the best intentions, the Seal of the Prophets who brought to mankind the perfection of the Ultimate Message from God. And how is it possible to carry on a useful dialogue with a Christian or a Jew on the nature of the Qur'an? To the mystery of the incarnation of Christ and of the redemption corresponds, in Islam, the no less difficult mystery of the taking of a concrete form by the Word of God consubstantial with Being, and therefore eternal, which yet descended (*tanzil*) into this world of contingent phenomena. So perhaps it may not be by pure chance that in the Middle Ages there were such heated arguments among Christians, on the one hand, concerning the nature of Christ, and among Muslims on the other, concerning the nature of the Qur'an. The Mu'tazilites, who were particularly sensitive to the human aspect of the Qur'an and who consequently considered it to be something purely created—thus doing away with the mystery of its double nature—were in a way the Arians of Islam. It was the Sunnites who prevailed and their understanding of the mystery was accepted by the majority, just as the doctrine of the dual nature of Christ prevailed among Christians. This is what makes it so difficult to subject the Qur'an to a type of textual criticism based on historicism and methods which are applicable to texts unquestionably written by human beings. Islam and Christianity have not the same conception of revelation. So, for certain questions, it is better to accept the situation as it is, at least for the time being, rather than bang one's head against a brick wall. G. C. Anawati is quite right when he remarks: "the more one is firm about the classical points that divide us the better we know where we stand, and our discussion becomes surprisingly open and fruitful."*23

PURPOSE OF DIALOGUE

Now although the usefulness and scope of dialogue are limited, there is no limit to its purpose. This is to shake people up and to make them get a move on, and to prevent them from remaining bogged down by their own convictions. Naturally everyone has the right to refuse to adopt any given point of view, but he has no excuse at all for not finding out first exactly what that point of view is and getting to know more about it. Before pontificating on someone, even if there are points on which it would serve no useful purpose to dialogue with him, one should at least listen to what he has to say. For Muslims in particular let me say that sometimes ideas which are considered very dangerous can turn out to be very salutary, if only as a scouring agent. Naturally this only takes place when they act as a type of revulsive on a well-formed and attentive conscience. Otherwise, the sole result could be to hasten the collapse and complete disintegration of worm-eaten structures. Such a danger is so real, in the present state of Islam, that attention has to be called to it.

However neither Islam nor any other belief in God has any choice today other than to accept the challenge. Science is advancing daily, and more deeply, into areas of the universe which were formerly shrouded in mystery, and asking questions which no philosophy and theology dare ignore if they wish to respect the fundamental nature of man. Science obliges us all to think more, and it constrains believers to re-read their Revelation in the light of new problems. Is it necessary to stress that our answer cannot be some simple but vague form of concordism, such as has often been proposed by Muslims since the *nahda*? Hence the need to explore every avenue and to tune into every transmission.

A new exegesis, which does not have to turn its back on past wealth and positive advances, will have to be worked out in a climate of adventure, of exchange of ideas, and of urgency to keep up to date and to settle all the doubts of our day. By creating such a fertile climate of tension, which has so dramatically been lacking in Islam for centuries, dialogue could play the role of shaking Muslims out of their false sense of security and could make their hearts and ears once more attentive to the Message of God. For if the Word of God is eternal, as every Muslim believes, it follows necessarily that, though revealed in time and space, it transcends all temporal and spatial characteristics, and remains always and everywhere perceptible, present, and forever new. It must therefore be perceived and accepted, not in a static manner, but rather as a set of properties and potentialities which are to be brought into actual existence by means of ceaseless research. This is not necessarily a revolutionary request. Many exegetes in the past have felt the need for just this sort of thing, because they had rightly become fascinated by the depths of meaning in the Qur'anic word whose exuberant vitality sweeps aside all linguistic barriers. Hence the necessity of listening to God with our present-day understanding, listening to Him in the here-and-now of the present moment. The re-launching of a modern type of exegesis, inspired by both daring and prudence, and well aware of the anguish, restlessness and questioning of our day, is therefore imperative if God is not to be banished from the world, but is to become present again in human activity. But it can develop only in a climate of dialogue open to all, both believers and non-believers.

Such an exegesis has a bounden duty to incorporate everything it can absorb, without any sort of fear or complex. Certainly there is a real danger of crises arising, of deviations taking place and of people losing their way, and such dangers should not be minimized. But is it not the natural vocation of a religion to be in a perpetual state of crisis, always striving to develop fully? In his efforts to understand correctly the Message of God the believer cannot afford to ignore the advances, even of a provisional nature, made by modern scholars in every branch of the exact sciences and human disciplines. Besides, the problem today does not concern orthodoxy or heterodoxy. Has there ever been such a thing as Truth pure, limpid and impervious? Is such Truth within man's grasp? Is not Truth like the distant star that guides the traveller on his way, rather than a burning torch that is carried with confidence? The Qur'an tells us: "Hold you fast to God's bond together, and do not scatter" (Qur'an 3:103). Is not this bond both mooring rope and Ariadne's thread? Tradition adds: whoever makes a sincere effort to reflect and reach his destination is doubly rewarded; whoever makes a sincere effort to reflect but fails to reach his destination will nevertheless be rewarded once. In fact only the fearful, who refuse the rope which draws them nearer to God and prefer to wallow in stagnation, will be refused a reward. The reward will be reserved for those who make an effort, examine their consciences, and practice their faith in all sincerity and with fervor. Now the precise purpose of dialogue, whatever the circumstances, is to reanimate constantly our faith, to save it from tepidity, and to maintain us in a permanent state of *itijihad*, that is a state of reflection and research.

Conclusion: The Horizon before Us

Where will such research, carried on in an open-minded spirit and not in isolation, lead us? Nobody can say precisely. It is an adventure which we must engage in day by day. Will religious unity be found at the end of the maze? "In the long term, of course," writes W. Montgomery Watt, "it is to be expected that there will be one religion for the whole world, though it may contain within itself permitted variations, comparable to the four permitted legal rites (*madhahib*) in Sunni Islam."*24 This perspective is not necessarily at variance with Islam. To the verses we have already quoted let us add one:

> The Messenger believes in what has been sent down to him from his Lord. He and the believers (in Islam), all of them believe in God and His angels and in His Books and His Messengers; we make no division between any one of His Messengers. They say "We have heard and we obey. Our Lord, grant us Thy forgiveness; unto thee is the home-coming" (Qur'an 2:285).

As far as classical Muslim theology is concerned, it has always proclaimed that the Light of God will finally disperse all darkness and will shine equally for all. "They desire to extinguish with their mouths the Light of God; but God will perfect His light, though the unbelievers be adverse" (Qur'an 61:8).

Meanwhile divergences continue and show little sign of fading away, at least in the foreseeable future. One must believe that they have their role to play in the economy of salvation and of the world, among other things by giving an impetus to evolution. Let me give some further quotations from the Qur'an:

> To every one of you We have appointed a right way and an open road. If God had willed, He would have made you one Community; but that He might try you in what has come to you. So be you forward in good works; unto God shall you return all together; and He will tell you of that whereon you were at variance (Qur'an 5:48).

> Mankind were only one community, then they fell into variance. But for a word that proceeded from thy Lord, it had been decided between them already touching their differences. They say: "If only a sign (casting light on this mystery) had been sent down on him from his

Lord." Say: "The mystery (*ghayb*) of God is inscrutable. Then watch and wait; I shall be with you watching and waiting" (Qur'an 10:18–19).

Say: "O my God, Creator of the Heavens and the Earth, who knowest all things visible and invisible, Thou wilt judge in the end between Thy servants touching that whereon they are at variance" (Qur'an 39:46).

Thus when all is said and done, we find ourselves faced with the unfathomable mystery of God's Plan and of man's condition. So we must accept our differences and disagreements, and by competing with one another in good works, shorten the time in which the trial of our disagreements will come to an end. We must also forego expecting too much from dialogue if we are to avoid bitterness and discouragement and be able to make progress, come wind or wild weather. For we must not have any illusions on this point: whatever the precautions we take there will be many discordant voices. Nobody has ever found in the past a magic wand which could eliminate misunderstandings and radically change the world. We should not expect one to turn up in the future. Dialogue means unending patience. If it helps us to draw gradually nearer to one another, to replace indifference or hostile reserve by real friendship, by true brotherhood even, in spite of our different beliefs and opinions, it will have already accomplished much. Dialogue does not necessarily mean finding a common solution; still less does it imply an absolute need to come to an agreement. Its role is rather to clarify and open up the debate still more, allowing all those engaged to progress, instead of becoming immutably fixed in their own convictions. The way towards the Kingdom of Light will prove to be a long one, and God has chosen to enshroud it in mystery.

There is no need to stress, of course, that these ideas come not from a professional theologian but from an historian who, by specializing in Medieval History, has come to realize how equally sincere love of God and of Truth was able to degenerate till it led to catastrophe. Besides, living as we do today in a century of re-examination, of contestation, in which the bounds of the Universe are continually expanding, we can no longer practice *qu'ud* or *kitman*, that is to say we cannot afford to give ourselves up to an easygoing, lukewarm indifference while we wait for some miracle or other which would re-instate Islam in History by enchantment, without effort or suffering on our part.

Work, and God will surely see you work, and His Messenger, and the believers (Qur'an 9:105).

7

"The People of the Book and the Diversity of 'Religions' ""[1]

FAZLUR RAHMAN

INTRODUCTION

Fazlur Rahman (1921–88) was professor of Islamic thought at the University of Chicago and the author of many books on the intellectual history of Islam. He was concerned, among many other things, to reinterpret Islam in such a way as to preserve its essence as he saw it, and at the same time to criticize its aberrations. In this essay he attempts to disentangle the Qur'anic attitude to religious pluralism; to show how Islamic attitudes to Christians and Jews have changed through Islamic history; and to recommend an attitude of openness on the part of Muslims toward Christians, provided always that Christians abandon their exclusivistic emphasis on the doctrine of the incarnation. He protests also against traditional Islamic exclusivism, branding it as non-Qur'anic. Especially important here is Rahman's stress on the idea of different religious communities being created by God and given the gifts they have so that they may compete in goodness rather than compete for members through evangelization. Being a good Muslim, in this view, need not entail wishing to make all non-Muslims into Muslims.

"THE PEOPLE OF THE BOOK AND THE DIVERSITY OF 'RELIGIONS' "

Islam's attitude to Christianity is as old as Islam itself, since Islam partly took shape by adopting certain important ideas from Judaism and Christianity and criticizing others. Indeed, Islam's self-definition is partly the result of its attitude to these two religions and their communities.

That there was messianism among certain Meccan Arab circles at the

102

time Muhammad appeared has been amply documented. Instead of accepting either Judaism or Christianity, these Arab circles were looking for a new revealed religion of their own, so that "they might be even better guided" than the two older communities. After the advent of Muhammad as God's Messenger, the Qur'an repeatedly refers to a group of people about whom it says, "We had already given them the Book [i.e., the Torah and the Gospel] and they also believe in the Qur'an." These verses clearly show that some Jews or Christians or Judeo-Christians had also entertained messianic hopes and encouraged Muhammad in his mission. The Qur'an, indeed, taunts the Meccan pagans, saying that whether or not they believed in the Qur'an (or the Prophet), "those to whom We had already given the Book, believe in it [or him]."

There are several important and interesting issues connected with this phenomenon. For example: was Islam entirely the result of Jewish or Christian "influences," or was it basically an independent native growth that picked up some important ideas from the Judeo-Christian tradition? A number of Jewish and Christian scholars have vied with each other to show that Islam was genetically related to one or other religion. Recently several Western scholars, among them Montgomery Watt, Maurice Gaudefroy-Demombynes, and, above all, H. A. R. Gibb, have argued convincingly that in its nativity Islam grew out of an Arab background, although in its formation and development there have been many important influxes from the Judeo-Christian tradition.[*2] But the issue with which we are directly concerned here is not the "originality" of Islam but Muhammad's perception of himself and his mission, which is intimately connected with his perception of his relationship to other prophets, their religion(s), and their communities.

It is quite obvious from the Qur'an that from the beginning to the end of his prophetic career Muhammad was absolutely convinced of the divine character of the earlier revealed documents and of the divine messengership of the bearers of these documents. This is why he recognized without a moment of hesitation that Abraham, Moses, Jesus, and other Old and New Testament religious personalities had been genuine prophets like himself. This acceptance was undoubtedly strengthened when some followers of these earlier religions recognized Muhammad as a true prophet and the Qur'an as a revealed book. Hence the falsity of the view popular among Western Islamists (originally enunciated by the patriarchs of Western Islamic studies like Snouck Hurgronje and Nöldeke-Schwally[3]) that in Mecca the Prophet Muhammad was fully convinced that *he was giving to the Arabs what Moses and Jesus had previously given to their respective communities*, and that it was at Madina, where the Jews refused to recognize him as God's Messenger, that he instituted the Muslim community as separate from Jews and Christians.

There is no mention of any fixed religious communities in the earlier parts of the Qur'an. True, different prophets have come to different peoples and nations at different times, but their messages are universal and identical. All these messages emanate from a single source: "the Mother of the Book" (43:4; 13:39) and "the Hidden Book" (56:78). Since these messages are universal and identical, it is incumbent on all people to believe in all divine messages. This is why Muhammad felt himself obligated to believe in the prophethood of Noah, Abraham, Moses, and Jesus, for God's religion is indivisible and prophethood is also indivisible. Indeed, the Prophet is made to declare in the Qur'an that not only does he believe in the Torah and the Gospel but "I believe in whatever Book God may have revealed (42:15). This is because God's guidance is universal and not restricted to any nation or nations: "And there is no nation wherein a warner has not come" (35:24) and "For every people a guide has been provided" (13:7). The word "Book" is, in fact, often used in the Qur'an not with reference to any specific revealed book but as a generic term denoting the totality of divine revelations (see 2:213, for example).

If Muhammad and his followers believe in all prophets, all people must also and equally believe in him. Disbelief in him would be equivalent to disbelief in all, for this would arbitrarily upset the line of prophetic succession. In the late Meccan period, however, the Prophet became more aware that Jews and Christians would not believe in him, nor would they recognize each other. Recent scholarship has shown that this awareness came to Muhammad in Mecca and not in Madina, as is often believed. At this point, Jews and Christians are called *al-ahzab* (sectarians, partisans, people who are divisive of the unity of religion and disruptive of the line of prophetic succession), each *hizb* (also *shi'a*) or party rejoicing in what it has to the exclusion of the rest. Muslims are warned not to split up into parties. It is at this point that the religion of Muhammad is described as "straight" and "upright," the religion of the *hanif* (i.e., of an upright monotheist who does not follow divisive forces) and is linked and identified with the religion of Abraham.

The awareness of the diversity of religions, despite the unity of their origin, sets Muhammad a theological problem of the first order. It so persistently and painfully pressed itself on his mind that from the beginning of his awareness until well into the last phase of his life, the Qur'an treats this question at various levels. The fact that religions are split not only from each other but even within themselves is recurrently deplored. But a somewhat different point of view on the problem also emerges in the Qur'an. Humankind had been a unity, but this unity was split up because of the advent of divine messages at the hands of the prophets. The fact that the prophets' messages act as watersheds and divisive forces is rooted in some divine mystery, for if God so willed, He could surely bring them to one path:

Mankind were one single community. Then God raised up prophets who gave good tidings and warnings and God also sent down with them The Book in truth, that it may decide among people in regard to what they differed. But people did not differ in it (i.e., with regard to the Truth) except those to whom it had been given (and that only) after clear signs had come to them; (and this they did) out of (sheer) rebelliousness among themselves (2:213).

If your Lord so willed, He would have made mankind one community, but they continue to remain divided (11:118).

Men were but one community; then they began to differ. But for a decree of your Lord that had already preceded, a decision would have been made with regard to that wherein they differ (10:19).

In Madina, the terms "sectarians" and "partisans" are dropped, and Jews and Christians are recognized as "communities," although, of course, they continue to be invited to Islam. As we noted earlier, the Qur'an, in the early stages at Mecca, does not speak at all in terms of communities and certainly not in terms of exclusivist communities. It was the awareness and subsequent recognition of the existence of the mutually exclusive Jewish and Christian communities (and probably equally exclusivist subgroups in Christianity) that led the Qur'an first to call them "sectarians" and "partisans" and subsequently to recognize them (in Madina) as communities. It was the solidification of these communities that led to the announcement of Muslims as a separate community:

The Jews say, The Christians have nothing to stand on, and the Christians say, The Jews have nothing to stand on, —while both recite the same Book (2:113).

They say, No one shall enter the paradise except those who are Jews or Christians—these are their wishful thoughts (2:111).

Jews and Christians will never be pleased with you (O Muhammad!) unless you follow their religion(s); say (to them): the guidance of God (not of Jews or Christians) is the guidance (2:120).

The Qur'an's reply to these exclusivist claims and claims of proprietorship over God's guidance, then, is absolutely unequivocal: Guidance is not the function of communities but of God and good people, and *no* community may lay claims to be uniquely guided and elected. The whole tenor of the Qur'anic argument is against election:

When God tested Abraham by some words and he (Abraham) fulfilled them, God said (to Abraham), I am going to make you a leader of men. What about my progeny? asked Abraham; He (God) replied, My promise does not extend to the unjust ones (2:124).

The whole mystique of election is undermined by the repeated statements of the Qur'an after mentioning Biblical prophets and their people:

That is a community that is by-gone: to them belongs what they earned and to you (O Muslims!) will belong what you will earn, and you will not be asked for what they had done (2:134, 141).

In conformity with this strong rejection of exclusivism and election, the Qur'an repeatedly recognizes the existence of good people in other communities — Jews, Christians and Sabaeans[4] — just as it recognizes the people of faith in Islam:

Those who believe (Muslims), the Jews, the Christians, and the Sabaeans — whosoever believe in God and the Last Day and do good deeds, they shall have their reward from their Lord, shall have nothing to fear, nor shall they come to grief (2:62; cf. 5:69).

In both these verses, the vast majority of Muslim commentators exercise themselves fruitlessly to avoid having to admit the obvious meaning: that those — from any section of humankind — who believe in God and the Last Day and do good deeds are saved. They either say that by Jews, Christians, and Sabaeans here are meant those who have actually become "Muslims" — which interpretation is clearly belied by the fact that "Muslims" constitute only the first of the four groups of "those who believe" or that they were those good Jews, Christians, and Sabaeans who lived before the advent of the Prophet Muhammad — which is an even worse *tour de force*. Even when replying to Jewish and Christian claims that the hereafter was theirs and theirs alone, the Qur'an says, "On the contrary, whosoever surrenders himself to God while he does good deeds as well, he shall find his reward with his Lord, shall have no fear, nor shall he come to grief" (2:112).

The logic of this recognition of universal goodness, with belief in one God and the Last Day as its necessary underpinning, demands, of course, that the Muslim community be recognized as a community among communities. Here, the Qur'an appears to give its final answer to the problem of a multi-community world:

And We have sent down to you the Book in truth, confirming the Book that existed already before it and protecting it. . . For each one of you (several communities) We have appointed a Law and a Way of Conduct (while the essence of religion is identical). If God had so willed, He would have made all of you one community, but (He has not done so) that He may test you in what He has given you; so compete in goodness. To God shall you all return and He will tell you (the Truth) about what you have been disputing (5:48).

The positive value of different religions and communities, then, is that they may compete with each other in goodness (cf. 2:148; 2:177; where, after announcing the change in the *quibla* from Jerusalem to Mecca, it is emphasized that the *quibla* per se is of no importance, the real worth being in virtue and *competing in goodness*).[5] The Muslim community itself, lauded as the "median Community" (2:144) and "the best community produced for mankind" (3:110), is given no assurance whatever that it will be automatically God's darling unless, when it gets power on the earth, it establishes prayers, provides welfare for the poor, commands good, and prohibits evil (22:41, etc.). In 47:38, the Muslims are warned that "If you turn your backs [upon this teaching], God will substitute another people for you who will not be like you" (cf. 9:38).

According to the Qur'an, the most fundamental distinction between God and creatures is that God is infinite – All-Life, All-Power, All-Knowledge, etc. – whereas all creatures are finite. God, the Infinite, has created everything "according to a measure" (e.g., 54:49). He alone is the "Measurer [*qadir*]," while everything else is "measured [*maqdur*]." This idea is ubiquitous in the Qur'an. This is not a doctrine of "pre-determinism," as many Muslim theologians of the medieval ages understood it to be. "Measuring" in this context simply means "finitude" of potentialities, despite their range. Human beings, for example, are acknowledged by the Qur'an to be possessed of great potentialities: Adam outstripped the angels in a competition of creative knowledge and angels were thus ordered to honor him (2:30ff.); yet human beings cannot be God.

It is because of the infinitude of God that both absolute mercy and absolute power are attributable to God alone. God's mercy is literally limitless (40:7; 7:156) – indeed mercy is a law written into God's nature (6:12). And the very fact that there exists the plenitude of being rather than the emptiness of nonbeing is an expression of the primal act of God's mercy. God's power is commensurate with God's mercy. You may not point to any human being, with delimitations and a date of birth, and say simply, "That person is God." To the Qur'an, this is neither possible, nor intelligible, nor pardonable.

The severity of the Qur'an's judgments on incarnation and trinity has varied. There are verses that regard the Christian doctrine simply as "extremism in faith":

O People of the Book! do not go to extremes in your faith and do not say about God except truth. The Messiah, Jesus, son of Mary, was but a Messenger of God and his Word that He cast into Mary and a Spirit from Him. So believe in God and in His Messengers and say not, (God) is there, desist from this, it is better for you. God is but one and only God—far above He be from having a son; to Him belong whatever is in the heaven and in the earth ... the Messiah (Jesus) will not be too proud to be God's servant, nor will those angels who are very near God (disdain to be His servants). And whosoever should disdain to do service to Him and be too proud (for this), God will gather all of them to Himself (on the Last Day) (4:171–72; cf. 5:77).

But there are much stronger verses reminiscent of the Qur'anic statements against idolators:

Those are infidels who say: God is the Messiah, son of Mary. Say: who will be of any help against God, if he should want to destroy the Messiah, son of Mary, his mother and all those who live on the earth? To God belongs the kingdom of heaven and earth and whatever is between them; He creates whatever He wills, and God is powerful over everything (5:17).

Again:

Committed to infidelity are those who say: God is the same as the Messiah, son of Mary. .... Committed to infidelity are those who say: God is one among three—while there is no God but the Unique one; if they do not desist from what they say, a painful punishment will touch those of them as commit infidelity. Why do they not repent to God and seek His pardon, for God is forgiving and merciful? The Messiah, son of Mary, was but a Messenger—before him had gone many other messengers; his mother was the truthful one; they both used to eat food (like other men). Just see how We make the signs clear to them and also see how they are being deceived! (5:72–75).

The Qur'an speaks in the same vein about and to Muhammad:

Muhammad is but a Messenger—before him have gone many other messengers. Should he then die or be slain (in battle) will you turn back upon your heels (O Muslims!)? (3:144).

Say (to the pagan Arabs), Tell me, if God were to destroy me and all those who are with me, or should have mercy upon us, who will provide refuge? (67:28).

Muhammad cannot take it for granted that God will automatically continue to send him revelatory messages:

Do they say that he (Muhammad) concocts lies and attributes them to God? But if God so will, He may seal up your heart (O Muhammad!

so that no revealed messages will issue forth from it) — indeed, God (not Muhammad) obliterates the falsehood and confirms what is true, through His Words (42:24).

For the Qur'an, then, Jesus can be as little an incarnation of God as Muhammad himself or, indeed, any other prophet. But it is true that the Qur'an speaks with tenderness of Jesus and also his followers (see 5:82: "You shall find the nearest of all people in friendship to the Believers (Muslims) those who say they are Christians. This is because among them there are priests and monks and they are not a proud people"; also 57:27: "Then we followed up (these Messengers) with Jesus, son of Mary, to whom We gave the Evangel, and We put in the heart of his followers kindness and mercy").

This attitude toward Christianity has no parallel toward other communities mentioned in the Qur'an. Because the Qur'an is sometimes very mild, indeed highly tender, toward Christians (although at times highly critical of them) some Western scholars have thought that Muhammad was a fellow-traveler and perhaps almost a Christian. It has been argued that political motivations prevented him from a full and explicit identification with Christianity. Some have also seen his increasing hostility toward Byzantium as the cause of the increasingly severe criticism of Christianity in the Qur'an. Some also think that he did not correctly understand the nature of the doctrine of Jesus in Christianity because it was misrepresented to him by Christians. But it is difficult to see how the doctrine of incarnation, for example, could be misunderstood. The trouble with the first view is that it is impossible to prove that the severely critical passages of the Qur'an are necessarily later than other passages. For example, 57:27 seems to be quite late Madinan. The truth, then, appears to be that Muhammad must have encountered various views at the hands of various representatives of Christianity and that the Qur'an appears to address different groups at different points.

In any case, the unacceptability of Jesus' divinity and the Trinity to the Qur'an is incontrovertible, as is the fact that Jesus and his followers are regarded as exceptionally charitable and self-sacrificing. The Qur'an would most probably have no objections to the Logos having become flesh if the Logos were not simply identified with God and the identification were understood less literally. For the Qur'an, the Word of God is never identified simply with God. Jesus, again, is the "Spirit of God" in a special sense for the Qur'an, although God had breathed His spirit into Adam as well (15:29; 38:72). It was on the basis of some such expectations from the self-proclaimed monotheism of Christians—and, of course, Jews—that the Qur'an issued its invitation: "O People of the Book! Let us come together upon a formula which is common between us—that we shall not serve anyone but God, and that we shall associate none with Him" (3:64). This invitation, probably issued at a time when Muhammad thought not all was yet lost among the three self-proclaimed monotheistic communities, must have appeared specious to Christians. It has remained unheeded. But I believe something can still be worked out by way of positive cooperation, provided the Muslims hearken more to the Qur'an than to the historic formulations of Islam and provided that recent pioneering efforts continue to yield a Christian doctrine more compatible with universal monotheism and egalitarianism.

8

Extracts from "Secular-Secularization-Secularism"[1]

SYED MUHAMMAD NAQUIB AL-ATTAS

INTRODUCTION

Syed Muhammad Naquib al-Attas was born in Indonesia in 1931 and educated largely in England. He teaches at the National University of Malaysia in Kuala Lumpur and has been a visiting professor at many universities in Europe, the Middle East, and the United States. He has published extensively on Islamic history, Islamic education, and the nature of the Islamic state.

The essay reprinted here is part of a chapter from a book on the future of Islam. In this chapter al-Attas gives a historical and theoretical analysis of the development of secularization in the Christian West. His interlocutors — to whom he refers as "they" throughout the first part of this piece — are Christian theologians who claim that the historical developments traced by al-Attas are a good thing, part of Christianity's internal dynamic, and that the current state of Western Christianity is to be judged positively. Al-Attas's view is different: as he sees it, "There were, and still are, from the Muslim point of view, two Christianities: the original and true one and the Western version of it." The original and true Christianity was, like Islam, a religion of revelation in which a single unified message was offered by Jesus to the Jews. This message embraced every aspect of human life, including the political, the social, and the intellectual. But the historical development of Christianity in the West broke this all-embracing unity, issuing eventually in what al-Attas sees as Christianity's irredeemable dualism in religion, politics, and sexuality. Christianity can therefore no longer act as a mediator of God's will to the human race: its corruption has gone too far. It has become either trivial or actively opposed to God.

Secularization as al-Attas sees it is a process by which more and more dimensions of human life are separated from God's will and law. The inevitable *result is that those aspects of human life so separated become demonic. Sexuality becomes promiscuity, politics becomes oppression, and intellectual activity becomes useless theorizing whose products cannot serve God. All these failures characterize Christianity. Islam, because it is not subject to them, holds the key to the religious future of the human race: "Islam totally rejects any application to itself of the concepts secular, or secularization, or secularism as they do not belong and are alien to it in every respect; and they belong and are natural only to the intellectual history of Western-Christian religious experience and consciousness."*

"SECULAR-SECULARIZATION-SECULARISM"

The term *secular*, from the Latin *saeculum* conveys a meaning with a marked dual connotation of *time* and *location*; the time referring to the "now" or "present" sense of it, and the location to the "world" or "worldly" sense of it. Thus *saeculum* means "this age" or "the present time," and this age or the present time refers to events in this world, and it also then means "contemporary events." The emphasis of meaning is set on a particular time or period in the world viewed as a *historical process*. The concept *secular* refers to the *condition* of the world at this particular time or period or age. Already here we discern the germ of meaning that easily develops itself naturally and logically into the existential context of an ever-changing world in which there occurs the notion of relativity of human values. This spatio-temporal connotation conveyed in the concept secular is derived historically out of the experience and consciousness born of the fusion of the Graeco-Roman and Judaic traditions in Western Christianity. It is this "fusion" of the mutually conflicting elements of the Hellenic and Hebrew world views which have deliberately been incorporated into Christianity that modern Christian theologians and intellectuals recognize as problematic, in that the former views existence as basically *temporal* in such wise that the arising confusion of world views becomes the root of their epistemological and hence also theological problems. Since the world has only in modern times been more and more understood and recognized by them as historical, the emphasis on the temporal aspect of it has become more meaningful and has conveyed a special significance to them. For this reason they exert themselves in efforts emphasizing their conception of the Hebrew vision of existence, which they think is more congenial with the spirit of "the times," and denouncing the Hellenic as a grave and basic mistake.

Secularization is defined as the deliverance of man "first from religious and then from metaphysical control over his reason and his language."[*2] It is

> the loosing of the world from religious and quasi-religious understandings of itself, the dispelling of all closed world views, the breaking of all supernatural myths and sacred symbols ... the "defatalization of

history," the discovery by man that he has been left with the world on his hands, that he can no longer blame fortune or the furies for what he does with it. ... [it is] man turning his attention away from worlds beyond and towards this world and this time.*³

Secularization encompasses not only the political and social aspects of life, but also inevitably the cultural, for it denotes "the disappearance of religious determination of the symbols of cultural integration."*⁴ It implies "a historical process, almost certainly irreversible, in which society and culture are delivered from tutelage to religious control and closed metaphysical world views."*⁵ It is a "liberating development," and the end product of secularization is historical relativism.*⁶ Hence according to them history is a process of secularization.*⁷ The integral components in the dimensions of secularization are the disenchantment of nature, the desacralization of politics, and the deconsecration of values.*⁸ By the "disenchantment" of nature—a term and concept borrowed from the German sociologist Max Weber*⁹—they mean as he means, the freeing of nature from its religious overtones; and this involves the dispelling of animistic spirits and gods and magic from the natural world, separating it from God and distinguishing man from it, so that man may no longer regard nature as a divine entity, which thus allows him to act freely upon nature, to make use of it according to his needs and plans, and hence create historical change and "development." By the "desacralization" of politics they mean the abolition of sacral legitimation of political power and authority, which is the prerequisite of political change and hence also social change allowing for the emergence of the historical process. By the "deconsecration" of values they mean the rendering transient and relative of all cultural creations and every value system, which for them includes religion and world views having ultimate and final significance, so that in this way history, the future, is open to change, and man is free to create the change and immerse himself in the "evolutionary" process. This attitude towards values demands an awareness on the part of secular man of the relativity of his own views and beliefs; he must live with the realization that the rules and ethical codes of conduct which guide his own life will change with the times and generations. This attitude demands what they call "maturity," and hence secularization is also a process of "evolution" of the consciousness of man from the "infantile" to the "mature" states and is defined as "the removal of juvenile dependence from every level of society . . . the process of maturing and assuming responsibility . . . the removal of religious and metaphysical supports and putting man on his own."*¹⁰ They say that this change of values is also the recurrent phenomenon of "conversion" which "occurs at the intersection of the action of history on man and the action of man on history," which they call "responsibility, the acceptance of adult accountability."*¹¹ Now we must take due notice of the fact that they make a distinction between secularization and *secularism*, saying that whereas the former implies a continuing and open-ended process in which values and world views are continually revised in accordance with "evolutionary" change in history, the latter, like religion, projects a closed world view and an absolute set of values in line with an ultimate historical purpose having a final significance for man. Secularism, according to them, denotes an *ideology.*[*12] Whereas the ideology that is secularism, like the process that is secularization, also disenchants nature and desacralizes politics, it never quite deconsecrates values since it sets up its own system of values intending it to be regarded as absolute and final, unlike secularization which relativizes *all* values and produces the openness and freedom necessary for human action and for history. For this reason they regard secularism as a menace to secularization, and urge that it must be vigilantly watched and checked and prevented from becoming the ideology of the state. Secularization, they think, describes the inner workings of man's "evolution." The context in which secularization occurs is the urban civilization. The structure of common life, they believe, has "evolved" from the primitive to the tribal to the village to the town to the city by stages—from the simple social groupings to the complex mass society; and in the state of human life, or the stage of man's "evolution," this corresponds to the "development" of man from the "infantile" to the "mature" states. The urban civilization is the context in which the state of man's "maturing" is taking place; the context in which secularization takes place, patterning the form of the civilization as well as being patterned by it.

The definition of secularization [is that] which describes its true nature to our understanding and corresponds exactly with what is going on in the spiritual and intellectual and rational and physical and material life of Western man and his culture and civilization; and it is true only when applied to describe the nature and existential condition of Western culture and civilization. The claim that secularization has its roots in biblical faith and that it is the fruit of the Gospel has no substance in historical fact. Secularization has its roots not in biblical faith, but in the *interpretation* of biblical faith by Western man; it is not the fruit of the Gospel, but is the fruit of the long history of philosophical and metaphysical conflict in the religious and purely rationalistic *world view* of Western man. The interdependence of the interpretation and the world view operates in history and is seen as a "development"; indeed it has been so logically in history because for Western man the truth, or God Himself, has become incarnate in man in time and in history.

Of all the great religions of the world Christianity alone shifted its center of origin from Jerusalem to Rome, symbolizing the beginnings of the *westernization* of Christianity and its gradual and successive permeation by Western elements that in subsequent periods of its history produced and accelerated the momentum of secularization. There were, and still are, from the Muslim point of view, two Christianities: the original and true one and the Western version of it. Original and true Christianity conformed with

Islam. Those who before the advent of Islam believed in the original and true teachings of Jesus (on whom be Peace!)[13] were true believers (*mu'min* and *muslim*). After the advent of Islam they would, if they had known the fact of Islam and if their belief (*iman*) and submission (*islam*) were truly sincere, have joined the ranks of Islam. Those who from the very beginning had altered the original and departed from the true teachings of Jesus (Peace be upon him!) were the creative initiators of Western Christianity, the Christianity now known to us. Since their holy scripture, the Gospel, is derived partly from the original and true revelation of Jesus (upon whom be Peace!) the Holy Qur'an categorizes them as belonging to the People of the Book (*Ahl al-Kitab*). Among the People of the Book, and with reference to Western Christianity, those who inwardly did not profess real belief in the doctrines of the Trinity, the Incarnation and the Redemption and other details of dogma connected with these doctrines, who privately professed belief in God alone and in the Prophet Jesus (on whom be Peace!), who set up regular prayer to God and did good works in the way they were spiritually led to do, who while in this condition of faith were truly and sincerely *unaware* of Islam, were those referred to in the Holy Qur'an as nearest in love to the Believers in Islam.*[14] To this day Christians like these and other People of the Book like them are found among mankind; and it is to such as these that the term *mu'min* (believer) is also sometimes applied in the Holy Qur'an.

Because of the confusion caused by the permeation of Western elements, the religion from the outset and as it developed resolutely resisted and diluted the original and true teachings of Christianity. Neither the Hebrews nor the original Christians understood or knew or were even conscious of the presently claimed so-called "radicalism" of the religion as understood in the modern sense after its development and secularization as Western Christianity, and the modern interpretation based upon reading—or rather misreading—contemporary experience and consciousness into the spirit and thought of the past is nothing but conjecture. The evidence of history shows early Christianity as consistently opposed to secularization, and this opposition engendered by the demeaning of nature and the divesting of it of its spiritual and theological significance, continued throughout its history of the losing battle against the secularizing forces entrenched paradoxically within the very threshold of Western Christianity. The separation of Church and State, of religious and temporal powers was never the result of an attempt on the part of Christianity to bring about secularization; on the contrary, it was the result of the secular Western philosophical attitude set against what it considered as the anti-secular encroachment of the ambivalent Church based on the teachings of the eclectic religion. The separation represented for Christianity a status quo in the losing battle against secular forces; and even that status quo was gradually eroded away so that today very little ground is left for the religion to play any significant social and political role in the secular states of the Western world. Moreover the

Church when it wielded power was always vigilant in acting against scientific enquiry and purely rational investigation of truth, which seen in the light of present circumstances brought about by such "scientific" enquiry and "rational" investigation as it developed in Western history is, however, partly now seen to be justifiable. Contrary to secularization Christianity has always preached a "closed" metaphysical world view, and it did not really "deconsecrate" values including idols and icons; it assimilated them into its own mold. Furthermore, it involved itself consciously in sacral legitimation of political power and authority, which is anathema to the secularizing process. The westernization of Christianity, then, marked the beginning of its secularization. Secularization is the result of the misapplication of Greek philosophy to Western theology and metaphysics, which in the seventeenth century logically led to the scientific revolution enunciated by Descartes, who opened the doors to doubt and skepticism; and successively in the eighteenth and nineteenth centuries and in our own times, to atheism and agnosticism, to utilitarianism, dialectical materialism, evolutionism and historicism. Christianity has attempted to resist secularization but has failed, and the danger is that having failed to contain it the influential modernist theologians are now urging Christians to join it. Their fanciful claim that the historical process that made the world secular has its roots in biblical faith and is the fruit of the Gospel must be seen as an ingenious way of attempting to extricate Western Christianity from its own self-originated dilemmas. While it is no doubt ingenious it is also self-destructive, for this claim necessitates the accusation that for the past two millennia Christians including the apostles, saints, theologians, theorists and scholars had misunderstood and misinterpreted the Gospel, had made a grave fundamental mistake thereby, and had misled Christians in the course of their spiritual and intellectual history. And this is in fact what they who make the claim say. If what they say is accepted as valid, how then can they and Christians in general be *certain* that those early Christians and their followers throughout the centuries who misunderstood, misinterpreted, mistook and misled on such an important, crucial matter as the purportedly secular message of the Gospel and secularizing mission of the Church, did not also misunderstand, misinterpret, mistake and mislead on the paramount, vital matter of the religion and belief itself; on the doctrine of the Trinity; on the doctrine of the Incarnation; on the doctrine of the Redemption and on the *reporting* and *formulation* and *conceptualization* of the revelation? Since it ought to be a matter of absolute, vital importance for them to *believe* that the *report* of the very early Christians about the nature of the God Who revealed Himself to them was *true*, it would be futile for them to overcome this problem by resorting to belief in human "evolution" and historicity and the relativity of truths according to the experience and consciousness of each stage of human "evolution" and history, for we cannot accept an answer based merely on subjective experience and consciousness and "scientific" conjecture where no criteria for knowledge and certainty exist. What they say amounts to meaning that God sent His revelation or revealed Himself to man when man was in his "infantile" stage of "evolution." "Infantile" man then interpreted the revelation and conceptualized it in dogmatic and doctrinal forms expressing his faith in them. Then when man "matures" he finds the dogmatic and doctrinal conceptualizations of "infantile" man no longer adequate for him to express his faith in his time, and so he must develop them as he develops, otherwise they become inadequate. Thus they maintain that the dogmatic and doctrinal conceptualizations "evolve," but they "evolve" not because they are from the very beginning necessarily inadequate, but because as man "develops" they become inadequate if they fail to develop correspondingly. This in our view of course does not solve the problem of the reliability of the *reporting* of the revelation, the more so when it was the work of "infantile" man. Moreover this way of integrating religion with the evolutionary theory of development seems to lead logically to circular reasoning. Why should God send His revelation or reveal Himself to "infantile" man and not to "mature" man, especially since God, Who created man, must know the stage of growth at which he was at the moment of the revelation? Even a man would not send a vitally important message or reveal himself meaningfully to an infant. They may answer that God did not send His revelation or reveal Himself to "mature" man but to "infantile" man instead precisely in order to initiate the process of "maturing" in him so that when he "developed" to "maturity" he would be able to know its true meaning and purpose. But then, even in his allegedly "mature" stage in this modern, secular age, Western man is still inadequately informed about God and still groping for a meaning in God. It seems then that Western man who believes in this version of Christianity must either admit that man is *still* "infantile," or that the revelation or the conceptualization of its meaning and purpose is from the very beginning necessarily inadequate. As regards the revelation itself, it would be impossible for them to ascertain beyond doubt that it was reliably formulated and reported, for there exist other reports, apart from that of St. Barnabas, and both from the Ante-Nicene and Post-Nicene Fathers,[15] which contradicted the report on which the conceptualization which became the "official" version of Christianity now known to us is based.

Western man is always inclined to regard his culture and civilization as man's cultural vanguard; and his own experience and consciousness as those representative of the most "evolved" of the species, so that we are all in the process of lagging behind them, as it were, and will come to realize the same experience and consciousness in due course sometime. It is with this attitude that they, believing in their own absurd theories of human evolution, view human history and development and religion and religious experience and consciousness. We reject the validity of the truth of their assertion, with regard to secularization and their theories and interpretation of knowledge based on their experience and consciousness and belief, to speak on our behalf. The secularization that describes its true nature clearly when applied to describe Western man and his culture and civilization cannot be accepted as true if it is intended to be a description of what is going on in and to the world and man in which it is also meant to be applicable to the religion of Islam and the Muslims, and even perhaps to the other Eastern religions and their respective adherents. Islam totally rejects any application to itself of the concepts secular, or secularization, or secularism as they do not belong and are alien to it in every respect; and they belong and are natural only to the intellectual history of Western-Christian religious experience and consciousness. We do not, unlike Western Christianity, lean heavily for theological and metaphysical support on the theories of secular philosophers, metaphysicians, scientists, paleontologists, anthropologists, sociologists, psychoanalysts, mathematicians, linguists and other such scholars, most of whom, if not all, did not even practice the religious life, who knew not nor believed in religion without doubt and vacillation; who were skeptics, agnostics, atheists, and doubters all. In the case of religion we say that in order to know it man's self itself becomes the "empirical" subject of his own "empiricism," so that his study and scrutiny of himself is as a science based upon research, investigation and observation of the self by itself in the course of its faith and sincere subjugation to Revealed Law. Knowledge about religion and religious experience is therefore not merely obtained by purely rational speculation and reflection alone. Metaphysics as we understand it is a science of Being involving not only contemplation and intellectual reflection, but is based on knowledge gained through practical devotion to that Being Whom we contemplate and sincerely serve in true submission according to a clearly defined system of Revealed Law. Our objection that their authorities, on whose thoughts are based the formulation and interpretation of the facts of human life and existence, are not reliable and acceptable insofar as religion is concerned on the ground stated above is valid enough already. We single out religion because we cannot discuss the issue of secularization without first coming to grips, as it were, with religion by virtue of the fact that religion is the fundamental element in human life and existence against which secularization is working. Now in their case it seems that they have found it difficult to define religion, except in terms of historicity and faith vaguely expressed, and have accepted instead the definition of their secular authorities who when they speak of religion refer to it as part of culture, of tradition; as a system of beliefs and practices and attitudes and values and aspirations that are created out of history and the confrontation of man and nature, and that "evolve" in history and undergo a process of "development," just as man himself "evolves" and undergoes a process of "development." In this way secularization as they have defined it will of course be viewed by the theists among them as a critical problem for religion precisely because man believes that his belief cast in a particular form—which according to the atheists is an illusion—is real and permanent;

whereas in point of fact—at least according to the modern theists—it must change and "develop" as man and history "develop." Now the view that religion undergoes "development" in line with human "evolution" and historicity is indeed true in their case, just as secularization is true and seen as a historical development in their experience and consciousness.*[16] We say this because, from the point of view of Islam, although Western Christianity is *based on revelation*, it is not a *revealed religion* in the sense that Islam is. According to Islam the paramount vital doctrines of Western Christianity such as the Trinity, the Incarnation and the Redemption and other details of dogma connected with them are all cultural creations which are categorically denied by the Holy Qur'an as divinely inspired. Not only the Holy Qur'an, but sources arising within early Christianity itself, as we have just pointed out, denied their divinely inspired origin in such wise that these denials, historically valid as succinct evidence, present weighty grounds for doubting the reliability and authenticity of the reporting and subsequent interpretation and conceptualization of the revelation. The Holy Qur'an indeed confirms that God sent Jesus (Peace be upon him!) a revelation in the form known as *al-Injil* (the Evangel), but at the same time denies the authenticity of the revelation as transmitted by the followers of some of the disciples. In the Holy Qur'an Jesus (on whom be Peace!) was sent as a messenger to the children of Israel charged with the mission of correcting their deviation from their covenant with God and of confirming that covenant with a second covenant; of conveying Glad Tidings (Gospel) of the approaching advent of the Universal Religion (Islam) which would be established by the Great Teacher whose name he gave as Ahmad (Muhammad). The second covenant was meant to be valid until the advent of Islam when the Final and Complete Revelation would abrogate previous revelations and be established among mankind.*[17] So in the Holy Qur'an God did not charge Jesus (on whom be Peace!) with the mission of establishing *a new religion* called Christianity. It was some other disciple and the apostles including chiefly Paul who departed from the original revelation and true teachings based on it, and who began preaching a new religion and set about establishing the foundations for a new religion which later came to be called Christianity. At the beginning even the name "Christian" was not known to it, and it developed itself historically until its particular traits and characteristics and attributes took form and became fixed and clarified and refined and recognizable as the religion of a culture and civilization known to the world as Christianity. The fact that Christianity also had no revealed Law (*shari'ah*) expressed in the teachings, sayings and model actions (i.e., *sunnah*) of Jesus (on whom be Peace!) is itself a most significant indication that Christianity began as a new religion not intended as such by its presumed founder, nor authorized as such by the God Who sent him. Hence Christianity, by virtue of its being created by man gradually developed its system of rituals by assimilation from other cultures and traditions as well as originating its own fabrications; and through successive stages clarified its creeds such as those at Nicea, Constantinople and Chalcedon. Since it had no Revealed Law it had to assimilate Roman laws; and since it had no coherent world view projected by revelation, it had to borrow from Graeco-Roman thought and later to construct out of it an elaborate theology and metaphysics. Gradually it created its own specifically Christian cosmology, and its arts and sciences developed within the vision of a distinctly Christian universe and world view.

From its earliest history Western Christianity, as we have pointed out, came under the sway of Roman influences with the concomitant latinization of its intellectual and theological symbols and concepts which were infused with Aristotelian philosophy and world view and other Western elements that gradually "disenchanted" nature and deprived it of spiritual significance. This divesting and demeaning of nature to a mere "thing" of no sacred meaning was indeed the fundamental element that started the process of secularization in Western Christianity and the Western world. Christianity failed to contain and Christianize these elements, and unwittingly, then helplessly, allowed the secularizing elements engendered by alien forces within its very bosom to proceed relentlessly and inexorably along logical lines in philosophy, theology, metaphysics and science until its full critical impact was realized almost too late in modern times.

The Western concept of religion does not in our view come under the category of *revealed* religion in the strict sense as applicable to Islam. We cannot accept, to mention a scientific example, Nathan Söderblom's categorization of Christianity as a revealed religion according to his typology of religion.*[18] For us it is for the most part a sophisticated form of culture religion, distinguished only by the fact that it claims possession of a revealed Book which, though partly true, it nevertheless was not intended nor authorized by that Book to call upon mankind universally in the manner that a revealed religion was called upon to do from the very beginning without need of further "development" in the religion itself and its sacred laws. A revealed religion as we understand it is complete and perfect in its adequacy for *mankind* from the very beginning. The Holy Qur'an says that Islam is already made complete and perfect for mankind, and this claim to completion and perfection is substantiated from its very beginning by history. The name *Islam* was given to the religion from the very beginning just as the name *Muslim* was given to denote the adherents of the religion from the very start. The Revelation itself was completed during the lifetime of the Holy Prophet, who may God bless and give Peace!, who himself interpreted it in his life and whose Sacred Law he patterned in his teachings, his thoughts and sayings and model actions (*sunnah*). Even his Companions and contemporaries acted and behaved in a manner divinely inspired to become the standard and criterion for the future; and they questioned him urgently while he was yet among them on every conceivable and actual problem of daily life and right conduct and thought and action and guidance that summarized the needs of mankind and whose answers would suffice for man for all ages and generations to come. They all acted in a concerted and significantly knowing manner emphasizing their consciousness that this was the Final Revelation from God, the Ultimate Religion for mankind, the Last Prophet to appear among men. That age in history became the Criterion for the future, as the future truth and values that guide to it were all there, so that Islam and the time of the Holy Prophet (may God bless and give him Peace!) is always relevant, is always adequate, is always "modern" or new, is always ahead of time because it transcends history. In this way the essentials of what made the religion a truly revealed one were completed and perfected, and for this reason we say that Islam knew and recognized its realization from the moment of its actual existence. As such it transcends history and is not subject to the kind of self-searching "evolution" and "development" that Christianity experienced and will continue to experience. Though some of us use the terms "tradition" and "traditional" in the context of Islam yet these terms do not and are not meant to refer to the kind of tradition that originated in man's creative activity which evolves in history and consists of culture.*[19] They always refer to the Holy Prophet, who may God bless and give Peace!, and to the religious way and method of the Prophets of the Abrahamic "tradition"; and this tradition is originated by revelation and instruction from God, not created and passed on by man in history. So now we who follow that religious way and method are following that "tradition." Since Islam is the religion which transcends the influences of human "evolution" and historicity, the values embodied in it are absolute; and this means that Islam has its own absolute vision of God, of the Universe, of Reality, of Man; its own ontological, cosmological, psychological interpretation of reality; its own world view and vision of the Hereafter having a final significance for mankind. As such therefore it completely rejects the notion of "deconsecration" of values if that were to mean the relativization of all values continually recurring in history as they mean. Islam certainly deconsecrates *all* values in the sense of all *unislamic* values; in the sense of values that run counter to Islam and to the truth which is partially found in the other world religions and in the good traditions of man and his society (*al ma'ruf*). There cannot be for Islam a deconsecration of every value system including its own because in Islam all value systems that need deconsecration, all human and cultural creations including idols and icons, have *already* been deconsecrated by it so that there is need of no further "evolution" of values or of relativization of values since its values, which include the truth as partially found in other world religions and in the good in man and his society, are already the ultimate for mankind. The same is the case with the "desacralization" of politics, of political power and authority. In Islam, more so even than in Christianity, the desacralization of politics was not originally just an *idea* that came to be gradually realized in history; it was recognized from the very beginning and began with Islam itself. Islam indeed desacralizes politics, but not to the extent they mean, for Islam itself is based on Divine

Authority and on the sacred authority of the Holy Prophet (may God bless and give him Peace!), which is no less than the reflection of God's Authority, and on the authority of those who emulate his example. Thus every Muslim individually, and collectively as society and nation and as a Community (*ummah*) all deny to anyone, to any government and state, sacral legitimacy unless the person or the government or the state conforms with the practice of the Holy Prophet (may God bless and give him Peace!) and follows the injunctions of the Sacred Law revealed by God. Indeed, the Muslim in fact does not owe real allegiance and loyalty even to legitimate king and country and state; his real allegiance and fealty and loyalty is to God and to His Prophet to the exclusion of all else. And the same is true with regard to the "disenchantment" of nature, which is the most fundamental component in the dimensions of secularization. It is the disenchantment of nature that brought about the chaos of secularization which is ravaging the Western world and Christianity in contemporary life; and because the crisis caused is so ominously portentous for the future of man and his world—seeing that secularization is becoming a global crisis—I think it proper to show in a brief and generalized but fairly accurate sketch the salient features marking its origins and history of development in the Western world.*[20]

Before the rise of Christianity, in the Olympian age of Antiquity nature was not separated from the gods. But when degeneration and decadence of religion began to set in among the Greeks, the gods were gradually banished from nature, which then became devoid of spiritual significance. Originally the Greek cosmology, like those of the other peoples of Antiquity, was permeated with spiritual forces governing and maintaining and sustaining the universe. Their philosophers sought to discover the underlying principle—what they called the arche—the spiritual substance that forms the ground of all reality. As the gods were driven away from their respective domains in nature, Greek philosophy was transformed from the symbolic interpretation of nature to become more and more concerned with explaining nature in plain naturalistic and purely rational terms reducing its origin and reality to mere natural causes and forces. When Aristotle introduced Greek philosophy to the Roman world where Christianity was later to formulate and establish itself as the religion of the Roman Empire and of the West, this pure rationalism and concomitant naturalism, stripping nature of its spiritual meaning that the intellect alone could recognize and seek to fathom, were already prevalent factors in the interpretation of the Roman world view. No doubt other forms of philosophy that recognized the spiritual significance of nature, a contemplative intellectualism or metaphysics, still existed in both the Greek and Roman worlds, but Aristotelianism held sway over the rest, so that by the time Christianity appeared on the scene pure rationalism and naturalism had already dominated the life and mind of the Latin peoples. Christianity itself came under the influence of this naturalistic portrayal of nature devoid of symbolic significance, and reacted to this influence by demeaning the Kingdom of Nature and neglecting serious contemplation of it in favor of the Kingdom of God having no connection whatever with the world of nature. That is why the only connection that could happen between the two Kingdoms in Christianity would logically be the *supernatural* one. Elements of Greek cosmology which stressed the paramount role of the intelligence as the prime means by which man is able to interpret the spiritual significance of nature were then still prevalent, and this obviously led to a confrontation with Christian theology which had come under the sway of naturalistic rationalism. The outcome of this religio-philosophical confrontation was that Christian theology began to suppress the role of intelligence, and hence also the knowledge of spiritual truth, and at the same time urged unquestioning faith through the exercise not of human intelligence and reason but of sheer human will which made love the basis of faith. Thus knowledge and certainty, which are both aspects of the same truth and which constitute the very essence of the intellect, were relegated to a somewhat inferior status in comparison with a purely rational theology. We have distinguished the intelligence or the intellect from the rational mind or reason in this way in order to describe the case in Western intellectual history. In our view, however, the intelligence is both the intellect (*al-'aql*) as well as its projection in the human mind which creates and organizes its mental activity, that is, the *ratio* or reason which we also designate as *'aql*. The fact that we use the same term to designate both concepts demonstrates that we make neither dichotomy nor separation between the activities of the two aspects of the same cognitive principle in man. Thus it is therefore obvious that when we apply in English the same term *rational* to describe an aspect of Islam, we do not mean the same thing as when the same term is applied in the discussion of Western intellectual history and its influence on Christian theology and metaphysics and on the development of Christianity as in the above case. What is considered "rational" in Islam does not merely pertain to the mind's systematic and logical interpretation of the fact of experience; or its rendering intelligible and manageable to reason the data of experience; or its abstraction of facts and data and their relationships; or the grasping of nature by the mind, and the law-giving operation the mind renders upon nature. Since reason is a projection of the intellect, it functions in conformity with the intellect, which is a spiritual substance inherent in the spiritual organ of cognition known as the "heart" (*al-qalb*). Hence the understanding of spiritual realities is also within the province of reason and is not necessarily divorced from rational understanding of them. In the case of Christian theology and its latinized vocabulary, the two terms *intellectus* and *ratio* corresponding with sapiential and scientific knowledge respectively, have been understood not as being in conformity with each other, and each has been stressed over the other in different periods of its history; the *intellectus* in the case of Augustine, and the *ratio* in the case of Aquinas. Christian theology suppressed the sapiential role of the intellect and stressed the scientific role of the purely rational, which can only operate on nature devoid of spiritual significance and follow its own naturalistic logic to its final conclusion. Once the rational became more or less severed from the intellectual, the world of nature is seen as a material, physical object with no connection with the spiritual reality and truth underlying it. As such nature became rejected as it was of no use and even obstructive to the Christian endeavor to attain to the world of spirit. It was inevitable that Aristotelianism became absorbed into Christian theology and metaphysics, and this assimilation of Aristotelian philosophy into Christian theology was finally accomplished in the thirteenth century when Aquinas achieved what came to be known in the intellectual history of the West as the Thomistic Synthesis. Rational philosophy and theology, without the intellectual criterion, naturally led to doubt about the existence of objects as Ockham, deriving from the Thomistic metaphysics of being, was to demonstrate soon after.*[21] In the development of science in the West, the logical result of this rationalism and secularization of nature was highlighted by the Copernican revolution in physics in which the decentralization of the earth in the cosmos brought repercussions that reduced the importance of man himself therein. It finally led to man being deprived of cosmic significance; he became terrestrialized and his transcendence was denied him. Already in the Western Christian world view he was conceived as a fallen creature, and this terrestrialization indeed seemed to conform with the salvific purport assigned to the doctrine of Redemption. Perhaps more important in its secularizing effect to the development of science in the West, the Cartesian revolution in the seventeenth century effected a final dualism between matter and spirit in a way which left nature open to the scrutiny and service of secular science, and which set the stage for man being left only with the world on his hands. Western philosophy developed resolutely and logically alongside the secularizing science. Man began to be conceived more and more in terms emphasizing his humanity, individuality and freedom. Already he was rid of the gods of nature who all fled from his rational onslaughts which made nature natural for him to act upon, and now his self-assertion by means of a secularizing philosophy and science sought to wrench his freedom from the God of the Universe so that he might act freely upon the nature confronting him. While in the seventeenth and eighteenth centuries Christian philosophers still believed in the possibility of a science of metaphysics with which to interpret and prove the reality of spiritual truths such as God, the soul and its immortality, the world as a whole, the trend and methods of secular thought and logic had already penetrated, as we have briefly seen, into its metaphysical structure at least since the thirteenth century. In the fifteenth and sixteenth centuries, during the period known as the Renaissance, Western men seemed already to have lost interest in Christianity as a religion. They engaged eagerly in the pursuit of knowledge and the revival of ancient civilization which they were beginning to acquaint themselves with again after what was to them a period of decay, a period in which Christianity seemed included. They emphasized the importance of the newly discovered ancient sources and rejected medieval standards and methods. They were thrilled by the "discovery" of the world and of man, and lost interest in medieval theology and metaphysics as the interpreter of reality in favour of the "new" or modern scientific interpretation. In this interpretation they laid emphasis on man and his place in the universe. The very name *renaissance*, which means "to be born," surely reflects the intellectual atmosphere of the period in which Western man felt himself being born into a new world of new possibilities; a new realization of his powers and potential. From the seventeenth to the nineteenth centuries the European Enlightenment was related to, and indeed was a continuation of the Renaissance. This period was characterized by its zeal for the materialization and secularization of the ideal man in an ideal society. Naturalist philosophers wrote on natural law, natural religion, and stressed humanity, freedom, liberty, justice. Their ideas were turned to reality in America, and served as the basic philosophy of Independence. If *renaissance* means "to be born," then *enlightenment* refers to Western man's "coming of age" from the state of infancy in which his reason had to depend on the aid of others, but which is now realized as matured and fully fledged to lead on its own. Thus while Christian philosophers sought to erect a science of metaphysics, they were in fact — by virtue of the secular elements that had since many centuries penetrated into its metaphysical structure — only leading their metaphysics towards final dissolution, corroded, as it were, from within by those very elements it harbored. Christianity was ultimately blamed as having forfeited the confidence of Western man in revealed religion. After Kant in the eighteenth century, metaphysics was considered an unnecessary and deceptive guide to reality and truth which should be abandoned by rational, thinking men, as it was demonstrated by philosophy that spiritual realities and truths cannot be known and proved, and that none can be certain of their existence. It is the fruits of secularizing philosophy and science, which were altogether alien to the soil of true Christianity, which eventually led Western man to believe in human evolution and historicity. Now in our time that belief and secularization going hand in hand has almost supplanted Western Christianity in the heart and mind of Western man. The disenchantment of nature and terrestrialization of man has resulted, in the former case, in the reduction of nature to a mere object of utility having only a functional significance and value for scientific and technical management and for man; and in the latter case, in the reduction of man of his transcendent nature as emphasizing his humanity and physical being, his secular knowledge and power and freedom, which led to his deification, and so to his reliance upon his own rational efforts of enquiry into his origins and final destiny and his own knowledge thus acquired, which he now sets up as the criterion for judging the truth or falsehood of his own assertions.

9

"The Islamic View of Christianity"[1]

SEYYED HOSSEIN NASR

INTRODUCTION

Seyyed Hossein Nasr (1933-) was educated largely in the United States (MIT and Harvard) and is currently professor of Islamic Studies at George Washington University. He has published many works on the history of Islamic thought, notably Knowledge and the Sacred, *his 1981 Gifford Lectures.*

In the piece reprinted here Nasr presents Islam in part esoterically, as a religion "based on the absolute and not its manifestations," and in part exoterically, as a religion which has managed to find and to a considerable extent preserve the proper balance between the mystical and the practical, the other-worldly and the this-worldly. He is happy to find similarities between (esoteric) Christianity and (esoteric) Islam—hence his considerable emphasis upon the mystics and their teachings—but is less happy with what he sees as a Christian lack of concern with the things of this world. As he puts it:

> *Christianity is seen by Muslims as a religion devoid of an exoterism which then substitutes a message of an essentially esoteric nature as the exoteric, thereby creating disequilibrium in human society.*

The "disequilibrium" in question is most evident in Christian ethical theory and practice. The fact that Christianity, unlike both Judaism and Islam, has no divine law upon which to base its ethic, is seen as a weakness because it leads to a lack of realism about what human beings are capable of ethically and a concomitant lack of concern to regulate human appetites and desires in a way that takes them seriously as gifts of God. Nasr's comments on Christian attitudes to sexuality and to war are very revealing in this connection.

126

"THE ISLAMIC VIEW OF CHRISTIANITY"

The Traditional View of Christianity

In considering the vast subject of the Islamic view of Christianity it is important to bear in mind the presence of an Islamic doctrine concerning Christianity rooted in the Qur'an and *Hadith*,[2] the Muslims' continuous experience of living with Eastern Christians for fourteen hundred years, over a millennium of battle with a West which for most of that period was Christian and the diversity of the experience of various parts of the Islamic world during the European domination of the colonial period which in any case cannot be divorced in the Muslim mind from Christianity. It is also essential to bear in mind the hierarchic structure of the Islamic revelation in the sense that it possesses levels of meaning ranging from the most exoteric to the most esoteric and the grades of those who attach themselves to the religion to which the Qur'an itself refers as those who follow the injunction of the religion *al-islam*, those who possess faith in its more inward sense, *al-iman*, and those who possess spiritual virtue, *al-ihsan*. The attitude of Muslims belonging to these various categories vis-à-vis other religions and especially Christianity has never been the same. Muslim saints and even philosophers have had Christian disciples or teachers while a certain religious authority living in the same city at the same time may have been writing polemics against Christians. Likewise, Muslims living in a particular area without much contact with Christianity have held a different attitude toward Christians than those who fought against the Crusaders, or were expelled from Spain or were put under various kinds of pressures by Christian missionaries. Nevertheless, despite these geographical and historical variations, there remains the Islamic view of Christianity rooted in certain chapters of the Qur'an mostly dealing with Christ and the Virgin Mary and remaining as a permanent background for Muslim reflections upon the religion which from the beginning was considered to be the closest to Islam not only in time in the historic unfolding of the Abrahamic religions but also in structure and beliefs. In contrast to Christianity, which obviously does not possess a specifically Christian doctrine of Islam rooted in its Sacred Scripture, Islam possesses its own revealed knowledge of Christianity, a knowledge which has been interpreted over the ages on many levels from the juridical and theological to the gnostic and mystical, but which nevertheless has remained over the centuries as the central determining factor in the way Muslims have viewed Christianity. Even today one cannot gain an in-depth understanding of the Islamic view of Christianity without knowledge of what the Islamic tradition, based upon the Qur'anic revelation, has taught the Muslims about the religion of Christ.

The traditional Islamic view of Christianity is founded first of all upon accepting *Christianity as a religion revealed by God*, of Christ as being sent by Him and even possessing miraculous characteristics including his virgin birth,*³ and of the gospels as being a revealed book. Hence, Christianity became juridically and theologically accepted as a *"religion of the book"* and the Christians as *"the people of the book"* (*ahl al-kitab*), with all that such a status implied for them according to the Divine Law (*al-Shari'ah*)*⁴ of Islam, including the recognition and protection of their religion wherever and whenever they would be under Muslim rule. The Islamic view of Christianity possesses of course its own doctrine of *Christ*, his mission, his being taken to Heaven in body without suffering death upon the cross and his eschatological role in bringing the present cycle of human history to a close. It also includes clear teachings about *Mary*, the most blessed of women, the only woman mentioned by name in the Qur'an after whom even a chapter of the Sacred Text is named, and the person who accompanies the soul of blessed Muslim women to paradise. The Qur'anic and Islamic doctrine of Christ and the Virgin, who moreover, appear nearly always together in the Qur'an, remains a part of the Islamic religion itself independent of Christianity. But the presence of such teachings cannot but affect the Muslims' views towards Christians, and indeed, over the centuries, despite all the enmity and distrust that has characterized much of the history of the two religions when in confrontation with each other, Islam and all traditional Muslims have continued to revere the two figures who also stand at the heart of the Christian religion.

Rejection of Trinity and Incarnation

There is, however, on the basis of the acceptance of the Divine Origin of the Christian message and reverence of an exceptional character for Christ and the Virgin, a rejection in the Qur'an itself of both the doctrine of the Trinity and the incarnation. Since Islam is based on the Absolute and not its manifestations and seeks to return Abrahamic monotheism to its original purity as the religion of the One, any emphasis upon a particular manifestation of the One in the direction of the many is seen by Islam as a veil cast upon the plenary reality of *Divine Unity* which Islam seeks to assert so categorically and forcefully. Therefore, the trinitarian doctrine, not only of certain Oriental churches to which the Qur'anic account seems to be closer than Western interpretations of the doctrine, but of any other kind which would not place the trinitarian relationship below the level of Divine Oneness, is rejected by the Islamic perspective. Needless to say, Islam would accept an interpretation of the Trinity which would not in any way compromise Divine Unity, one which would consider the persons of the Trinity to be "Aspects" or "Names" of God standing below His Essence which, being the Absolute, must be One without condition and above all relations. Likewise, the idea of a Divine Descent in the form of *incarnation* is excluded from the Islamic point of view. The chapter which is entitled

"Unity" or "Sincerity" in the Qur'an and which summarises Islamic beliefs concerning the nature of God is as follows:

> Say: "He God is One.
> God, the Self-sufficient Besought of all;
> He begetteth not, nor is He begotten,
> And none is like unto Him."[5]

These verses not only define the Islamic perspective but almost seem to oppose directly the doctrines of the Trinity (*tathlith*) and incarnation (*hulul*), both being such an anathema to the Muslim mind, as these doctrines were usually understood in the world in which Islam spread.

The question thus appeared to the earliest Muslims as to why a religion revealed by God through such a major prophet as Christ to a people some of whom the Prophet of Islam met and respected, should possess such teachings which should be so directly opposed to what Muslims consider as the obvious truth concerning the nature of the Divine. Few Muslim theologians of the earlier or even later centuries sought to examine the works of Christian theologians themselves on these issues, especially writings emanating from the Latin Church, while certain Sufis such as Ibn 'Arabi[6] and many of the Persian Sufi poets saw both the doctrine of Trinity and incarnation as symbolic ways of speaking about the Absolute and Its manifestations without in any way destroying the doctrine of Divine Unity.*[7] Moreover, a theologian and Sufi like al-Ghazzali[8] tried expressly to absolve Christ himself from having ever taught either the trinitarian or the incarnationist doctrine, he being a prophet who cannot, according to Islam, but claim God's Oneness without any reserve or compromise.*[9]

Belief in Abrogation

By and large, however, Muslims tended toward the elaboration of the Qur'anic teaching itself concerning the changes and modifications brought about in the text of earlier revelations as a result of the passage of time and lack of care of the followers of these religions to preserve the actual texts revealed to them, not to speak of purposeful distortions. To this view was added the belief in *abrogation* (*naskh*), according to which a later revelation abrogates an earlier one. Some argued on the basis of this idea that the gospels abrogated the Torah and the Qur'an the gospels, and that with the coming of Christianity all Jews should have embraced Christianity and likewise with the coming of Islam all Christians should have become Muslims. But many perceptive religious thinkers of Islam realized that the doctrine of abrogation could not be applied so simply because in the case of the Qur'an itself certain verses directly concerned with the Divine Law abrogated earlier verses without the earlier verses becoming false or ceasing to be the Word of God. Moreover, Christians continued to live and practice their religion as did the Jews, and both obviously according to God's Will. Therefore, their religion could not simply be dismissed as being abrogated. The commonly held view thus remained one of accepting the Divine Origin of Christianity and that Christians would be saved if they practiced their religion,*[10] while there was the general feeling that somehow changes had taken place in the Sacred Scripture of the Christians leading them to such doctrines as that of the Trinity and incarnation, neither of which could have been taught by a prophet of God, as Muslims envisaged the prophetic function in its totality from Adam to the Prophet of Islam.

Problems with Christian Ethics

The Islamic view of Christianity is also as much concerned with the *moral and practical aspects of religion* as with the theological. Here, two very different forms of morality have examined and judged the other in the light of their own precepts and norms. Islam criticizes Christianity for not having a Divine Law, a *Shar'iah*, in the strict sense of the term, and does not understand why Christianity did not follow Mosaic Law or bring a law of its own. Christianity is seen by Muslims as a religion devoid of an exoterism which then substitutes a message of an essentially esoteric nature as the exoteric, thereby creating disequilibrium in human society. Christian ethics is seen by Muslims as being too sublime for ordinary human beings to follow, the injunction to turn the other cheek being meant only for saints. That is why Sufis call Christ the prophet of inwardness and the spiritual life. But since all human beings are not saints, this Christian morality is seen by Muslims as neglecting the reality of human nature, and of substituting an unattainable ideal, as far as the collectivity is concerned, for a realism based on human nature and capable of creating equilibrium for man in his earthly life and felicity in the hereafter based upon this equilibrium.

Nowhere is this opposition of moral views more evident than in the question of *sexuality* which is seen as being tainted with sin in the mainstream of Christian theology especially as it developed in the West, while being seen as a sacrament in Islam as long as it is practiced according to the Divine Law. Islam sees the indissoluble, monogamous marriage of Latin Christianity as being certainly a possibility, but not as exhausting all the possibilities of human nature. Moreover, Islam opposes celibacy and therefore cannot accept the Christian doctrine of the virtue of celibacy over married life. Muslims are especially surprised when Christians attack the Islamic attitude toward sexuality and such practices as polygamy, while in the West, in which Christianity has been the religion of the vast majority, sexual promiscuity is of a dimension inconceivable to a traditional Muslim.

This *lack of realism* in promulgating Christian ethics is seen by Muslims to be also at the root of the Christian opposition to the world and worldly power. The Muslims have always asked if Christianity is opposed to war, for Christ said, "He who uses the sword shall perish by the sword." Then why is it that Christian people over the centuries have not carried out less wars than others, and certainly have not shown any more restraint in war than have non-Christians? The whole attitude of Christianity towards the world, whether it be its political and economic aspects or the enjoyments of the flesh, is seen by Islam to contain an ambiguity where the ideal preached and the practice followed have often little to do with each other. This opposition issues in fact from the very different conception of the "world" in the religious perspectives of Christianity and Islam. "For the Christian 'what is of this world *ipso facto* takes one away from God'; for the Abrahamic Semites [Muslims and also Jews] 'what takes one away *de facto* from God is of this world alone.' "*11

Lest it be thought that the evaluation of Christian morality by Muslims is simply negative, it must be emphasized that for traditional Muslims the ethical teachings of Christ are to be criticized not for being imperfect but for being too exalted to be realized by most human beings and therefore not widely applicable. All Muslims who still remain faithful to their tradition revere and respect the Sermon on the Mount and have great reverence for those who put such sublime teachings into practice. They criticize Christianity on this score in being too spiritual, not that it lacks spiritual character. In fact there is a widespread Islamic belief according to which in the Abrahamic cycle of revelations, Judaism represents the Law and the religion of this world; Christianity the Way and the religion of the heart or of the other world; and Islam the synthesis of both in which a balance is created between the Law and the Way, between the demands of the body and of the spirit. It is no accident that Christ plays such an important role in Islamic esoterism, totally independent of historical influences, for he represents the esoteric dimension in the Abrahamic tradition, while Sufism is esoterism in Islam which seeks to return to the Unity and synthesis of the religion of Abraham before its particularization into the Judaic and Christian religions.

Appreciation for Christianity

The appreciation of the spiritual nature of Christian morality is especially evident where Muslims live near pious Christians. In lands such as Syria and Egypt, as well as the Holy Land before recent tragedies, there was hardly a devout Muslim who did not revere and deeply respect some pious Christian friend or neighbor. Reverence for Christian piety and beauty of soul of certain Christians in daily contact with Muslims constitutes a most important element of the Islamic view of Christianity, one which is often left out of account in theological or historical discussions and also one which unfortunately tends to become destroyed in those lands where the fruit of centuries of harmonious relationship between Muslims and

Christians is being destroyed as a result of internal wars as well as intrusion of alien factors and forces.

The appreciation of Christianity is, however, not confined to human contacts on an every day basis. In spite of polemics written by Muslim theologians and jurists, there exists a notable body of Islamic literature, especially in Arabic and Persian, which is based on profound respect for Christianity. Most of this literature is of a mystical nature where Christ plays a crucial role but in a Muhammadan universe. No one can read the poetry of Hafiz or Rumi[12] without becoming immediately aware of the ever present power of the "breath of the Messiah" to enliven the soul of man in the same way that the historical Christ brought the dead back to life. One must not forget that a saint like Rumi had many Christian disciples and even a Christian wife who did not convert to Islam, and that he visited Christian monasteries where he held friendly discourse with monks. It was only a bit over a century ago when, in Isafahan, where many Armenians lived across the Zayanderud River from the Muslim quarters, a poet like Hatif could claim that while trying to debate with a Christian concerning the Trinity, he heard from the church bells themselves that there is but one God worshipped by Muslims and Christians alike. Likewise, an Ibn 'Arabi, who hailed from southern Spain where he had encountered numerous Christians, could write many an illuminating page on the Christic reality and its function in the whole cycle of prophecy.*[13]

Problems of the Common History

Historical contingencies and events such as the Crusades and the expulsion of Muslims from Spain have had of course a great deal of effect upon the view of certain Muslims about Christians, if not Christianity itself. But by and large before the present period Muslims have remained remarkably indifferent to Western Christianity and have not been at all interested in studying it. Accounts of West European Christianity do not appear in Muslim sources until the seventeenth and eighteenth centuries, and then in chronicles of Ottoman and Moroccan ambassadors rather than in the works of theologians. In general in these sources some description is given of the institution of the papacy, which Muslims did not understand fully and which they usually opposed. In fact something of the anti-clericalism of the French Revolution entered into the Islamic world and even affected those Muslims who were opposed to modernism, but who saw this European anti-clericalism as affirming their own opposition to the presence of a priesthood in Christianity. Again, they contrasted the situation of Islam in which every man is his own priest with that of Christianity, especially Catholic Christianity, with an elaborate ecclesiastic hierarchy, and thought of the latter as being a later invention opposed to the original simple teachings of Christ. As Muslims came to know also more about the post-medieval religious art of Europe, especially that of the Baroque period with its extremely ornate and naturalistic patterns and designs, they grew in their opposition to the practices of Christians and criticized their possession of power, both economic and military, combined with an art which appeared to Muslim eyes as an idolatry.*[14] Such was not the case in either medieval Spain or Byzantium, but then Muslims were facing a Christian civilization of traditional character, possessing a spirituality and an otherworldliness of which the more perceptive among Muslim observers were fully aware.

Likewise, *missionary activity*, whether Catholic or Protestant, usually combined with political and economic domination, played a major role in determining Muslim attitudes toward Christians, to the extent that in the Arab world to this day missionary activity (*tabshir*) is practically identified with colonialism (*isti'mar*). Since the Western powers, while opposing religion within their borders, usually helped the missionaries from their countries when they went abroad, most Muslims came to identify practically all the activities of Western powers with Christianity. A distrust was created of Western Christianity which did not exist during the Crusades when European nations were openly Christian. This distrust has become aggravated as a result of political machinations and such colossal tragedies as recent events in Palestine and Lebanon. As a result, an atmosphere of bitterness has been created in many quarters vis-à-vis Christianity, an atmosphere which did not exist even half a century ago, and certainly not in the Middle Ages, when Christians and Muslims often fought, but as enemies who respected one another.

To these negative elements must be added the rise of what in the West is called *Islamic fundamentalism*. Many of the movements grouped under this name have in fact much in common with modernism and are not to be confused with traditional Islam. One of the major points of difference between them is in fact their attitude towards Christianity. To the extent that these movements, many of which are fanatical and seek to redress grievances through violence, spread among traditional Muslims, the base of faith of the Muslims who accept their rhetoric and so-called ideology becomes narrowed. A simple peasant in the countryside of Tunisia or a merchant in the Lahore bazaar is usually more open to Christianity and appreciative of its spiritual values than an educated Muslim student caught in the web of one of such so-called fundamentalist movements. The fire of hatred burns bonds of amity and shrivels the soul of the faithful, whether they be Muslim or Christian.

Coexistence and Mutual Acceptance

There are, however, those within the Islamic world who realize that the destinies of Islam and Christianity are intertwined, that God has willed both religions to exist and to be ways of salvation for millions of human beings, that the enemy of both religions is modern agnosticism, atheism and secularism, and that Christianity is a dispensation willed by heaven not only as a historical background to Islam but as a revelation destined to guide a sector of humanity until the second coming of its founder. Such Muslims can draw from a vast resource of traditional Islamic writings which is able to provide ample basis for a veritable ecumenical encounter with Christianity, based not on reducing each religion to a bare minimum to accommodate the other, but grounded in that transcendent unity which unites all authentic religions, and especially Christianity and Islam. Such Muslims, far from surrendering to the fads and fashions of the day in the name of keeping up with the times, or of loosening the reins which control the passions in order to express anger in the name of indignation, base themselves on the eternal message of the Qur'an in their dealings with Christians. They develop, in the light of present needs, the expressly Qur'anic doctrine of the universality of revelation, and even practice the Christian virtue of turning the other cheek when it comes to the matter of religious truth; that is, they accept the validity of Christianity even if Christians deny the authenticity of the Islamic revelation. They let the matter of who is saved be decided by the Supreme Judge who judges according to the truth, not the "fashions of the times" and expediency. The voice of such Muslims might seem to be drowned out at the moment by the cry and fury of those who preach hatred in the name of justice, and who even insult other religions in direct opposition to the injunctions of the Qur'an. But the voice of understanding and harmony cannot but triumph at the end, for it is based upon the truth, and surely Christ whose second coming is accepted by both Christians and Muslims shall not come but in truth and shall not judge but by truth, that truth which he asserted himself to be, according to the Gospel statement, and which the Qur'an guarantees as being triumphant at the end for there will finally arrive the moment when it can be asserted with finality that "the Truth has come and falsehood has perished" (Qur'an 17:81).

Part III

Buddhist Perceptions of Christianity in the Twentieth Century

INTRODUCTION TO PART THREE

Buddhists have had contacts with Christians since almost the beginning of the Christian era. The name of Buddha is mentioned by Clement of Alexandria in the second century, and, given the relatively free and open trade routes between what we now think of as the Middle East and those areas further east in which Buddhism then had a substantial presence, contacts between Christians and Buddhists must have been relatively frequent.

These contacts, though, have left rather few traces in the literature produced by the intellectuals of both traditions. In spite of the fact that some knowledge of Buddhism was current among Christians in Alexandria in the second century, this knowledge remained fragmentary and inaccurate for the next fifteen hundred years, and Buddhism had only indirect influence upon Christianity until the beginning of European colonial expansion in the sixteenth century. Insofar as Buddhist ideas were known or Buddhist literary themes appropriated, this happened through intermediaries: Zoroastrianism mediated some Buddhist ideas to the Christian West, as, probably, did some of the gnostic movements; and some Buddhist fables, through long and complex chains of transmission, became naturalized into Christian thinking, though no longer with the explicit knowledge that they had once been Buddhist.[1]

Traces of direct knowledge of Christians and Christianity in Buddhist literature are even fewer. There may possibly be some references to Christianity in some late Indian Buddhist texts, from the ninth century and after. But there is no evidence of detailed knowledge, much less of any real interest, until quite late in the history of the European colonial domination of Buddhist countries. For Buddhist discussions of Christianity based upon any detailed or direct knowledge, therefore, there are no sources earlier than the nineteenth century.

The Conceptual Basis for Buddhist Assessments of Christianity

Buddhists have, however, been accustomed to thinking about religious pluralism since the very beginning. The Buddha himself was active in India about five hundred years before the beginning of the Christian era,[2] during a period when a number of new religious movements were being founded and when the orthodox Brahmanism of the time was being challenged. Buddhists therefore quickly developed some conceptual tools to deal with the questions raised by the existence of manifold and apparently incompatible religious claims and communities.

First, and perhaps most important, there is a methodological principle, a principle that has to do with the nature of religious doctrines. Briefly and rather crudely, this principle suggests that religious doctrines have utility rather than truth; that their importance lies in the effects they have upon those who believe in them; and that since the condition of religious believers varies enormously, identical doctrines will not have identical effects upon all believers. This principle opens the door to a flexible and interesting method of dealing with apparently incompatible religious claims. Since the condition of religious believers is variable, it may be perfectly appropriate for different individuals to assent to incompatible claims and to engage in incompatible practices, for a belief that has appropriate effects upon some believers may have quite inappropriate effects upon others.

From this principle is derived the idea that the Buddha himself frequently taught different and incompatible doctrines to different hearers. The Buddha's perfect skill in doing this, his perfect knowledge of what any hearer needs to hear in order to advance along the path to Nirvana, is denoted by the technical term *upayakaushalya*, often translated "skill in means."[3] This capability, although possessed to its full extent only by Buddhas, is a virtue recommended to all Buddhists; its workings are traditionally explained by appeal to a story in the *Lotus Sutra*, an important text of Mahayana Buddhism.[4] The story tells of a compassionate father who discovers that his sons are caught in a burning house, but, not realizing that the house is burning, refuse to listen to his pleas that they should leave the house. In order to get them out he promises each of them a different reward: one is offered a goat-drawn carriage, another a deer-drawn carriage, and a third an ox-drawn carriage. Since these things are exactly what each wants, these promises induce them to leave. When they get outside each child is presented with a single magnificent carriage, drawn by a white ox. Only the third child got exactly what was promised, but each was given a promise that had the desired effect. So also with the Buddha's preaching of religious doctrines.[5]

The Buddhist view of religious doctrines as instruments for transformation rather than descriptions of reality is illustrated by a standard simile, that of the raft, presented in the following words traditionally ascribed to Gautama Buddha:

> Monks, as a man going along a highway might see a great stretch of water, the hither bank dangerous and frightening, the further bank secure, not frightening, but if there were not a boat for crossing by or a bridge across for going from the not-beyond to the beyond, this might occur to him: "This is a great stretch of water . . . suppose that I, having collected grass, sticks, branches and foliage, and having tied a raft, depending on that raft, and striving with hands and feet, should cross over safely to the beyond?" To him, crossed over, gone beyond, this might occur: "Now, this raft has been very useful to me. I, depending on this raft, and striving with my hands and feet, crossed safely over to the beyond. Suppose now that I, having put this raft on my head, or having lifted it on to my shoulder, should proceed as I desire?" What do you think about this, monks? If that man does this, is he doing what should be done with that raft?[6]

The expected answer, of course, is no. Rafts are for crossing rivers, for getting you somewhere. If you continue to carry them on dry land your progress will be slowed or halted. Similarly with religious doctrines: When their use, their function, is exhausted, undue attachment to them will only hinder progress. They should be discarded at that point.

These views about the nature of religious doctrine influence how Buddhists have looked at the doctrines and practices of non-Buddhists. They have tended to focus more upon the effects of these doctrines and practices upon their believers and practitioners, and less upon the truth of the doctrines or the desirability of the practices considered in abstraction from particular situations. This thrust is evident in almost all of the essays reprinted here, but perhaps most especially in K. N. Jayatilleke's distinction between "satisfactory" and "unsatisfactory" religions (Chapter 10), and in the Dalai Lama's emphasis on the common goal of all religious communities (Chapter 12).

But it is not possible for all Buddhist assessments of non-Buddhist doctrines and practices to consider only the utility of those doctrines and practices. The question of truth cannot be bracketed entirely, even if only because Buddhists clearly regard some claims as simply true, in a fairly straightforward sense, and others as equally evidently false. And a concern to argue against claims that seem to Buddhists just false (and, therefore, often religiously unproductive) has therefore been present within the Buddhist tradition from the earliest times.

Among many other things, Buddhists have frequently argued against theists—originally Hindus, but latterly both Muslims and Christians. Theism, in the sense of belief in a deity who is self-caused and self-existent, independent of all other existents, is a false belief for almost all Buddhists, and there is a long tradition of anti-theistic apologetics within the tradition. This strand of thought is very clear in the extracts from Gunapala Dharmasiri's book *A Buddhist Critique of the Christian Concept of God* reprinted as Chapter 11 of this volume, and more comments upon it are offered in the introductory notes to that chapter. Here it will suffice to note that this traditional Buddhist atheism—"principled atheism" as one scholar has called it[7]—has had significant effects upon Buddhist perceptions of Christianity.

While, in accordance with the principle of *upayakaushalya* and the idea that different doctrines are useful for different individuals, it is accepted that theism may be of some use for some people at some times—and the Dalai Lama is explicit about this in Chapter 12—it is still universally held that theism is ultimately a barrier to the attainment of Nirvana and thus that Christians must, finally, be disabused of their adherence to it.

Buddhist discussions of Christianity tend, therefore, to center upon theism or ethics. Interest in the former is for the reasons just canvassed; interest in the latter springs from the fact that the inculcation and application of compassion are of central importance in Buddhism. Buddhists are therefore naturally attracted to and interested in the ideals of selfless love evident within Christianity. This also is very clear in the Dalai Lama's contribution, as it also is, though to a lesser extent, in all of the other contributions. It is very noticeable that there are almost no Buddhist discussions of Christ or of Christology, much less of complex doctrinal matters such as the doctrines of the trinity or of the atonement. This lack is partly due to the fact that Buddhists have been sufficiently interested in Christianity to produce discussions of it for only a short time, and thus have as yet not had enough opportunity to develop expertise in these obscure and difficult questions. But it is also, I think, due to the fact that such doctrines hold little appeal for Buddhists; it is not obvious to them how such doctrines help Christians achieve salvation.

Historical Influences upon Buddhist Assessments of Christianity

Buddhist assessments of Christians and Christianity developed almost exclusively in response to the linked challenges of colonialism and Christian missionary activity. It was evident to Buddhists in those countries that were directly subject to European rule that Christianity was a vital part of the culture that was dominating them. Naturally, therefore, Christianity was often simultaneously reviled, rejected, and imitated. Reviled and rejected because of its identification with political, military, and social domination;

imitated because of the need to meet it on its own ground with its own weapons.

The rejection grew in strength as Buddhists became aware that a rediscovery and re-assertion of Buddhist identity would require a critique of Christianity. So, to take an example fairly extreme (but not entirely atypical) in its rhetoric, we find Anagarika Dharmapala (1864–1933), a Sinhalese Buddhist reformer, writing:

The semitic religions have neither psychology nor a scientific background. Judaism was an exclusive religion intended only for the Hebrews. It is a materialistic monotheism with Jehovah as the architect of a limited world. Christianity is a political camouflage. Its three aspects are politics, trade, and imperial expansion. Its weapons are the Bible, barrels of whisky, and bullets.[8]

Anti-Christian rhetoric of this kind became common in many of the Buddhist countries of South and Southeast Asia as the nineteenth century progressed, especially as Protestant Christian missionaries became more explicit and aggressive in their attempts at conversion.[9] At the same time, Buddhists in many countries began to adopt, more and more openly, Protestant Christian institutional forms and methods of evangelization. So, for example, in 1898 a Young Men's Buddhist Association was founded in Sri Lanka (then Ceylon), and Buddhists began to write and publish anti-Christian and pro-Buddhist apologetical pamphlets in a number of Buddhist countries.[10] Buddhism became Protestantized even as it became more anti-Christian.

These trends are still visible in the writings of Buddhist intellectuals from the Theravada countries of South and Southeast Asia. Some of them are evident in Chapters 10 and 11 of this volume. The experience of Buddhists in Central and East Asia was different: Tibetans were affected by European colonialism only marginally, although Tibetan Buddhism has recently been almost destroyed by the Chinese variety of colonialist expansionism. The Dalai Lama's view of Christians and Christianity (Chapter 12) has been affected by the recent experience Tibetans have had of Christians as helpers in the fight to resist communism; there is therefore little anti-Christian animus in his work. Japan, also, was scarcely touched by European colonialism, and has, since its defeat in World War II, become one of the leading economic world powers. The question for contemporary Japanese Buddhists, then, is not so much whether they are able to reaffirm Buddhism in such a way as to resist Christian missionary activity, but rather whether and to what extent Christians are able to learn from and appropriate the conceptual and religious riches of Buddhism. This explains much of the tone adopted by Masao Abe and Daisaku Ikeda in Chapters 13 and 14.

In sum: a full understanding of the works reprinted in Part 3 will have to take into account both the conceptual constraints that Buddhists typically operate under in thinking about non-Buddhists, and also the historical and political influences that have shaped specific instances of that thought.

SUGGESTIONS FOR FURTHER READING

The resources for studying Buddhist perceptions of Christianity are as yet very limited. There is an enormous and growing literature by Christians about various aspects of Buddhism — Buddhism seems to hold more fascination for Christians than any other world religon, perhaps because of deep conceptual difference coupled with superficial similarity as a multicultural missionary religion — but as yet rather little by Buddhists about Christianity.

An excellent bibliographical introduction to Christian writing about Buddhists, as well as to what little there is by Buddhists about Christians, may be found in Joseph J. Spae, *Buddhist-Christian Empathy* (Chicago: The Chicago Institute of Theology and Culture, 1980), 245–52. See also the bibliography in Minoru Kiyota et al., eds., *Japanese Buddhism: Its Tradition, New Religions and Interaction with Christianity* (Los Angeles: Buddhist Books International, 1987), 202–5.

Journals with occasional articles by Buddhists on Christianity are: *The Eastern Buddhist* (Kyoto); *Buddhist-Christian Studies* (Honolulu); and *Dialogue* (Colombo, Sri Lanka).

A useful collection of Anagarika Dharmapala's essays and addresses, many of which contain a vehement anti-Christian polemic, is Anagarika Dharmapala, *Return to Righteousness: A Collection of Speeches, Essays, and Letters of the Anagarika Dharmapala*, ed. Ananda Guruge (Colombo, Sri Lanka: Government Press, 1965). This is fairly representative of the late nineteenth and early twentieth century Protestantization of Buddhism already referred to. More recently, Daisetz Teitaro Suzuki (1870–1966), perhaps the greatest apologist for Zen Buddhism that Japan has yet produced, offered a number of observations on Christianity in several of his works. Relevant here is D. T. Suzuki, *Mysticism: Christian and Buddhist* (London: Allen & Unwin, 1957); *Outlines of Mahayana Buddhism* (New York: Schocken Books, 1963), 24–29; David W. McKain, ed., *Christianity: Some Non-Christian Appraisals* (New York: McGraw-Hill, 1964), 121–31.

Recently, Japanese thinkers influenced by the Kyoto School (on which see the notes to Chapter 13) have offered scattered comments on Christianity. See Keiji Nishitani, *Religion and Nothingness*, translated by Jan Van Bragt (Berkeley: University of California Press, 1982), especially chapters 5 and 6. Anthologies of Christian views on Buddhism (of which there are now many) are also beginning to include the occasional essay by a Buddhist on Christianity. See, for a good recent example, Shohei Ichimura, "Shunyata and Religious Pluralism," in Paul O. Ingram and Frederick J. Streng, eds., *Buddhist-Christian Dialogue: Mutual Renewal and Transformation* (Honolulu: University of Hawaii Press, 1986), 95–114.

10

Extracts from "The Buddhist Attitude to Other Religions"[1]

K. N. JAYATILLEKE

INTRODUCTION

Kulatissa Nanda Jayatilleke was trained both in traditional Buddhist learning in Sri Lanka and in the kind of philosophy taught in English universities in the 1950s and 1960s. His magnum opus, Early Buddhist Theory of Knowledge, *turns this combination of skills to good account, and Jayatilleke's interests in Western philosophy are evident also in the piece reprinted here.*

On 4 April 1966 Jayatilleke delivered a lecture entitled "The Buddhist Attitude to Other Religions" at what was then the University of Ceylon. Roughly half of that lecture is reproduced here. The lecture was then and still remains the clearest and most comprehensive statement in English of a Theravada Buddhist view of non-Buddhist religions.[2]

Jayatilleke sees Buddhism as tolerant and pragmatic but not relativistic in its attitude to non-Buddhist religious communities. He stresses that from the beginning, from the time of the Buddha himself, Buddhists were familiar with cultural and intellectual situations in which religious pluralism was the norm. They therefore evolved a pragmatic approach to adjudicating rival religious claims. If some particular set of such claims is found to be antithetical to the development of a good moral life and to taking responsibility for one's own actions, then the religious community that espouses that set of claims is judged to be following a "pseudo-religion" or a "religion-surrogate."

If, by contrast, some other set of such claims does foster these virtues among those who believe them, but is in some respects nevertheless opposed to Buddhism — say, as to belief in God, denial of rebirth, or some such — then these claims are judged to be part of an "unsatisfactory" religion. It is into this category that most forms of Christianity would fall, according to Jayatilleke.

There is, of course, only one set of religious claims that is both "verifiably true," to use Jayatilleke's phrase, and fully conducive to the moral life which issues, ultimately, in Nirvana. This set comprises the central claims of Buddhism as Jayatilleke understands them.

It is interesting to note that Jayatilleke treats both Buddhism and non-Buddhist religions from the perspective of a philosopher and a rationalist. What matters, for him, about any set of religious doctrines is its truth-value and its utility; he exhibits very little interest in Buddhism as a set of religious practices. And in this he is perhaps somewhat atypical of the tradition.

"THE BUDDHIST ATTITUDE TO OTHER RELIGIONS"

The following oft-quoted passage, which is not always accurately translated, contains the essence of the attitude recommended by the Buddha in choosing between conflicting ideologies as a basis for living:

There are certain religious teachers who come to Kesaputta. They speak very highly of their own theories but oppose, condemn and ridicule the theories of others. At the same time there are yet other religious teachers who come to Kesaputta and in turn speak highly of their own theories, opposing, condemning and ridiculing the theories of these others. We are now in a state of doubt and perplexity as to whom out of these venerable recluses spoke the truth and who spoke falsehood.

O Kalamas, you have a right to doubt or feel uncertain for you have raised a doubt in a situation in which you ought to suspend your judgment. Come now, Kalamas, do not accept anything on the grounds of revelation, tradition or report or because it is a product of mere reasoning or because it is true from a standpoint or because of a superficial assessment of the facts or because it conforms with one's preconceived notions or because it is authoritative or because of the prestige of your teacher. When you, Kalamas, realise for yourself that these doctrines are evil and unjustified, that they are condemned by the wise and that when they are accepted and lived by, they conduce to ill and sorrow, then you should reject them.[*3]

This critical attitude should be focussed on Buddhism itself:

If anyone were to speak ill of me, my doctrine or my Order, do not bear any ill-will towards him, be upset or perturbed at heart; for if you were to be so it will only cause you harm. If on the other hand, anyone were to speak well of me, my doctrine, and my Order, do not be overjoyed, thrilled, or elated at heart; for if so it will only be an obstacle in the way of forming a realistic judgment as to whether the qualities praised in us, are real and actually found in us.[*4]

The later tradition often underlines this attitude. The following verse attributed to the Buddha is to be found in a Sanskrit Buddhist text called the *Tattvasamgraha* and a Tibetan work called the *Jnanasamuccayasara*:

Just as the experts test gold by burning it, cutting it and applying it on a touchstone, my statements should be accepted only after critical examination and not out of respect for me.[5]

This does not, however, mean that faith is no requirement at all in Buddhism. Far from it. One cannot test a theory unless one accepts it at least tentatively as one's basis of life. The Buddhist accepts the "right philosophy of life" (*samma-ditthi*) as the basis of his living because he finds it reasonable and in fact more reasonable than any other way of life. Such faith which eventually culminates in knowledge is called a "rational faith" (*akaravati saddha*) as opposed to a blind or "baseless faith" (*amulika saddha*).

Going along with this critical outlook is the causal conception of nature, which is conceived of as a causal system in which there operate physical laws (*utu-niyama*), biological laws (*bija-niyama*), psychological laws (*citta-niyama*), as well as moral and spiritual laws (*kamma-dhamma-niyama*). These laws are said to operate whether a Buddha comes into existence or not and all that the Buddha does is to discover them and reveal to us those which are of relevance to the moral and spiritual life, which is both possible and desirable in the universe in which we live. It is said:

Whether Tathagatas[6] arise or not, this order exists, namely the fixed nature of phenomena, the regular pattern of phenomena or conditionality. This the Tathagata discovers and comprehends; having discovered and comprehended it, he points it out, teaches it, lays it down, establishes, reveals, analyses, clarifies it and says "Look."[*7]

This dispassionate and impartial but critical outlook, the causal conception of the universe and the conception of the Buddha as a being who discovers the operation of certain moral and spiritual laws and reveals them to us, may be said to be the first plank on which Buddhist tolerance rests. A scientist does not ask a fellow-scientist to accept a theory on faith though his fellow-scientist must have enough faith in the theory on his preliminary examination of it before he thinks of testing it out. In the same way, the Buddha shows us the way but we have to do the hard work of treading on it before we can get anywhere — *tumhe hi kiccam attappam akkhataro tathagata*. The Dhamma[8] if well-proclaimed (*svakkhato*) produces results without delay in this very life (*sanditthiko akaliko*), it invites anyone to verify it for himself (*ehipassiko*), it leads to the desired goal (*opanayiko*) and it is to be realised by the wise, each person for himself (*paccattam veditabbam viññuhi*). It looks as if the Buddha was addressing a modern mind of the twentieth century for the outlook that the Buddha recommends is what we today call the scientific outlook, except for the fact that it does not make a dogma of materialism.

The concept of the Buddha as one who discovers the truth rather than as one who has a monopoly of the truth is clearly a source of tolerance. It leaves open the possibility for others to discover aspects of the truth, or even the whole truth, for themselves. The Buddhist acceptance of Pacceka-Buddhas,[9] who discover the truth for themselves, is a clear admission of this fact. Referring to certain sages (*munayo*), who had comprehended the nature of their desires and had eliminated them, crossing over the waves of samsaric[10] existence, the Buddha says: "I do not declare that all these religious men are sunk in repeated birth and decay."*[11] Yet, as it is pointed out, the Dhamma is to be preached to all beings though all beings may not profit by it just as much as all sick people are to be treated although some may get well or succumb to their illnesses despite the medicines given.*[12] This is because there are beings who would profit only from the Dhamma.

This assertion of the possibility of salvation or spiritual growth outside Buddhism does not mean that Buddhism values all religions alike and considers them equally true. It would be desirable to determine the Buddhist use of the word for religion before examining this question. In early Buddhism, a "religious doctrine" was denoted by the word *dhamma*. *Ditthi* was a "religio-philosophical theory" and for it the word *darshana* was later used in Indian thought. But for "religion," which includes both beliefs as well as practices, the word used was *dhamma-vinaya*, which literally means "doctrine and discipline."

But the term, which was common to the Vedic tradition as well, was *brahma-cariya*, which literally means the "religious life." It was used in a very wide sense, because of the intellectual tolerance of the Vedic tradition at this time, to denote any "ideal life." It could be interpreted to mean any way of life, which was considered to be the ideal as a result of accepting a certain view of life concerning the nature and destiny of man in the universe. In this sense, the way of life of a materialist is also an ideal life from his point of view.

Indian thought has been accused of failing to divorce religion from philosophy. The accusation is unjustified. For what happened in the history of Indian thought is that the theoretical aspect of each religion was considered its philosophy, whereas its practical aspect was the religion. Every philosophy, including materialism, thus had both a view of life as well as a way of life, and consistency was demanded not only in each sphere (i.e., within each "view of life" and within each "way of life") but also between both. A materialist philosopher who did not live in accordance with material values was thus considered inconsistent. The Buddha claimed that there was consistence between his theory and practice (*yathavadi tathakari*). Western classical metaphysics, on the other hand, latterly came to be divorced from living. It was for this reason that Existentialism had to come in to fill the void. In Indian thought, however, every philosophical system had its theory as well as its practice and a philosophy was not entertained in isolation from its practical bearing on life. Today, we call those non-theistic philosophies, which have a practical bearing on life and often claim the sole allegiance of an individual, religion-surrogates since they take the place of traditional religions and act as substitutes for religion. Humanism, certain forms of Existentialism not related to traditional religions and certain materialist philosophies like Marxism, which have a practical bearing on life, may be considered such religion-surrogates.

Buddhism considers some of those religion-surrogates on the same footing as practical religions (*brahmacariyavasa*) in stating its attitude to various types of religion. In the *Sandaka Sutta*, Ananda, reporting the ideas of the Buddha, says that there are four pseudo-religions (*abrahmacariyavasa*) or false religions in the world, and four religions which are unsatisfactory (lit. *anassasikam*, unconsoling) but not necessarily false.

The pseudo-religions are first Materialism, which asserts the reality of the material world alone and denies survival, secondly a religious philosophy which recommends an amoral ethic, thirdly one which denies free will and moral causation and asserts that beings are either miraculously saved or doomed, and fourthly deterministic evolutionism, which asserts the inevitability of eventual salvation for all.*[13]

The four unsatisfactory but not necessarily false religions are presumably those which in some sense recognise the necessity for a concept of survival, moral values, freedom and responsibility and the non-inevitability of salvation. They are described as follows. The first is one in which omniscience is claimed for its founder in all his conscious and unconscious periods of existence. The second a religion based on revelation or tradition. The third a religion founded on logical and metaphysical speculation and the fourth is one which is merely pragmatic and is based on sceptical or agnostic foundations.

We note here that the relativist valuation of religion in early Buddhism does not presuppose or imply the truth of all religions or religion-surrogates. Some types of religion are clearly condemned as false and undesirable, while others are satisfactory to the extent to which they contain the essential core of beliefs and values central to religion, whatever their epistemic foundations may be. Those based on claims to omniscience on the part of the founder, revelation or tradition, metaphysical speculation or pragmatic scepticism, being unsatisfactory insofar as they are based on uncertain foundations.

Revelations and revelational traditions contradict each other and it is said that they may contain propositions which may be true or false. In the case of religions based on metaphysical argument and speculation, "the reasoning may be valid or invalid and the conclusions true or false."*[14] Buddhism is, therefore, by implication a religion which asserts survival, moral values, freedom and responsibility, the non-inevitability of salvation, and is also verifiably true.

I do not propose in this lecture to examine any of the specific doctrines of another religion and compare or contrast them with Buddhism, but it will be observed that the definition of the Buddhist "right view of life" (*samma ditthi*) comprehends the basic beliefs and values of the higher religions. The definition reads as follows:

> There is value in alms, sacrifices and oblations; there is survival and recompense for good and evil deeds; there are moral obligations and there are religious teachers, who have led a good life and who have proclaimed with their superior insight and personal understanding the nature of this world and the world beyond.*15

This "right view of life" (*samma ditthi*) is said to be of two sorts, (a) one of which is mixed up with the inflowing impulses (*sasava*) and (b) the other not so mixed up. These impulses are the desire for sensuous gratification (*kamasava*), the desire for self-centered pursuits (*bhavasava*) and illusions (*avijjasava*). Thus a right view of life mixed up with a desire for a belief in personal immortality in heaven or a belief in sensuous heavens would be a *sasava sammaditthi.*

The above summary of the right philosophy of life, it may be observed, is comprehensive enough to contain, recognise and respect the basic truths of all higher religions. All these religions believe in a Transcendent, characterised as Nirvana which is beyond time, space and causation in Buddhism, as an Impersonal Monistic principle such as Brahman or Tao in some religions, and as a Personal God in others. They all assert survival, moral recompense and responsibility. They all preach a "good life," which has much in common and whose culmination is communion or union with or the attainment of this Transcendent. The early Buddhist conception of the nature and destiny of man in the universe is, therefore, not in basic conflict with the beliefs and values of the founders of the great religions so long as they assert some sort of survival, moral values, freedom and responsibility and the non-inevitability of salvation. But at the same time it is not possible to say that in all their phases of development and in all their several strands of belief in varying social contexts they have stood for this central core of beliefs and values. This applies to Buddhism as well, particularly when we consider some of the developments in Tantric Buddhism.

One of the last questions put to the Buddha was by the wandering Ascetic Subaddha. He wanted to know whether the leading philosophies and religions proclaimed in his day by the six outstanding teachers, who had a large following each, were all true, all false, or whether some were true and some were false. The Buddha did not give a specific answer to this question since he generally avoided making specific criticisms of particular religions unless he was invited or challenged to do so, but he says that any religion is true to the extent to which it would incorporate the noble eight-fold path:[16]

> In whatever religion the noble eight-fold path is not found, that religion would not have the first saint, the second, the third, and the fourth; in whatever religion the noble eight-fold path is found, that religion would have the first, second, third and fourth saints. Void are these other religions of true saints. If these monks were to live righteously, the world would never be devoid of saints.*[17]

The first saint (the "stream-enterer" or *sotapanna*) is the person who has given up preconceptions about a soul to be identified with or located in aspects or the whole of his psycho-physical personality, and is convinced that no permanent and secure existence is possible within the cosmos of becoming (i.e., he has given up *sakkaya ditthi*, "personality belief"),[18] has by study and understanding cleared his doubts about the Buddha, the Dhamma, and the saintly Sangha (i.e., had got rid of *vicikiccha*),[19] has given up obsessional attachments to religious rites and rituals (i.e., has discarded *silabbata-paramasa*), and leads a pure moral life. As such he is not likely to fall below the level of human existence in any of his future births (*avinipata-dhammo*) and is assured of final realisation. The third saint*[20] is the person, who in addition to the above, tends to act out of selfless charity (*caga*), compassion (*metta*) and understanding (*vijja*), rather than out of greed (*lobha*), hatred (*dosa*) and ignorance (*moha*). Ignorance comprises all the erroneous beliefs and illusions we entertain about the nature and destiny of man in the universe. Hatred is the source of our aggressive (*vibhava-tanha*) tendencies, and greed includes the desire for sensuous gratification (*kama-tanha*) as well as the desire for self-centered pursuits (*bhava-tanha*), such as the desire for power, fame, etc. The fourth saint is the person, who attains final realisation in this life itself.*[21]

Leaving out Nigantha Nataputta, the founder of Jainism,[22] the other five out of the six outstanding teachers in the day of the Buddha represent standard types of philosophies or religions. In Sañjaya we have the Sceptic or Agnostic or Positivist, who argued that questions pertaining to survival, moral responsibility and values, spiritual beings and transcendent existence were beyond verification. Ajita Kesakambali was a Materialist, who denied any value in religious activities, denied survival, moral recompense, and moral obligations, and denied that there were any religious teachers who had led a good life and who have proclaimed with their superior insight and understanding the nature of this world and the world beyond; his view was that the fools and the wise alike were annihilated at death. Makkhali Gosala has been called a theist (*issara-karana-vadi*); as a theist who believed in God he seemed to have argued that salvation is essentially predestined for all. Everything is preplanned and takes place in accordance with the fiat of God; it is like the unravelling of a ball of thread thrown on the ground. Fools and wise alike evolve in various forms of existence high and low, in the course of which they gather experience under the impact of diverse forces, living in accordance with the sixty-two philosophies of life in different lives. Man himself has no will of his own since everything is predetermined by the divine will, which guarantees final salvation for all.

The theism of Makkhali is severely criticised since it gave a false sense of security to people and encouraged complacency by denying free will, the value of human effort and ensuring eventual salvation. The Buddha says that he knows of no other person than Makkhali born to the detriment and disadvantage of so many people, comparing him to a fisherman casting his net at the mouth of a river for the destruction of many fish.*[23] There are two arguments against belief in such a personal God (*ishvara*) mentioned in the Buddhist scriptures. The first is that the truth of theism entails a lack of man's final responsibility for his actions: "If God designs the life of the entire world — the glory and the misery, the good and the evil acts — man is but an instrument of his will and God is responsible."*[24] The other is that some evils are inexplicable if we grant the truth of such a theism: "If God is the lord of the whole world and the creator of the multitude of beings, then why has he ordained misfortune in the world without making the whole world happy, for what purpose has he made a world that has injustice, deceit, falsehood and conceit, or: the lord of the world is unrighteous, in ordaining injustice where there could have been justice."*[25]

The fact that such a theistic philosophy is severely criticised does not mean that all forms of theism are condemned. For a theistic religion and philosophy, which stresses the importance of human freedom, responsibility, and effort, encourages the cultivation of moral and spiritual values and the attainment of moral perfection, and offers the hope of fellowship with God (Brahma), who is represented as a perfect moral being, wise and powerful but not omniscient or omnipotent, is commended on pragmatic grounds. Addressing some personal theists among the Brahmins,[26] the Buddha describes the path to fellowship (*sahavyata*, literally "companionship") with God (Brahma) and speaks of the necessity of cultivating selflessness, compassion, freedom from malice, purity of mind, and self-mastery for this purpose:

> Then you say too, Vasettha, that the Brahmins bear anger and malice in their hearts and are impure in heart and uncontrolled, whilst God is free from anger and malice, pure in heart, and has self-mastery. Now can there be concord and harmony between the Brahmins and God?
>
> Certainly not, Gotama!
>
> Very good, Vasettha, that those Brahmins versed in the Vedas[27] and yet bearing anger and malice in their hearts, sinful and uncontrolled, should after death when the body is dissolved, attain fellow-

ship with God, who is free from anger and malice, pure in heart and has self-mastery—such a state of things can in no wise be.*28

Whatever the basis of the theistic myth they believed in, so long as these Brahmins could be persuaded to cultivate these virtues grounded in their faith in God, it was a step in the right direction. Thus on pragmatic grounds the belief in a Personal God is not discouraged in so far as it is not a hindrance but an incentive for moral and spiritual development. At the same time we must not forget that even according to the Buddhist conception of the cosmos, such a heaven had a place in the scheme of things, though the God who ruled in it, worshipped as the Almighty, was only very wise, powerful and morally perfect though not omniscient and omnipotent.

It will be worthwhile drawing attention to this conception of the cosmos in order to clarify this statement. The early Buddhist description of the cosmos as far as the observable universe goes, is claimed to be based on extrasensory clairvoyant perception. It is remarkably close to the modern conception of the universe:

As far as these suns and moon revolve, shedding their light in space, so far extends the thousand-fold universe. In it there are thousands of suns (*sahassam suriyanam*), thousands of moons, thousands of inhabited worlds of varying sorts . . . thousands of heavenly worlds of varying grades. This is the thousand-fold Minor World System (*culanika lokadhatu*). Thousands of times the size of a thousand-fold Minor World System is the twice-a-thousand Middling World System (*majjhimika lokadhatu*). Thousands of times the size of the Middling World System is the thrice-a-thousand Great Cosmos (*maha lokadhatu*).*29

This conception of the universe as consisting of hundreds of thousands of clusters of galactic systems containing thousands of suns, moons, and inhabited worlds is not to be found in the Hindu or Jain scriptures and was much in advance of the age in which it appears. In later Theravada it gets embedded in and confused with mythical notions about the universe. In the Mahayana, the conception is magnified and there are references to the "unlimited and infinite number of galactic systems (*lokadhatu*) in the ten quarters,"*30 but the original conception of a "sphere of [a] million millions of galactic systems"*31 survives. Brahma occupies a place in the highest of heavens and although he is morally perfect, he is still within the cosmic scheme of things and his knowledge does not extend as far as that of a Buddha. In the *Brahmajala Sutta*, the Buddha points out that the origins of some forms of theistic religion and philosophy are to be traced to the religious teachings of beings from this heaven, who are born on earth and leading a homeless life preach a doctrine which leads to fellowship with Brahma. It is said that in ages past Sunetta (Fair-Eyed) and five other such teachers taught the path to heaven and fellowship with God.*³² Such teachings are commended since they help man in bettering his condition.

On the other hand, when the Buddha addressed Materialists, Sceptics, Determinists, or Indeterminists, who denied survival, freedom and responsibility, he does not presuppose the truth of these latter concepts but uses a "wager argument" reminiscent of Pascal, to show that on pragmatic grounds it was better to base one's life on the assumptions of survival, freedom, and responsibility; for, otherwise, whatever happens, we stand to lose whereas on the other alternative we stand to gain.*³³

It would be possible for scholars and students of Buddhism to take these texts in isolation and, ignoring the rest of the material in the Canon, argue that either the Buddha was a Theist or an Agnostic, a Sceptic or a Materialist, as the case may be. There seem to be even "Buddhists" who, on the basis of the erroneous belief that the doctrine of *anatta* ("no-soul") precludes any possibility of a belief in survival, argue that the Buddha could not have entertained any belief in survival. This would make Buddhism a form of Materialism, perhaps a Dialectical Materialism with the emphasis on the doctrine of impermanence (*anicca*), or a Scepticism, doctrines from which Buddhism has been clearly distinguished in all its phases of expansion. It has even been said that rebirth is not taught in the First Sermon, which no one dared tamper with, whereas even this sermon quite clearly refers to "the desires which tend to bring about rebirth or re-becoming" (*tanha ponobbhavika*). So does the last sermon to Subaddha emphasise the noble eight-fold path, whose first member is the "right view of life" which underlines the reality of this world as well as the world beyond (*atthi ayam loko, atthi paro loko*). Likewise, on the question of theism, we find that a scholar like Mrs. Rhys Davids³⁴ latterly believed that Buddhism was no different in principle from a theistic religion, making the Buddha a Personal Theist. Radhakrishnan³⁵ saw the Buddha as an Impersonal Theist or an Implicit Monist. For Keith,³⁶ the Buddha was an Agnostic, and for Stcherbatsky³⁷ an Atheist. In actual fact none of these labels are adequate to describe Buddhism, which transcends them all, but it is important to distinguish Buddhism from all of them for the Buddhist attitude to other religions would depend on the view we take of Buddhism itself.

It is important to distinguish Buddhism on the one hand from Personal Theism and on the other hand from atheistic Materialism, although Buddhism has common ground with both. The Buddha was quite emphatic about this. The Buddha referred to the former as *bhava-ditthi*, "the personal immortality view" and the latter as *vibhava-ditthi*, the "annihilation view." Distinguishing Buddhism from both these views, which he says are found in the world and are mutually opposed to each other, the Buddha states: "These religious teachers who do not see how these two views arise and cease to be, their good points and their defects and how one transcends them in accordance with the truth, are under the grip of greed, hate and ignorance . . . and will not attain final redemption from suffering."*³⁸

We have already talked about the common ground that Buddhism has with some forms of theism in urging the validity of moral and spiritual values and of a transcendent reality. It will be worthwhile summarising the common ground that Buddhism has with some forms of Materialism.

The Buddha refused to preach to a hungry man and what Buddhism requires of man in society is the pursuit of one's material as well as spiritual well-being, such a quest being practicable where one's wealth is righteously earned and righteously spent for one's good as well as that of others, without squandering or hoarding it. The man who is valued is the person who "possesses the capacity to acquire wealth that he could not acquire before and also to increase it and at the same time possesses that insight which makes it possible for him to distinguish good and evil."*³⁹ Buddhism upholds the reality of this world as well as the next and the Buddha speaks of the happiness of the average man as deriving from economic security (*atthi-sukha*), the enjoyment of one's wealth (*bhoga-sukha*), freedom from debt (*anana-sukha*) and a blameless moral and spiritual life (*anavajja-sukha*). All forms of asceticism, which mortify the flesh are condemned even for monks since a strong and healthy body was necessary for both material and spiritual endeavours.

The Buddha was the first to proclaim the equality of man in the fullest sense of the term. There are differences of species, points out the Buddha, among plants and animals, but despite differences in the colour of the skin, the shape of the nose or the form of the hair, mankind is biologically one species. There was absolute spiritual equality as well for man, for anyone could aspire to become a Brahma or a Buddha; there are no chosen castes, chosen churches or chosen individuals. The Buddha gives a dynamic conception of society and holds that the economic factor is one of the main determinants of social change. Social disintegration and the division of the world into the haves and have-nots, resulting in tensions, the loss of moral values in human society and destructive wars originate from the maldistribution of goods: "As a result of goods not accruing to those bereft of goods, poverty becomes rampant, poverty becoming rampant, stealing becomes rampant."*⁴⁰ Tracing the cause of this poverty, which leads to such dire consequences, it is said that the mistake that the kings made was to consider that their task was merely to preserve law and order without developing the economy; the king "provided for the righteous protection and security of his subjects but neglected the economy."*⁴¹ The ideal state was one in which there was both freedom as well as economic security. This freedom embraces the recognition of human rights, the freedom to propagate any political or religious doctrine as well as freedom for "birds and beasts" (*mighapakkhisu*) to live without being wantonly attacked by humans. In advising a king, the Buddha says that the best way to ensure peace and prosperity in one's kingdom is not by wasting the country's resources in performing religious sacrifices but by ensuring full employment and thereby developing the economy.*⁴² The emperor Asoka, who was imbued with these ideals, has been credited with being the first king in history to conceive of a welfare state.[43] Imbued with these same ideals Sinhalese kings set up tremendous irrigation works for the welfare of man. It was King Parakrama Bahu[44] who said: "Truly in such a country not even a little water that comes from the rain must flow into the ocean without being made useful to man. . . . For a life of enjoyment of what one possesses, without having cared for the welfare of the people, in no wise benefits one like myself."[*45]

I think these few observations would suffice to show how strongly Buddhism stressed the importance of the material realities of life and how practical the advice has been. Both freedom as well as economic security are necessary ingredients for man's material and spiritual advancement. And freedom includes the freedom to criticise each others' political or religious philosophies without rancour or hatred in our hearts. I said earlier that the dispassionate and impartial quest for truth, the causal conception of the universe and the conception of the Buddha as a discoverer and proclaimer of truth was one of the planks of Buddhist tolerance. The other has throughout been compassion. We cannot force the truth on others. All we can do is to help them to discover it, and the greatest help we can give others especially in imparting spiritual truth is to try not to speak out of greed, hatred and ignorance, but out of unselfishness, compassion and wisdom.

Truth is immortal speech— this is the eternal law.
Hatred does not cease by hatred—hatred ceases by love.
This is the eternal law.

11

Extracts from *A Buddhist Critique of the Christian Concept of God*[1]

GUNAPALA DHARMASIRI

INTRODUCTION

Gunapala Dharmasiri was born and partly educated in Sri Lanka where he studied both Western philosophy and traditional Buddhism. He received his doctorate from the University of Lancaster in England and has written articles and books on both Buddhism and Western thought. He currently teaches philosophy at the Peradeniya campus of the University of Sri Lanka.

Dharmasiri is, in the best possible sense of the term, an apologist for the truth of the central claims of the Buddhist tradition as he understands them. He takes these claims with intellectual seriousness and judges them to be true; this requires him, when disagreement is evident, to engage in argument against the claims of religious communities other than his own. The book from which the extracts reprinted here are taken is an example of this; it is best understood as an extended intellectual engagement with Christian theism. The first chapter, of which about half is given here, deals with the intimate relationship, as Dharmasiri sees it, between Christian ideas about the soul and Christian ideas about God. Since Dharmasiri, like almost all Buddhists, rejects the possibility that the soul exists, he also rejects the possibility that the soul can be an image of God. And since, in his view, Christian theology makes God and soul conceptually interdependent, the nonexistence of the latter strongly suggests the nonexistence of the former.

Dharmasiri judges that to believe in a self-subsistent eternal changeless creator of everything is to have a false belief; that having such a belief is both a product of, and itself gives rise to, various unpleasant emotional attachments;

and that the belief's falsity can be demonstrated. The extracts reprinted here sketch some preliminary arguments in the service of such a demonstration and provide an idea of one kind of Buddhist philosophical reaction to Christian theism.

Dharmasiri represents, with great clarity and force, one important dimension of Buddhist perceptions of and responses to Christianity: the uncompromising rejection of a metaphysics constructed around the idea of enduring substances. Neither God nor human persons can, from a Buddhist viewpoint, be regarded as such, and the development of arguments to show that there are no substances and, ex hypothesi, *that an eternal deity cannot exist, has been an important part of the Buddhist apologetical arsenal since long before the encounter with Christianity.*[2] *Where Dharmasiri is perhaps less typical is in his tendency toward a strong and fairly crude kind of verificationism and empiricism. These proclivities are clearly evident in the extracts reprinted here and are probably a result of Dharmasiri's exposure to British "analytical" philosophy. A similar intellectual tone can be seen in K. N. Jayatilleke's work (Chapter 10).*

A BUDDHIST CRITIQUE OF THE CHRISTIAN CONCEPT OF GOD

1.1 The idea of self or soul is very closely related to the idea of God. According to contemporary Christian theologians, this relationship takes on various forms. One form is to treat the soul as an analogy of God. Thus Reinhold Niebuhr emphasizes the significance of the concept of *imago dei*.*[3] James Richmond speaks of a clue to understanding God. "The clue, that is to say, consists of the fact that the only conceivable *analogy* which would enable the cartographer to speak intelligibly and significantly of God . . . is a certain type of human discourse or explanation referring to the human soul or self as some unobservable, non-spatio-temporal, enduring principle or entity, 'involved in' the world certainly, yet somehow (and mysteriously) referrable to as 'beyond' or 'outside' what is empirically perceptible."*[4] Therefore an understanding of the soul contributes much to the understanding of God. About the degree of analogy some (e.g., Karl Barth) would significantly differ. Others (e.g., Paul Tillich) may go much further and speak of a closer and more intimate relationship of the soul with God. According to their theses, the understanding of the soul may more or less amount to an understanding of God and this is made obvious when they make their typical equations: ground of being = God; existence = God. This way of approach to the Reality or the source of salvation which is God, according to them, may be interestingly compared with the Buddha's ideas that were extremely critical of the concept of soul. In other words, the Christian and the Buddhist systems try to give two completely contrasting ways of approaching a similar problem. The Buddha's criticisms become relevant in this context because he was mainly criticizing the then prevalent Upanishadic[5] and other theories of soul which are extremely similar to the traditional or contemporary Christian theories of soul.

1.2 Many contemporary theologians accept the traditional ideas concerning the existence and nature of the soul. Some discuss it again (e.g., Maritain). But some try to contradict the traditional doctrine or claim to do so (e.g., Barth) while still others do in fact contradict it (e.g., Bishop Robinson). Maritain accepts the traditional doctrine of the soul as an immaterial, spiritual substance intrinsically independent of the body. The Buddha's verificatory attitude would strongly reject such an idea because it goes beyond any possibility of knowing the soul's existence. Maritain states, "Concerning *what is* our soul, concerning its essence, or its quiddity, this experience tells us nothing."*6 But Maritain puts forward a non-empirical form of verification. "My (soul or my substance) cannot be experienced by itself in its essence; a quidditative experience of the soul is possible only for a separated soul."*7

1.3 This is, on the one hand, to accept the empirical meaninglessness of the soul in its essence. On the other hand, it is an attempt to make the idea of soul meaningful in a non-empirical manner. For that, Maritain proposes an eschatological form of verification. But such a method of verification would make sense only if the concept to be verified is a meaningful one. Let us see whether it can be a meaningful concept.

1.4 In traditional Christianity, the reality of the soul is somehow dependent on God, in terms of the Spirit. It is in this sense that Maritain speaks of the soul as a permanent principle in man. "The person is a substance whose substantial form is a spiritual soul."*8 "A soul which is spiritual in itself, intrinsically independent of matter in its nature and existence, cannot cease existing."*9 It is here when they talk of the soul as a permanent principle within the personality that it becomes really vulnerable to empirical verification. Here, it is important to notice, one of the central Christian dogmas becomes exposed to empirical investigation.

1.5 The soul as a permanent principle was a favorite idea of the Upanishads too, and the Buddha was therefore very familiar with this conception. The Buddhist critique starts by inquiring into the possibility of finding such a permanent soul in man's personality. The Buddha takes the basic constituents of personality and looks into them, viz., (i) body, (ii) feelings, (iii) sensations, (iv) dispositions, (v) consciousness.[10] The Buddha questions his disciples:

"Is body (consciousness, etc.) permanent or impermanent?"
"Impermanent, revered sir."
"But is what is impermanent non-satisfying, or is it satisfying?"
"Non-satisfying, revered sir."
"And is it right to regard that which is impermanent, non-satisfying, liable to change, as 'This is mine, this am I, this is my self'?"
"No, revered sir."*11

The Buddha emphasizes that the selflessness of the body, consciousness, etc., are seen when they are seen as they really are (*yathabhuta*).*12 If one cannot see any such soul, the burden of proof falls on the soul-theorist.

1.11 If there is no reason to believe in a soul theory, why do some people have such a view? The Buddha maintained that if a rational explanation cannot be given to a belief, then its origin should be traced to an emotional bias. Therefore he called the ideas about "I" and "self" to be the "thoughts haunted by craving concerning the inner self."*¹³ For example, the desire for an immortal life (*bhavatanha*) might prompt one to believe and find security in the idea of an eternal soul. Also, the Buddha points out that there is another form of desire at work here. It is the desire and attachment for the consciousness and its types. "Whatever is desire, whatever is attachment, whatever is delight, whatever is craving, for all types of consciousness as eye-consciousness and for the mind, mental states, mental consciousness with mental states cognizable through mental consciousness . . . (these are called to be) dogmas, emotional biases, tendencies."*¹⁴ Therefore the idea of the soul is essentially an emotional bias. The Buddha addresses Kaccayana Thera:

> Grasping after systems, imprisoned by dogmas is this world, Kaccayana, for the most part. And the man who does not go after that system-grasping, that mental standpoint, that dogmatic bias, who does not grasp at it, does not take up his stand upon it, (does not think) — "it is my soul."*¹⁵

1.12 The Buddhist, of course, has to clear up certain problems before he formulates the no-soul theory. A soul theorist can point out that without accepting the existence of a soul there would be no way of explaining the facts of personal identity and moral responsibility. The Buddhist can give two answers. One is to show the defective nature of the soul theorist's contention. He is presupposing the meaningfulness of the concept of soul in advancing his argument. But we have tried to show how the concept of soul becomes absolutely meaningless when it is subjected to a proper and detailed analysis. Therefore, the soul theorist, before he advances his argument, has to show that the idea of soul is a meaningful concept. Thus his contention becomes meaningless because his essential presupposition is meaningless.

1.13 The fact that the Buddha rejected the idea of the soul does not mean that he did away with the concept of a person or a being. According to him, the person is, as we saw above, a conglomeration of psychic and material factors. The standard example to illustrate this was that of the chariot. "Just as the word 'chariot' is used when the parts are put together, just so when the (psycho-physical) factors are present arises the convention of 'a being.' "*¹⁶ For the Buddha the question was not how to account for a person if all we see in him are only groups of ever changing factors. Therefore, one cannot speak of "*dukkha*¹⁷ as done by oneself (*sayamkatam*) or by another (*parakatam*)" because there is no substantial entity persisting through actions and their fruitions. Also, one cannot say that *dukkha* is not done by oneself (*asayamkatam*) because one is responsible for actions done by oneself. Why? It is because, the Buddha states, one has achieved "the right view of cause and the causal origin of things."*18

1.14 However, there is the problem of explaining moral responsibility in terms of the no-soul theory. This was raised as a problem during the time of the Buddha himself. It is said, "The following doubt arose in the mind of a certain monk: If body, feelings, ideas, dispositions, and consciousness are without self, then what self can be affected by deeds not done by a self?"*19 To explain this further, one can do no better than quote Buddhaghosa[20] who tried to give a lucid and perceptive solution to this problem:

Whose is the fruit since there is no experiencer? . . . Here is the reply. . . . When a fruit arises in a single continuity, it is neither another's nor from other (*kamma*)[21] because absolute identity and absolute otherness are excluded there. The formative processes of seeds establish the meaning of this. For once the formative processes of a mango seed, etc., have been set afoot, when the particular fruit arises in the continuity of the seed's (growth), later on owing to the obtaining of conditions, it does so neither as the fruit of other seeds nor from other formative processes as condition; and those seeds or formative processes do not themselves place where the fruit is. This is the analogy here. And the meaning can also be understood from the fact that the arts, crafts, medicine, etc., learned in youth give their fruit later on in maturity. Now it was also asked, "Whose is the fruit since there is no experiencer?" Herein, "experiencer" is a convention for the mere arising of the fruit; they say, "it fruits" as a convention when on a tree appears its fruit. Just as it is simply owing to the arising of tree fruits, which are one part of the phenomena called a tree, that it is said "the tree fruits" or "the tree has fruited," so it is simply owing to the arising of the fruit consisting of the pleasure and pain called experience, which is one of the aggregates called "deities" and "human beings," that it is said "a deity or a human being experiences or feels pleasure or pain." There is therefore no need at all here for a superfluous experiencer.*22

Thus the problems of moral responsibility can be explained in terms of the memory and the causal continuity of the processes involved.

1.15 Moral responsibility, in turn, amounts to an explanation of the problem of personal identity. The latter assumes a significant position in the context of rebirth. Buddhaghosa explains personal identity with special reference to rebirth. Referring to the starting, co-originating consciousness of a new birth, he says, "here let the illustration of this consciousness be such things as an echo, a light, a seal impression, a looking-glass image, for the fact of its not coming here from the previous becoming (birth) and for the fact that it arises owing to causes that are included in past becomings. For just such an echo, a light, a seal impression, and a shadow, have respectively sound, etc., as their cause and come into being without going elsewhere, so also this consciousness."

> And with a stream of continuity there is neither identity nor otherness. For if there were absolute identity in a stream of continuity, there would be no forming of curd from milk. And yet if there were absolute otherness, the curd would not be derived from milk. And so too with all causally arisen things. And if that were so there would be an end to all worldly usage, which is hardly desirable. So neither absolute identity nor absolute otherness should be assumed here.*[23]

1.16 A "person" is not only a series of momentary events but also a causal continuum and therefore an identity is preserved in terms of the causal continuum. That is why, "He who does the deed and he who experiences are the same" or different are said to be two wrong extremes.*[24] This does not mean that one can speak of the mind or consciousness as the persisting principle of identity. The Buddha states that one cannot speak of consciousness as running on or faring on because consciousness itself is generated by conditions.*[25] A "person" (a group of psycho-physical factors) in the present moment inherits qualities of the preceding causal continuum of which the present moment is only a conditioned result. In a similar sense "he" is responsible for "his" future. Here one's continuity is felt through one's memory. It is important to remember that the Buddha attached a great significance to the unconscious part of the mind (*asampajana mano sankhara*).*[26] This was how the Buddha accounted for the nature of a person or a being.

1.24 According to the Buddha, it was an arbitrary abstraction to talk of soul as cognizer and thinker, etc., because these functions involved various factors like sense organs and the body. Thinking or thoughts were essentially conditioned by these factors so that it was structurally impossible to trace thoughts to a pure principle like soul. What happened with the soul theorists who argued against Ryle[27] was that their devotion to analysis that started with criticizing Ryle suddenly stopped after coming to the stage of proving the existence of mind and mental states. It is here that the Buddhist parts company with them in carrying the analysis further. If one is not interested in further analysis, there is no reason why one should not have stopped with Ryle rather than with the soul theory. The Buddha analyzes the mind into further factors and finds them all dynamic and essentially changing. Even the mind was not "a thing" but only another group of activities. It was necessarily dependent on body, but not in an epiphenomenalistic sense and therefore the Buddha accepted interactionism (*vinnanapaccaya namarupam namarupapaccaya vinnanam*). Though it was dependent on the body, the mind was regarded as a strong causal factor because it had paranormal capacities and powers like telepathy and psychokinesis. Here the Buddha would be at his strongest against any form of reductionism. The rejection of reductionist positions does not make the Buddhist position dualistic. The concept of "person" is only a conventional one that refers to a composite of five factors. Therefore a Buddhist would agree with Strawson[28] when the latter says, "that one's states of consciousness, one's thoughts and sensations, are ascribed *to the very same thing* to which these physical characteristics, this physical situation, is ascribed."*[29] In this sense, as in Strawson, "person" is a primitive concept*[30] in Buddhism. The knowledge of the existence of other minds is not a problem for the Buddhist because he accepts telepathy as a means of knowledge. Therefore, Wisdom's*[31] and Plantinga's*[32] arguments from the rational mystery of other minds to an analogical rational mystery with regard to God's existence, do not make much sense in the Buddhist context.

1.25 The Buddha's empirical theory of mind can be a fruitful alternative to the extremes of reductionism and soul theories. It should be emphasized that the Buddha did not preach the doctrine of no-soul *as a theory*. Once he clarified that if he upheld the theory of no-soul it would presuppose the meaningfulness of the concept of "soul." As he could not give any meaning to the concept of soul he at last rejected the theory of soul as well as the theory of no-soul. The Buddha keeps silent when Vacchagotta asks him whether there is a self or is not. The Elder Ananda later questions the Buddha:

"How is it, lord, that the Exalted One gave no answer to the question of the wanderer Vacchagotta?"

"Ananda, when asked by Vacchagotta, the Wanderer: 'Is there not a self?' had I replied that there is not, it would have been more bewilderment for the bewildered Vacchagotta. For he would have said: 'Formerly indeed I had a self, but now I have not one any more.' "*[33]

1.26 Therefore, to a Buddhist, the conception of God either as analogous to or as identical with the soul would not be able to make any sense. From the point of view of salvation, such a conception would be regarded as positively harmful.

1.35 It is instructive to see the Buddhist and Christian attitudes to the pragmatic value of the idea of the soul. The Christian believes that the idea of the soul is spiritually and morally satisfying and is positively conducive to moral and spiritual progress. The Buddhist reaction follows partly from the epistemological and ontological arguments discussed earlier, e.g., a fiction cannot lead to any real and enlightening moral and spiritual progress. But the Buddha opposed the idea of the soul on moral and spiritual grounds too. Answering the Buddhist, Tillich maintains that a perfect society is possible only on the idea of everyone possessing a substantial self:

> The Buddhist says, "Your two answers are incompatible; if every person has a substance, no community is possible." To which the Christian replies, *"Only* if each person has a substance of his own is community possible, for community presupposes separation. You, Buddhist friends, have identity but not community."*34

However, the issue is to be decided on the relative merits of the two alternatives. The Buddha strongly maintained that the idea of a personal self is a harmful concept communally as well as individually. Referring to the fundamentals, the notion of the self gives rise to the feelings and ideas that center round the self. This is a form of conceit.

> "I am"—that is a conceit (*mannitam*). "This am I"—that is a conceit. "I shall be"—that is a conceit . . . a conceit is, brethren, a lust . . . an imposthume,35 a barb.*36

This leads to an egoism (*asmimana*).*37 This conceit is generated in the following manner:

> Owing to the existence, dependent on, by adhering to the eye . . . tongue . . . body . . . mind . . . comes the notion of "better am I," or "equal am I" or "inferior am I."*38

A Buddhist would agree that a community needs separation but he would maintain that separation does not presuppose the existence of substances and usually it never does. On the other hand, the existence of substances might lead to the possibility of an absolute separatedness which will make community impossible. The Buddha was repeatedly clarifying how hatred, jealousy, the ideas of possessiveness, etc., do always depend on the wrong idea of self and therefore how such a notion can be socially harmful. To achieve the ideals of selflessness, disinterestedness and renunciation the idea of no-soul (*anatta*) is logically more conducive than the idea of soul.

> When he regards this body as impermanent, suffering, as a disease, an imposthume, a dart, a misfortune, an affliction, as other, as decay, empty, not-self, whatever is regard for body, desire for body, affection for body, subordination to body—this is got rid of.*39

1.36 Maritain believes that the possibility of spiritual depth necessitates the existence of a soul.*40 Also, according to Maritain, understanding myself involves understanding of my "self" which is noble, etc.*41 Barth is anxious to emphasize the intrinsic value of the soul as it is constituted by the Spirit, which is identical with God.*⁴² On the contrary, the Buddha sees the soul as an essentially evil idea that leads to spiritually harmful results. One cannot gain any spiritual satisfaction by seeking a soul in the mind and clinging to it because the mind is liable to changes.

> The uninstructed average person regards consciousness (body, feelings, etc.) as self, or self as having consciousness, or consciousness as in self, or self as in consciousness. His consciousness alters and becomes otherwise; with the alteration and otherwiseness in his consciousness, his consciousness is occupied with the alteration in his consciousness; mental objects, arising, persist in obsessing his thought; because of this obsession of his thought he is afraid and annoyed and full of longing and he is disturbed by grasping. This, your reverences, is what is being disturbed by grasping.*⁴³

By identifying oneself with a changing entity like mind one cannot be happy because it is "of little strength, fading away and comfortless."*⁴⁴ The identification of soul with God or the noumenal reality (Upanishadic) can also lead to harmful results. "Here is one of this view: my soul is great. He, having thought that the whole world is the space for his soul thinks that 'my soul is in everything.' This is his view. (Therefore) to his very soul he gets attached and because of that he starts to feel conceited. This should be known as greed and conceit."*⁴⁵

1.37 A person who has achieved enlightenment does not think "I have achieved it." "And inasmuch as this venerable one beholds, 'Tranquil am I, without grasping am I,' this too is known as grasping on the part of that worthy recluse or Brahman."*⁴⁶ In fact, the Buddha did positively inquire into the possibility of finding salvation by believing in the existence of a soul and found it was impossible. "Could you, monks, grasp that grasping of the theory of self, so that by grasping that theory of self there would not arise grief, suffering, anguish, lamentation, despair? No, revered sir."*⁴⁷

1.38 Thus a Buddhist would not find soul a morally and spiritually edifying concept. Therefore, in that sense, he would maintain that the soul cannot be a good analogy to a morally and spiritually perfect God either.

12

"Religious Harmony" and Extracts from *The Bodhgaya Interviews*[1]

H. H. THE XIVTH DALAI LAMA

INTRODUCTION

Tenzin Gyatso, the fourteenth Dalai Lama of Tibet, was born in 1935 in Amdo, in what was then Northeastern Tibet. Since 1959 he has lived in exile, mostly in Dharamsala, India, but also as a frequent visitor to Europe and the United States. His exile is due to the Chinese annexation of Tibet — the latter is now known as an autonomous region of the People's Republic of China — and to the demonstrated Chinese hostility to traditional Tibetan Buddhism.

To Tibetan Buddhists the Dalai Lama is an incarnation of Avalokiteshvara, "the lord who looks down with mercy," a Bodhisattva or spiritual genius of great power and compassion. Tenzin Gyatso is therefore himself a charismatic figure, and is regarded with awe and reverence by most Tibetans. He is both temporal and spiritual leader of the Tibetan people, and is head of the Tibetan government in exile.[2] In the Fall of 1989 Tenzin Gyatso was awarded the Nobel Prize for Peace in recognition of his efforts toward a nonviolent resolution of the struggle between China and the Tibetan people.

The first piece reprinted here, "Religious Harmony," is a short address delivered to various audiences in the United States in the early 1980s, together with some questions and responses. The second piece contains some extracts from an interview given at Bodhgaya, India, in 1981.

The central theme throughout, elaborated in a number of different ways, is the Dalai Lama's instrumentalist view of religion. For him, religion is an instrument designed to have certain effects upon those who choose to use it. All religions are designed to further human compassion and to reduce human suf-

162

fering. Insofar as any particular religion does this—and the Dalai Lama asserts that all have this as their goal—it is good and desirable, and its followers have no need to look elsewhere.

On this basis the Dalai Lama, as a Buddhist, is able to offer a positive appreciation of Christianity and is able to give the doctrinal differences between the traditions a very secondary position. Religious doctrines, it would seem, are only important to the extent that they foster compassion. In spite of this there is still, perhaps, a hint that Buddhist doctrines are preferable to Christian ones; the way the Dalai Lama responds to his questioner at the very end of the extract from the interview at Bodhghaya will repay careful study on this point.

"RELIGIOUS HARMONY"

That we have here a common gathering of various believers is a positive sign. Among spiritual faiths, there are many different philosophies, some just opposite to each other on certain points. Buddhists do not accept a creator; Christians base their philosophy on that theory. There are great differences, but I deeply respect your faith, not just for political reasons or to be polite, but sincerely. For many centuries your tradition has given great service to humankind.

We Tibetans have benefited greatly from the help offered by Christian relief organizations, such as the World Council of Churches, as well as the many others that have helped Tibetan refugees when we were passing through our most difficult period. Our Christian friends all over the world showed us great sympathy along with substantial material assistance, and I would like to express my deepest thanks to them all.

All of the different religious communities accept that there is another force beyond the reach of our ordinary senses. When we pray together, I feel something, I do not know what the exact word is—whether you would call it blessings or grace—but in any case there is a certain feeling that we can experience. If we utilize it properly, that feeling is very helpful for inner strength. For a real sense of brotherhood and sisterhood that feeling—that atmosphere and experience—is very useful and helpful. Therefore I particularly appreciate these ecumenical gatherings.

All of the different religious faiths, despite their philosophical differences, have a similar objective. Every religion emphasizes human improvement, love, respect for others, sharing other peoples' suffering. On these lines every religion has more or less the same viewpoint and the same goal.

Those faiths which emphasize Almighty God and faith in and love of God have as their purpose the fulfillment of God's intentions. Seeing us all as creations of and followers of one God, they teach that we should cherish and help each other. The very purpose of faithful belief in God is to accomplish His wishes, the essence of which is to cherish, respect, love, and give service to our fellow humans.

Since an essential purpose of other religions is similarly to promote such beneficial feelings and actions, I strongly feel that from this viewpoint a central purpose of all the different philosophical explanations is the same. Through the various religious systems, followers are assuming a salutary attitude toward their fellow humans — our brothers and sisters — and implementing this good motivation in the service of human society. This has been demonstrated by a great many believers in Christianity throughout history; many have sacrificed their lives for the benefit of humankind. This is true implementation of compassion.

When we Tibetans were passing through a difficult period, Christian communities from all over the world took it upon themselves to share our suffering and rushed to our help. Without regard for racial, cultural, religious, or philosophical differences, they regarded us as fellow humans and came to help. This gave us real inspiration and recognition of the value of love.

Love and kindness are the very basis of society. If we lose these feelings, society will face tremendous difficulties; the survival of humanity will be endangered. Together with material development, we need spiritual development so that inner peace and social harmony can be experienced. Without inner peace, without inner calm, it is difficult to have lasting peace. In this field of inner development religion can make important contributions.

Although in every religion there is an emphasis on compassion and love, from the viewpoint of philosophy, of course, there are differences, and that is all right. Philosophical teachings are not the end, not the aim, not what you serve. The aim is to help and benefit others, and philosophical teachings to support those ideas are valuable. If we go into the differences in philosophy and argue with and criticize each other, it is useless. There will be endless argument; the result will mainly be that we irritate each other — accomplishing nothing. Better to look at the purpose of the philosophies and to see what is shared — an emphasis on love, compassion, and respect for a higher force.

No religion basically believes that material progress alone is sufficient for humankind. All religions believe in forces beyond material progress. All agree that it is very important and worthwhile to make strong effort to serve human society.

To do this, it is important that we understand each other. In the past, due to narrow-mindedness and other factors, there has sometimes been discord between religious groups. This should not happen again. If we look deeply into the value of a religion in the context of the worldwide situation, we can easily transcend these unfortunate happenings. For, there are many areas of common ground on which we can have harmony. Let us just be side by side — helping, respecting, and understanding each other — in common effort to serve humankind. The aim of human society must be the compassionate betterment of human beings.

Politicians and world leaders are trying their best to achieve arms control and so forth, and this is very useful. At the same time, we who have certain beliefs have a duty and responsibility to control our own bad thoughts. This is the real disarmament, our own arms control. With inner peace and full control of bad thoughts, external control is not particularly significant. Without inner control, no matter what steps are taken, external efforts will not make much difference. Therefore, under the present circumstances, we in the religious community have a special responsibility to all humanity — a universal responsibility.

The world situation is such that continent to continent all are heavily dependent on each other, and under such circumstances genuine cooperation is possible. This depends on good motivation. That is our universal responsibility.

Questioner: As a religious leader, are you interested in actively encouraging others to join your faith? Or do you take the position of being available if someone should seek knowledge of your faith?

Dalai Lama: This is an important question. I am not interested in converting other people to Buddhism but in how we Buddhists can contribute to human society, according to our own ideas. I believe that other religious faiths also think in a similar way, seeking to contribute to the common aim.

Because the different religions have at times argued with each other rather than concentrating on how to contribute to a common aim, for the last twenty years in India I have taken every occasion to meet with Christian monks — Catholic and Protestant — as well as Muslims and Jews and, of course in India, many Hindus. We meet, pray together, meditate together, and discuss their philosophical ideas, their way of approach, their techniques. I take great interest in Christian practices, what we can learn and copy from their system. Similarly, in Buddhist theory there may be points such as meditative techniques which can be practiced in the Christian church.

Just as Buddha showed an example of contentment, tolerance, and serving others without selfish motivation, so did Jesus Christ. Almost all of the great teachers lived a saintly life — not luxuriously like kings or emperors but as simple human beings. Their inner strength was tremendous, limitless, but the external appearance was of contentment with a simple way of life.

Questioner: Can there be a synthesis of Buddhism, Judaism, Christianity, Hinduism, and all religions, gathering the best in all and forming a world religion?

Dalai Lama: Forming a new religion is difficult and not particularly desirable. However, in that love is essential to all religions, one could speak of the universal religion of love. As for the techniques and methods for developing love as well as for achieving salvation or permanent liberation, there are many differences between religions. Thus, I do not think we could make one philosophy or one religion.

Furthermore, I think that differences in faith are useful. There is a richness in the fact that there are so many different presentations of the way. Given that there are so many different types of people with various predispositions and inclinations, this is helpful.

At the same time, the motivation of all religious practice is similar — love, sincerity, honesty. The way of life of practically all religious persons is contentment. The teachings of tolerance, love, and compassion are the same. A basic goal is the benefit of humankind — each type of system seeking in its own unique ways to improve human beings. If we put too much emphasis on our own philosophy, religion, or theory, are too attached to it, and try to impose it on other people, it makes trouble. Basically, all the great teachers, such as Gautama Buddha, Jesus Christ, or Mohammed, founded their new teachings with a motivation of helping their fellow humans. They did not mean to gain anything for themselves nor to create more trouble or unrest in the world.

Most important is that we respect each other and learn from each other those things that will enrich our own practice. Even if all the systems are separate, since they each have the same goal, the study of each other is helpful.

Questioner: Sometimes when we hear Eastern religions compared with Western culture, the West is made to seem materialistic and less enlightened than the East. Do you see such a difference?

Dalai Lama: There are two kinds of food — food for mental hunger and food for physical hunger. Thus a combination of these two — material progress and spiritual development is the most practical thing. I think that many Americans, particularly young Americans, realize that material progress alone is not the full answer for human life. Right now all of the Eastern nations are trying to copy Western technology. We Easterners such as Tibetans, like myself, look to Western technology feeling that once we develop material progress, our people can reach some sort of permanent happiness. But when I come to Europe or North America, I see that underneath the beautiful surface there is still unhappiness, mental unrest, and restlessness. This shows that material progress alone is not the full answer for human beings.

THE BODHGAYA INTERVIEWS

From the 1981 Interview

Questioner: Do you see any possibility of an integration of Christianity and Buddhism in the West? An overall religion for Western society?

Dalai Lama: It depends upon what you mean by integration. If you mean by this the possibility of the integration of Buddhism and Christianity within a society, where they co-exist side by side, then I would answer affirmatively. If, however, your view of integration envisions all of society following some sort of composite religion which is neither pure Buddhism nor pure Christianity, then I would have to consider this form of integration implausible.

It is, of course, quite possible for a country to be predominantly Christian, and yet that some of the people of that country choose to follow Buddhism. I think it is quite possible that a person who is basically a Christian, who accepts the idea of God, who believes in God, could at the same time incorporate certain Buddhist ideas and techniques into his/her practice. The teachings of love, compassion, and kindness are present in Christianity and also in Buddhism. Particularly in the Bodhisattva vehicle[3] there are many techniques which focus upon developing compassion, kindness, etc.; these are things which can be practiced at the same time by Christians and by Buddhists. While remaining committed to Christianity it is quite conceivable that a person may choose to undergo training in meditation, concentration, and one-pointedness of mind, that, while remaining a Christian, one may choose to practice Buddhist ideas. This is another possible and very viable kind of integration.

Questioner: Is there any conflict between the Buddhist teachings and the idea of a creator God who exists independently from us?

Dalai Lama: If we view the world's religions from the widest possible viewpoint, and examine their ultimate goal, we find that all of the major world religions, whether Christianity or Islam, Hinduism or Buddhism, are directed to the achievement of permanent human happiness. They are all directed toward that goal. All religions emphasize the fact that the true follower must be honest and gentle, in other words, that a truly religious person must always strive to be a better human being. To this end, the different world religions teach different doctrines which will help transform the person. In this regard, all religions are the same, there is no conflict. This is something we must emphasize. We must consider the question of religious diversity from *this* viewpoint. And when we do, we find no conflict.

Now from the philosophical point of view, the theory that God is the creator, is almighty and permanent, is in contradiction to the Buddhist teachings. From this point of view there is disagreement. For Buddhists, the universe has no first cause and hence no creator, nor can there be such a thing as a permanent, primordially pure being. So, of course, doctrinally, there is conflict. The views are opposite to one another. But if we consider the purpose of these different philosophies, then we see that they are the same. This is my belief.

Different kinds of food have different tastes: one may be very hot, one may be very sour, and one very sweet. They are opposite tastes, they conflict. But whether a dish is concocted to taste sweet, sour or hot, it is nonetheless made in this way so as to taste good. Some people prefer very spicy hot foods with a lot of chili peppers. Many Indians and Tibetans have a liking for such dishes. Others are very fond of bland tasting foods. It is a wonderful thing to have variety. It is an expression of individuality; it is a personal thing.

Likewise, the variety of the different world religious philosophies is a very useful and beautiful thing. For certain people, the idea of God as creator and of everything depending on his will is beneficial and soothing, and so for that person such a doctrine is worthwhile. For someone else, the idea that there is no creator, that ultimately one is oneself the creator — in that everything depends upon oneself is more appropriate. For certain people, it may be a more effective method of spiritual growth, it may be more beneficial. For such persons, this idea is better and for the other type of person, the other idea is more suitable. You see, there is no conflict, no problem. This is my belief.

Now conflicting doctrines are something which is not unknown even within Buddhism itself. The Madhyamikas and Cittamatrins, two Buddhist philosophical subschools,[4] accept the theory of emptiness. The Vaibhashikas and Sautrantikas,[5] two others, accept another theory, the theory of selflessness, which, strictly speaking is not the same as the doctrine of emptiness as posited by the two higher schools. So there exists this difference, some schools accepting the emptiness of phenomena and others not. There also exists a difference as regards the way in which the two upper schools explain the doctrine of emptiness. For the Cittamatrins, emptiness is set forth in terms of the non-duality of subject and object. The Madhyamikas, however, repudiate the notion that emptiness is tantamount to idealism, the claim that everything is of the nature of mind. So you see, even within Buddhism, the Madhyamikas and Cittamatra schools are in conflict. The Madhyamikas are again divided into Prasangikas and Svatantrikas,[6] and between these two subschools there is also conflict. The latter accept that things exist by virtue of an inherent characteristic, while the former do not.

So you see, conflict in the philosophical field is nothing to be surprised at. It exists even within Buddhism itself.

Questioner: It is generally said that teachers of other religions, no matter how great, cannot attain liberation without turning to the Buddhist path. Now suppose there is a great teacher, say he is a Shaivite,[7] and suppose he upholds very strict discipline and is totally dedicated to other people all of the time, always giving of himself. Is this person, simply because he follows Shiva, incapable of attaining liberation, and if so, what can be done to help him?

Dalai Lama: During the Buddha's own time, there were many non-Buddhist teachers whom the Buddha could not help, for whom he could do nothing. So he just let them be.

The Buddha Shakyamuni[8] was an extraordinary being. He was the manifestation (*nirmanakaya*), the phsyical appearance, of an already enlightened being.[9] But while some people recognized him as a Buddha, others regarded him as a black magician with strange and evil powers. So, you see, even the Buddha Shakyamuni himself was not accepted as an enlightened being by all of his contemporaries. Different human beings have different mental predispositions, and there are cases when even the Buddha himself could not do much to overcome these — there was a limit.

Now today, the followers of Shiva have their own religious practices and they reap some benefit from engaging in their own forms of worship. Through this, their life will gradually change. Now my own position on this question is that Shiva-ji's[10] followers should practice according to their own beliefs and traditions, Christians must genuinely and sincerely follow what they believe, and so forth. This is sufficient.

Questioner: But they will not attain liberation!

Dalai Lama: We Buddhists ourselves will not be liberated at once. In our own case it will take time. Gradually we will be able to reach *moksha* or *nirvana*,[11] but the majority of Buddhists will not achieve this within their own lifetimes. So there's no hurry. If Buddhists themselves have to wait, perhaps many lifetimes, for their goal, why should we expect that it be different for non-Buddhists? So, you see, nothing much can be done.

Suppose, for example, you try to convert someone from another religion to the Buddhist religion, and you argue with them trying to convince them of the inferiority of their position. And suppose you do not succeed, suppose they do not become Buddhist. On the one hand, you have failed in your task, and on the other hand, you may have weakened the trust they have in their own religion, so that they may come to doubt their own faith. What have you accomplished by all this? It is of no use. When we come into contact with the followers of different religions, we should not argue. Instead, we should advise them to follow their own beliefs as sincerely and as truthfully as possible. For if they do so, they will no doubt reap certain benefit. Of this there is no doubt. Even in the immediate future they will be able to achieve more happiness and more satisfaction. Do you agree?

This is the way I usually act in such matters, it is my belief. When I meet the followers of different religions, I always praise them, for it is enough, it is sufficient, that they are following the moral teachings that are emphasized in every religion. It is enough, as I mentioned earlier, that they are trying to become better human beings. This in itself is very good and worthy of praise.

Questioner: But is it only the Buddha who can be the ultimate source of refuge?

Dalai Lama: Here, you see, it is necessary to examine what is meant by liberation or salvation. Liberation in which "a mind that understands the sphere of reality annihilates all defilements in the sphere of reality" is a state that only Buddhists can accomplish. This kind of *moksha* or *nirvana* is only explained in the Buddhist scriptures, and is achieved only through Buddhist practice. According to certain religions, however, salvation is a place, a beautiful paradise, like a peaceful valley. To attain such a state as this, to achieve such a state of *moksha*, does not require the practice of emptiness, the understanding of reality. In Buddhism itself, we believe that through the accumulation of merit one can obtain rebirth in heavenly paradises like the Tushita.[12]

Questioner: To what do you attribute the growing fascination in the West, especially in America, with Eastern religions? I include many, many cults and practices which are becoming extremely strong in America. To what do you attribute, in this particular age, the reasons for this fascination, and would you encourage people who are dissatisfied with their own Western way of life, having been brought up in the Mosaic religions (Christianity, Judaism, and Islam), dissatisfied with their lack of spiritual refreshment, would you encourage them to search further in their own religions or to look into Buddhism as an alternative?

Dalai Lama: That's a tricky question. Of course, from the Buddhist viewpoint, we are all human beings and we all have every right to investigate either one's own religion or another religion. This is our right. I think that on the whole a comparative study of different religions is useful.

I generally believe that every major religion has the potential for giving any human being good advice; there is no question that this is so. But we must always keep in mind that different individuals have different mental predispositions. This means that for some individuals one religious system or philosophy will be more suitable than another. The only way one can come to a proper conclusion as to what is most suitable for *oneself* is through comparative study. Hence, we look and study and we find a teaching that is most suitable to our own taste. This, you see, is my feeling.

I cannot advise everyone to practice Buddhism. That I cannot do. Certainly, for some people the Buddhist religion or ideology is most suitable, most effective. But that does not mean it is suitable for *all*.

13

"Self-Awakening and Faith – Zen and Christianity"[1]

MASAO ABE

INTRODUCTION

Masao Abe, perhaps the best known and most prolific expositor of Zen Buddhism to the West since the death of D. T. Suzuki, was professor of philosophy at Nara University of Education from 1952–80 and has since then served on the faculty of the Claremont Graduate School in California and at the University of Hawaii. He studied and practiced Zen as a young man in Japan and has served as visiting professor at a large number of universities in the United States. Abe's thought is influenced by that of the important school of Japanese philosophical thought centered in Kyoto[2]; he offers a philosophical version of Zen Buddhism, insofar as such a thing is possible.

The word Zen *is a Japanese representation of a Chinese term* Ch'an, *which in turn represents the sound of a Sanskrit word* dhyana. *The word means, roughly, "meditation," and meditational practice is absolutely central to Zen. In some of its forms it claims for itself a direct wordless transmission of truth from awakened sage to awakened sage, a transmission independent of Buddhist sacred texts (*sutra*) – and indeed of anything to do with words. The aim of Zen practice – though it is improper to make a separation between the practice and its aim, for the practice* is *the aim – is to attain a direct nonverbal apprehension of the way things really are, and so to liberate oneself from attachment, desire, and suffering.*[3]

The piece reprinted here was originally delivered as a lecture at a seminar on Zen Buddhism for Christian missionaries in Kyoto, Japan, in September 1974. Excerpts from the discussion between Abe and the participants are also included. In the lecture, Abe points to three basic contrasts between Zen Buddhism and Christianity. The first is that between God and Nothingness; for Abe,

171

Nothingness⁴ denotes not simply nothing, but rather the radical interdependence of all things. The contrast with God, understood as the independent source of everything other than God, is very clear.

The second contrast is between faith and enlightenment. Faith, according to Abe, is other-directed, while enlightenment is self-produced, being simply a recognition of what one already is. Abe doubts that faith, in the Christian sense, is radical enough to produce salvation: "Man's finitude is so deep and so radical that it cannot even be overcome by faith, not even through the work of the divine other power. Hence the need for the realization of absolute Nothingness." This second contrast then entails the third, that between salvation and self-awakening. Self-awakening is a present reality that only needs to be acknowledged and realized; the Christian striving for salvation and the overcoming of good by evil is, from Abe's perspective, rooted necessarily and irredeemably in dualism.

Some of these contrasts are taken up and developed in the discussion between Professor Abe and the participants in the seminar. I give an edited version of this discussion in the version reprinted here. It will suffice to note at this point that Abe's presentation of Christianity is a common Buddhist one. Christianity is seen as a metaphysical dualism whose toils make true liberation and enlightenment impossible, even while they may be of some preliminary and provisional use for those not yet sufficiently advanced for Zen practice. This, I think, is the upshot of Abe's affirmation of Christianity's axiology (theory of value) and its ethic, but his rejection of its ontology.

"SELF-AWAKENING AND FAITH – ZEN AND CHRISTIANITY"

The dialogue between Zen and Christianity has been becoming more serious and important during the past decade or so. Those of us involved in it are pleased with this development because we maintain that such a dialogue is necessary for the development of mutual understanding between East and West.

To make this sort of dialogue effective and fruitful, we have to be very frank and open, as well as sincere. To be frank, I find it necessary to clarify the difference rather than the affinity between Christianity and Zen. Of course it is necessary for such a dialogue to elucidate both affinities and differences between the two religions. It is rather easy to point out the affinity between Christianity and Zen, because both of them are equally, in their essence, religions. So, naturally, there are some kinds of similarity. However, the emphasis on similarity, although important, does not necessarily create something new. On the other hand, an attempt to disclose the differences, if properly and relevantly done, promotes and stimulates mutual understanding and inspires both religions to seek further inner development of themselves. I hope my emphasis on differences in this talk is not understood as a rejection or exclusion of Christianity from a Zen point of view, or as a presumption of the superiority of Zen to Christianity.

My point is to reach a real and creative mutual understanding. My understanding of Christianity is, however, insufficient and limited, so I hope you will correct me later, my discussion being completely open to your criticism.

To simplify the point to be discussed in connection with the theme, "Self-Awakening and Faith — Zen and Christianity," I will try to contrast some central motifs in Zen and Christianity: the difference between Christianity and Zen could be formulated in the contrasts of God — Nothingness, Faith — Enlightenment, Salvation — Self-Awakening.

A Zen master once said, "There is one word I do not like to hear, that is 'Buddha.'" Rinzai, a Chinese Zen master of the T'ang Dynasty (618–907) said, "Encountering a Buddha, kill the Buddha. Encountering a patriarch, kill the patriarch . . . only thus does one attain liberation and detachment from all things, thereby becoming completely unfettered and free." As you can understand from these words, Zen rejects or denies the idea of Buddha and emphasizes the idea of no-Buddha or non-Buddha. So, in that sense, Zen is not theistic but atheistic.

One of the well-known utterances of Zen is this: "When all things are reduced to the one, where is that one to be reduced?" Zen does not end with that one, which is beyond any particular and transcends any form of duality. Rather, Zen starts with the question: Where is that one to be reduced? It emphasizes the necessity of abandoning even the one. Zen transcends not only dualism but also monism and monotheism. It is essential "not to maintain even the one." To go beyond the absolute means to go to Nothingness. The absolute oneness must be turned into absolute Nothingness.

This realization of absolute Nothingness is in Zen the realization of one's true Self. For the realization of absolute Nothingness opens up the deepest ground of one's Subjectivity which is beyond every form of subject-object duality, including the so-called divine-human relationship. Enlightenment takes place only through the realization of absolute Nothingness which is beyond every form of duality. This is not faith in the divine mercy nor salvation by a divine other power, but Self-Awakening — the Self-Awakening of true Self. In the realization of Absolute Nothingness, the true Self awakens to itself. This Self-Awakening is not something to be sought for sometime in the future or somewhere outside yourself, but it is originally and already realized in yourself, here and now. If enlightenment is something to be sought for somewhere outside yourself or in the future, that so-called enlightenment will not be true. It is not absolute Nothingness, but rather a sort of somethingness which would be realized beyond the present *now* and outside the *here*. So Zen always emphasizes that you are originally in enlightenment. You are already inseparable from Self-Awakening.

On the other hand, if I am not wrong, the affirmation of the absolute oneness of God is taken for granted in Christian thinking. When a scribe wanted to know if Jesus was in agreement with the Biblical tradition, he tempted him by asking about the greatest commandment in the Law. Jesus answered by quoting the Old Testament passage about loving God with all the heart, soul and mind, mentioning the classical Biblical confession: "Hear, O Israel, the Lord our God, the Lord is one" (Mark 12:29). The scribe then said to him, "You are right, teacher, you have truly said that he is one and there is no other but he" (Mark 12:32). In Christianity God is the one and only living God. He is father, creator, judge and ruler of the universe and of history.

Why does Zen not accept the only and absolute one and instead emphasize Noth-ngness? What is the doctrinal background for Zen's emphasis of *Mu*, absolute Nothingness? As you know, one of the most basic ideas of Buddhism is expressed in the Sanskrit term *pratitya-samutpada*, which we call *engi* in Japanese. It is translated in various ways, as "dependent co-origination," "relationality," "relativity," "dependent co-arising," "interdependent causation," etc. The Buddhist idea of *engi*, dependent origination, indicates that everything without exception is dependent on something else. Nothing whatsoever is independent or self-existing. This idea is generally expressed by the formulation, "When this exists, that comes to be. When this does not exist, that does not exist. When this is destroyed, that is destroyed." In this formulation, "this" and "that" are completely interchangeable and are mutually dependent on each other. This idea must be applied to things not only in the universe but also beyond the universe. It applies also to the relation between immanence and transcendence, between the human and the divine.

Christianity teaches that all men are equal before God. So they should all be relative and interdependent. But God is not dependent upon man, while man definitely is dependent upon God. We can therefore say with full justification that when God exists, the world comes into existence. When God does not exist, the world will not exist. However, is it possible to say that when the world exists, God comes into being? Or, when the world does not exist, God does not exist? At least the last statement is impossible in Christian thinking. The world cannot exist without God, but God can exist without the world. Because God is the self-existing deity, God can or does exist by himself without depending on anything else.

Against this basic Christian standpoint, Zen may raise the question: How is God's self-existence possible? What is the *ground* of God's self-existence? God said to Moses, "I am that I am." Theologians . . . have said that the Hebrew word *hayah*, which is the root of *ehyeh* (I am), does not simply mean to *be*, but to *become*, to *work* and to *happen*. So in God, his being is his action and vice versa. This dynamic character of God's being stresses his independence. His being is not to be understood in terms of dependent origination.

From a Buddhist point of view this idea of a self-sustaining God is ultimately inadequate, for Buddhists cannot see the ontological ground of this one and self-sustaining God. This is the reason why the Buddha rejected the traditional Upanishadic view of Brahman as the ultimate power of the universe and proclaimed that everything without exception is transitory and perishable, nothing being unchangeable and eternal. The idea that everything is transitory is inseparably connected to the idea of interdependent co-origination. So again, from this point of view we have to ask: What is the *ground* of the one God? How can we accept the one God as the ruler of the universe and history? The Christian might answer this question by stressing the importance of faith in God, this faith being nothing but the "assurance of things hoped for, the conviction of things not seen" (Hebrews 11:1).

Before discussing the concept of faith, however, I must return to the Christian concept of God. If I am not wrong, the truth that God is a *living* God is more evident in Christianity than that he is the *one* true God. Being a living and personal God, he calls men through his word, and man must respond to his word. Hence the I-thou relationship between man and God.

In Jesus Christ, this I-thou relationship is most deeply and significantly actualized. Jesus is the mediator between man and God. He has the nature of *homooūsios*, consubstantiality, in which the immanence and transcendence are paradoxically one. Thus, Jesus Christ may be said to be a symbol of the Buddhist idea of relationality or interdependent causation. With full justification Buddhists regard Jesus as a Buddha or as an Awakened one. The new life through death is clearly realized in him.

However, the Christian idea of the I-thou relationship in terms of faith, although interdependent and relational, is not completely reciprocal. Having faith in Jesus Christ, the Christian believes that if we die with him, we shall also live with him. So the Christian *participates* in the death and resurrection of Jesus Christ. He is the savior and we are the saved; he is the redeemer and we are the redeemed, not vice versa.

In faith Jesus Christ and I are, ultimately speaking, not in the relationship of interdependent causation. This is the case because man's finitude, that is his sinfulness, is deeply and keenly realized in Christianity. The faith in Jesus Christ is inseparably connected to the realization of man's sinfulness. Death is for the Christian nothing but "the wage of sin." From this Christian point of view, I am afraid that the Zen expression, "Encountering a Buddha, kill the Buddha. . . . Only thus does one attain liberation," may sound blasphemous. The Zen saying that man is originally a Buddha and an Enlightened one, may sound arrogant or self-deceptive. And the Buddhist realization of man's finitude merely in terms of transiency may appear quite insufficient.

Frankly speaking, however, from the Zen point of view, the Christian realization of man's finitude in terms of sinfulness, and consequently, the idea of salvation through Jesus Christ, does not seem thoroughgoing enough to reach the ultimate Reality. Can man's finitude in terms of sinfulness be fully overcome through faith? What is the ground of this faith and hope in which our death and sin can be redeemed? Is man's finitude the kind of finitude which can be overcome by faith? These questions imply that for

Zen, man's finitude is so deep and so radical that it cannot even be overcome by faith, not even through the work of the divine other power. Hence the need for the realization of absolute Nothingness.

Let me develop this question by considering the question of good and evil. In Buddhism in general, and Zen in particular, good and evil are, like every other thing, interdependently originated. There is no good without evil and vice versa. How is it possible that good can stand without evil? Good and evil are in Buddhism entirely interdependently originated. There is no priority of one over the other.

Questioner: If you are born in enlightenment, is not that in itself a priority of good over evil?

Abe: Enlightenment is not something good in the relative sense, as distinguished from evil. Enlightenment is the realization of my being prior to the duality of good and evil.

Questioner: But that realization in itself is good, or are we talking in different terms?

Abe: When you say that realization in itself is good, from which point of view are you so doing? I am afraid you are from the outset talking about good and evil from the dualistic point of view. Good has no priority over evil. The priority of good over evil is an ethical imperative but not an actual human situation. In human beings good and evil have equal power: I cannot say that my good is stronger than my evil although I should try to overcome my evil by my good. The Buddhist shares the Pauline thought that the more we try to do good, the more we become aware of evil in ourselves. This dilemma between good and evil in our being is so deep that it cannot be solved by the power of good. In faith in God as the Supreme Good, the dilemma is believed to be solved in the future in the form of hope. This is not, however, a complete solution of the dilemma *at the present*, but a pushing away of the solution into the eternal future. The dilemma of good and evil is so radical that there is no way for us to escape it even in the future. It is not that I *have* a dilemma between good and evil, but that I *am* that dilemma. It is not that I *have* an aporia, but that I *am* an aporia in this sense. In the final and deepest realization of the dilemma between good and evil, the structure of my ego collapses and I come to the realization that I am not simply good, or simply bad. I am neither good nor bad. I am nothing whatsoever. However, this realization is not negative but positive, because in the full realization of Nothingness we are liberated from the dichotomy of good and evil, life and death. At that point we awaken to our true nature prior to dualistic consciousness. That is the reason why Zen often asks us to see our "original face" as it is prior to any distinction between good and evil. Enlightenment is precisely to see one's "original face."

To return to my discussion. Practically speaking, I have no way to overcome evil by the power of good. This applies to not only the non-religious humanistic dimension, but also to the transcendental religious dimension. The reason that the dilemma between good and evil is so deep and thoroughgoing is because good and evil are interdependently originated, negating each other with equal power. Therefore, it cannot be overcome even through faith in God who is absolutely good. If God is absolutely good, what is the origin of the evil in man and in the world?

Tillich said, "In God evil is conquered not by being annihilated, but by not being actualized. It is actualized in the finite world, but not in the infinite ground of being, i.e., God."*[5] This means that the actuality of evil is never in God, but evil is left as a potentiality in God. I think this is to be regarded as a sort of theodicy regarding the origin of evil. God created everything but he is not responsible for the actuality of evil. Thus, the dichotomy between good and evil can be solved in Christianity by saying that in eternity evil is conquered by being reduced to mere potentiality. I am afraid this Christian view may be that of a false endlessness. The problem of evil is moved from actuality to potentiality, from time to eternity, but without a definitive solution.

The point in which you are not limited by the duality of good and evil can be realized in yourself *right here* and *right now*, through the realization that you *are* the dilemma of good and evil. Once you thoroughly realize that you *are* the dilemma of good and evil you can break through this dilemma and come to a standpoint which is neither good nor evil. Thus, from the Zen point of view, the essential point is not faith in God, but realization of Nothingness and awakening to one's true nature. This is the inevitable conclusion of the Buddhist idea of dependent co-origination. Not only good and evil, but life and death, God and man, are interdependent. Therefore Buddha, when understood as something beyond man, must be killed to realize our own true nature and to attain Self-Awakening.

Though contrasting Zen and Christianity, I want to stress that it is an oversimplification to say that Zen is based on Nothingness, while Christianity is based on God as Being, in contrast to non-being. If this were the case, Zen and Christianity would be entirely without any correspondence.

According to my understanding, when Christianity emphasizes the one God who is the ruler of the universe and of history, who is the absolute good and eternal life, who can overcome death and evil, etc., this is not simply an ontological issue, but rather an *axiological* issue.[6] In Christianity the most significant point is not the issue of being and non-being, but the question of what I as a human being ought to do. The idea of righteousness is very important, although righteousness must be fulfilled as an aspect of love. The Christian idea of love always includes the idea of justice. Without justice, there is no real love. In that sense the "ought" or "divine imperative" is important. When Christians confess God as the one, self-existing God, it is not primarily because He is the only divine Being, but because He is the personal God who rules the whole universe and calls for man's response to His commandments. The idea of justice represented by the "ought" is rather lacking, or at least very weak in Buddhism, particularly in Zen, while the idea of being and non-being, life and death, is very strong.

The Christian idea of the one God should not be understood merely ontologically, but also axiologically. The Christian faith in the one God is more concerned with justice and love than the ontological questions of God's being. In that sense Zen's criticism of the Christian view of the one God, based upon the Buddhist idea of dependent co-origination, does not necessarily hit the core of, or do justice to, the essence of Christianity.

Both in Zen and Christianity ontological and axiological aspects are inseparably connected. But in Zen the ontological aspect, the question of being and non-being, life and death, is much more central than the issue of good and evil. On the other hand, in Christianity the issue of good and evil is much more strongly emphasized than the question of being and non-being.

So we may try to draw the lines from Zen and its ontological under-standing of Nothingness to the Christian faith with its axiological emphasis on God's "ought" and find the crossing point.

The strength in Zen is the weakness in Christianity and vice versa. Based on this recognition of these mutual strengths and weaknesses, we must enter into dialogue.

Questioner: In my reading and study of Buddhism, what has always puzzled me and still puzzles me is the concept of Nothingness. As you said in your lecture, "The realization of one's Nothingness is the realization of one's True Self," and "I am nothing whatsoever." If that is true, both in the ontological and in the actual sphere of life, what is the use of talking? What are we doing in this life if we are absolutely nothing? And how can we do something to improve the society which is also nothing?

Abe: Do you think that the self is something?

Questioner: We have to realize the absolute nothingness in order to realize our own true Self, as you said. That means that I am absolutely nothing. If that is true, what are we doing here in this world, both in the ontological and actual sphere of life? What is the meaning of our life personally — if we *are* persons? What can we do for society — *if* society exists?

Abe: My counterquestion is this: do you think that the human self is something?

Questioner: I think so, Professor, I do!
Abe: What is it who thinks of yourself as something?

Questioner: My consciousness of being something, a somebody. And I believe that people around me are real people, that this house is a real thing, that the universe is a real thing. I am conscious of that in my mind.
Abe: What is it that has such consciousness?

Questioner: The human being.
Abe: Human being in general?

Questioner: Each human being! It is difficult to say if it is up here in the head or in the heart—I don't know. But as a human being I have that consciousness.
Abe: Who is talking about "I" as a human being—what has that consciousness?

Questioner: My own consciousness of myself and of the relationship to each other.
Abe: I am afraid you always objectify yourself when you talk about yourself or your own consciousness. Whenever I ask you "What is it that is so talking?" you say that it is your consciousness, it is your own consciousness of yourself, your personality, or so on. Thus you objectify your own consciousness, your own existence, your own self, and in that way *you yourself* move back step by step. When you answered my questions in that way, you were always regressing, trying to present something more inner including your "self." However, your *true* "Self" can never be presented in that way because it is always standing "behind" your presentation, "behind" your regression.

You may, of course, objectify your "self." An objectified self, however, is not the true Self. The true Self must be the true Subjectivity which is beyond objectification. The "Self" is the unobjectifiable. As soon as the self is objectified it becomes "something." However, the true Self, as the unobjectifiable, is not "anything" whatsoever, but "nothing" in the sense that it is beyond objectification. And "Nothingness" in this sense is not simply negative but rather positive, because it indicates one's true Subjectivity as the root source of one's activity of objectification.

Questioner: Can we say that the concept of Nothingness is in some way positive?
Abe: Yes, the Buddhist idea of Nothingness is a positive and dynamic idea. It is *neither* somethingness *nor* nothingness, yet it includes both. It is

the dynamic whole which attaches itself to neither. There is nothing outside Nothingness. You and I and everything else are included without losing our particularity in the dynamic structure of this *positive* Nothingness.

Questioner: Is Nothingness the ultimate in the same way as we talk about God as the ultimate? This seems to be founded on a sort of belief. How can you say that there is not an equivalent somethingness related to Nothingness, just as in the relation between good and evil? Why is Nothingness unrelated?

Abe: Good and evil are completely interdependent. There is no good without evil and vice versa. There is no nothingness without somethingness and vice versa. Yet good and evil, nothingness and somethingness, are principles contrary to one another. They are negating one another and yet are inseparably connected with one another. At the extreme limit of opposition they turn into a single mass, becoming a serious contradiction. This is the most critical issue for man. As I said: it is not I that *have* a dilemma, but I *am* a dilemma. When we come to the point of *total* realization of this existential dilemma, it is overcome from within. And I come to the point where there is neither good nor evil, neither life nor death, neither nothingness nor somethingness. This is the root and source for good and evil, life and death, etc. This is the existential ground for life and activity, in which we can work without being limited by any kind of duality. This is freedom. Nothingness related to somethingness does not indicate freedom or openness just as good related to evil does not. Freedom is fully realized by going beyond the duality of somethingness and nothingness, good and evil, and so forth. This is why the Buddhist Nothingness is beyond both somethingness and nothingness. . . . In the beginning of my lecture I said that the emphasis on similarity of the two religions [i.e., Buddhism and Christianity], though necessary, is not sufficient to develop a creative dialogue. My emphasis on difference does not intend to judge which one is better. I would like to reach a deeper and more creative understanding beyond the essential differences. So we should not overlook even subtle differences. Speaking from the Zen point of view, Zen must raise the question: what is the ground of the one God; what is the ground of faith in God? This Zen question will not destroy but rather deepen the Christian faith in God. However, it is more ontologically oriented than the Christian action-oriented understanding of God's Being. Christianity is justified in its idea of the one God in the sense that He is the living personal God with ethical character who justifies man in spite of his sinfulness through unconditional love. Zen must learn more about this ground of the Christian faith in God.

14

"Scholastic Philosophy and Modern Civilization"[1]

DAISAKU IKEDA

INTRODUCTION

Daisaku Ikeda was born in 1928, became the third president of the Soka Gakkai ("Value-Creating Society") in 1960, and served in that office until 1979. Since then he has been honorary president. The Soka Gakkai is perhaps the largest and most influential of Japan's twentieth-century new religious movements. It looks to Nichiren Daishonin (1222–82) for its basic ideas, and sees itself as a vehicle for spreading Nichiren's teachings. Nichiren's teaching, revolutionary for thirteenth-century Japan, emphasized the chanting of an invocation of praise and homage to a Buddhist text, the Lotus Sutra.[2] *The Soka Gakkai has continued this, developed it philosophically, and applied it both religiously and politically.*[3]

The address reprinted here was given at the Soka University on the occasion of the Second Takiyama Festival in July 1973. In it, Ikeda reveals a fairly intimate knowledge of the development of Christian Scholastic thought in medieval Europe. He sketches the history of this thought with respect, and tries to show that the philosophico-theological synthesis of the medieval thinkers was a key factor in the development of modern European thought and civilization and was a bearer of culture in the fullest sense of that term.

Significantly — and here he echoes themes found in at least two of our Islamic critics of Christianity (see Chapters 5 and 8) — Ikeda points to what he sees as the separation of faith and reason that began to take place during this period. Although he is much less explicit and much less harsh than our Islamic thinkers, it would not be inaccurate, I think, to say that Ikeda shares their negative evaluation of the intellectual developments that grew from this medieval dichotomy.

He also thinks (this is very evident toward the end of the address reproduced here) that modern Christianity, the inheritor of the intellectual legacy of medieval Scholasticism, carries no hope for the future of the human race. That hope is located elsewehere, in the Soka Gakkai itself; it is to this that Ikeda refers in the closing paragraphs of his address. It should not be forgotten that the Soka Gakkai is an aggressively missionary movement; from the viewpoint of its honorary president it is scarcely surprising that Christianity should be perceived as a phenomenon of considerable historical significance but no real religious vitality. This perception may, in turn, be linked to the history of Christianity in Japan.

"SCHOLASTIC PHILOSOPHY AND MODERN CIVILIZATION"

In the remarks I delivered concerning the origin of Soka University at the opening ceremonies on April 9, I touched on the spirit of the Renaissance, from which modern civilization grew. I explained how the startling flowering of the Renaissance was not the result of the sudden mutation, but was the outcome of the inevitable tide of the times and of constant, inconspicuous, upward human strivings over a long preceding period. Further, I said that the buds from which this flowering developed had already started growing in the winter of the Middle Ages, or the Dark Ages, as they are often called.

At present, the trees around this university are gleaming with new green leaves. The buds from which those leaves grew did not suddenly develop in the springtime. Preparations for them were steadily being made during the severe cold of winter. The true origin of budding takes place in the winter, but the trees put forth their misty, fresh greenery only in the spring. Something very similar can be said about human life. The inconspicuous daily efforts all of us are making now, during the early period of the growth of this university, as well as our many trials and errors, are preparations for a brilliant future flowering of world culture.

Scholastic philosophy is often thought of as verdureless. Today, I should like to shed some light on that philosophy, in order to show that it, too, represents a period in which a persistent process of budding was taking place for the sake of the civilization of the succeeding age. I want to do this, because a sure understanding of the facts of the vivid transitions in the history of the past is the key to the history of the future.

Birth and Background of Scholastic Philosophy

Scholasticism is a general term for the philosophy that flourished in Europe during the twelfth and thirteenth centuries. The word *schola*, which refers to the schools attached to the monasteries of the time is, as you all know, the source of the English word "school." Often considered no more than an official philosophy, Scholasticism is sometimes called the handmaiden of theology, because it advocated the authority of Christian doctrines. Undeniably, philosophers and thinkers known by the name "scholastics" strove to justify faith in the teachings of the Bible.

For this reason, European medieval philosophy in general, including Scholasticism, has come to be regarded as a dark valley between the brilliant peaks of Greece and Rome and the equally brilliant mountain range of the Renaissance. This interpretation has been advanced by modern rationalist philosophers, but is it correct? Now that modern rationalism has reached an impasse, as we enter a new age, what evaluation should we make of Scholasticism? Answering this question is the main theme of my talk today.

First we must take into consideration the conditions of the age and society in which Scholasticism was born and cultivated. European medieval philosophy can be divided into two main stages. The initial stage, which lasted from the first century of the Christian era until the eighth and ninth centuries, was patristic philosophy, named in honor of the Church Fathers, who wrote works explaining the teachings of Christianity.

Christianity first spread throughout the Roman Empire. After the collapse of that empire, it spread to the world of the Germanic tribes, who were then making their first major appearance on the stage of history. In other words, in this early period, the Church was in an active missionary phase. The primary duty of the Church Fathers, the nucleus of the missionary activity, was to systematize the teachings of Christianity and find a way to adapt them to the traditional ways of thinking of the Romans and the Germanic tribes. Consequently, during this stage, establishment of all-pervading faith was emphasized. Some of the outstanding Church Fathers include Justin, Tertullian, Origen, and Saint Augustine, who was famous as a universal philosopher.[4] In the well-known phrase that is considered to be a summary of Tertullian's philosophy—"It is impossible, therefore I believe"[5]—it is possible to see a crystallization of patristic philosophy as the advocate of absolute faith.

In *The City of God*, Saint Augustine laid an ideological foundation for the system of rule of the Catholic Church by teaching that, as the City of God made manifest on earth, it would continue eternally, even after the fall of Rome, the City of Man.

The age of patristic philosophy came to a close when Christianity was firmly established throughout Europe. The period between the ninth century and the Renaissance was the age of Scholasticism. The causes for the emergence of this philosophy must be analyzed from many angles; but some important elements can be stated simply: unification of Germanic society under Charlemagne, withdrawal of the forces of Islam, the Carolingian renaissance, and what today is called the rise of the arts and learning. The church and monastery schools that I mentioned earlier as the *schola* were instituted with the encouragement of Charlemagne.

When the age of missionary activity and development was over, with the opportunities presented by the flourishing of art and letters, a deepening and a formalizing of the doctrines of Christianity were required. Augustine and others of the Fathers had already perfected the basic doctrines. The problems in this later period were to prove them, to order them in relation to each other, and to systematize them.

Medieval Europe inherited the seven liberal arts—grammar, rhetoric, dialectic, arithmetic, geometry, astronomy, and music—from ancient Greece and Rome. The problem that scholars faced in the period before the Renaissance was to connect those seven arts with theology. The great influence exerted by Aristotelian philosophy by way of contacts with Islamic society made it essential to touch not only on individual sciences but also on basic human issues, such as the relationships between reason and the revelations of the Bible, between intellect and faith, and between philosophy and theology.

Separation of Intellect and Reason from Faith

Outstanding figures in the Scholastic movement were John Scotus Erigena, in the ninth century; Saint Anselm and Saint Abelard, in the eleventh century; Albertus Magnus, Thomas Aquinas, and Duns Scotus, from the end of the twelfth to the thirteenth century; and Roger Bacon, a forerunner of modern natural science. I do not intend to cover today the major aspects of the history of this philosophy, one by one, for the entire four centuries. I shall, however, abstract a few basic issues and, with the addition of some reflections, examine the general current of development from a modern viewpoint.

Erigena, who was born in Ireland and who spent his active life in Paris, is called either the First Father of Scholasticism or the Charlemagne of Scholasticism, because he laid the foundation for European medieval Scholastic philosophy just as the great emperor laid the foundations for medieval politics.

Erigena's philosophical basis is summed up in this proposition: True religion is true philosophy; at the same time, true philosophy is true religion; consequently, philosophy rejects skepticism in relation to religion. This proposition certainly holds true in the case of Buddhism. The major Scholastic conviction of the oneness of religion and philosophy and of faith and reason and the desire to prove that conviction are clearly revealed in the intention expressed in Erigena's proposition.

It must be recognized that, from its inception, Scholastic philosophy was seriously restricted by the need to provide intellectual and rational verification for faith; that is, it was indeed a handmaiden to theology. The absoluteness of faith was a major premise for all of the Scholastic philosophers, including Anselm, who said, "I believe because I do not know."

Thomas Aquinas and Duns Scotus

Nonetheless, subtle shifts in nuance occurred with the passing of time. For instance, Thomas Aquinas said: "Faith, within the limits apprehensible by reason, ought to be in concordance with theology. But, not all of the sphere of faith is necessarily acknowledged by reason. Therefore, in the area where reason cannot reach, truth can only be grasped by faith." His position, a subtle swing from the standpoint initially adopted by Scholasticism — that faith and reason are one — can be interpreted as a slight step in the direction of skepticism toward Christianity.

By the time of Duns Scotus, we have already reached a clear separation between reason and faith. He said: "Nothing restrains the Divine Will. It is free. It is something transcending reason. Reason, therefore, can neither perceive it nor discover its foundations. Theology is not a thing of reason but is solely a thing of action."

Though the process of change did not shake the faith of the Scholastic philosophers, it did impart to reason a special position, in which it was free of bondage to faith and theological doctrines. As a result of reason — once it had been placed in this new position — modern philosophy developed, learning flowered, and, as a consequence of learning, contradictions in the doctrines of the church were exposed. This shook the very teachings themselves; and, in this sense, the germination of the modern age and the modern world was gradually being accomplished within Scholastic philosophy.

The Middle Ages and Their Distinctive Culture

This discussion shows that it is possible to interpret Scholastic philosophy as more than the handmaiden of theology and the symbol of the Dark Ages: it can be seen as the point of origin of the modern world. But still deeper inquiry shows that, in this very trait, Scholasticism represents an illustrious period in which a great culture glowed.

As I have mentioned, it is the modern rationalist philosophers who describe the European Middle Ages as a time of darkness between the ancient and the modern periods. But this is an inappropriate description, since the Middle Ages produced a distinctive culture, in no way inferior to the cultures of the ancient and modern worlds. Essentially, it is in this culture that I see the germination of the modern world.

Stressing this point makes it possible to interpret modern civilization as a period of latter-day confusion and dehumanization caused by the decline of medieval Christian civilization.

In the truest meaning, the European Dark Ages lasted from the first century and the fall of the Roman Empire until the ninth or tenth century.[6] During this time, the great Germanic migrations took place, social law and order were destroyed, and commerce came to a halt. An age that is forced to undergo constant pillage and slaughter can truly be called dark. But from the ninth into the tenth century, social stability was achieved, people applied themselves diligently to productive activities, and the trend toward creating a new culture began to gain impetus. All of this was greeted by the age of Scholastic philosophy.

The churches and cathedrals that survive in many European towns and cities today were built or begun in the age of Scholasticism. Great memorials to the civilization of the Middle Ages, such works of Gothic architecture as Notre Dame, Chartres, and the Cologne Cathedral, were not built by political authority. Instead, they were the outcome of the application of the techniques and wealth assembled and put to use by religious faith.

Moreover, these buildings remain today as symbols of European cities, the history of the peoples, and European civilization in general. In Paris, any number of buildings as noteworthy as Notre Dame from an architectural point of view could be cited — the Louvre, the Arc de Triomphe, the Eiffel Tower, and so on. But these are only remnants of the glory of monarchs or of people of the privileged classes. As a crystallization of a culture, supported by the hearts and minds of the ordinary citizenry, they cannot approach Notre Dame in importance.

Just as the cathedrals, soaring examples of Gothic architecture, are physical symbols of the flourishing culture of the Middle Ages, so Scholasticism itself symbolizes the elevated spirit of that same period. The flourishing of learning gave birth to numerous such centers of education as those in Paris, Bologna, Oxford, and Cambridge, where teachers and students gathered to form universities. Indeed, the university of today is a heritage from the age of Scholasticism.

The things studied by the Scholastic philosophers — and of course taught in the universities — seem somewhat naive and mistaken in the light of modern knowledge. For instance, the scholastics believed that knowledge is not something gained from observation but something written down by such ancient philosophers as Plato, Aristotle, and Euclid. Scholastic scholars engaged in subtle demonstrations for the sake of systematizing knowledge, proving doctrines of theology, and organizing what they knew. For this reason, they earned the name "followers of the complicated philosophy." Nonetheless, even when these faults are admitted, we cannot fail to recognize the important contributions that Scholasticism made on a more fundamental level.

Contributions of Scholastic Philosophy

First and most important is Scholasticism's clear guide to human behavior in life. This guide was drawn up on the basis of a complete comprehensive world view. The Spanish philosopher Ortega y Gasset,[7] in his book *Mission of the University*, refers to this point in a most interesting way. "What is called 'general culture' today was something very different in the Middle Ages. It was not an ornament for the mind or mere character training. It was, on the contrary, the system of ideas, concerning the world and humanity, which man at that time possessed. It was, consequently, a repertory of convictions which became an effective guide for his existence."

Although this passage deals with general culture in university education, its significance goes beyond college courses, for it is an important pronouncement on the basic nature of the kind of culture that human beings ought to possess. At present, what is called culture has a very vague content and is what Ortega y Gasset calls an "ornament for the mind" or at best "character training." True culture, however, is a "system of ideas concerning the world and man" (or human existence) that enables a person to guide himself from within.

In another passage, Ortega y Gasset says, "Life is chaos, a tangled and confused jungle in which man is lost. But his mind reacts against the sensation of bewilderment: he labors to find 'roads,' 'ways' through the woods, in the form of clear, firm ideas concerning the universe, positive convictions about the nature of things. The ensemble, or system, of these ideas is culture in the true sense of that term; it is precisely the opposite of external ornament. Culture is what saves human life from being a mere disaster; it is what enables man to live a life which is something above meaningless tragedy or inward disgrace."

In the Middle Ages, Scholasticism was the source of this kind of culture. Earlier I said that one of the significances of Scholasticism was the preparations it made for the development of learning in the modern world. But I call Scholasticism a peak of the civilization of the Middle Ages not for this reason alone but also because it was the source of the kind of culture described by Ortega y Gasset. Although the role it plays in preparing for the succeeding age is an important part of the contribution of a culture, I believe what it does for the people of its own time and for their improvement is more important still.

Of course, Scholasticism did not deliberately deal with questions of humanity and its improvement. As I said at the opening of my talk, its real aims were to endorse faith by means of reason, to unify the branches of learning under theology, and in this way to strengthen the authority of the Christian faith and the doctrines of the Church. In effect, however, what Scholasticism did was to fuse Hebraism and Hellenism, which Europe had inherited separately from the ancient world; incarnate them in itself; and thus forge a true Europe and a truly European view of humanity.

A Prototype of European Civilization

In terms of cultural history, Scholasticism played an important part in marking the decisive epoch of transition from a Mediterranean to a European culture. Of course, the political, economic, and industrial conditions for this change had been in preparation earlier. In the vital spiritual and intellectual fields, however, it was during the age of Scholasticism that

Europe broke away from dependence on Mediterranean civilization.

From the time of its origin until the eighth or ninth century, Christianity's major stage of activity was the ancient world around the Mediterranean. The centers of primitive and early Christianity were Alexandria, Cappadocia, and Rome. Saint Augustine was born and was active in Hippo, in Numidia, which is now part of Algeria.

The expansion of the field of authority of Islam in the seventh and eighth centuries put an end to the cultural supremacy of Mediterranean civilization. The followers of Islam seized control of the Mediterranean Sea, and Christianity was shut up within the continent of Europe itself. Later, Charlemagne effected unification of the Germanic world, and even though the area broke up politically after his death, it continued to move in the direction of cultural unity.

Through many vicissitudes, including the Renaissance, the Reformation, and modern nationalism, European civilization has developed and disseminated itself throughout the world to become what can be called the civilization of today. Essentially, it was completed in the twelfth or thirteenth century in the age of Scholasticism, which is the basic spiritual prototype of modern European civilization. Further, the continued fundamental importance to learning of such places as Paris, Oxford, and Cambridge — all centers of Scholastic study — indicates that the original spiritual current of that philosophy continues to flow.

The long series of historical developments that began with Scholasticism has produced some gross, disfigured, and ugly forms and now faces a tragic ending. The loss of humanity and the distortions of civilization symbolized by environmental pollution are obvious to all. The university, once a source of cultural creative energy, is at the brink of destruction. It is no exaggeration to say that the traditional university is about to lose its position of leadership as a place of learning and human development.

At this passing of an old age and the opening of a new one, a novel university is needed. Perhaps the form of the university is of secondary importance. The vital thing is that it represents a new philosophy, the flourishing of a modern Scholasticism in the best sense. Such a new philosophy of human revival is one that is based on true religion and centered on true faith, one that unites all fields of learning, reason, emotion, desire, and impulse and puts each in its proper place. We must build a true culture that will clarify man's place in universal life and blaze a trail to show man how to live in the dense, chaotic forest of today.

Forming such a university is equivalent to bringing together human beings determined to find the required kind of philosophy and to put that philosophy to practical use. People and ideas, not buildings and facilities, make up a university. Any place where people with a philosophy that enables them to cope with the chaos of life come together — any place that is a source of energy to influence the age and to create culture — is a university in the richest sense.Today Scholasticism has crumbled, because the religion on which it rested has lost its power. Perhaps no other age in history has lost the religious spirit to the extent that ours has; and no other age in history has been in greater need of salvation. We face this fact, and we must continue to live with it. We must be aware that our most pressing tasks today are to establish a philosophy that can cope with and take the lead in the current situation and to found a new religion as the basis of that philosophy.

What is the mission of a university whose pride it will be to bear the responsibility of the future? With the firm conviction that all of you already have the answer to this question in your hearts, I conclude my message.

PART IV

Hindu Perceptions of Christianity in the Twentieth Century

INTRODUCTION TO PART FOUR

The classical Sanskrit texts of traditional Brahmanical Hinduism show almost no interest in any non-Indian religious community. In spite of a very long history of social and political interaction with Muslims and Christians (the former present in northern and western India since the beginning of the second millennium of the Christian era, and the latter present in southern India since at least the third century), Hindu intellectuals paid these religious communities very little systematic attention until the nineteenth century. Christians and Muslims were simply unimportant for Hindu self-consciousness and Hindu religious practice.

This lack of interest has deep roots in classical Brahmanical thought. Foreigners, non-Indians, those outside the hierarchically ordered and ritually defined caste society of traditional India, are called *mleccha*, an onomatopoeic word meant to represent the way non-Sanskritic speech sounds to an Indian; such speech is ludicrously incomprehensible, to be called "speech" only by courtesy. True speech is Sanskritic speech. *Mleccha*, then, is a term heavily laden with value-judgments: *mlecchas* are the excluded, the irrelevant, the other, the ritually impure. They are opposed to the *arya*, the "noble one" (in modern terms, though somewhat anachronistically, the "Hindu"), who is a full and proper member of caste society and who has ritual and religious duties (*dharma*) that make him such. Hence, insofar as classical Sanskrit texts talk of *mlecchas* at all, they do so only to provide regulations governing the intercourse of Hindus with them, or to explain how an *arya* monarch should behave toward *mlecchas* who happen to come under his rule. Foreigners are certainly not dignified by entering into discussion of their religious beliefs and habits. Indeed, it is almost inconceivable that a traditional Hindu would think of such beliefs and habits as being in any significant way like his own practice of religious duty—of *dharma*. Wilhelm Halbfass puts this traditional position thus:

The Indocentrism developed in "orthodox" Hindu thought transcends by far what is ordinarily called "ethnocentrism." It is not simply an unquestioned perspective or bias, but a sophisticated theoretical structure of self-universalization and self-isolation. Seen from within this complex, highly differentiated structure, the *mlecchas* are nothing but a faint and distant phenomenon at the horizon of the indigenous tradition.[1]

There is therefore no traditional Hindu position on Christians or Christianity, and no systematic discussions of the phenomenon by Hindu intellectuals in classical times.

This began to change only in the nineteenth century. Hindu intellectuals by that time, both those trained as pandits in the classical Sanskritic traditions, and those trained in the English-speaking schools set up in India by the British, could scarcely avoid taking Christianity and Christians seriously and saying something specific about them. Christianity was perceived as the dominant ideology of an occupying power whose technological and military superiority were unmistakable. The language of this occupying power was also the language of Christianity—at least as perceived by most Indians—and fluency in it became, increasingly throughout the latter half of the nineteenth century, a necessity for success in any of the professions controlled by the British—most obviously the law and the civil service. Finally, Christian missionaries of various types were increasingly insistent in their public statements upon the obvious superiority of all things Christian to the heathen idolatry and decadence of all things Hindu. Some considered systematic response was necessary.

This response initially took two forms. The first was that of the traditionally trained Sanskritic pandits, the intellectuals and scholastics of the Hindu tradition who were, on the whole, both anti-Christian and relatively uninfluenced by Western thought-forms and religious practices. This traditional response began to occur only when Christian missionaries initiated debate in Sanskrit through the composition of polemical works in that language aimed at the pandits. The most influential example of this was J. S. Muir's *Matapariksha* ("Investigation of Religious Opinions"), an intellectual attack on some key Hindu doctrines and an attempt to establish the truth of Christian doctrines; it was published in India around 1840. This work was the subject of several more-or-less vitriolic replies (also in Sanskrit) by traditional Hindus.[2]

These debates have considerable intellectual interest, but because they were conducted entirely in the learned language of Sanskrit—a necessary condition for participation in them by the pandits – they have had little effect upon Hindu-Christian dialogue in the present century. Also, these debates were almost exclusively upon doctrinal questions, issues such as the truth of the doctrine of rebirth or the possibility of divine forgiveness of sins. The connections of these doctrinal questions with the political context in which it became possible to discuss them and their implications for broader practical and ethical questions are present only in the subtext of these works; they never reach the surface.

The second kind of response is that which has come to be called "neo-Hindu." While those thinkers included under this rubric, from Rammohan Roy (1772–1833) to Vivekananda himself (1863–1902, see Chapter 16), do not speak with a unified voice and do not have a single perspective upon Christianity and Christians, there are some common themes evident in their work. I shall speak to three of these.

The first is the theme of Westernization. Most neo-Hindus, so-called because they were concerned to reconstitute and reform Hinduism in the light of its interactions with Western culture and religion, often in ways significantly different from any that would have been recognized and given approval by traditional Brahmanism, were very self-conscious about their own relations, conceptual, linguistic, and institutional, with the West. Most of them wrote a good number of their works in English. Many were educated largely or exclusively in British-run, English-speaking schools. Several visited Europe. And virtually all have it as a central concern to redefine Hinduism in the light of Christianity. This is perhaps most evident on the institutional level. The nineteenth century saw the founding of a number of Hindu reform movements, notably the Brahmo Samaj and the Arya Samaj, which, both in their institutional forms and in their explicit ideologies, mirrored much in Protestant Christianity. Consider, for example, the following statement by Keshab Chandra Sen (1838–84), the founder of a new branch of the Brahmo Samaj in 1866 and the proclaimer of a "new dispensation"(*nava vidhana*), which would transcend and fulfil the dispensations of the Old and New Testaments and bring all religions into harmony:

I believe in the Church Universal which is the deposit of all ancient wisdom and the receptacle of all modern science, which recognizes in all prophets and saints a harmony, in all scriptures a unity, and through all dispensations a continuity, which abjures all that separates and divides, always magnifies unity and peace, which harmonizes faith and reason, yoga and bhakti, asceticism and social duty in their highest forms and which shall make of all nations and sects one kingdom and one family in the fullness of time.[3]

Themes such as these echo through the works and institutional practices of the neo-Hindus, though it is probably true to say that Sen is more positive in his assessment of Christianity—and Judaism—than most neo-Hindus.

Second, it is possible to see in the thought of neo-Hindus a nationalistic awareness, a desire to affirm the importance of India (*Bharata* in Sanskrit) as a nation-state with something important to contribute to the world, and also to identify Hinduism as the religion of the inhabitants of that nation-state. Typical here is Vivekananda's attempt (see Chapter 16) to represent India (and Hinduism—the two can scarcely be distinguished in his thought) as the possessor of the highest spiritual goods in contrast to the West's possession of the best in material and technological goods. Typical also—though much more polemical—is Dayananda Sarasvati's (see Chapter 15) attempt to portray Hinduism (and thus also India) as the apex of civilization and rationality. Along with all this goes a strong tendency to identify Christianity straightforwardly with Western colonialism, and thus to reject it as a possible religious option for Indians. Gandhi's comments on his emotional and intellectual responses to Christian missionaries (see Chapter 17) are very representative of this.

Third, and finally, there is a tendency toward an inclusivistic view of the relations between Hinduism and non-Hindu religions in the thought of almost all neo-Hindus. This is present also in some of the more recent examples of Hindu reflections on Christianity included in this volume (see Chapter 18). The Hindu inclusivist typically does not reject the doctrines of Christianity as false or the practices of Christians as undesirable. Rather, the inclusivist judges them to be partially true, included within and super-seded by the more embracing and complete truths evident within Hinduism. So the divinity of Jesus Christ is not denied; it is affirmed, but judged simply to be one more somewhat imperfect example of a phenomenon available much more fully and perfectly within Hinduism. Neo-Hindus will often say that all religions are true, or that all religions are aimed at the same goal, or that all religions are describing the same ultimate reality differently. The *Rgveda* itself is often quoted in support of this position: "Truth is one, but wise men name it variously."[4] But when those who say this are pressed, the truth that is named, the reality that is pointed to, and the goal that is aimed at almost always turn out to be precisely those espoused by the variety of neo-Hinduism being defended. And this is a hallmark of inclusivism in all its varieties.

Neo-Hinduism is still with us and still influences what Hindus have to say about Christianity. The export of Hinduism to the West, effectively begun by Vivekananda at the beginning of this century, but reaching new heights with the West's passionate interest in Indian gurus during the last three decades, also shows this tendency toward inclusivism. It is clearly present in the essay by Bithika Mukerji (Chapter 18) and in many of the statements of those Hindu teachers whose activities have become such a public and well-publicized part of American religious life since 1970.[5] Christianity is always, in this view, subsumed within Hinduism, becoming a small part of the eternal truth, the *sanatanadharma*, in which Hinduism, according to Hindus, essentially consists.

There is, finally, another trend in Hindu thinking about Christianity and Christians observable in recent years. This is the reaction by contemporary Hindu intellectuals, often trained by and teaching in the academies of the West, to the theories about them developed by Christian theologians. Bibhuti S. Yadav's critique of Hans Küng's theories, included as Chapter 19 of this volume, is representative. Christian universalism is rejected as imperialistic; its emphasis on the specificity of God's saving act in Christ is criticized as entailing a narrow-minded and inappropriate representation of God; and, as with all earlier trends in Hindu thinking about Christianity, Christian theology is finally subsumed as an insignificant variant of Vaishnavism or Shaivism[6] or whatever particular sectarian variety of Hinduism is being defended.

SUGGESTIONS FOR FURTHER READING

The definitive historical work on the intellectual and religious relations between India and Europe is Wilhelm Halbfass's *India and Europe: An Essay in Understanding* (Albany, NY: State University of New York Press, 1988). I have drawn heavily upon this, especially chapters 11–14 and 22, in the remarks made here. A useful survey may be found in Harold Coward's *Pluralism: Challenge to World Religions* (Maryknoll, NY: Orbis Books, 1985), 72–78. Important collections of essays are to be found in two recent volumes: Harold Coward, ed., *Modern Indian Responses to Religious Pluralism* (Albany, NY: State University of New York Press, 1987); Arvind Sharma, ed., *Neo-Hindu Views of Christianity* (Leiden: E.J. Brill, 1988). The essays in these volumes often cover the same or similar ground, but are useful for the different and often complementary perspectives they provide upon it. Some of the classic papers by Paul Hacker — the indologist responsible for the coinage of the term *neo-Hinduism* and for its characterization as "inclusivist" — are still indispensable. See especially, "Aspects of Neo-Hinduism as Contrasted with Surviving Traditional Hinduism," in Hacker, *Kleine Schriften*, edited by Lambert Schmithausen (Wiesbaden: Harrassowitz, 1978), 580–608. There is much useful material also (though most of it in German) in Gerhard Oberhammer, ed., *Inklusivismus: eine indische Denkform* (Vienna: De Nobili Research Library, 1983). A useful anthology, with contents of direct relevance to the topic of this book, is that edited by Glyn Richards: *A Sourcebook of Modern Hinduism* (London: Curzon Press, 1985).

15

Extracts from *The Light of Truth*[1]

DAYANANDA SARASVATI

INTRODUCTION

Dayananda Sarasvati (1824–83) was born a Brahmin in Kathiawari. In 1845, according to his autobiographical account, he renounced home and family, determined to reject idolatry, to purify Hinduism, and to attain liberation. In 1875 he founded the Arya Samaj in Bombay, an organization devoted to the recovery and promulgation of pure Vedic Hinduism. This involved, among many other things, the rejection of Christianity as an undesirable influence upon India. Dayananda sees Christianity as a religion of a book — the Bible — and his criticisms of it attempt to show that the Bible is irrational and barbaric, and that any religion based upon it must share these characteristics.

Dayananda is a rationalist. He is profoundly opposed to idol worship and to everything that might be construed as superstition. He criticized such things when he thought he found them within Hinduism and, as will be evident from the extracts that follow, also within Christianity. His religion, and that propounded by the Arya Samaj, is one to which morality and rationality are central. The Veda, as the inerrant source of all true beliefs, is its basis, and there is little doubt that Dayananda's view of the Veda was influenced by what he had learned of then-current Protestant Christian views of the Bible. One book is replaced by another. Dayananda's works show, both in the extracts that follow and elsewhere, that he was aware of positivist thought in the West; many of his criticisms of Christianity are foreshadowed and paralleled by arguments constructed by anti-Christian rationalists in Europe.

Dayananda is also a nationalist. Much of his critique of Christianity is in the service of Indian nationalistic self-consciousness. Christianity is seen as a foreign import, an integral part of colonialist oppression, and its rejection is therefore judged to be an essential part of Indian (Hindu) self-discovery and self-assertion. Interestingly, Dayananda is also concerned to present Hindu-

ism — proper Vedic Hinduism — as a rational and scientific religion in contrast to the irrationality and superstition evident in Christianity. This latter theme is evident in his criticisms of the Bible given below; the former theme runs through-out Dayananda's exegetical work on the Veda. He presents the Veda as not only inerrant, but also as containing all scientific truths.[2]

While Dayananda, like Vivekananda, represents neo-Hinduism, he does so in a very different way. He claims superiority for India and Vedic Hinduism not only in the spiritual sphere, as does Vivekananda, but also in the scientific and rational spheres, where Vivekananda was prepared to cede superiority to the West. For Dayananda, India has nothing to learn from the West.

THE LIGHT OF TRUTH

Now we shall discuss the Christian religion in order to make it clear to all whether this religion is free from faults and its sacred book called the Bible is the Word of God or not.[3] . . . We shall write a little about the New Testament that comprises gospels according to St. Matthew, etc., and is held in great reverence by the Christians who call it the Bible. We should now examine it and see what kind of book it is.[4]

On the Birth Narrative from the Gospel of Matthew

Now the birth of Jesus Christ was this wise: When as his mother Mary was espoused to Joseph, before they came together, she was found with child of the Holy Ghost ... behold the angel of the Lord appeared unto him in a dream, saying, Joseph, thou son of David, fear not to take unto thee Mary thy wife: for that which is conceived in her is of the Holy Ghost (Matthew 1:18, 20).[5]

No educated man can ever believe in such things as are opposed to all kinds of evidence (such as direct cognition, inference, etc.[6]) and to the laws of nature. Only people in a state of barbarism can believe them. It does not become educated and civilised men to do so. Breathes there a man who could violate the laws of God? Should anyone succeed in subverting His law, no one will ever obey His commandments, nor would God himself break his own laws as He is Omniscient and infallible. If this story of the birth of Christ were held to be true, any unmarried girl that happens to conceive could say that she was with child of the Holy Ghost. She could also falsely say that the angel of the Lord told her in a dream "that which is conceived in her is of the Holy Ghost"! This story is as possible as that recorded in the Puranas about Kunti being conceived of the Sun.[7] Only those who have "more money than brains" can believe in such things and fall an easy prey to superstition. It must have happened like this that Mary cohabited with someone and thereby became *enceinte*. She or someone else gave out (such an impossible thing) that she had conceived of the Holy Ghost.

On the Temptation Narrative from the Gospel of Matthew

Then was Jesus led up of the Spirit into the wilderness to be tempted of the devil. And when he had fasted forty days and forty nights, he was afterwards an hungered. And when the tempter came to him, he said, If thou be the Son of God, command that these stones be made bread (Matthew 4:1–3).

This conclusively proves that the Christian God was not Omniscient, otherwise why should He have had Jesus tempted of the devil? He would have known all about him by His Omniscience. Will a Christian live if he be kept without food for 40 days and 40 nights? It also proves that Jesus was neither the son of God nor did he possess any miraculous power or why would he not have turned stones into bread? Why would he have himself suffered the pangs of hunger? The truth is that what God has created as stones no one could ever turn into bread, nor could God Himself subvert His laws ordained by Himself since He is Omniscient and all His works are free from error.

On the Story of the Paralyzed Man

And, behold, they brought to him a man sick of the palsy, lying on a bed: and Jesus seeing their faith said unto the sick of the palsy: Son, be of good cheer; thy sins be forgiven thee . . . For I am not come to call the righteous, but sinners to repentance (Matthew 9:2,13).

Now this thing is as impossible as others that have been mentioned before. As regards the forgiveness of sins it is only a bait thrown to simpletons to ensnare them. Just as alcohol, Indian hemp, or opium taken by one person cannot affect another, likewise, a sin committed by one cannot affect another. On the other hand, it is he alone who suffers sins. Verily, this is Divine Justice! God would indeed be unjust if good or bad deeds done by one man should affect another, or if the judge should take on himself the consequences of the crimes of the criminal. Remember righteousness alone is the cause of felicity (happiness), not Christ or any other saint or prophet. The righteous do not at all stand in need of Christ, etc., nor do the sinners as their sins can never beforgiven.

On Rewards and Works

. . . And then he shall reward every man according to his works (Matthew 16:27).

When all men shall be rewarded according to their works, it is useless for the Christians to preach the doctrine of the forgiveness of sins. If the latter be true, the former must be false. If the Christians say that those that deserve to be forgiven shall be forgiven, while those that do not deserve it shall not be forgiven, it cannot be right, since justice and mercy consist only in awarding punishment and reward for all works.

On Faith

O [ye] faithless and perverse generation, how long shall I be with you? How long shall I suffer you? Bring him hither to me ... For verily I say unto you, If ye have faith as a grain of mustard seed, ye shall say unto this mountain, Remove hence to yonder place; and it shall remove; and nothing shall be impossible unto you (Matthew 17:17, 20).

The Christians go about preaching: "Come, embrace our religion, get your sins forgiven and be saved." All this is untrue, since had Christ possessed the power of having sins remitted, instilling faith in others and purifying them, why would he have not freed his disciples from sin, made them faithful and pure? When he could not make those who went about with him pure, faithful and sinless, how could he now, that no one knows where he is, purify anyone? Now disciples of Christ were destitute of as much faith as a grain of mustard seed and it is they that wrote the Bible, how could then such a book be held as an authority? Those who seek happiness should not believe in the works of the faithless, the impure (at heart) and the unrighteous. It also proves that if the word of Christ be held to be true, no Christian possesses as much faith as a grain of mustard. If a Christian should say that he possessed it more or less, let him then be asked to remove a *mountain* from one place to another. Even if he succeeded in doing it, he could not be said to possess perfect faith but only about as much as a grain of mustard. On the contrary, if he did not succeed, he was then destitute even of an atom of faith or righteousness. If anyone were to say that all this is allegorical and the word mountain here stands for pride and other evil qualities of the mind, it cannot be right, as raising the dead, curing the blind, the lepers and those possessed of devils could also be allegorical. Christ raising the dead, etc., may mean curing the lazy of their laziness, curing the blind, dispelling the ignorance of the mentally blind, the licence of licentiousness and the superstitions of those who were superstitious.

Even this interpretation would not hold water, since had this been the case, why would he have not been able to cure his disciples of their faithlessness, ignorance, etc.? Hence Christ betrays his ignorance by saying such impossible things. Had Christ possessed even a little knowledge, why would he have talked such nonsense like a savage? However as it has been said,

"In a country where no trees are seen to grow, even the castor oil plant is considered to be the biggest and the best tree"; in like manner in a country where none but the most ignorant savages lived, Christ was rightly considered a great man but Christ can be of no count among the learned and wise men of the present day.

On the Words of Institution from the Gospel of Matthew

And as they were eating, Jesus took bread, and blessed it and broke it, and gave it to his disciples, and said, Take, eat; this is my body. And he took the cup, and gave thanks, and gave it to them, saying, Drink ye all of it; for this is my blood of the new testament (Matthew 26:26–28).

Can a cultured man ever do such a thing? Only an ignorant savage would do it. No enlightened man would ever call the food of his disciples his flesh nor their drink his blood. This is called *Lord's Supper* by the Christians of the present day. They eat and drink imagining all the time that their bread was the flesh of Christ and their drink his blood. Is not it an awful thing? How could those, who could not even keep aloof from the idea that their food and drink were the flesh and blood of their saviour, abstain from the flesh and blood of others?

On Christ as the Way to Salvation

Let not your heart be troubled: ye believe in God, believe also in me. In my father's house are many mansions: If it were not so, I would have told you. I go to prepare a place for you. And [if] I go and prepare a place for you, I will come again, and receive you into myself; that where I am, there ye may be also . . . Jesus saith unto him, I am the way, the truth, and the life: no man cometh unto the Father, but by me. [If] ye had known me, ye should have known my Father also (John 14:1–4,6–7).

Now reader mark the words of Christ! Are they a bit better than what the popes say to their dupes? Had he not set up this fraud, who would have been caught into his net? Has Christ got the monopoly of his Father? If He be under his control, he will no longer remain independent and consequently could never be God. To say that no man cometh unto the Father but by me can never be true as God does not stand in need of any mediator. Had no one attained God before Christ? All this boasting about his Father's mansions and about his going to prepare a place for his followers and speaking with his own lips about his being the way, the truth and the life were nothing but a hoax and hence can never be true.

Dayananda Sarasvati on His Own Beliefs

I believe in a religion based on universal and all-embracing principles which have always been accepted as true by mankind, and will continue to command the allegiance of mankind in ages to come. Hence it is that the religion in question is called the *primeval eternal religion*,[8] which means that it is above the hostility of all human creeds whatsoever. Whatever is believed in by those who are steeped in ignorance or have been led astray by sectaries is not worthy of being accepted by the wise. That faith alone is really true and worthy of acceptance which is followed by *Aptas*, i.e., those who are true in word, deed and thought, promote public good and are impartial and learned; but all that is discarded by such men must be considered as unworthy of belief and false.

My conception of God and all other objects in the universe is founded on the teachings of the Veda and other true Shastras,[9] and is in conformity with the beliefs of all the sages from Brahma*[10] down to Jaimini.[11] I offer a statement of these beliefs for the acceptance of all good men. That alone I hold to be acceptable which is worthy of being believed by all men in all ages. I do not entertain the least idea of founding a new religion or sect. My sole aim is to believe in truth and help others to believe in it, to reject falsehood and help others to do the same. Had I been biased, I would have championed any one of the religions prevailing in India. But I have not done so. On the contrary, I do not approve of what is objectionable and false in the institutions of this or any other country, nor do I reject what is good and in harmony with the dictates of true religion, nor have I any desire to do so, since a contrary conduct is wholly unworthy of man. He alone is entitled to be called a man who possesses a thoughtful nature and feels for others in the same way as he does for his own self, does not fear the unjust, however powerful, but fears the truly virtuous, however weak. Moreover, he should always exert himself to his utmost to protect the righteous and advance their good, and conduct himself worthily towards them even though they be extremely poor and weak and destitute of material resources. On the other hand, he should constantly strive to destroy, humble, and oppose the wicked, sovereign rulers of the whole earth and men of great influence and power though they be. In other words, a man should, as far as it lies in his power, constantly endeavour to undermine the power of the unjust and to strengthen that of the just, he may have to bear any amount of terrible suffering, he may even have to quaff the bitter cup of death in the performance of this duty, which devolves on him on account of being a man, but he should not shirk it.

Now I give below a brief summary of my beliefs . . .

(1) He who is called *Brahma* or the Most High; who is *Paramatma* or the Supreme Spirit Who permeates the whole universe; Who is a true personification of Existence, Consciousness, and Bliss; Whose nature, attributes, and characteristics are Holy; Who is Omniscient, Formless, All-

pervading, Unborn, Infinite, Almighty, Just and Merciful; Who is the author of the universe, sustains and dissolves it; Who awards all souls the fruits of their deeds in strict accordance with the requirements of absolute justice and is possessed of the like attributes — even Him I believe to be the Great God.

(2) I hold that the four Vedas — the repository of Knowledge and Religious Truths — are the Word of God. They comprise what is known as the *Sanhita-Mantra*[12] portion only. They are absolutely free from error and are an authority unto themselves. In other words, they do not stand in need of any other book to uphold their authority. Just as the sun (or a lamp) by his light, reveals his own nature as well as that of other objects of the universe, such as the earth — even so are the *Vedas*.

16

"Christ, the Messenger"[1]

VIVEKANANDA

INTRODUCTION

Vivekananda (1863–1902) was born to a high-caste family in Calcutta, educated largely in British schools, and intended for a legal career. In 1881 he came under the influence of the mystic and visionary Ramakrishna; he thereafter devoted himself to the study and preaching of a version of Ramakrishna's thought and to the attempt to spread that gospel in the West (especially in the United States). In 1893 he attended the World's Parliament of Religions in Chicago as a representative of Hinduism, and there made an international name for himself. He founded the Ramakrishna mission in California in the late 1890s and spent the last few years of a short but very active life lecturing in Europe, India, and the United States.

The piece reprinted here appears to have been delivered as a public lecture on many occasions during the middle and late 1890s in both Europe and the United States. In it Vivekananda argues strongly for the superiority of the Orient to the West in matters religious, while acknowledging Western superiority in matters political and military. This attitude is entirely typical of neo-Hindu thinkers of this period; given their political position as part of the British empire they had to find a way to assert the value of Hinduism that would not be misunderstood by the British as seditious and would yet allow them to advance Hinduism as of value even (perhaps especially) for the Western world. The usual move made — and this is very evident in Vivekananda's work — was to separate the religious from the socioeconomic and the military, and to claim superiority for India in the religious sphere.

As part of this strategy Vivekananda claims Jesus Christ as an Oriental and rejects Western misrepresentations of him as a Caucasian. The doctrine of the incarnation in its usual orthodox Christian form is also rejected, and its acceptance is linked explicitly with Western colonialism. None of this means that

204

Vivekananda has a negative view of the person and significance of Christ. Instead, using the flowery late Victorian rhetoric typical of Indian intellectuals educated primarily in English schools, he claims Christ as a "Messenger" and a "Prophet," one among many to represent God to human beings and one whose teaching is of sacred significance. Proper Christian discipleship, in this view, may very well include the worship of Christ, but it cannot include an exclusivist rejection of all other prophets and messengers, much less a claim that salvation is located solely among those who acknowledge Christ as savior. This is the link, in Vivekananda's eyes, between traditional Christian doctrines of the incarnation and Western (European) colonialism.

Underlying Vivekananda's view of Christ and Christianity are elements of a traditional Vedantic nondualist metaphysics.[2] According to this metaphysics, all distinctions—between subject and object, word and referent, religion and religion—are ultimately illusory. What is real is single, undifferentiated, inaccessible to language. The function of prophets, incarnations, and messengers, is to communicate as much of this transcendental truth as human beings are able to comprehend at any particular time. The apparent differences among the messages of the various prophets and religious teachers are due to their different social and cultural contexts, not to any fundamental religious disagreement among them. All good religious teachers teach exactly the same thing. It is into this mold that Jesus Christ is here fitted.

"CHRIST, THE MESSENGER"

The wave rises on the ocean, and there is a hollow. Again another wave rises, perhaps bigger than the former, to fall down again; similarly, again to rise—driving onward. In the march of events, we notice the rise and fall, and we generally look towards the rise, forgetting the fall. But both are necessary and both are great. This is the nature of the universe. Whether in the world of our thoughts, the world of our relations in society, or in our spiritual affairs, the same movement of succession, of rises and falls, is going on. Hence great predominances in the march of events, the liberal ideals, are marshalled ahead, to sink down, to digest, as it were, to ruminate over the past—to adjust, to conserve, to gather strength once more for a rise and a bigger rise.

The history of nations, also, has ever been like that. The great soul, the Messenger we are to study this afternoon, came at a period of the history of his race which we may well designate as a great fall. We catch only little glimpses here and there of the stray records that have been kept of his sayings and doings; for, verily it has been well said that the sayings and doings of that great soul would fill the world if they had all been written down. And the three years of his ministry were like one compressed, concentrated age, which it has taken nineteen hundred years to unfold, and who knows how much longer it will yet take! Little men like you and me are simply the recipients of just a little energy. A few minutes, a few hours, a few years at best, are enough to spend it all, to stretch it out, as it were, to its fullest strength, and then we are gone for ever. But mark this giant that came; centuries and ages pass, yet the energy that he left upon the world is not yet stretched, nor yet expended to its full. It goes on adding new vigour as the ages roll on.

Now what you see in the life of Christ is the life of all the past. The life of every man is, in a manner, the life of the past. It comes to him through heredity, through surroundings, through education, through his own rein-carnation — the past of the race. In a manner, the past of the earth, the past of the whole world is there, upon every soul. What are we, in the present, but a result, an effect, in the hands of that infinite past? What are we but floating wavelets in the eternal current of events, irresistibly moved forward and onward and incapable of rest? But you and I are only little things, bubbles. There are always some giant waves in the ocean of affairs; and in you and me the life of the past race has been embodied only a little; but there are giants who embody, as it were, almost the whole of the past and who stretch out their hands for the future. These are the sign-posts here and there, which point to the march of humanity; these are verily gigantic, their shadows covering the earth — they stand undying, eternal! As it has been said by the same Messenger, "No man hath seen God at any time, but through the Son." And that is true. And where shall we see God but in the Son? It is true that you and I, and the poorest of us, the meanest even, embody that God, reflect that God. The vibration of light is every-where, omnipresent; but we have to strike the light of the lamp before we can see the light. The Omnipresent God of the universe cannot be seen until He is reflected by these giant lamps of the earth — the Prophets, the man-Gods, the Incarnations, the embodiments of God.

We all know that God exists, and yet we do not see Him, we do not understand Him. Take one of these great Messengers of light, compare his character with the highest ideal of God that you ever formed, and you will find that your God falls short of the ideal, and that the character of the Prophet exceeds your conceptions. You cannot even form a higher ideal of God than what the actually embodied have practically realised, and set before us as an example. Is it wrong, therefore, to worship these as God? Is it a sin to fall at the feet of these man-Gods, and worship them as the only divine beings in the world? If they are really, actually, higher than all our conceptions of God, what harm is there in worshipping them? Not only is there no harm, but it is the only possible and positive way of worship. However much you may try, by struggle, by abstraction, by whatsoever method you like, still so long as you are a man in the world of men, your world is human, your religion is human, and your God is human. And that must be so. Who is not practical enough to take up an actually existing thing, and give up an idea which is only an abstraction, which he cannot grasp, and is difficult of approach except through a concrete medium?

Therefore, these Incarnations of God have been worshipped in all ages and in all countries.

We are now going to study a little of the life of Christ, the Incarnation of the Jews. When Christ was born, the Jews were in that state which I call a state of fall between two waves; a state of conservatism, a state where the human mind is, as it were, tired for the time being of moving forward and is taking care only of what it has already; a state when the attention is more bent upon particulars, upon details, than upon the great, general, and bigger problems of life; a state of stagnation, rather than a towing ahead; a state of suffering more than of doing. Mark you, I do not blame this state of things. We have no right to criticise it—because had it not been for this fall, the next rise, which was embodied in Jesus of Nazareth, would have been impossible. The Pharisees and Sadducees might have been insincere, they might have been doing things which they ought not to have done; but whatever they were, these factors were the very cause of which the Messenger was the effect. The Pharisees and Sadducees at one end were the very impetus which came out at the other end as the gigantic brain of Jesus of Nazareth.

The attention to forms, to formulas, to the everyday details of religion, and to rituals, may sometimes be laughed at, but nevertheless within them is strength. Many times in the rushing forward we lose such strength. As a fact the fanatic is stronger than the liberal man. Even the fanatic, therefore, has one great virtue, he conserves energy, a tremendous amount of it. As with the individual, so with the race, energy is gathered to be conserved. Hemmed in all around by external enemies, driven to focus in a centre by the Romans, by the Hellenic tendencies in the world of intellect, by waves from Persia, India, and Alexandria—hemmed in physically, mentally, and morally—there stood the race with an inherent, conservative, tremendous strength, which their descendants have not lost even today. And the race was forced to concentrate and focus all its energies upon Jerusalem and Judaism. But all power when once gathered cannot remain collected; it must expend and expand itself. There is no power on earth which can be kept long confined within a narrow limit. It cannot be kept compressed too long to allow of expansion at a subsequent period.

This concentrated energy amongst the Jewish race found its expression at the next period in the rise of Christianity. The gathered streams collected into a body. Gradually, all the little streams joined together, and became a surging wave on the top of which we find standing out the character of Jesus of Nazareth. Thus, every Prophet is a creation of his own times, the creation of the past of his race; he, himself, is the creator of the future. The cause of today is the effect of the past and the cause for the future. In this position stands the Messenger. In him is embodied all that is best and greatest in his own race, the meaning, the life, for which that race has struggled for ages; and he, himself, is the impetus for the future, not only to his own race but to unnumbered other races of the world.

We must bear another fact in mind: that my view of the great prophet of Nazareth would be from the standpoint of the Orient. Many times you forget, also, that the Nazarene himself was an Oriental of Orientals. With all your attempts to paint him with blue eyes and yellow hair, the Nazarene was still an Oriental. All the similes, the imageries, in which the Bible is written—the scenes, and locations, the attitudes, the groups, the poetry and symbol—speak to you of the Orient: of the bright sky, of the heat, of the sun of the desert, of the thirsty men and animals; of men and women coming with pitchers on their heads to fill them at the wells; of the flocks, of the ploughmen, of the cultivation that is going on around; of the water-mill and wheel, of the millpond, of the millstones—all these are to be seen today in Asia.

The voice of Asia has been the voice of religion. The voice of Europe is the voice of politics. Each is great in its own sphere. The voice of Europe is the voice of ancient Greece. To the Greek mind, his immediate society was all in all. Beyond that, it is Barbarian—none but the Greek has the right to live. Whatever the Greeks do is right and correct; whatever else there exists in the world is neither right nor correct, nor should be allowed to live. It is intensely human in its sympathies, intensely natural, intensely artistic, therefore. The Greek lives entirely in this world. He does not care to dream. Even his poetry is practical. His gods and goddesses are not only human beings, but intensely human, with all human passions and feelings, almost the same as with any of us. He loves what is beautiful, but, mind you, it is always external nature: the beauty of the hills, of the snows, of the flowers; the beauty of forms and of figures; the beauty in the human face, and, more often, in the human form—that is what the Greeks liked. And the Greeks, being the teachers of all subsequent Europeanism, the voice of Europe is Greek.

There is another type in Asia. Think of that vast, huge continent, whose mountain-tops go beyond the clouds, almost touching the canopy of heaven's blue; a rolling desert of miles upon miles, where a drop of water cannot be found, neither will a blade of grass grow; interminable forests and gigantic rivers rushing down to the sea. In the midst of all these surroundings, the Oriental love of the beautiful and the sublime developed itself in another direction. It looked inside, and not outside. There is also the thirst for Nature, and there is also the same thirst for power; there is also the same thirst for excellence, the same idea of the Greek and the Barbarian; but it has extended over a larger circle. In Asia, even today, birth or colour or language never makes a race. That which makes a race is its religion. We are all Christians; we are all Mohammedans; we are all Hindus or all Buddhists. No matter if a Buddhist is a Chinaman, or is a man from Persia, they think that they are brothers, because of their professing the same religion. Religion is the tie, the unity of humanity. And then again, the Oriental, for the same reason, is a visionary, is a born dreamer. The ripples of the waterfalls, the songs of the birds, the beauties of the sun and moon and stars and the whole earth are pleasant enough; but they are not sufficient for the Oriental mind. He wants to dream a dream beyond. He wants to go beyond the present. The present, as it were, is nothing to him. The Orient has been the cradle of the human race for ages, and all the vicissitudes of fortune are there. Kingdoms succeeding kingdoms; empires succeeding empires; human power, glory, and wealth, all rolling down there: a Golgotha of power and learning. That is the Orient: a Golgotha of power, of kingdoms, of learning. No wonder, the Oriental mind looks with contempt upon the things of this world and naturally wants to see something that changeth not, something which dieth not, something which in the midst of this world of misery and death is eternal, blissful, undying. An Oriental Prophet never tires of insisting upon these ideas; and, as for Prophets, you may also remember that without one exception, all the Messengers are Orientals.

We see, therefore, in the life of this great Messenger of life, the first watchword: "Not this life, but something higher"; and, like the true son of the Orient, he is practical in that. You people of the West are practical in your own department, in military affairs, and in managing political circles and other things. Perhaps, the Oriental is not practical in those ways, but he is practical in his own field: he is practical in religion. If one preaches a philosophy, tomorrow there are hundreds who will struggle their best to make it practical in their lives. If a man preaches that standing on one foot would lead to salvation, he will immediately get five hundred to stand on one foot. You may call it ludicrous; but, mark you, beneath that is their philosophy—that intense practicality. In the West, plans of salvation mean intellectual gymnastics, plans which are never worked out, never brought into practical life. In the West, the preacher who talks the best is the greatest preacher.

So, we find Jesus of Nazareth, in the first place, the true son of the Orient, intensely practical. He has no faith in this evanescent world and all its belongings. No need of text-torturing, as is the fashion in the West in modern times, no need of stretching out texts until they will not stretch any more. Texts are not India-rubber, and even that has its limits. Now, no making of religion to pander to the sense of vanity of the present day! Mark you, let us all be honest. If we cannot follow the ideal, let us confess our weakness, but not degrade it; let not any try to pull it down. One gets sick at heart at the different accounts of the life of the Christ that Western people give. I do not know what he was or what he was not! One would make him a great politician; another, perhaps, would make of him a great military general; another, a great patriotic Jew, and so on. Is there any warrant in the books for all such assumptions? The best commentary on the life of a great teacher is his own life. "The foxes have holes, and the birds of the air have nests, but the Son of man hath not where to lay his head." That is what Christ says as the only way to salvation; he lays down no other way. Let us confess in sackcloth and ashes that we cannot do that.

We still have fondness for "me" and "mine." We want property, money, wealth. Woe unto us! Let us confess and not put to shame that great Teacher of Humanity! He had no family ties. But do you think that that Man had any physical ideas in him? Do you think that this mass of light, this God and not-man, came down to earth, to be the brother of animals? And yet, people make him preach all sorts of things. He had no sex ideas! He was a soul! Nothing but a soul, just working a body for the good of humanity; and that was all his relation to the body. In the soul there is no sex. The disembodied soul has no relationship to the animal, no relationship to the body. The ideal may be far away beyond us. But never mind, keep to the ideal. Let us confess that it is our ideal, but we cannot approach it yet.

He had no other occupation in life; no other thought except that one, that he was a Spirit. He was a disembodied, unfettered, unbound Spirit. And not only so, but he, with his marvellous vision, had found that every man and woman, whether Jew or Gentile, whether rich or poor, whether saint or sinner, was the embodiment of the same undying Spirit as himself. Therefore, the one work his whole life showed was calling upon them to realise their own spiritual nature. Give up, he says, these superstitious dreams that you are low and you are poor. Think not that you are trampled upon and tyrannised over as if you were slaves, for within you is something that can never be tyrannised over, never be trampled upon, never be troubled, never be killed. You are all Sons of God, Immortal Spirit. "Know," he declared, "the Kingdom of Heaven is within you." "I and my Father are one." Dare you stand up and say, not only that "I am the Son of God" but I shall also find in my heart of hearts that "I and my Father are One"? That was what Jesus of Nazareth said. He never talks of this world and of this life. He has nothing to do with it, except that he wants to get hold of the world as it is, give it a push and drive it forward and onward until the whole world has reached the effulgent Light of God, until everyone has realised his spiritual nature, until death is vanquished and misery vanished.

We have read the different stories that have been written about him; we know the scholars and their writings, and the higher criticism, and we know all that has been done by study. We are not here to discuss how much of the New Testament is true, we are not here to discuss how much of that life is historical. It does not matter at all whether the New Testament was written within five hundred years of his birth, nor does it matter, even, how much of that life is true. But there is something behind it, something we want to imitate. To tell a lie, you have to imitate a truth, and that truth is a fact. You cannot imitate that which never existed. You cannot imitate that which you never perceived. But there must have been a nucleus, a tremendous power that came down, a marvellous manifestation of spiritual power—and of that we are speaking. It stands there. Therefore, we are not afraid of all the criticism of the scholars. If I, as an Oriental, have to worship Jesus of Nazareth, there is only one way left to me, that is, to worship him as God and nothing else. Have we no right to worship him in that way, do you mean to say? If we bring him down to our own level and simply pay him a little respect as a great man, why should we worship at all? Our scriptures say, "These great children of Light, who manifest the Light themselves, who are Light themselves, they being worshipped, become, as it were, one with us and we become one with them."

For, you see, in three ways man perceives God. At first the undeveloped intellect of the uneducated man sees God as far away, up in the heavens somewhere, sitting on a throne as a great Judge. He looks upon Him as a fire, as a terror. Now, that is good, for there is nothing bad in it. You must remember that humanity travels not from error to truth, but from truth to truth; it may be, if you like it better, from lower truth to higher truth, but never from error to truth. Suppose you start from here and travel towards the sun in a straight line. From here the sun looks only small in size. Suppose you go forward a million miles, the sun will be much bigger. At every stage the sun will become bigger and bigger. Suppose twenty thousand photographs have been taken of the same sun, from different standpoints; these twenty thousand photographs will certainly differ from one another. But can you deny that each is a photograph of the same sun? So all forms of religion, high or low, are just different stages towards that eternal state of Light which is God Himself. Some embody a lower view, some a higher, and that is all the difference. Therefore, the religions of the unthinking masses all over the world must be, and have always been, of a God who is outside of the universe, who lives in heaven, who governs from that place, who is a punisher of the bad and a rewarder of the good, and so on. As man advanced spiritually, he began to feel that God was omnipresent, that He must be in him, that He must be everywhere, that He was not a distant God, but clearly the Soul of all souls. As my soul moves my body, even so is God the mover of my soul. Soul within soul. And a few individuals who had developed enough and were pure enough went still further, and at last found God. As the New Testament says, "Blessed are the pure in heart, for they shall see God." And they found at last that they and the Father were one.

You find that all these three stages are taught by the Great Teacher in the New Testament. Note the Common Prayer he taught: "Our Father which art in Heaven, hallowed be Thy name," and so on — a simple prayer, a child's prayer. Mark you, it is the "Common Prayer" because it is intended for the uneducated masses. To a higher circle, to those who had advanced a little more, he gave a more elevated teaching: "I am in my Father, and ye in me, and I in you." Do you remember that? And then, when the Jews asked him who he was, he declared that he and his Father were one, and the Jews thought that that was blasphemy. What did he mean by that? This has been also told by your old Prophets: "You are gods and all of you are children of the Most High." Mark the same three stages. You will find that it is easier for you to begin with the first and end with the last.

The Messenger came to show the path: that the Spirit is not in forms, that it is not through all sorts of vexatious and knotty problems of philosophy that you know the Spirit. Better that you had no learning, better that you never read a book in your life. These are not at all necessary for salvation — neither wealth, nor position, nor power, not even learning — but what is necessary is that one thing, purity: "Blessed are the pure in heart," for the Spirit in its own nature is pure. How can it be otherwise? It is of God, it has come from God. In the language of the Bible, "It is the breath of God." In the language of the Koran, "It is the soul of God." Do you mean to say that the Spirit of God can ever be impure? But, alas, it has been, as it were, covered over with the dust and dirt of ages, through our own actions, good and evil. Various works which were not correct, which were not true, have covered the same Spirit with the dust and dirt of the ignorance of ages. It is only necessary to clear away the dust and dirt, and then the Spirit shines immediately. "Blessed are the pure in heart, for they shall see God." "The Kingdom of Heaven is within you." Where goest thou to seek for the Kingdom of God, asks Jesus of Nazareth, when it is there, within you? Cleanse the Spirit, and it is there. It is already yours. How can you get what is not yours? It is yours by right. You are the heirs of immortality, sons of the Eternal Father.

This is the great lesson of the Messenger, and another, which is the basis of all religions, is renunciation. How can you make the Spirit pure? By renunciation. A rich young man asked Jesus, "Good Master, what shall I do that I may inherit eternal life?" And Jesus said unto him, "One thing thou lackest: go thy way, sell whatsoever thou hast, and give to the poor, and thou shalt have treasures in heaven: and come, take up thy cross, and follow Me." And he was sad at that saying, and went away grieved: for he had great possessions. We are all more or less like that. The Voice is ringing in our ears day and night. In the midst of our pleasures and joys, in the midst of worldly things, we think that we have forgotten everything else. Then comes a moment's pause and the Voice rings in our ears: "Give up all that thou hast and follow me." "Whosoever will save his life shall lose it; and whosoever shall lose his life for My sake shall find it." For whoever gives up this life for His sake, finds the life immortal. In the midst of all our weakness there is a moment of pause and the Voice rings: "Give up all that thou hast; give it to the poor and follow Me." This is the one ideal he preaches, and this has been the ideal preached by all the great Prophets of the world: renunciation. What is meant by renunciation? That there is only one ideal in morality: unselfishness. Be selfless. The ideal is perfect unselfishness. When a man is struck on the right cheek, he turns the left also. When a man's coat is carried off, he gives away his cloak also.

We should work in the best way we can, without dragging the ideal down. Here is the ideal. When a man has no more self in him, nothing to call "me" or "mine," has given himself up entirely, destroyed himself as it were — in that man is God Himself; for in him self-will is gone, crushed out, annihilated. This is the ideal man. We cannot reach that state yet; yet, let us worship the ideal, and slowly struggle to reach the ideal, though maybe with faltering steps. It may be tomorrow, or it may be a thousand years hence, but that ideal has to be reached. For it is not only the end, but also the means. To be unselfish, perfectly selfess, is salvation itself, for the man within dies, and God alone remains.

One more point. All the teachers of humanity are unselfish. Suppose Jesus of Nazareth was teaching, and a man came and told him: "What you teach is beautiful. I believe that it is the way to perfection and I am ready to follow it; but I do not care to worship you as the only begotten Son of God." What would be the answer of Jesus of Nazareth? "Very well, brother, follow the ideal and advance in your own way. I am not a shopkeeper. I do not trade in religion. I only teach truth, and truth is nobody's property. Nobody can patent truth. Truth is God himself. Go forward." But what the disciples say nowadays is: "No matter whether you practise the teachings or not, do you give credit to the Man? If you credit the Master, you will be saved; if not, there is no salvation for you." And thus the whole teaching of the Master is degenerated and all the struggle and fight is for the personality of the Man. They do not know that in imposing that difference they are, in a manner, bringing shame to the very Man they want to honour — the very Man that would have shrunk with shame from such an idea. What did he care if there was one man in the world that remembered him or not? He had to deliver his message, and he gave it. And if he had twenty thousand lives he would give them all up for the poorest man in the world. If he had to be tortured millions of times, for a million despised Samaritans, and if for each one of them the sacrifice of his own life would be the only condition of salvation, he would have given his life. And all this without wishing to have his name known even to a single person. Quiet, unknown, silent, would he work, just as the Lord works. Now, what would the disciple say? He will tell you that you may be a perfect man, perfectly unselfish, but unless you give the credit to our Teacher, to our Saint, it is of no avail. Why? What is the origin of this superstition, this ignorance? The disciple thinks that the Lord can manifest Himself only once. There lies the whole mistake. God manifests Himself to you in man. But throughout nature, what happens once must have happened before, and must happen in future. There is nothing in nature which is not bound by law, and that means that whatever happens once, must go on and must have been going on.

In India, they have the same idea of the incarnations of God. One of their great Incarnations, Krishna, whose grand Sermon, the Bhagavad-Gita,[3] some of you might have read, says:

Though I am unborn, of changeless nature, and Lord of beings, yet subjugating My Prakriti, I come into being by My own Maya. Wherever virtue subsides and immorality prevails, I body Myself forth. For the protection of the good, for the destruction of the wicked, and for the establishment of Dharma, I come into being in every age.[4]

Whenever the world goes down, the Lord comes to help it forward; and so He does from time to time and place to place. In another passage He speaks to this effect: Wherever thou findest a great soul of immense power and purity struggling to raise humanity, know that he is born of My splendour, that I am there working through him.

Let us, therefore, find God not only in Jesus of Nazareth but in all the Great Ones that have preceded him, in all that came after him, and all that are yet to come. Our worship is unbounded and free. They are all manifestations of the same Infinite God. They are all pure and unselfish; they struggled and gave up their lives for us, poor human beings. They each and all suffer vicarious atonement for every one of us, and also for all that are to come hereafter.

In a sense you are all Prophets; every one of you is a Prophet, bearing the burden of the world on your own shoulders. Have you ever seen a man, have you ever seen a woman, who is not quietly, patiently, bearing his or her little burden of life? The great Prophets were giants—they bore a gigantic world on their shoulders. Compared with them we are pigmies, no doubt, yet we are doing the same task; in our little circles, in our little homes, we are bearing our little crosses. There is no one so evil, no one so worthless, but he has to bear his own cross. But with all our mistakes, with all our evil thoughts and evil deeds, there is a bright spot somewhere, there is still somewhere the golden thread through which we are always in touch with the divine. For, know for certain, that the moment the touch of the divine is lost, there would be annihilation. And because none can be annihilated, there is always somewhere in our heart of hearts, however low and degraded we may be, a little circle of light which is constant touch with the divine.

Our salutations go to all the past Prophets whose teachings and lives we have inherited, whatever might have been their race, clime, or creed! Our salutations go to all those God-like men and women who are working to help humanity, whatever be their birth, colour, or race! Our salutations go to those who are coming in the future—living Gods—to work unselfishly for our descendants!

17

Extracts from *The Story of My Experiments with Truth*[1]

MOHANDAS KARAMCHAND GANDHI

INTRODUCTION

Mohandas Karamchand (Mahatma) Gandhi (1869–1948) was an Indian political and religious leader. He was partly educated in London, where he studied law and was called to the bar in 1891. He spent time in South Africa, where he founded the Natal Indian Congress, an organization devoted to publicizing and redressing some of the wrongs suffered by the Indian community in that part of Africa. Finally, he was instrumental in the movement that eventually led India to independence from the British in 1947. He was assassinated in 1948.

Gandhi's political and religious thinking was influenced by that of Leo Tolstoy (1823–1900), and he was a radical religious reformer, especially in regard to the question of caste. As the extracts from his autobiography reprinted here show, he was always ambivalent in his attitudes toward Christianity: extremely positive in his assessment of a certain (largely ethical) interpretation of the New Testament, but equally negative in his perceptions of much connected with ecclesiastical Christianity. He made much of the connections between Christianity and colonialism and was explicit in his rejection of what he perceived as Christian intolerance and imperialism, especially in connection with Christian attempts to convert non-Christians.

Like many Westernized neo-Hindus, Gandhi's knowledge of the sacred texts of his own religious tradition came to him at first largely through English translations. His Western education, as he was himself aware, had separated him from his own religious roots, and so his comments on religion in general—and on Christianity in particular—appear often as those of an uncommitted individual taking whatever seems best to him from each tradition.

The extracts supplied here from Gandhi's autobiography deal with the early period of his life, before his final return to India in 1914. His later more developed thinking on religion affirmed religious pluralism as a value and attempted also to affirm the equality of all religious traditions,[2] but it is probably fair to say that he never lost his distaste for traditional Christian exclusivism and imperialism and the attitudes to which it typically leads.

THE STORY OF MY EXPERIMENTS WITH TRUTH

Glimpses of Religion

From my sixth or seventh year up to my sixteenth I was at school, being taught all sorts of things except religion. I may say that I failed to get from the teachers what they could have given me without any effort on their part. And yet I kept on picking up things here and there from my surroundings. The term "religion" I am using in its broadest sense, meaning thereby self-realization or knowledge of self.

Being born in the Vaishnava faith,[3] I had often to go to the *Haveli*.[4] But it never appealed to me. I did not like its glitter and pomp. Also I heard rumours of immorality being practised there, and lost all interest in it. Hence I could gain nothing from the *Haveli*.

But what I failed to get there I obtained from my nurse, an old servant of the family, whose affection for me I still recall. I have said before that there was in me a fear of ghosts and spirits. Rambha, for that was her name, suggested, as a remedy for this fear, the repetition of *Ramanama*.[5] I had more faith in her than in her remedy, and so at a tender age I began repeating *Ramanama* to cure my fear of ghosts and spirits. This was of course short-lived, but the good seed sown in childhood was not sown in vain. I think it is due to the seed sown by that good woman Rambha that today *Ramanama* is an infallible remedy for me.

Just about this time, a cousin of mine who was a devotee of the *Ramayana*[6] arranged for my second brother and me to learn *Ram Raksha*.[7] We got it by heart, and made it a rule to recite it every morning after the bath. The practice was kept up as long as we were in Porbandar. As soon as we reached Rajkot, it was forgotten. For I had not much belief in it. I recited it partly because of my pride in being able to recite *Ram Raksha* with correct pronunciation.

What, however, left a deep impression on me was the reading of the *Ramayana* before my father. During part of his illness my father was in Porbandar. There every evening he used to listen to the *Ramayana*. The reader was a great devotee of Rama—Ladha Maharaj of Bileshvar. It was said of him that he cured himself of his leprosy not by any medicine, but by applying to the affected parts *bilva* leaves which had been cast away after being offered to the image of Mahadeva[8] in Bileshvar temple, and by the regular repetition of *Ramanama*. His faith, it was said, had made him whole. This may or may not be true. We, at any rate, believed the story. And it is a fact that when Ladha Maharaj began his reading of the *Ramayana* his body was entirely free from leprosy. He had a melodious voice. He would sing the *Dohas* (couplets) and *Chopais* (quatrains), and explain them, losing himself in the discourse and carrying his listeners along with him. I must have been thirteen at that time, but I quite remember being enraptured by his reading. That laid the foundation of my deep devotion to the *Ramayana*. Today I regard the *Ramayana* of Tulsidas[9] as the greatest book of all devotional literature.

A few months after this we came to Rajkot. There was no *Ramayana* reading there. The *Bhagavat*,[10] however, used to be read on every *Ekadashi**[11] day. Sometimes I attended the reading, but the reciter was uninspiring. Today I see that the *Bhagavat* is a book which can evoke religious fervour. I have read it in Gujarati with intense interest. But when I heard portions of the original read by Pandit Madan Mohan Malaviya during my twenty-one days' fast, I wished I had heard it in my childhood from such a devotee as he is, so that I could have formed a liking for it at an early age. Impressions formed at that age strike roots deep down into one's nature, and it is my perpetual regret that I was not fortunate enough to hear more good books of this kind read during that period.

In Rajkot, however, I got an early grounding in toleration for all branches of Hinduism and sister religions. For my father and mother would visit the *Haveli* as also Shiva's and Rama's temples, and would take or send us youngsters there. Jain monks would also pay frequent visits to my father, and would even go out of their way to accept food from us — non-Jains. They would have talks with my father on subjects religious and mundane.

He had, besides, Musalman[12] and Parsi friends, who would talk to him about their own faiths, and he would listen to them always with respect, and often with interest. Being his nurse, I often had a chance to be present at these talks. These many things combined to inculcate in me a toleration for all faiths.

Only Christianity was at the time an exception, I developed a sort of dislike for it. And for a reason. In those days Christian missionaries used to stand in a corner near the high school and hold forth, pouring abuse on Hindus and their gods. I could not endure this. I must have stood there to hear them once only, but that was enough to dissuade me from repeating the experiment. About the same time I heard of a well known Hindu having been converted to Christianity. It was the talk of the town that, when he was baptized he had to eat beef and drink liquor, that he also had to change his clothes, and that thenceforth he began to go about in European costume, including a hat. These things got on my nerves. Surely, thought I, a religion that compelled one to eat beef, drink liquor, and change one's own clothes did not deserve the name. I also heard that the new convert had already begun abusing the religion of his ancestors, their customs and their country. All these things created in me a dislike for Christianity.

But the fact that I had learnt to be tolerant to other religions did not mean that I had any living faith in God. I happened, about this time, to come across *Manusmriti**13 which was amongst my father's collection. The story of the creation and similar things in it did not impress me very much, but on the contrary made me incline somewhat towards atheism. There was a cousin of mine, still alive, for whose intellect I had great regard. To him I turned with my doubts. But he could not resolve them. He sent me away with this answer: "When you grow up, you will be able to solve these doubts yourself. These questions ought not to be raised at your age." I was silenced, but was not comforted. Chapters about diet and the like in *Manusmriti* seemed to me to run contrary to daily practice. To my doubts as to this also, I got the same answer. "With intellect more developed and with more reading I shall understand it better," I said to myself.

Manusmriti at any rate did not then teach me *ahimsa*.14 I have told the story of my meat-eating. *Manusmriti* seemed to support it. I also felt that it was quite moral to kill serpents, bugs and the like. I remember to have killed at that age bugs and such other insects, regarding it as a duty.

But one thing took deep root in me—the conviction that morality is the basis of things, and that truth is the substance of all morality. Truth became my sole objective. It began to grow in magnitude every day, and my definition of it also has been ever widening.

A Gujarati didactic stanza likewise gripped my mind and heart. Its precept—return good for evil—became my guiding principle. It became such a passion with me that I began numerous experiments in it. Here are those (for me) wonderful lines:

> For a bowl of water give a goodly meal;
> For a kindly greeting bow thou down with zeal;
> For a simple penny pay thou back with gold;
> If thy life be rescued, life do not withhold.
> Thus the words and actions of the wise regard;
> Every little service tenfold they reward.
> But the truly noble know all men as one,
> And return with gladness good for evil done.

Acquaintance with Religions

Towards the end of my second year in England15 I came across two Theosophists, brothers, and both unmarried. They talked to me about the *Gita*.16 They were reading Sir Edwin Arnold's translation—*The Song Celestial*—and they invited me to read the original with them. I felt ashamed, as I had read the divine poem neither in Sanskrit nor in Gujarati. I was constrained to tell them that I had not read the *Gita*, but that I would gladly read it with them, and that though my knowledge of Sanskrit was meagre, still I hoped to be able to understand the original to the extent of telling where the translation failed to bring out the meaning. I began reading the *Gita* with them. The verses in the second chapter:

> If one
> Ponders on objects of sense, there springs
> Attraction; from attraction grows desire,
> Desire flames to fierce passion,
> passion breeds recklessness;
> then the memory—all betrayed—
> Lets noble purpose go, and saps the mind,
> Till purpose, mind, and man are all undone.[17]

made a deep impression on my mind, and they still ring in my ears. The book struck me as one of priceless worth. The impression has ever since been growing on me with the result that I regard it today as the book *par excellence* for the knowledge of Truth. It has afforded me invaluable help in my moments of gloom. I have read almost all the English translations of it, and I regard Sir Edwin Arnold's as the best. He has been faithful to the text, and yet it does not read like a translation. Though I read the *Gita* with these friends, I cannot pretend to have studied it then. It was only after some years that it became a book of daily reading.

The brothers also recommended *The Light of Asia*[18] by Sir Edwin Arnold, whom I knew till then only as the author of *The Song Celestial*, and I read it with even greater interest than I did the *Bhagavadgita*. Once I had begun it I could not leave off. They also took me on one occasion to the Blavatsky Lodge and introduced me to Madame Blavatsky and Mrs. Besant.[19] The latter had just then joined the Theosophical Society, and I was following with great interest the controversy about her conversion. The friends advised me to join the Society, but I politely declined saying, "With my meagre knowledge of my own religion I do not want to belong to any religious body." I recall having read, at the brothers' insistence, Madame Blavatsky's *Key to Theosophy*. This book stimulated in me the desire to read books on Hinduism, and disabused me of the notion fostered by the missionaries that Hinduism was rife with superstition.

About the same time I met a good Christian from Manchester in a vegetarian boarding house. He talked to me about Christianity. I narrated to him my Rajkot recollections. He was pained to hear them. He said, "I am a vegetarian. I do not drink. Many Christians are meat-eaters and drink, no doubt; but neither meat-eating nor drinking is enjoined by Scripture. Do please read the Bible." I accepted his advice and he got me a copy. I have a faint recollection that he himself used to sell copies of the Bible, and I purchased from him an edition containing maps, concordance, and other aids. I began reading it, but I could not possibly read through the Old Testament. I read the book of Genesis, and the chapters that followed invariably sent me to sleep. But just for the sake of being able to say that

I had read it, I plodded through the other books with much difficulty and without the least interest or understanding. I disliked reading the book of Numbers.

But the New Testament produced a different impression, especially the Sermon on the Mount which went straight to my heart. I compared it with the *Gita*. The verses, "But I say unto you, that ye resist not evil: but whosoever shall smite thee on thy right cheek, turn to him the other also. And if any man . . . take away thy coat let him have thy cloak too,"[20] delighted me beyond measure and put me in mind of Shamal Bhatt's "For a bowl of water give me a goodly meal" etc. My young mind tried to unify the teaching of the *Gita*, the *Light of Asia* and the Sermon on the Mount. That renunciation was the highest form of religion appealed to me greatly. This reading whetted my appetite for studying the lives of other religious teachers. A friend recommended Carlyle's *Heroes and Hero-Worship*.[21] I read the chapter on the Hero as a prophet and learnt of the Prophet's greatness and bravery and austere living.

Beyond this acquaintance with religion I could not go at the moment, as reading for the examination[22] left me scarcely any time for outside subjects. But I took mental note that I should read more religious books and acquaint myself with all the principal religions.

And how could I help knowing something of atheism too? Every Indian knew Bradlaugh's name and his so-called atheism.[23] I read some book about it, the name of which I forget. It had no effect on me, for I had already crossed the Sahara of atheism. Mrs. Besant who was then very much in the limelight, had turned to theism from atheism, and that fact also strengthened my aversion to atheism. I had read her book *How I Became a Theosophist*.

It was at about this time that Bradlaugh died. He was buried in the Woking cemetery. I attended the funeral, as I believe every Indian living in London did. A few clergymen were also present to do him the last honours. On our way back from the funeral we had to wait at the station for our train. A champion atheist from the crowd heckled one of these clergymen.

"Well, sir, you believe in the existence of God?"

"I do," said the good man in a low tone.

"You also agree that the circumference of the Earth is 28,000 miles, don't you?" said the atheist with a smile of self-assurance.

"Indeed."

"Pray tell me then the size of your God and where he may be?"

"Well, if we but knew, He resides in the hearts of us both."

"Now, now, don't take me to be a child," said the champion with a triumphant look at us.

The clergyman assumed a humble silence.

This talk still further increased my prejudice against atheism.

Christian Contacts

The next day at one o'clock I went to Mr. Baker's prayer-meeting. There I was introduced to Miss Harris, Miss Gabb, Mr. Coates and others. Everyone kneeled down to pray, and I followed suit. The prayers were supplications to God for various things, according to each person's desire. Thus the usual forms were for the day to be passed peacefully, or for God to open the doors of the heart.

A prayer was now added for my welfare: "Lord, show the path to the new brother who has come amongst us. Give him, Lord, the peace that Thou hast given us. May the Lord Jesus who has saved us save him too. We ask all this in the name of Jesus." There was no singing of hymns or other music at these meetings. After the supplication for something special every day, we dispersed, each going to his lunch, this being the hour for it. The prayer did not take more than five minutes.

The Misses Harris and Gabb were both elderly maiden ladies. Mr. Coates was a Quaker. The two ladies lived together, and they gave me a standing invitation to four o'clock tea at their house every Sunday.

When we met on Sundays, I used to give Mr. Coates my religious diary for the week, and discuss with him the books I had read and the impression they had left on me. The ladies used to narrate their sweet experiences and talk about the peace they had found.

Mr. Coates was a frank-hearted staunch young man. We went out for walks together, and he also took me to other Christian friends.

As we came closer to each other, he began to give me books of his own choice, until my shelf was filled with them. He loaded me with books, as it were. In pure faith I consented to read all those books, and as I went on reading them we discussed them.

I read a number of such books in 1893. I do not remember the names of them all, but they included the *Commentary* of Dr. Parker of the City Temple, Pearson's *Many Infallible Proofs* and Butler's *Analogy*.[24] I liked some things in them, while I did not like others. *Many Infallible Proofs* were proofs in support of the religion of the Bible, as the author understood it. The book had no effect on me. Parker's *Commentary* was morally stimulating, but it could not be of any help to one who had no faith in the prevalent Christian beliefs. Butler's *Analogy* struck me to be a very profound and difficult book, which should be read four or five times to be understood properly. It seemed to me to be written with a view to converting atheists to theism. The arguments advanced in it regarding the existence of God were unnecessary for me, as I had then passed the stage of unbelief; but the arguments in proof of Jesus being the only incarnation of God and the Mediator between God and man left me unmoved.

But Mr. Coates was not the man to easily accept defeat. He had great affection for me. He saw, round my neck, the Vaishnava necklace of *Tulasi* beads. He thought it to be a superstition and was pained by it. "This superstition does not become you. Come, let me break the necklace."

"No, you will not. It is a sacred gift from my mother."

"But do you believe in it?"

"I do not know its mysterious significance. I do not think I should come to harm if I did not wear it. But I cannot, without sufficient reason, give up a necklace that she put round my neck out of love and in the conviction that it would be conducive to my welfare. When, with the passage of time, it wears away and breaks of its own accord, I shall have no desire to get a new one. But this necklace cannot be broken."

Mr. Coates could not appreciate my argument, as he had no regard for my religion. He was looking forward to delivering me from the abyss of ignorance. He wanted to convince me that, no matter whether there was some truth in other religions, salvation was impossible for me unless I accepted Christianity which represented *the* truth, and that my sins would not be washed away except by the intercession of Jesus, and that all good works were useless.

Just as he introduced me to several books, he introduced me to several friends whom he regarded as staunch Christians. One of these introductions was to a family which belonged to the Plymouth Brethren, a Christian sect.[25]

Many of the contacts for which Mr. Coates was responsible were good. Most struck me as being God-fearing. But during my contact with this family, one of the Plymouth Brethren confronted me with an argument for which I was not prepared:

"You cannot understand the beauty of our religion. From what you say it appears that you must be brooding over your transgressions every moment of your life, always mending them and atoning for them. How can this ceaseless cycle of action bring you redemption? You can never have peace. You admit that we are all sinners. Now look at the perfection of our belief. Our attempts at improvement and atonement are futile. And yet redemption we must have. How can we bear the burden of sin? We can but throw it on Jesus. He is the only sinless Son of God. It is His word that those who believe in Him shall have everlasting life. Therein lies God's infinite mercy. And as we believe in the atonement of Jesus, our own sins do not bind us. Sin we must. It is impossible to live in this world sinless. And therefore Jesus suffered and atoned for all the sins of mankind. Only he who accepts His great redemption can have eternal peace. Think what a life of restlessness is yours, and what a promise of peace we have."

The argument utterly failed to convince me. I humbly replied:

"If this be the Christianity acknowledged by all Christians, I cannot accept it. I do not seek redemption from the consequences of my sin. I seek to be redeemed from sin itself, or rather from the very thought of sin. Until I have attained that end, I shall be content to be restless."

To which the Plymouth Brother rejoined: "I assure you, your attempt is fruitless. Think again over what I have said."

And the Brother proved as good as his word. He knowingly committed transgressions, and showed me that he was undisturbed by the thought of them.[26]

But I already knew before meeting with these friends that all Christians did not believe in such a theory of atonement. Mr. Coates himself walked in fear of God. His heart was pure, and he believed in the possibility of self-purification. The two ladies also shared this belief. Some of the books that came into my hands were full of devotion. So, although Mr. Coates was very much disturbed by this latest experience of mine, I was able to reassure him and tell him that the distorted belief of a Plymouth Brother could not prejudice me against Christianity.

My difficulties lay elsewhere. They were with regard to the Bible and its accepted interpretation.

Religious Ferment

It is now time to turn once again to my experiences with Christian friends.

Mr. Baker was getting anxious about my future. He took me to the Wellington Convention. The Protestant Christians organize such gatherings every few years for religious enlightenment or, in other words, self-purification. One may call this religious restoration or revival. The Wellington Convention was of this type. The chairman was the famous divine of the place, the Rev. Andrew Murray. Mr. Baker had hoped that the atmosphere of religious exaltation at the Convention, and the enthusiasm and earnestness of the people attending it, would inevitably lead me to embrace Christianity.

But his final hope was the efficacy of prayer. He had an abiding faith in prayer. It was his firm conviction that God could not but listen to prayer fervently offered. He would cite the instances of men like George Muller of Bristol, who depended entirely on prayer even for his temporal needs. I listened to his discourse on the efficacy of prayer with unbiased attention, and assured him that nothing could prevent me from embracing Christianity, should I feel the call. I had no hesitation in giving him this assurance, as I had long since taught myself to follow the inner voice. I delighted in submitting to it. To act against it would be difficult and painful to me.

So we went to Wellington. Mr. Baker was hard put to it in having "a coloured man" like me for his companion. He had to suffer inconveniences on many occasions entirely on account of me. We had to break the journey on the way, as one of the days happened to be a Sunday, and Mr. Baker and his party would not travel on the sabbath. Though the manager of the station hotel agreed to take me in after much altercation, he absolutely refused to admit me to the dining room. Mr. Baker was not the man to give way easily. He stood by the rights of the guests of a hotel. But I could see his difficulty. At Wellington also I stayed with Mr. Baker. In spite of his best efforts to conceal the little inconveniences that he was put to, I could see them all.

This Convention was an assemblage of devout Christians. I was delighted at their faith. I met the Rev. Murray. I saw that many were praying for me. I liked some of their hymns, they were very sweet.

The Convention lasted for three days. I could understand and appreciate the devoutness of those who attended it. But I saw no reason for changing my belief — my religion. It was impossible for me to believe that I could go to heaven or attain salvation only by becoming a Christian. When I frankly said so to some of the good Christian friends, they were shocked. But there was no help for it.

My difficulties lay deeper. It was more than I could believe that Jesus was the only incarnate son of God, and that only he who believed in him would have everlasting life. If God could have sons, all of us were His sons. If Jesus was like God, or God Himself, then all men were like God and could be God Himself. My reason was not ready to believe literally that Jesus by his death and by his blood redeemed the sins of the world. Metaphorically there might be some truth in it. Again, according to Christianity only human beings had souls, and not other living beings, for whom death meant complete extinction; while I held a contrary belief. I could accept Jesus as a martyr, an embodiment of sacrifice, and a divine teacher, but not as the most perfect man ever born. His death on the Cross was a great example to the world, but that there was anything like a mysterious or miraculous virtue in it my heart could not accept. The pious lives of Christians did not give me anything that the lives of men of other faiths had failed to give. I had seen in other lives just the same reformation that I had heard of among Christians. Philosophically there was nothing extraordinary in Christian principles. From the point of view of sacrifice, it seemed to me that the Hindus greatly surpassed the Christians. It was impossible for me to regard Christianity as a perfect religion or the greatest of all religions.

I shared this mental churning with my Christian friends whenever there was an opportunity, but their answers could not satisfy me.

Thus if I could not accept Christianity either as a perfect, or the greatest, religion, neither was I then convinced of Hinduism being such. Hindu defects were pressingly visible to me. If untouchability could be a part of Hinduism, it could be but a rotten part or an excrescence. I could not understand the raison d'être of a multitude of sects and castes. What was the meaning of saying that the Vedas were the inspired Word of God? If they were inspired, why not also the Bible and the Koran?

As Christian friends were endeavouring to convert me, even so were Musalman[27] friends. Abdulla Sheth had kept on inducing me to study Islam, and of course he had always something to say regarding its beauty.

I expressed my difficulties in a letter to Raychandbhai.[28] I also corresponded with other religious authorities in India and received answers from them. Raychandbhai's letter somewhat pacified me. He asked me to be patient and to study Hinduism more deeply. One of his sentences was to this effect: "On a dispassionate view of the question I am convinced that no other religion has the subtle and profound thought of Hinduism, its vision of the soul, or its charity."

I purchased Sale's translation of the Koran and began reading it. I also obtained other books on Islam. I communicated with Christian friends in England. One of them introduced me to Edward Maitland, with whom I opened correspondence. He sent me *The Perfect Way*, a book he had written in collaboration with Anna Kingsford. The book was a repudiation of the current Christian belief. He also sent me another book, *The New Interpretation of the Bible*.[29] I liked both. They seemed to suppport Hinduism. Tolstoy's *The Kingdom of God is Within You*[30] overwhelmed me. It left an abiding impression on me. Before the independent thinking, profound morality, and the truthfulness of this book, all the books given me by Mr. Coates seemed to pale into insignificance.

My studies thus carried me in a direction unthought of by the Christian friends. My correspondence with Edward Maitland was fairly prolonged, and that with Raychandbhai continued until his death. I read some of the books he sent me. These included *Panchikaran, Maniratnamala, Mumukshu Prakaran of Yogavasishtha*, Haribhadra Suri's *Shaddarshana Samuchchaya* and others.[31]

Though I took a path my Christian friends had not intended for me, I have remained for ever indebted to them for the religious quest that they awakened in me. I shall always cherish the memory of their contact. The years that followed had more, not less, of such sweet and sacred contacts in store for me.

Comparative Study of Religions

If I found myself entirely absorbed in the service of the community,[32] the reason behind it was my desire for self-realization. I had made the religion of service my own, as I felt that God could be realized only through service. And service for me was the service of India, because it came to me without my seeking, because I had an aptitude for it. I had gone to South Africa for travel, for finding an escape from Kathiawad intrigues and for gaining my own livelihood. But as I have said, I found myself in search of God and striving for self-realization.

Christian friends had whetted my appetite for knowledge, which had become almost insatiable, and they would not leave me in peace, even if I desired to be indifferent. In Durban, Mr. Spencer Walton, the head of the South Africa General Mission, found me out. I became almost a member of his family. At the back of this acquaintance was of course my contact with Christians in Pretoria. Mr. Walton had a manner all his own. I do not recollect his ever having invited me to embrace Christianity. But he placed his life as an open book before me, and let me watch all his movements. Mrs. Walton was a very gentle and talented woman. I liked the attitude of this couple. We knew the fundamental differences between us. Any amount of discussion could not efface them. Yet even differences prove helpful, where there are tolerance, charity and truth. I liked Mr. and Mrs. Walton's humility, perseverance and devotion to work, and we met very frequently.

This friendship kept alive my interest in religion. It was impossible now to get the leisure that I used to have in Pretoria for my religious studies. But what little time I could spare I turned to good account. My religious correspondence continued. Raychandbhai was guiding me. Some friend sent me Narmadashanker's book *Dharma Vichar*.[33] Its preface proved very helpful. I had heard about the Bohemian way in which the poet had lived, and a description in the preface of the revolution effected in his life by his religious studies captivated me. I came to like the book, and read it from cover to cover with attention. I read with interest Max Müller's book *India – What Can it Teach Us?*[34] and the translation of the *Upanishads* published by the Theosophical Society. All this enhanced my regard for Hinduism, and its beauties began to grow upon me. I read Washington Irving's *Life of Mahomet and His Successors*[35] and Carlyle's panegyric on the Prophet.[36] These books raised Muhammad in my estimation. I also read a book called *The Sayings of Zarathustra*.

Thus I gained more knowledge of the different religions. The study stimulated my self-introspection and fostered in me the habit of putting into practice whatever appealed to me in my studies. Thus I began some of the Yogic practices, as well as I could understand them from a reading of the Hindu books. But I could not get on very far, and decided to follow them with the help of some expert when I returned to India. The desire has never been fulfilled.

I made too an intensive study of Tolstoy's books. *The Gospels in Brief, What to Do?* and other books made a deep impression on me. I began to realize more and more the infinite possibilities of universal love.

About the same time I came into contact with another Christian family. At their suggestion I attended the Wesleyan church every Sunday. For these days I also had their standing invitation to dinner. The church did not make a favourable impression on me. The sermons seemed to be uninspiring. The congregation did not strike me as being particularly religious. They were not an assembly of devout souls; they appeared rather to be worldly-minded people, going to church for recreation and in conformity to custom. Here, at times, I would involuntarily doze. I was ashamed, but some of my neighbours, who were in no better case, lightened the shame. I could not go on long like this, and soon gave up attending the service.

My connection with the family I used to visit every Sunday was abruptly broken. In fact it may be said that I was warned to visit it no more. It happened thus. My hostess was a good and simple woman, but somewhat narrow-minded. We always discussed religious subjects. I was then re-reading Arnold's *Light of Asia*. Once we began to compare the life of Jesus with that of Buddha. "Look at Gautama's[37] compassion!" said I. "It was not confined to mankind, it was extended to all living beings. Does not one's heart overflow with love to think of the lamb joyously perched on his shoulders? One fails to notice this love for all living beings in the life of Jesus." The comparison pained the good lady. I could understand her feelings. I cut the matter short, and we went to the dining room. Her son, a cherub aged scarcely five, was also with us. I am happiest when in the midst of children, and this youngster and I had long been friends. I spoke derisively of the piece of meat on his plate and in high praise of the apple on mine. The innocent boy was carried away and joined in my praise of the fruit.

But the mother? She was dismayed.

I was warned. I checked myself and changed the subject. The following week I visited the family as usual, but not without trepidation. I did not see that I should stop going there. I did not think it proper either. But the good lady made my way easy.

"Mr. Gandhi," she said, "please don't take it ill if I feel obliged to tell you that my boy is none the better for your company. Every day he hesitates to eat meat and asks for fruit, reminding me of your argument. This is too much. If he gives up meat, he is bound to get weak, if not ill. How could I bear it? Your discussions should henceforth be only with us elders. They are sure to react badly on children."

"Mrs. —," I replied, "I am sorry. I can understand your feelings as a parent, for I too have children. We can very easily end this unpleasant state of things. What I eat and omit to eat is bound to have a greater effect on the child than what I say. The best way, therefore, is for me to stop these visits. That certainly need not affect our friendship."

"I thank you," she said with evident relief.

18

"Christianity in the Reflection of Hinduism"[1]

BITHIKA MUKERJI

INTRODUCTION

Professor Mukerji was born and educated in India, and has devoted a good deal of her writing to an exposition of neo-Vedanta. She has studied and taught at several universities in North America and Europe and has taught in the department of philosophy at Banaras Hindu University. In the essay reprinted here she shows Christianity as it appears when interpreted through the conceptual categories of Advaita Vedanta,[2] a radically nondualistic philosophical perspective.

Especially important in this essay is her use of the idea of a "self-authenticating experience" as the basis for the way in which Hinduism can make room for a multiplicity of different religious communities. What is revealed in such an experience, Professor Mukerji suggests, is "the reality of the dimension of the unspoken," in which no formulation of religious truth in words can hope to encapsulate reality. Variety in such verbal formulations is precisely to be expected, and even to be celebrated when it occurs. So the verbal formulae that Christians have often taken to be definitive of their faith are not judged false; they are simply judged to be one more piece of the puzzle. There is, of course, a paradox here: if Professor Mukerji's position is that all verbal formulae purporting to describe ultimate reality do so equally well, then it will follow that any verbal formula that claims to describe ultimate reality better and more fully than any other such formula must describe that reality just as well as those other formulae, which make no such exclusivist claim. And such a conclusion should lead to a certain amount of uneasiness.

"CHRISTIANITY IN THE REFLECTION OF HINDUISM"

"The History of the study of alien religious experience in Judaism, Islam, Hinduism, Buddhism and Confucianism remains to be written."*[3] Since these lines were written by Joachim Wach nearly thirty years ago, no significant contribution has been made in this direction by any of the religions named by him. Christianity, on the other hand, is distinguished by its preoccupation with other faiths. From within the region of exclusivity which he learns to cherish and guard, the Christian is constantly called upon to address "the other," to bring him to a realisation of the need for the saving grace of Christ. The role of "the other" therefore, is crucial as the partner in this on-going process of dialogue, where dialogue is used as the adumbration of the Christian message.*4

The Hindu scholar has nothing to show as against the bulk of literature compiled by Christian missionaries or the stupendous work done by Indologists. It could be a rewarding undertaking to examine the reasons for this lack of awareness of alien religions in the reflection of Hinduism, but for the purpose of this paper one factor alone needs to be stressed as relevant to the issue. The Hindu, in general, is not called upon to preach his religion to "the other." "The other," to the Hindu is a *fellow-pilgrim* rather as if a mirror which reflects his own self-understanding. Since evangelisation forms no part of his own faith he can easily countenance any alternate scheme of worship as a viable way of religious life. His appreciation for "the other's" devotional attitude would preclude him from making any belittling criticisms, even in self-defence. That, indeed, would be "anathema" to the Hindu.

The Hindu does not or need not recognise situations of "challenges" or "confrontations" in the sphere of commitment to God. He would rather feel called upon to view with utmost sensitivity the *dimension of the sacred being presented to him*. It must be acknowledged however, that ordinarily no such demand is made upon the Hindu by Christians. As far as Christianity is concerned, Hinduism comprises of the entire gamut of heresies from paganism to pantheism and thus the Hindu may be an ideal partner in a dialogue but never the spokesman for a way to God-realisation.

Christianity in the reflection of Hinduism, consequently could be seen only as it presents itself to an alien culture. In order to clarify this, the first part of the paper takes up the assessment of the changing order of the role of Christianity with regard to Hinduism. As a complementary thesis, in the second part of the paper, an attempt is made to delineate the Hindu meaning of "revelation." It is true that Hinduism is not considered to be a revealed religion by Christianity, nevertheless a focussing on its source of inspiration may make it clear how a commonwealth of religions is not only acceptable but rather a matter of celebration to the Hindu. By this separation of issues it is hoped that the possibility of mutual understanding could be envisaged at a deeper level than that of a dialogue.

Christianity in Confrontation with Other Traditions

The long history of Christianity is enriched by the dedicated work of men who devoted themselves to the task of carrying out the commandment:

All power is given unto me in heaven and in earth. Go ye, therefore, and teach all nations, baptising them in the name of the Father, and of the Son, and of the Holy Ghost: teaching them to oberve all things whatsoever I have commanded you: and lo, I am with you always, even unto the end of the world. Amen (Matthew 28:18–20).

The coming of Christ was the supremely unique event in history which gave a new direction to human destiny. The cross symbolises the intersection of transcendence and immanence, the vertical descent of the Divine onto the horizontal plane of the mundane. Out of compassion, God chose to participate in the human condition as Man so that men by taking refuge in this act for grace, may overcome death and attain salvation.

The small band of disciples who preached this Gospel to all nations became the Church of Christ. All alien religions came into contact with Christianity through the ministry of the Church. Thus the Church is important as the gateway to Christianity. The movement of evangelisation is of some interest to the Hindu because thus far his experience of Christianity has had no chance to go beyond it. Hinduism, prepared to revel in its so-called "paganism," was required to view it as a "defilement."[*5] His most cherished philosophical ideas regarding the unity of the self with Brahman were trivialised as the natural reaction of a tropical people against robust individualism.[*6]

More recently, Hinduism has been seen as an ancient culture which can rise to sublime heights of spirituality. In this the case of Hinduism is comparable to Hellenic culture. The Church Fathers had conceded that philosophy is admissible as preparation for the coming of the Church. The same criterion could be applied to Hinduism as well. All ancient cultures have produced or are capable of producing men of outstanding faith who are no doubt moved by the spirit of God, and as such eligible for entry into the Church.

Christianity in confrontation with other traditions, cultures, ways of worship, remained unshaken in its self-confidence as the unique message of God for mankind. The combination of faith and dogma cast in the mould of providential eschatology was a powerful force which rode the crest of missionary zeal for many centuries.

The present century has brought about many changes in the outlook of the Church. We live now under the shadow of a crisis situation. This has created a new mood of sensitivity regarding inter-religious confrontations. The movement of ecumenism within the Protestant Church as well as the II Vatican Council have brought about an openness toward "the other" which has radicalised the methodology of conversion.

Hinduism would welcome this change but it is obliged to see that evangelisation lies at the heart of Christianity. Because the acceptance of the authenticity of other religions by the II Vatican Council seems bracketed by the suggestion that the non-Christian multitudes have the right to listen to the Gospels and so the idea of the Christian mission would seem to remain. It is true that a few eminent theologians have sought to minimise the "otherness" of alien religions. Karl Rahner's theory of Anonymous Christianity[7] has found wide favour in this context. The orthodox Christian, however dismisses it as amounting to an equalisation of all religions and to the Hindu it seems another form of being forced into the matrix of pre-paredness for the Church.

In truth, the Hindu is such a stranger to the concept of an institution-alised religion that he is unable to appreciate the prescriptive role of the Church. The Church has a peculiarly singular way as it were of looking at the spiritual map of the world. The totality of the perspective is transfixed to one unique vantage point. If we consider the meaning of the word "per-spective" as used by Shakespeare we can see the implication of the Chris-tian interpretation of human destiny:

> . . . perspectives, which when rightly gazed upon, Show nothing but confusion; ey'd awry Distinguish form (Richard Second II.11.18).

The world, to the Christian, is a jumbled facade which must be "ey'd awry" through the slant of the New Covenant. He is unable to see meaning or truth in "the other's" way of worship. In this context we may refer to the famous sermon by Paul which serves as a model for evangelists at all times:

> For as I passed by, and beheld your devotions, I found an altar with this inscription, TO THE UNKNOWN GOD. Whom therefore ye ignorantly worship, him I declare to you (Acts 17:23).

The question may be raised whether the Athenians could have said to Paul: "Him that you have found now, we already render homage to because he is truly unknown but not unknowable." We must stretch our imagination further and say that Paul would then have identified the philosophy of the Athenians as the heresy of gnosticism.

This brings us to the second part of the paper. *Hinduism emphasises the "unknown-ness" of God but not his unknowability.* It is man's privilege to respond to the highest calling for engaging in the most worthwhile adven-ture of life. The certainty of success alone is stated by the Hindu scriptures, leaving him free to choose his own way of engaging in this endeavour. All religions have a ritualistic structure of worship. A *wide range of possibilities seems* almost inevitable because men do not react in the same way to the quest for God-realisation. The Hindu scriptures therefore, celebrate the infinite ways of God's participation in human affairs, not seeking to deny that every occasion of the manifestation of his grace is unique in itself.

The Authenticating of Many Religions in Hinduism

Revelation pertains to the unmanifest, the unspoken, the ultimately hidden mystery of existence. The stirring of interest in the meaning of the givenness of the many-splendored universe is felt within the heart.*⁸ The Indian scriptures always mention the heart in this context possibly because the brain is too ready with resolutions which makes opaque what it seeks to understand. It is not in the nature of reason to await answers. Thus an inwardisation of the questing spirit marks the beginning of an awareness of the longing for penetrating the mystery of existence.

The heart experiences a yearning for the supreme felicity of a "home coming" which is endemic to the human condition itself. It is natural for the traveller, who finds himself out of tune with his surroundings, to seek to return whence he came and where he could be himself. To such a pilgrim the scriptures speak of the final state of self-realisation which is in the nature of a supreme gain.*⁹

The nature of this "supreme gain" is stated obliquely in many ways, in paradoxes in anecdotes and also in the form of the dialogue between teacher and disciple. The "Unknown-ness" of the nature of the final finding is not disclosed because in the ultimate analysis the supreme living experience cannot be communicated as a commensurable commodity. It is felt within the being of the aspirant and needs no confirmation because the experience is self-authenticating. The man of enlightenment, thereafter, by his way of being in the world forges another link in the chain of living exemplars in the tradition who inspire other pilgrims toward the way of spiritual life.

The man of realisation is a seer, a sage who can bear witness to the reality of the dimension of the unspoken, but eminently speakable which manifests itself in the unity of soundless resonance and the vision of divine prefigurement of letters known as the mantra. The mantra, a pulsating unity of sound and vision, by flashing into the consciousness of the seer, irradiates his understanding so that he is in tune with the cosmic rhythm of the universe. This experiencing of the unveiling of the ultimate mystery is celebrated in the sacred language of the *Vedas*.¹⁰ The Vedas are therefore a celebration of the experience of fulfilment which imparts authenticity to the promise of "supreme gain." The language of the Veda itself is of the nature of Truth itself. It is distinguished from secular language by virtue of the particular order of the arrangement of syllables, the sequence of words and the rhythm which holds them together. The unity of all three is the mantra.

The Vedic tradition has been preserved by a very exact system of memorising and recitation. The mantra is not created by man and has its being in the enlightened consciousness of the seer, the poet, and thus it perpetuates a living tradition of spiritual quest and its fulfillment.

Much has been written on the nature of this self-realisation. For the advaita philosophy it is the knowledge of the unity of the self with Brahman. All other vedantic traditions, which comprise the framework of Hinduism, reject this position. All religions use the language of God-realisation. The devotional prayers of God-intoxicated men have enriched all the languages of India. In the sphere of religious commitment no dogma can operate because God has infinite ways of disclosing Himself to his devotee. Thus variety is a matter of celebration and rejoicing as evidence of the myriad possibilities of the coming together of man and the Person (the *Ishta*[11]) who is dear to his heart. The wealth of man's outpourings of the heart at the feet of the Lord is truly immeasurable and no limits are sought to be put to channelise them in one direction. No one can legislate for another as to the true image of God because his images are legion. All forms are his because he is formless, all auspicious qualities are his because he is the ultimate repository of all magnificence.

This fluidity is anchored on the rock of the nature of a spiritual aspiration. The spiritual journey of a pilgrim begins when he feels the yearning for a restoring of his fragmented existence in the world or in the language of religion when he engages in a steadfast, onepointed, untrammelled seeking for refuge in God. Times and conditions of human existence keep on changing but the yearning for penetrating the mystery of our givenness in the world survives. The living voice of Sruti[12] sustains this questioning, inspires the seeker to become a pilgrim and promises that the quest is not in vain but will be crowned with success. Revelation, therefore, in the Indian context perpetuates the asking of questions promising the worthwhileness of the quest.*[13] The answer remains in the region of grace. It is the region of mystery which indeed makes spiritual life the greatest adventure of human existence.

The highest truth is preserved in concealment. There is no will to truth here or a rationalising of dogmatic faith; what is sought to be preserved is the relevance of yearning toward truth.

Christianity in the reflection of Hinduism is yet another dimension in which God has disclosed himself to his People. The commitment to Christ is easily understood by a Hindu who is committed to a particular way of devotion in his own tradition. The nature of commitment demands that it should be exclusive, as well as involve the whole being of the pilgrim in search of spiritual fulfillment. It could be said that the Hindu would believe in a community of committed people which is a free association of friends who come together to celebrate each other's way of seeking God-realisation.*[14]

19

"Vaishnavism on Hans Küng: A Hindu Theology of Religious Pluralism"[1]

BIBHUTI S. YADAV

INTRODUCTION

Bibhuti Yadav is professor of religious studies at Temple University in Philadelphia. He holds a Ph.D. in philosophy from Banaras Hindu University and has written extensively on Indian philosophy and, more recently, on Christian views of Hinduism.[2] He represents, in the piece reprinted here, Vaishnava Hinduism, both as a scholar and as a practitioner. "Vaishnavas" are followers of the God Vishnu, particularly in his incarnation or avatar *as Krishna. The legendary and mythological accounts of the life of Krishna in the large body of sacred literature known as* Purana *is of special importance to Vaishnavas, and Yadav refers to these texts often in the essay that follows.*

Yadav's essay, of which only about half is reprinted here—the second half, sketching a Vaishnava theology of religious pluralism in opposition to that of Hans Küng, analyzed and criticized in the first half, could not be included—is of special interest for the purposes of this volume, since it is the only one of the essays in Part 4 to self-consciously and polemically engage the thought of a particular Christian theologian on religious pluralism. Yadav chooses Hans Küng to be his interlocutor, basing his exposition and critique upon a relatively early work of Küng's, Freedom Today *(1966).*

Küng is professor of ecumenical theology at the University of Tübingen in West Germany. He is a Roman Catholic theologian, who during the last two decades has become famous for questioning the teaching of the Vatican on a number of key theological issues, ranging from papal infallibility to Christology. He has also shown an increasing interest in the problem of developing a Chris-

tian theology of non-Christian religions; while the version of his position that Yadav chooses to attack may not be precisely representative of Küng's most recent stance on this matter,[3] the interest of Yadav's work for us lies not so much in whether it accurately represents Küng as in the kinds of argument it develops against a particular Christian position on religious pluralism.

Yadav expounds Küng's position in the first part of the extract that follows and criticizes it in the second. In doing both he adopts a highly flavored rhetorical tone and a polemical stance. For him Küng represents both hypocrisy and ambiguity, an attempt to hide old-style Christian imperialism behind a rhetoric of love and compassion. Küng's attempt to locate "special revelation" in Jesus Christ and to restrict the non-Christian religions to a "general revelation" that, while it contains truth and may even be salvific, is inferior to and different in kind from that available to Christians is, to Yadav, "a methodology that perceives fantasies as facts," and, moreover, one that "does not let God be God."

Yadav, being a theist and one who believes strongly, as do most Christians, in God's universal salvific will and in God's ability to make salvation available to human beings by becoming incarnate among them, is offended at the particularity and universality of Küng's claims for the incarnation of God in Christ. All those criteria that Küng applies to distinguish the "genuine" incarnation from the "mythological" or "false" incarnations appear to Yadav as no more than an attempt to give metaphysical grounding to personal and cultural fantasies of superiority. And — although Yadav does not himself make this connection — there can be little doubt that such "fantasies" are all the more objectionable to him because of their historical rooting in European colonialism.

"VAISHNAVISM ON HANS KÜNG: A HINDU THEOLOGY OF RELIGIOUS PLURALISM"

Christian theology of redemptive history has taken an unusual turn in recent times. It has finally acknowledged that non-Christian religions exist, and that they too are in some way committed to the Ultimate. "It will," says a leading Christian theologian, "be increasingly apparent, and it is already essentially true, that to be a Christian in the modern world or [a] Jew or agnostic, is to be so in a society in which other men, intelligent, devout and religious, are Buddhists, Muslims, and Hindus."[4]

The world after all has become a small place, thanks to economic interdependence of nations, communications, and travel of ideas. For reasons that were not always spiritual, Christians could afford to say whatever they wanted to say about non-Christian religions. Not any more. Words such as "Hare Krishna,"[5] "Dhyani Buddhas"[6] are being heard in Western societies, words that come from lands which were supposed to be those of God and His only Son. Populism apart, Christianity has noted with seriousness the words of liberal humanists such as Gandhi, who said: "I believe in the Gita. I regard all the great faiths of the world as equally true with my own."

Such a humanist form of life required a form of thinking, a philosophical construction of the world in which all religions are equal, and in which one inflicts injury on one's own religion by devaluating the religions of others. The idea was to establish the universality of mankind, so to conceive the Ultimate that it sustains history, especially religious history, in terms of the logic of "both/and," unity as well as difference. Radhakrishnan[7] promoted this ontology of universal humanity in most of his works, particularly in his *Eastern Religions and Western Thought.* He posited the sort of Absolute which has not only become *actio immanent*[8] in all revelations, but is especially and differently present in them all. Such an Absolute is the ground of transcendental unity as well as the historical differences of religions. To claim "special revelation" for a religion is anthropomorphic; it is an argument to kill the Absolute and to enthrone oneself as Absolute. Radhakrishnan further argued that the Absolute is larger than its revelations, that no revelation is as absolutely true as the Absolute, and that all revelations are equally true but relative in relation to the Absolute.

Hans Küng's Theology of Religions

Such is Radhakrishnan's ontology of religious tolerance, an argument for a form of life lived in peaceful coexistence. No thinking Christian would disagree with Radhakrishnan's efforts towards religious pluralism and tolerance. What worries them is his method of arriving at the conclusion, the necessity of relativising all religions between themselves and in relation to God. It challenges the Christian claim of universality and uniqueness, and has caused a sense of methodological inadequacy among thinking Christians. Needless to say, Christian theology has traditionally been confident, rooted as it was in the jealous God who had said "I am the first and I am the last; besides me there is no God. Who is like me? Let him proclaim it." Such a God housed himself in the Church, whose self-defined task was to divinise herself by accepting on faith this self-congratulation of God by God. As the house of God, the Church has been living in terms of the following conviction: "I am the first and I am the last house of God; beside me there is no house of God. Who is like me? If there is let him be proclaimed." The Church was no less jealous than the God whom it housed. It declared: "Outside the church [there is] no salvation." The jealous God would not tolerate any other God before or after him, and he would not tolerate any other in between. Honest to God, new-Israel[9] was committed to equate what it wished to see with what there was to see in fact; it reduced history to a theological space. It would not recognize any other form of reducing "nature" to history, the world of things to a worldview. The Church outsmarted God in being jealous; it declared as "natural" a worldview which had no place for the natural humanity crucified in the second Adam and symbolised by the Cross.

But history is equally jealous. It has finally impressed upon the Church that it is easier for God to be jealous, not so easy to implement this non-historical jealousy in history. The Vedas are after all older than the Bible, Banaras[10] exists besides Jerusalem, and the Ganges keeps on flowing in spite of the Jordan. This alienation between promise and performance has forced the Church to be realistic.

Outside church no salvation: can you actually keep on saying this when you look with honesty at the present time, and consider that of the more than three billion present inhabitants of the earth only about 950 million are Christians, and of these only about 584 million are Catholics. That in India only 2.4% are Christians and only 1.2% Catholics, while in China and Japan only about 0.5% are Christians. . . . Consider the years of humanity's existence before Christ and without Christ. What have you to say about the salvation of the countless millions who have lived in the past outside the Catholic Church and altogether outside Christianity . . . what have you to say about the innumerable millions and billions who are going to live in the future outside the Catholic church and altogether outside Christianity? [Küng].

Such expressions are not mere naive lamentations. Hans Küng, a leading Christian theologian and spokesman of the Vatican II, made them several years ago in his *Freedom Today*. These expressions call for a reassessment of history, a quest of what thinking Christians have to say to themselves and to the world religions that have survived in spite of Christianity. The task is not simple, however, for it involves a reinterpretation of [*extra*] *ecclesiam nulla salus*,[11] the Bible, the history of dogma and the concept of God. It requires raising brave new questions as well. "Do non-Christian religions stay in any relation of whatever kind to one living God, to the only God there is? What significance, despite their knowledge of God, revelation and morality, is to be ascribed to world religions from the point of view of the eschatological reality of the new life dawned?" [Küng].

Needless to say these questions are not innocent, not proposals for gathering information in order to arrive at probable and therefore falsifiable conclusions. They are implied answers, the sort of questions through which a theology has come to utterance. They reinforce a frame of reference, a dogmatic *blik*,[12] which necessarily reduces what is there to see to what it is committed to see. The questions reveal a theology that is out to reduce history to sacred history and for so doing to call itself a historical religion. Such a form of thinking acknowledges non-comparing them [i.e., Christian and non-Christian religions]. Understanding, however, is not autonomous; it is comprised of categories that are rooted in history and culture. The "facts" that scientific methodologies study are not "given." They are methodologically determined, and therefore constituted by a form of thinking which in turn is an expression of a form of life. Thus a scientific study of religion does not "describe" facts; it constitutes them by tacitly defining or recognising them, arranging them in a certain order and frame of reference, and by making them meet certain standards of intelligibility.

Theology of religion is honest. It does not hide its methodological subjectivity in the name of scientific objectivity. It does not take religions as empirical phenomena, and is thus not interested in empirical ascertainability of "facts" or verifiability of its claim. Theology of religion raises questions honestly and does not seek empathy with religions by asking: What does it mean to understand the Buddhas? It rather is interested in self-understanding and therefore asks: Where do the Buddha and Buddhism stand in relation to God and his only Son? The question seeks to situate, not compare, non-Christian religions in relation to Christianity. The act of relating is not an end in itself, however; it is a means of affirming the religions by identifying Christian truths in them. "The Catholic religion," proclaimed the Vatican II, "rejects nothing that is true and holy in these religions. She regards with sincere reverence those ways of conduct and of life, those precepts and teachings which, though differing in many aspects from the ones she holds and sets forth, nonetheless often reflect a ray of that Truth which enlightens all men."[13]

Such is the catholicity of new-Israel, the ecumenical spirit described by Christian theologians as the "great new fact of our times." Facts, however, do not explain themselves; they demand explanations. Hans Küng does it by going back to the Bible, history of dogma, and the concept of God. He has discovered that the Christian record in positively evaluating non-Christians is not entirely dismal; it is not new either. In spite of all the political and social situations, Jesuits like Ricci (1552–1610) and de Nobili (1577–1656) attempted accommodation in China and India respectively. They were not entirely without precedents in history. Committed to universalistic uniqueness, Christianity was driven to evaluative encounters with cultures outside the holy land. It was destined to produce thinkers like Nicholas of Cusa, Pico della Mirandola, and Erasmus.[14] Positive evaluation of the religions by Christianity is not just a matter of historical contingencies; it is a matter of theological necessity as well. "Ethiop or Israelite, what care I? The God that brought you here from Egypt was the God that brought the Philistines from Caphtor and brought the Syrians from Kir?" (Amos 9:7).[15] Hans Küng has discovered with relief that the God of the Bible is not just jealous but a loving Father as well, who lets history begin with Adam, not with the first Israelites. God made universal alliance with the whole of mankind, valid for ever with "every creature on earth" (Genesis 1:10; 9:12). God is the Father of all; His name is great among nations outside Israel. He is neither jealous nor partial in administering justice (Romans 2:6). God gives all history a *theme*, thus providing non-biblical religions with some form of revelation in their respective socio-historical situations. The *Logos* who took visible, definite form in Jesus Christ is the same *Logos* who has been enlightening mankind from the beginning of time. God was never far from them; it is another story if they did not recognize Him (Acts 14:16–17; 17:26–27).

This liberation of God from the ethnicity of Jerusalem has several implications. For the first time in her history, new-Israel has outgrown her cherished claim that non-Christian religions are expressions of naturalistic metaphysics, that they worship gods made by human hands. She is so earnestly digging passages like these in the Bible. "Then God said to Noah: 'Behold I establish my covenant with you and your descendants after you and with every creature living with you' " (Genesis 9:8–17). It follows from this universalistic covenant that history does not begin with the first Israelites but with Adam, that history is larger and older than Israel. It also implies universality of the lost vocation of the first Adam; all are involved in the second Adam situation and therefore "already redeemed in principle." Christianity is as old as the world, and the first Christians, albeit unconscious, did not live in Jerusalem. Such is the theological determination of humanity, the eschatological recognition that Jesus is "the creaturely being in whose existence God's act of deliverance has taken place for everyone else." In Christ, God not only gives the possibility of salvation but actual salvation as well.

This biblical *a priorism* demands that the Church be honest to God. The universality of the second Adam situation implies that *uroffenbarung*,[16] the world religions are not *cognitio dei naturalis*,[17] that there is no such thing as a purely natural life and destiny. "The present universal order of human existence is supernatural order: man is created for Christ." The death of the jealous God is an argument why the Church may not be jealous either; as the eschatological community of the people of God, the Church should love her newly recognised neighbours, the world religions. This in turn demands that the old attitude be discarded, the attitude that the world religions are false because Christianity alone is true. Christianity does not confront the non-Christian religions as mere non-Christians; it encounters them with the belief that revelation is not one-dimensional, and that all religions are instruments of God. Not all revelations are equally deep in dimension, however, for God's covenant with Noah was "general" and "ordinary" in character. It was followed by an "extra-ordinary" revelation, the "special covenant" that God made with Abraham, and for Israel alone. Out of many nations God chose a particular people whose destiny in history was to clear the confusion of tongues at Babel, to be morally responsible towards the whole of mankind in the name of what was done "once and for all." This decisiveness gives new-Israel a theological priority, a prior position to her special sacred history in the general history of salvation. It is God who willed the non-Christian religions, as it is God's will that He gave special revelation to a chosen people. What God willed is not open to discussion; it can only be testified to in humility and affirmed in faith. There is no reason behind God's will except that He wills; there is no other reason why God gave a "special revelation" to a people except that He did.

To question the propriety of God's will is to involve a criterion other than God's will; it is to be dishonest to God.

This theological priority of new-Israel is an argument for her immanent universality in history, making it an imperative that she understand, be linked with, and have moral obligations toward the world religions. It also demands that new-Israel think historically, that she be conscious of what the world was before she was, and what it is destined to be now that she has come to being. This witnessing of what the world was and what it shall be is history, a temporal destiny of deeds and events constituted by the functional identity of new-Israel. "Once we too were non-Christians, then transformed from the ordinary to the extraordinary way of salvation, not because we were better than the most of men ... but solely because it pleased God to reveal His glory." To be the sole medium of the eschatological reality is not an argument for arrogance; on the contrary, it is a humbling task which new-Israel has accepted in humility, without raising any voice of protest why God entrusted her with this burden. The theological priority of the special revelation demands its implementation in history, which is another way of saying that general sacred history has come to an end with and in Jesus Christ. Since then she exists for God, the Church is committed to the service of the world religions. "She was not called out from the religions of the world as new-Israel to exist for herself, but in order to be sent back again to the world religions. To this extent, mission (*missio*) belongs to the essence of her who is called out (*ek-klesis*)." The Church therefore is out to elevate sacred history to the special sacred history, to educate the world religions through and in the absolute eschatological life that is Christianity. "She knows what the situation of the world religions is. This is something the world religions do not know: whence they come, where they now stand, and where they are going, what the ultimate situation is between God and men, wherein lies true salvation and damnation." Such is the eschatological call for conversion, the implementation of the compassionate *inha* or Christian intolerance of the world religions. This is an act of "grace," the sole purpose of which is to help the religions recognise the Truth which is lying in them and of whose presence they are unconscious. This therapeutic conversion is spiritual, and not just psychological; it does not involve a passage from neurosis to psycho-physical relief. It rather is a catharsis of sacred forms of life, a discovery by the non-Christian peoples of their identity by returning to God the Father, who was all the time with them in spite of the fact that they did not recognise His presence. The therapeutic task of new-Israel is to help the religions discover their Christian identity. In so doing the Church is not asking them to become what they are not. It is only inviting them to psycho-spiritual peace by helping them make a passage from the unconscious to the conscious, from an indefinite and imperfect perception of their identity to the one that is definite and perfect. "The Church is this sign of invitation to the peoples so that from Christians *de jure* they can become Christians *de facto*;

from Christians *in spe*, Christians *in re*[18]; that from being Christians by designation and vocation they may become Christians by profession and witness."

All this should not be construed as religious imperialism, not as if the Church were greater than God. It only means that the Church is the *pars pro toto*,[19] the *signum levatum in nationes*,[20] the sign of the fulfillment of all things. The moral point behind this observation could not be simpler: Truth is Christian and it is open to all. This radical universalism is an argument against discrimination of any kind whatsoever, discrimination in the name of race, nationality, or religion. It signifies the Christian middle way, a commitment against exclusive particularism as well as enfeebling and relativistic mysticism. "Hence we have nothing to say for the totalitarian domination of one religion, which suppresses freedom. But neither have we anything to say for syncretist mingling of all religions, which suppresses truth." What new-Israel believes in is Jesus Christ, who stands for the unity of truth and freedom.

Such is the theology of religious freedom, a "confident, joyful, and victorious science" which Hans Küng has presented in his *Freedom Today*. He claims to have heard the word of God, and recommends that his theology be used as methodology of dialogue with world religions. He warns that dialogue is not an expression of the historical helplessness of Christianity, not a strategy invented by ecclesiastics in face of the *diaspora* situation of Christians. Rather, dialogue is a methodology of being honest to God, a technique of redemptive determination of the religions in Jesus Christ. "If the Son makes you free, you will be free indeed."

Criticism of Hans Küng's Position

I must say Hans Küng's magnanimity leaves me trembling. It forces me to recall Nietzsche[21] in anguish: "Freedom from what? I should see shining in your eyes: Freedom for what?" This recalling is no solace, however, and my eyes are not shining either. When Zarathustra's God dies, Nietzsche enthroned himself as God. The uniqueness of this new God was to perpetuate the confusion of tongues at Babel, to find freedom in the boredom of eternal recurrence. Zarathustra's was not the only God who dies, nor was Nietzsche the only figure who enthroned himself as God. When the Son of God, the indomitable defender of individual conscience against institutional formalism died, new-Israel declared itself as God. The uniqueness of this God is to enslave religions in the name of "loving" them, to not be bored with repeating what was done "once for all." What is common between will-to-power and will-to-love is self-love. Between Nietzsche and Hans Küng, between the "superman" and the super "sheep," poor humanity is lost.

The two differ in style, however, Nietzsche's passion to create truth drove him to a blunt form of life, his language being as powerfully to the point as his will-to-power. Hans Küng, on the contrary, is an institution who has "received" the Truth in "humility," his will-to-power over the religions is diplomatically expressed in self-abasing language. Honest to his being God, Nietzsche created a world to be lived in by a special breed of heroes who were committed to doing for the sake of having, to a moral holocaust of driving the "sheep" out of being. Hans Küng is only a "sheep." He represents a special revelation and a "chosen people," a people the *a priori* necessity of whose will-to-love is that they be committed to the moral obligation of "freeing" the religions, of liberating them from their function, values, and ultimately their reasons to exist. The exclusivity of this will-to-love demands that world religions be so conceived a priori that they call for their redemptive correction by Christianity. "How abruptly," says Hans Küng, "the religions fall either into an abrupt dualistic separation or an overweening monistic union with him [God]. How often, for instance, in Hinduism is the reality of the free and loving God either exaggerated in its transcendence into the impersonal absolute . . . or reduced, in its encounter with man, to the anthropomorphic, materialised object of a ritualistic and popular deity."

Hans Küng is under a moral obligation to misunderstand religions by using second hand data. He can say that the son of Joseph and Mary was the only Son of God, not an anthropomorphic projection but the flesh of the trinitarian God. This son of Joseph and Mary arose from the grave. His resurrection was the eschatological fulfilment of all history; it is a historical fact, not a myth. Hans Küng is under "grace" to say that Udayana, Ramanuja, Vallabhacharya, and a host of non-Advaitic schools of Hinduism are "abrupt," ignoring the fact that these are theistic traditions committed to writing rigorous exegesis of the scriptures, rational and dogmatic theology, realistic epistemology and theories of language.[22] All this the Hindu schools of thought did to defend a personal God who accounts for the dignity of man and the world. Krishna was born to Vasudeva and Devaki[23] as mysteriously and with as much commitment to moral justice as Jesus to Joseph and Mary. But Hans Küng is authorised to say that Krishna's birth was not a case of *Logos* becoming flesh, that Vaishnavism is based on a popular superstition and is unhistorical and mythical.

Küng's theology of religious freedom is an exercise in diplomatic ambiguity. Born of the enlightenment that the world is larger than Israel, Küng is in search of words which could gently show that the world is smaller than the Vatican. The Church has noted with anguish that non-Christians outnumber Christians, that she has failed the "loving Father" in spite of the fact that she was commissioned to "clear the confusion of tongues at Babel." The Church knows history will not let her do what she was out to do, and that she is committed to perpetuate herself by telling her that somehow she is doing what in fact she is not doing. Hence the theology of Hans Küng which is a methodology of perceiving fantasies as facts, theological space as history. It is a theology that does not kill God; it only lets

Him live a life of a thousand qualifications. Its *a priori* demand is that Christianity alone should be the absolute instrument of God in history, but historical compulsions force her to play a language game with world religions. Such compulsions demand that Hans Küng play the game with sophistication, that he should keep on saying until what he intends to say becomes so obvious that it need not be said.

His redemptive theology is too fat to be confined to diplomatic niceties, however; it makes God look naively ridiculous. God [being a] Christian and committed to [the] equality of man has revealed himself to all, but not as absolutely and conclusively as to those who happened to be in Jerusalem. Not that the world religions do not have truth concerning the true God; they indeed do. They are only in error, and proclaim that truth of the true God, in spite of the fact that they are in error. The reverse is more true. Despite whatever truth Christianity has concerning the true God, she is in truth (Christianity, though in truth, proclaims the truth) of the true God. God is gracious and the world religions speak the language of error. Only this error is not in vain. Though they contain errors, God has nevertheless graced the world religions to do good deeds unconsciously, although they do not know that it is God, the Father, who has asked them to do what they do. The religions indeed teach the truth of Christ, not knowing that they teach the truth of the Gospels. The same God revealed himself in Jerusalem and Rome, and Christians are consciously committed to Him, knowing what they do and say. God's grace works in strange ways.

Hans Küng does not let God be God. Driven by the will to become God in history, he makes God in his own image and then claims to have been made in the image of God. The collective wish of a people that they be unique and special is unconsciously transcendentalised in the garb of "special revelation." Hans Küng does love God, the almighty Father. In so doing, however, he would not let God, the Father, pay equal attention to His other children. Not that Hans Küng does not love his Buddhist and Hindu brothers. On the contrary, he finds no "foundation for any theory or practice that leads to discrimination between man and man or people and people." He only insists that the "just Father" loves him in a "special" way, an "extraordinary" way, and his brothers in a "general" way, an "ordinary" way. Küng's profession demands that he accept himself as a child of God, humble and serving. It is only that through his theology of religion he appoints himself as the father of God, dictating to Him what to do and where, to whom and to what extent. Küng admits that man's will, like Adam's, is sin; only he does not let God go against his own will. Implied in this will is the anxiety of the continuity of his collective identity, the *vasana*[24] which forces God, the creator and healer of all mankind, to universalise the particularity of the Imperious Vatican.

Küng's theology is a methodology of absolutising a particular form of life. He admits the world to be a problematic situation; only he so absolutises his definition of the problems that he alone can solve them. That something good be done in the world is not important; what is important is that the Church alone should do it. This moral egoism, as the Buddha said, is *anadi vasana*,[25] an *a priori* obsession which is concerned with what must be presupposed, given which what we do is all that can be done in the world. Such an obsession, as the Buddha would say, is not something man has learned in the world; it is to satisfy this moral uniqueness that there is a world. It demands a theological construction of reality, a reduction of history to sacred history in such a way that its moral uniqueness becomes the birthplace of the world. History is an *a priori* necessity of Christian uniqueness, a field to materialise what was done "once and for all." This moral uniqueness refuses to be alone, and it implies that there is nothing similar to it. It demands religions that are different from it; if there are no religions it will create them. The Christian uniqueness, the collective ego, is the mother of the world and world religions.

Such a collective ego has become flesh in Hans Küng's theology of religious freedom. It makes him select and grasp fact at his convenience; it drives him to measure, judge, and then to make historical claims. Hans Küng generalises, collectivises, and transcendentalises the obsession to be unique, and then thinks he is making theological claims. He confuses *seeing as* with *seeing*, and then evolves a theology which is in fact a methodology of divinising his psychosis of identity. In so doing he encounters the religions and proposes dialogue only to deny their right to decisive forms of sacred history. His commitment to uniqueness results in the phrase "non-Christian," implying that all those who are not Christians think alike, talk alike, go to the circus alike, make love alike, live and die alike, and then go to hell alike. Hans Küng distorts history. If the religions do not have any sense of history, if they do not believe in the close encounter with a God of the Christian kind, they have no idea of a personal God. If all mammals are whales, then cows are not mammals; if you do not eat meat you must be fasting.

Needless to say, the source of this logical fallacy is nobler than a bad logic. It is the redemptive universalism of Christianity, the essence of which could not be simpler: what Christianity can acknowledge in the world religions is determined by what she wants to do for them. Christianity defines the problematics of life in such a way that it is a *priori* impossible for the religions to solve them. That is why Küng is engaged in category formation in order to establish the neighbourhood of all religions under the saving grace of Jesus Christ. This he does by first alienating the facts of religions from their contexts, and then keeps on putting them in the wrong categories until they have a nervous breakdown. Buddhists like Dharmakirti and Ratnakirti, in Küng's theological scheme, could not do critical epistemology because they belonged to the "mystical East."[26] The Nyaya[27] did not cultivate rational theology because it is an *a priori* necessity of history that Thomas Aquinas alone could do it. If they did it, it is because of the signs of Christ. Religions talk of the Christian God for Christian reasons, although they do so unconsciously. The Vedas are unconscious Bible, the Ganges unconscious Jordan, and Banaras, of course, has always been unconscious Rome.

Such a vandalism of history in justification of the collective wish to be "special" is not new, however. It is not exclusively Christian, either. The Puranas did it, perhaps as efficiently as Hans Küng. Here is a sample. "God," records Shrimad Bhagavatam, "whose nature is not to be born and to die, will be born into the family of Yadavs out of the concern to relieve the world from the burden of evil ... the same God, at a later stage in history, will appear as the Buddha who, having witnessed that unauthorised people are doing Yajna,[28] will persuade them from doing it by taking recourse to the magic of logic and sophistry."[29]

It should be noted that the Shrimad Bhagavatam, the most respected Vaisnava Purana, was written a dozen centuries after the Buddha. It was written at a time when Vaisnava theology had run out of gas, having done its share of scriptural hermeneutics, epistemology, and theology of analogical predications. The Bhagavat Purana seeks to succeed in doing what Vaisnava theology could not do. Puranic mythology is a methodology of theological justification, a well thought out medium through which Indian theology, even metaphysics, accomplished in fantasy what it could not do in fact. When Hinduism could not stop the Buddha of history in history, it reduced history to a sacred history, where the Buddha says or does things he did not say or do in reality. The Buddha of history was opposed to Brahmins and Yajna; he had no time to believe in God and had no wish for personal immortality in heaven. But the Buddha of the Hindu sacred history does the opposite. As an incarnation of God, he establishes that Yajna should be done, and that Brahmins alone should do it.

Hans Küng's theology of religions is an unfortunate mythology in support of missiology that has fortunately failed. Having failed to convert Hindus and Buddhists in history, it is now out to liberate their *logos* in a fantasy, in a mythic and sacred universe.

In such a universe the Buddha, including Buddhism, is shut up, and Hans Küng performs conversion by conducting dialogue with the Buddha whose *a priori* destiny is to say what new-Israel wishes to hear. Dialogue thus becomes a technique of converting the forms of thinking of a people; it is the recent way of handling *depositum fidei*.[30] Hans Küng is honest to his predecessors. "Even before converting the world, nay in order to convert it, we must meet the world and talk to it."

Such a dialogue is done in humility. Its anonymous logic is not so humble, however. In effect what it says is this. "I am in the right and you are in the wrong. When you are stronger you ought to tolerate me, for it is your duty to tolerate truth. But when I am the stronger, I will prosecute you, for it is my duty to prosecute error." Prosecution need not always be physical; it could be conceptual in the name of creating a universal humanity. "To this," says John Pawlikowski, "all the dregs of humanity ... the Jews, the

Poles, the Gypsies ... had to be eliminated ... So often universalism has been nothing more than an attempt to rob people of their individuality and force them into my pattern of life, to elevate my culture, my ideas and my style of living to an universal plane. Those who do not conform must die, physically or at least religiously and culturally."[31]

Notes

INTRODUCTION

1. The Secretariat for Non-Christians (now the Pontifical Council for Interreligious Dialogue) has issued a quarterly *Bulletin* since 1965. This contains records of most official, quasi-official, and papal statements on non-Christian religions and their adherents. Especially important is the 1984 papal statement on dialogue to be found in #56 of the *Bulletin*. A useful review of Roman Catholic theological work in this area may be found in Sheard's *Interreligious Dialogue in the Catholic Church Since Vatican II.*

2. Two useful reviews of the earlier phases of this movement are Hallencreutz's *New Approaches to Men of Other Faiths, 1938–1968*, and Vallée's *Mouvement oécumenique et religions non-chrétiennes*. Among the more important of the World Council of Churches' publications on interreligious dialogue is its 1979 *Guidelines on Dialogue with People of Living Faiths and Ideologies.*

3. The only other collection of this kind of which I am aware is McKain's anthology *Christianity: Some Non-Christian Appraisals*, now published more than a quarter of a century ago and long out of print. The motivation behind that book appears to have been similar to that behind this. But the selection made by McKain and that made for this volume overlap scarcely at all; only two authors appear in both — Mohandas Gandhi and Franz Rosenzweig — and they are represented by different pieces.

4. I explore this question as it relates to the doctrine-expressing sentences produced by religious communities in more detail in "Denaturalizing Discourse: Abhidharmikas and Propositionalists."

5. I borrow this term from Christian. See especially his *Oppositions of Religious Doctrines* and *Doctrines of Religious Communities*. The analysis of doctrine-expressing sentences given here is heavily indebted to Christian's extraordinarily perceptive work, though I apply it in ways of which he might not entirely approve.

INTRODUCTION TO PART ONE

1. On Christian anti-Semitism see Davies, *Anti-Semitism and the Foundations of Christianity.*

2. Heschel adverts to this in Chapter 2 below. See also Peck, "The Very Depths of Our Pain."

3. The biblical story of the covenant with Noah is found in Genesis 9. Rabbinic discussions of it are extensive, often discerning seven commandments to which all Gentiles are theoretically subject. See Wyschogrod's use of this idea in Chapter 4 below.

4. On the idea of covenant from a Jewish point of view see, for example, Kroner and Klenicki, *Issues in the Jewish-Christian Dialogue*; Novak, "The Covenants We Share: A Jewish Perspective"; and Fisher, "Covenant Theology and Jewish-Christian Dialogue."

5. Even for a thinker as profoundly learned in Christian (and Islamic) theology as Maimonides (1135–1204), developing a Jewish position on Christians and Christianity was not of central interest.

6. Although it is not represented by any of the selections in this volume, it should be noted that the profound theological disagreement between Jews and Christians as to the person and work of Jesus of Nazareth has not made it impossible for Jews to develop an interest in Jesus as a Jew. This work on a "Jewish Jesus" has developed mostly in the United States of America in the twentieth century, and it is connected with reform and liberal Jewish attempts to extract a non-legalistic "essence" of Judaism and then to present Jesus as a teacher of that essence. For an excellent review of this trend, see Novak, "The Quest for the Jewish Jesus."

7. This image was used creatively in a recent essay by Signer: *"Speculum Concilii*: Through the Mirror Brightly."

1. EXTRACTS FROM THE ELEVENTH LETTER TO EUGENE ROSENSTOCK-HUESSY

1. Reprinted by permission from Rosenstock-Huessy, *Judaism Despite Christianity*, 107–15.

2. On Rosenzweig's life and thought see Glatzer, *Franz Rosenzweig: His Life and Thought*; Freund, *Franz Rosenzweig's Philosophy of Existence*; and Mendes-Flohr, *The Philosophy of Franz Rosenzweig*.

3. Rosenzweig is writing in late 1916.

4. Rosenzweig here refers to his pre-war realization, catalyzed by discussions with Rosenstock-Huessy, that he had to come to grips with the fact of his Jewishness, and that the best way to do this was by defining it (and himself) over against Christianity.

5. "Because we have no better alternative." (French)

6. Rosenstock-Huessy, in the letter to which Rosenzweig is here replying, had quoted Moliére's *Les fourberies de Scapin*, act II, scene 11, to express his puzzlement at Rosenzweig's attempt to make real his Jewishness to himself. Moliére says: *"Que diable allait-il faire dans cette galère?"* ("What the devil is he doing on that galley?"), and the motif of Judaism as a galley, a ship whose rowers do not have the freedom to stop rowing even if they should wish to, is one that Rosenzweig picks up here.

7. "Great strength." (Latin)

8. Marcion (85–165) developed an idiosyncratic brand of gnosticism according to which the God of the law and the prophets, of the Hebrew Bible, was not the Father of Jesus Christ. Marcion therefore thought that there is a fundamental opposition between the theology of the Hebrew Bible and that of the New Testament, and that Christians should not read the Old Testament any longer. Hence, "the Jews belong to the devil."

9. "Return to the mark." (Italian)

10. I omit here a paragraph of Rosenzweig's on the merits and demerits of a particular edition of Tertullian's (155–222) works that he happens to have been reading.

11. In the year 70 the Roman armies destroyed the second Temple in Jerusalem. This marked the beginning of the end of the Jewish nation (the final end came in 135, at least until the re-establishment of Israel in 1948) and had a great effect on the ways in which Jews perceived and thought of themselves.

12. This view is still evident in Heschel's thought. See Chapter 2.

13. These three individuals were, respectively, Islamic, Jewish, and Christian. All flourished in the eleventh or twelfth centuries. On al-Ghazzali see notes to Chapter 9.

14. Yehuda ha-Levi (or Jehuda Halevi) (1070–1143) was a Jewish philosopher and poet active in Spain and North Africa. He engaged in the Judeo-Christian-Islamic debates of the Middle Ages and argued for the superiority of Judaism to both Christianity and Islam.

15. Eduard König was a professor of Old Testament at Bonn during the first and second decades of the twentieth century. Rosenstock-Huessy referred to him several times in his letters of June and July 1916.

16. "Let there be truth and let reality perish." (Latin)

17. "Let there be the kingdom of God and let the world perish." (Latin)

18. "Let there be the name of One God and let humanity perish." (Latin)

19. "For what? To live and die there." (French)

2. "NO RELIGION IS AN ISLAND"

1. Reprinted by permission from *Union Seminary Quarterly Review* 21 (1966): 117–33.

2. A Hebrew word meaning literally "rule by which to go." It refers to the ordinances of the Talmud, the law that governs the life of the Orthodox Jew.

3. Tillich (1886–1965) was a German Protestant theologian, who lived and taught in the United States after 1933. His three-volume *Systematic Theology* (1951–63) makes use of some of the conceptual categories of existentialism. Toward the end of his life he became interested in the Christian encounter with non-Christian religions. Weigel was a Roman Catholic theologian (1906–64) who wrote extensively on ecumenism.

4. The last part of this sentence reads " . . . in fighting *anti*-Marcionite trends as an act of love" in the original version of Heschel's paper. I suspect that this was an error, since a central tenet of Marcion's (85–165) brand of gnosticism was that the God of the law and the prophets was not the Father of Jesus Christ and that there is therefore a fundamental opposition between the theology of the Hebrew Bible and that of the New Testament. I do not think that Heschel would have wished to defend Marcion as his original sentence suggests.

5. Ibn Gabirol, or Avicebron, was a Jewish philosopher (1020–70) with neo-platonist tendencies. The *Fons vitae* or *Fountain of Life* was one of his major works.

6. "To the greater glory of God." (Latin)

7. Niebuhr (1892–1971) was one of the most influential Christian ethicists in the United States during the middle of the twentieth century. Basing his theological thought upon Protestant neo-orthodoxy, Niebuhr was for a long time a socialist in politics.

*8. Niebuhr, *Pious and Secular America*, 108.

*9. Tillich, *Christianity and the Encounter of the World Religions*, 95.

*10. *Ecumenical Review* 16/1 (1963): 108.

11. Maimonides was a Jewish philosopher (1135–1204), born in Spain and active in North Africa. His most famous work is *The Guide of the Perplexed*. Heschel refers here, I think, to Maimonides' *Mishneh Torah*, a codification of Jewish law.

12. On Halevi see Chapter 1 n. 14.

13. "A preparation for the Messiah." (Latin)

14. "A preparation for the Gospel." (Latin)

15. Akiba (50–135) was an influential rabbi in Israel immediately after the fall of Jerusalem in 70. His connection with the Bar Kochba rebellion led to his imprisonment and execution by the Romans.

3. "CHRISTIANITY AND THE HOLOCAUST"

1. Reprinted by permission from Rosenberg's, *The Christian Problem*, 183–204.

*2. Cohen, *Myth of the Judeo-Christian Tradition*, 172.

*3. Cohen, *Myth of the Judeo-Christian Tradition*, 172. [Italics added by Rosenberg—ed.]

*4. The use of the word *Holocaust* in this connection was coined by author Elie Wiesel, probably around 1959. Yet even by mid-1961, when Adolf Eichmann was tried in a Jerusalem court, the word *Holocaust* was not yet in vogue. The words used more frequently were "genocide," "final solution," "catastrophe," or "destruction" of the Jews. In 1966 Gideon Hausner, Israel's state prosecutor of Eichmann published his account of these events. Even there the word *Holocaust* does not yet appear. See his *Justice in Jerusalem*.

*5. For the full story see Yahil's *The Rescue of Danish Jewry*.

*6. See Bierman, *Righteous Gentile: The Story of Raoul Wallenberg*.

*7. Friedman, *Roads to Extinction*, 416. See also the late Dr. Friedman's splendid account of Christians who saved Jewish lives in *Their Brother's Keeper*.

*8. See Morley, *Vatican Diplomacy and the Jews During the Holocaust, 1939–43*, 205. Also see relevant references to the information available to the Vatican concerning the Holocaust, and its reticence to act in any substantial way to prevent the slaughter of Jews in Laqueur, *The Terrible Secret*; and Penkower, *The Jews Were Expendable*.

*9. See Bauminger, *Roll of Honour*, Introduction.

*10. Bauer, *The Holocaust in Historical Perspective*, 77–78.

11. I omit here Rosenberg's discussion of Hilberg's work, *The Destruction of the European Jews*. Rosenberg suggests through this discussion that the history of Christian anti-Semitism in Europe was reflected in almost every particular by the anti-Semitic ordinances of Hitler's Germany.

*12. See Wyman, *Abandonment of the Jews*, xii.

*13. Brown and Weigel, *American Dialogue*, 32.

*14. Quoted in the *New York Times* National Edition (2 May 1985), 10.

15. I omit here Rosenberg's analysis of the reasons why Jews are now capable of breaking the silence about the Holocaust that followed immediately upon the end of World War II.

16. Rosenberg refers to the Council's "Declaration on the Relationship of the Church to Non-Christian Religions" (*Nostra Aetate*), the majority of which is devoted to a rejection of traditional Christian anti-Semitism and a call for dialogue (see especially §4 of *Nostra Aetate*).

*17. *New York Times* (16 October 1965), 8.

*18. Dawidowicz, in "Letters from Readers," *Commentary*, May 1985, 18.

19. I omit here a lengthy quotation from Eckardt on the silence of the Christian churches about the Six Day War.

*20. Littell, *The Crucifixion of the Jews*, 63.

*21. Quoted in Eliach, *Hasidic Tales of the Holocaust*, 185.

*22. Littell, *The German Phoenix*, 217.

*23. The medieval Jewish biblical commentator Rashi, expounding the reasons for the failure of idolaters at the Tower of Babel (Genesis 11:7) explains: "One man asked for a brick but [misunderstanding] the other gave him mortar, instead; whereupon the first man killed the second." To idolaters, human life is not as sacred as are trivial, material objects.

*24. Littell, *The Crucifixion of the Jews*, 47–48.

*25. Edward Alexander, "Stealing the Holocaust," *Midstream* (November 1980): 48.

26. I omit here some examples of what Rosenberg calls "Nazi gutter historiography" — attempts by some to deny that the Holocaust ever happened, or that it was in any special way significant if it did.

4. "JUDAISM AND EVANGELICAL CHRISTIANITY"

1. Reprinted by permission from Tanenbaum, Wilson, and Rudin, *Evangelicals and Jews in Conversation on Scripture, Theology, and History*, 34–52.

2. It is difficult to say exactly who is an evangelical Christian and who is not. I take the term here in its simple sense, much as Wyschogrod uses it in the piece that follows: evangelical Christians are those who place a high value on the Bible, a relatively low value on tradition, and an emphasis upon Jesus Christ's pivotal significance in God's plan for the salvation of humankind.

3. A reference to Karl Barth (1886–1968), one of this century's most influential Protestant theologians. His *Church Dogmatics* is a comprehensive attempt to construct a systematic theology based solely upon God's self-revelation in Jesus.

4. A reference to Rudolf Bultmann (1884–1976), a German New Testament theologian whose central premise was that the New Testament needed to have its mythological elements removed if it was to be acceptable to and usable by modern humans.

5. Wyschogrod here refers to the conciliar document *"Dei Verbum,"* §10. See Abbott, *Documents of Vatican II*, 117–18.

6. "Bar Kochba" means "son of a star." He was the leader of the final Jewish rebellion against the Roman occupying power, a rebellion which led, in spite of initial successes, to the complete destruction of Jerusalem and the scattering of the Jewish people in the 130s. Bar Kochba does not appear to have taken the title of Messiah for himself, but many others, including Rabbi Akiba, gave it to him.

*7. Barth, *Church Dogmatics*, II/2:287.

8. Ramm, *The Evangelical Heritage*.

INTRODUCTION TO PART TWO

1. This Islamic rejection of the incarnation is evident from the very earliest interactions between Muslim and Christian intellectuals. See, for example, Finkel,

trans., "A Risala of al-Jahiz," for an early Islamic instance. See also John of Damascus, "On the Heresy of the Ishmaelites," for the earliest Christian attempt to explore Christian-Muslim theological differences systematically.

2. al-Afghani died in 1897 and 'Abduh in 1905. Access to some of 'Abduh's ideas may be had through his *Theology of Unity*.

3. The former died in 1898 and the latter in 1928. Amir 'Ali was the author of the extremely influential work *The Spirit of Islam*.

4. Muhammad 'Abduh and Amir 'Ali are quite explicit about this. See also the work of Ahmad Amin (1886–1954), an introduction to which may be found in Shepard, "A Modernist View of Islam and Other Religions."

5. "THAT HIDEOUS SCHIZOPHRENIA"

1. Reprinted from Qutb, *Islam: The Religion of the Future*, 34–60.

2. This is a little confused. The consensus of scholars is that each of the four gospels was written in Greek, though Jesus himself probably spoke Aramaic.

3. This would certainly not have been Paul's own view of himself, but Qutb's reasons for saying it become evident in what follows.

4. This is not the usual view of New Testament scholars, who would place most of Paul's letters in the 50s of the first century of the Christian era.

*5. *Allah*, by Abbas El-Akkad. [Qutb gives no page reference, and I have not been able to locate a copy of this work—ed.]

6. Qutb here refers, in a slightly confused way, to the complex of Christological controversies that developed after the Council of Chalcedon in 451. For a useful and accurate capsule account of these controversies see Pelikan, *The Emergence of the Catholic Tradition*, 266–77.

7. The reference is to Heraclius, the Byzantine emperor (d. 641) who was involved in the Monothelite controversies in the 630s.

8. The Jacobites were Syrian Monophysite Christians, named after Jacob Baradeus (d. 578), the monophysite Bishop of Edessa.

9. By the usual numbering this would be the Fourth Lateran Council held at Rome in 1215.

10. I omit here a lengthy quotation given by Qutb from Nadawi's *What the World Lost by Muslim's Decadence* in support of this historical point. I have not been able to locate either this work or any references to it.

11. Martin Luther (1483–1546), John Calvin (1509–64), and Ulrich (Huldreich) Zwingli (1484–1531) were all key figures in the early history of the Reformation.

12. I omit here a lengthy quotation given by Qutb from Nadawi's *What the World Lost by Muslim's Decadence* in support of this historical point.

6. "ISLAM AND DIALOGUE"

1. Reprinted by permission from Rousseau, ed., *Christianity and Islam: The Struggling Dialogue*, 53–73.

2. Talbi refers to the Second Vatican Council (1962–65).

*3. We should mention two meetings organized by the World Council of Churches, the first at Geneva-Caryigny in March 1969, the second, a year later, at Beirut-Ajaltoun. Buddhists and Hindus assisted at this second meeting. The book [by M. Arkoun] *Les Musulmans* is also a form of dialogue. It clearly brings out the difficulties we have emphasized and on which we shall have to insist further. We should also mention a discussion, reported in the daily paper *Le Monde* (28 June 1971), which, on the initiative of the Fédération Protestante de France, brought together some sixty people in a meeting chaired by Professor Fathi Abd El-Moneim of Al-Azhar University, Cairo, and Professor Roger Arnaldez of the Université de Paris IV.

*4. See, for example, the review *Esprit* (October 1967), which deals with the topic of "Nouveau Monde et Parole de Dieu," as well as the issue of November 1971 where the following question is asked: "Réinventer l'église?"

5. *Chance and Necessity.*

6. *Chance and Life.*

7. Louis Massignon (1883–1962) was one of the greatest Western Islamicists of this century. He wrote extensively on the history of Islamic spirituality and probably trained more scholars of Islam in France than any other man of his generation.

8. Talbi uses this term to mean "expert in Christianity" rather than in its more usual sense of "theorist about Christ."

*9. Review of the book by Anawati and Gardet, *Les grands problémes de la théologie musulmane;* i.e., Gardet, "Dieu et la destinée de l'homme," 102.

*10. Cf. Qur'an 33:72.

11. *Supplication of a Muslim to Christians.*

*12. *Les Musulmans*, 125.

*13. Watt, *Islamic Revelation in the Modern World*, 121.

*14. Nusslé, *Dialogue avec l'Islam*, 147.

*15. Luccioni, "Le mythe aujourd'hui," *Esprit* (New Series, April 1971), 610–11.

16. This text given by Talbi here is close to, but not identical with, the standard English version of §3 of the conciliar document *Nostra Aetate*. See Abbott, ed., *Documents of Vatican II*, 663.

*17. Anawati, "Vers un dialogue islamo-chrétien," 627. See also Caspar, "La foi musulmane selon le Coran."

*18. Cairo edition 1319/1901, 75–78. See also Caspar, "Le salut des non-musulmans d'aprés Ghazali."

*19. Cf. Tafsir al-Manar (1st ed., 1346/1927–28), I:333–35. [I omit here a long discussion by Talbi of various traditional Islamic discussions of these Qur'anic verses, concentrating especially upon the question of whether 3:85 — "Whoso desires to profess a religion other than Islam it shall not be accepted of him; in the next world he shall be among the losers" — should properly be taken to abrogate 2:62, discussed above, or whether the two can be harmonized — ed.]

20. *Nostra Aetate* §1. See Abbott, ed., *Documents of Vatican II*, 661.

*21. Koenig, "Le monothéisme dans le monde contemporain."

22. I omit here a note in which Talbi provides some details about the works of these individuals. As far as I can ascertain, none of their writings is available in any language but Arabic.

*23. Anawati, "Vers un dialogue islamo-chrétien," 627.

*24. Watt, *Islamic Revelation in the Modern World*, 127.

7. "THE PEOPLE OF THE BOOK AND THE DIVERSITY OF 'RELIGIONS' "

1. Reprinted by permission from Rahman, *Major Themes of the Qur'an*, 162–70.

*2. Watt, *Muhammad at Mecca*; Gaudefroy-Demombynes, *Mahomet*, i-xxii; Gibb, "Pre-Islamic Monotheism in Arabia."

3. Chr. Snouck Hurgronje (1857–1936) and Theodor Nöldeke-Schwally (1836–1930) were prominent European Islamicists from the early part of this century.

4. The Sabaeans were the people of Saba (biblical Sheba) in what is today Yemen. They are mentioned often in the Qur'an, which enumerates them, along with Christians and Jews, as people who worship Allah in their own way but who should nevertheless be ready to receive the message brought by Muhammad.

5. The reference here is to the direction in which Muslims must face to say their prayers. The term *quibla* means literally "anything in front." Originally, Muslims faced Jerusalem; latterly Mecca. The change is discussed and defended in the Qur'an at the places noted.

8. EXTRACTS FROM "SECULAR-SECULARIZATION-SECULARISM"

1. Reprinted by permission from al-Attas, *Islam, Secularism and the Philosophy of the Future*, 13–46.

*2. By the Dutch theologian Cornelis van Peursen, who occupied the chair of philosophy in the University of Leiden. This definition is cited by the Harvard theologian Harvey Cox in *The Secular City* 2, and is quoted from a report on a conference held at the Ecumenical Institute of Bossey, Switzerland, in September 1959.

*3. Cox, *Secular City*, 2, 17.

*4. Cox, *Secular City*, 20.

*5. Cox, *Secular City*, 20.

*6. Cox, *Secular City*, 30–36.

*7. Cox, *Secular City*, passim, and see 109.

*8. Cox, *Secular City*, 21–23.

*9. The phrase "disenchantment of the world" was used by Friedrich Schiller and quoted by Weber. Another term Weber used in this connection is "rationalization." See Weber's *Essays in Sociology*; see also his *Sociology of Religion*. See chapter 3 and 5 of the former; and for Weber's concept of rationalization, see Talcott Parsons' explanation of it in the Introduction to the latter work, xxxi-xxxiii.

*10. Cox, *Secular City*, 109, 119.

*11. Cox, *Secular City*, 123.

*12. Cox, *Secular City*, 21.

13. This salutation, repeated at every mention of Jesus's name, indicates the deep reverence with which Muslims regard Jesus of Nazareth.

*14. *Al-Ma'idah* (5): 85–88.

15. al-Attas refers to the pivotal Council of Nicea (325) at which some of the key Christological and soteriological doctrines of the church were stated.

*16. Even philosophy in the West has now more and more come to be regarded as unable to give a conclusive answer to its permanent question about truth. Philosophy attempts to clarify only the "truth-perspective" of the age in which the crisis of truth occurs, and is hence now regarded as an "open science." Advocates of this view are clearly representatives of the spirit of secularization which demands "openness" in every vision of truth. See, for example, Rauche, *Contemporary Philosophical Alternatives and the Crisis of Truth*.

*17. See *al-Ma'idah* (5): 49, 75, 78, 119–21; *Al 'Imran* (3): 49–51, 77–79; *al-Nisa'* (4): 157, 171; *al-Tawbah* (9): 30–31; *al-Ra'd* (13): 38–39; *al-Shaff* (61): 6, 9; *al-Baqarah* (2): 106, 135–140; *Saba* (34): 28.

*18. See his *The Nature of Revelation*.

*19. We are referring here to the concept of *naql*.

*20. The following sketch is most cursory. A more comprehensive account than the one given in what follows is to be found in S. H. Nasr's [the author of Chapter 9 in this volume – ed.] penetrating study *Man and Nature*. The idea that I express in the following outline account is perhaps similar to what Professor Nasr has more adequately given in chapter 2 of the work cited.

*21. See Dewart, *The Future of Belief*, 152–59.

9. "THE ISLAMIC VIEW OF CHRISTIANITY"

1. Reprinted from Küng and Moltmann, eds., *Christianity Among World Religions*, 3–12.

2. The *Hadith* are "multi-volume collections of accounts called hadiths (from the Arabic *hadith*, 'story, tradition') that report or allege to report the sayings and deeds of the Prophet Muhammad. These hadiths provide an official guide for all aspects of Muslim daily life, for which Muhammad stands as an exemplar *par excellence*. Six canonical collections were compiled in the ninth century . . . the traditional Muslim view is that at least the 'sound' hadiths . . . are valid statements going back to Muhammad's contemporaries, and that orthodox Islamic life and thought must be based on the Qur'an and these hadiths" (Hinnells, ed., *Handbook of Living Religions*, 124).

*3. References to Jesus and Mary abound in the Qur'an. See especially *Surahs* 3, 5, 19, and 61.

*4. There is an extensive literature on the legal status of *dhimmah* and *dhimmis*, especially Christians. As far as the Western views of the subject are concerned, see Chéhata, *Essai d'une théorie générale de l'obligation en droit musulman*, Rose, "Islam and the Development of Personal Status Laws Among Christian *Dhimmis*." Muslims are in general very sensitive to the Christian criticism of the Islamic law on *dhimmis*, and nearly all Muslim apologetic literature from Amir 'Ali onward contains discussions of this subject.

5. This is Surah 112 of the Qur'an, cited by Nasr in a translation by Martin Lings.

6. Ibn 'Arabi, a Sufi mystic with inclinations toward philosophical monism, lived from 1165–1240.

*7. In his *Tarjuman al-ashwaq*, 70, Ibn 'Arabi has a poem which is as follows: "My Beloved is three although He is One, even as/ the (three) Persons (of the Trinity) are made/ one Person in essence." In his own commentary on the poem (71) he adds, "Number does not beget multiplicity in the Divine substance, as the Christians declare that the Three Persons of the Trinity are One God, and as the Qur'an declares (17: 110): 'Call on God or call on the Merciful; howsoever ye invoke Him, it is well, for to Him belong the most excellent Names.' The cardinal Names in the Qur'an are three, viz. Allah, al-Rahman and al-Rabb, by which One God is signified, and the rest of the Names serve as epithets of those Three." In his *al-Futuhat al-makkiyyah*, 172, Ibn 'Arabi states that the Christians in emphasizing the

Trinity still have a way open to God's uniqueness (*al-fardaniyyah*) since the number three is in a sense a return to the number one, and trinity being the first reflection of unity in the domain of multiplicity.

8. Al-Ghazzali (d. 1111) was one of the greatest thinkers of the Islamic tradition. Among many other things, he tried to show that the rationalism inherent in the natural theology of the practitioner of *kalam* was religiously unsatisfactory and always finally self-refuting. See especially his work *Tahafut al-Falasifa* ("The Incoherence of the Philosophers").

*9. See his *al-Radd al-jamil ala sarih al-injil.* [There is no English translation available and therefore I did not include it in Works Cited—ed.] Some contemporary scholars have doubted the authenticity of the attribution of this work to al-Ghazzali, while Louis Massignon and several other scholars consider it to be one of al-Ghazzali's authentic writings. In any case the work exemplifies the attitude we wish to point out.

*10. There were some Muslim religious authorities who did not accept this view, but the majority of them as well as of traditional Muslims in general have believed and continue to believe that the doors of both heaven and hell are open for Christians as they are for Muslims. Moreover, there are numerous *hadiths* concerning both Christ and Moses leading the virtuous members of their community to paradise on the Day of Judgment. The general use of the term *kafir* (usually translated as infidel) so common in Muslim sources when referring to Christians is more a custom than a strictly speaking theological definition. Some Muslim schools of thought have called their Muslim opponents *kafirs* as well without this implying damnation in principle as the doctrine of *extra ecclesiam nulla salus* would imply.

*11. Schuoun, *Christianity/Islam—Essays on Esoteric Ecumenism*, 111.

12. Both Hafiz (ca. 1325–89) and Jalal al-Din Rumi (d. 1273) were Sufi mystical poets who wrote in Persian. The standard work on Rumi in English is Nicholson, *Rumi: Poet and Mystic*.

*13. See especially his *Bezels of Wisdom*, chapter 15, "The Wisdom of Prophecy in the Word of Jesus"; and Ibn 'Arabi, *La sagesse des prophètes*, 109–29.

*14. This kind of reaction was not to be observed to the same extent as far as Protestantism was concerned. Many Muslims, who in fact encountered Protestantism for the first time, thought that it was closer to Islam and that Luther had moved in the direction of the Islamic understanding of religion.

INTRODUCTION TO PART THREE

1. The most famous example of this literary transmission is the story of Barlaam and Josaphat (to use the Latin versions of their names), a hagiographical story popular throughout the Christian West in the medieval period. This story was originally a Buddhist fable: "Josaphat" is in fact a corruption of the Indic word *bodhisattva*. On this see Smith, *Towards a World Theology*, 7–11.

2. The exact date of the Buddha is still a much disputed issue among scholars. A recent review of the evidence, Bechert's *Die Lebenszeit des Buddha*, discusses the two major contenders for the date of Buddha's death—the "long chronology," which places it 218 years before Ashoka's consecration (i.e., ca. 486 B.C.), and the "short chronology," which places it 100 years before Ashoka's consecration (i.e., ca. 368 B.C.)—and dismisses both datings as later constructions in the service of non-

historical ends (p. 52). He concludes that all indications suggest that the Buddha's life ended not long before Alexander's wars of conquest spread to the Indian subcontinent in the second half of the fourth century B.C. (pp. 54–55).

3. The only monographic treatment of this concept in English is Pye's *Skilful Means*. This is an excellent introduction and will direct the reader to numerous textual sources.

4. The *Lotus Sutra* was written in Sanskrit (in which language its title is *Saddharmapundarikasutra*) and translated into Chinese and Japanese. It was (and is) probably the single most influential text in the history of East Asian Buddhism. A good English translation is Hurvitz, *Scripture of the Lotus Blossom of the Fine Dharma*.

5. The story is found in Hurvitz, *Scripture of the Lotus Blossom*, 58–64.

6. Horner, trans., *The Collection of the Middle Length Sayings*, 1:173.

7. See Hayes, "Principled Atheism in the Buddhist Tradition."

8. Dharmapala, *Return to Righteousness*, 439.

9. For an excellent account of events in Sri Lanka in the latter half of the nineteenth century see Malalgoda, *Buddhism in Sinhalese Society 1750–1900*, 194–255.

10. On all this see Bechert's indispensable *Buddhismus, Staat und Gesellschaft in den Ländern des Theravada Buddhismus*. See also Gombrich, *Theravada Buddhism*, 172–97.

10. EXTRACTS FROM "THE BUDDHIST ATTITUDE TO OTHER RELIGIONS"

1. Reprinted, by permission, from Jayatilleke, "The Buddhist Attitude to Other Religions," 17–36.

2. *Theravada* means "doctrine [or school] of the Elders." The word refers to that form of Buddhism dominant in South and Southeast Asia, most especially in Sri Lanka, Burma, and Thailand. For a clear historical introduction to the Sri Lankan form of Theravada, see Gombrich, *Theravada Buddhism*.

*3. Morris et al., eds., *Anguttara Nikaya* 1:189.

*4. Rhys Davids and Carpenter, eds., *Digha Nikaya* 1:3.

5. The *Tattvasangraha* ("Compendium of Truth") is a systematic scholastic work, probably written in India in the eighth century of the common era by Shantarakshita, one of the more important of the Buddhist systematicians. A complete English translation is available: Jha, trans., *The Tattvasangraha of Shantarakshita*. The *Jnanasarasamuccaya* (a more likely version of the title than that given by Jayatilleke; the text does not survive in its original Sanskrit, so the title is a conjectural reconstruction from the Tibetan) may be from the same period, though its authorship is not certain. No English translation of this latter work has yet been made.

6. "Tathagata" is one of the many honorific titles given to the Buddha. It means, fairly literally, "he who has come [or gone] thus."

*7. Feer, ed., *Samyutta Nikaya* 2:25.

8. This is the Pali form of the more familar Sanskrit *dharma*. It means, in this context, simply "doctrine."

9. This term is usually taken to mean "individual Buddha" — someone who has attained Buddhahood independently, without reliance upon the teachings of another Buddha.

10. The Sanskrit term *samsara*, from which this adjective is derived, refers to the cyclic process of rebirth and redeath to which all sentient beings are subject in Buddhist theory. It is this cycle from which one is liberated when one attains Nirvana.

*11. See Andersen and Smith, eds., *Sutta Nipata*, v. 1082. [I omit here, and in several of the notes that follow, the Pali text that Jayatilleke supplies—ed.]

*12. Morris et al., eds., *Anguttara Nikaya* 1:120–21.

*13. Trenckner et al., eds., *Majjhima Nikaya* 1:515–18.

*14. Trenckner et al., eds., *Majjhima Nikaya* 1:520.

*15. Trenckner et al., eds., *Majjhima Nikaya* 3:72.

16. The eightfold path is the fourth of the four truths of Buddhism. It prescribes specific actions and intentions that will take the practitioner beyond the suffering of samsara into Nirvana. The eight components are: (1) right view; (2) right intention; (3) right speech; (4) right action; (5) right livelihood; (6) right effort; (7) right mindfulness; (8) right concentration.

*17. Rhys Davids and Carpenter, eds., *Digha Nikaya* 2:151.

18. *Sakkaya ditthi* is one of the most fundamental cognitive errors possible for a Buddhist. It consists in making the mistake of thinking that one is an enduring, changeless substance of some kind, that there is anything continuous connecting together the changing streams of thought and emotion that one experiences. From this error comes attachment and desire, and from these in turn come all suffering. On this see Collins, *Selfless Persons*.

19. The Sangha is the Buddhist monastic community. It is the third of Buddhism's "three jewels." The other two are the Buddha and his doctrine (*dhamma/ dharma*).

*20. The "Non-Returner" (to the world of sensuality, *anagami*). He has fully eliminated the fetters of sensuous desire and ill-will, which are still present—though weakened—in the second saint ("Once-Returner"), who is not mentioned in these texts.

*21. The Arahat. He has fully eliminated all the remaining five fetters: desire for fine-material and immaterial existence, conceit, restlessness and ignorance.

22. Jainism is the only non-Hindu religious movement (apart from Buddhism itself) to originate in India before the beginning of the Common Era and still to have a considerable number of adherents in India. Unlike Buddhism, it never spread significantly outside the sub-continent. The best introduction to Jainism is Jaini's *The Jaina Path of Purification*.

*23. Morris et al., eds., *Anguttara Nikaya* 1:33.

*24. Fausbøll, ed., *Jataka* 5:238.

*25. Fausbøll, ed., *Jataka* 6:208.

26. That is, Hindu priests.

27. The sacred texts of Hinduism. See Part 4 of this volume.

*28. *Tevijja Sutta* (Rhys Davids and Carpenter, eds., *Digha Nikaya* 1:235–53).

*29. Morris et al., eds., *Anguttara Nikaya* 1:227–28.

*30. *Sukhavativyuha* 1. [There are a number of Mahayana sutras with the title *Sukhavativyuha*; while selections from a number of them are available in English, Jayatilleke's reference is not sufficiently precise to make it possible to give an exact citation here—ed.]

*31. *Vajracchedika* 30. See Conze, trans., *The Short Prajnaparamita Texts*, 137–38.

*32. Morris et al., eds., *Anguttara Nikaya* 3:371.
*33. *Apannaka Sutta* (Trenckner et al., eds., *Majjhima Nikaya* 1:400–13).
34. Caroline A.F. Rhys Davids (1858–1942) was one of the early editors and translators of Pali Buddhist texts. Together with her husband, T. W. Rhys Davids, she was instrumental in the foundation of the Pali Text Society, a society devoted to making Theravada Buddhist texts available to Western scholars.
35. Sarvepalli Radhakrishnan (1888–1975) was president of India in the early 1960s and holder of the Spalding chair in Eastern Religions and Ethics at Oxford University. He is chiefly remembered for his expositions of Advaita Vedanta, a form of Hindu thought (on which see Part 4 of this book).
36. Arthur Berriedale Keith was Regius Professor of Sanskrit and comparative philology at the University of Edinburgh in the early part of the twentieth century. He published extensively on Indian philosophical thought and on Indian literature.
37. Th. Stcherbatsky (more fully, Fedor Ippolitovitch Shcherbatskoi) was born in 1866 in Poland and studied Indo-European linguistics at St. Petersburg in the 1880s. He became one of the greatest Western interpreters of Buddhist logic. He died in Russia in 1942.
*38. Trenckner et al., eds., *Majjhima Nikaya* 1:65.
*39. Morris, ed., *Puggalapannati*, §3.
*40. Rhys Davids and Carpenter, eds., *Digha Nikaya* 3:65.
*41. Rhys Davids and Carpenter, eds., *Digha Nikaya* 3:65.
*42. Rhys Davids and Carpenter, eds., *Digha Nikaya* 1:135.
43. Ashoka was ruler over much of the Indian subcontinent during the third century before the beginning of the Common Era. Buddhist legend makes of him the ideal Buddhist monarch.
44. There were two Sinhalese kings with this name. The first ruled from 1153–86 and the second from 1236–71. It is not entirely clear which one Jayatilleke has in mind.
*45. See Geiger, *The Culavamsa, 277.*

11. EXTRACTS FROM *A BUDDHIST CRITIQUE OF THE CHRISTIAN CONCEPT OF GOD*

1. Reprinted, by permission, from Dharmasiri, *A Buddhist Critique of the Christian Concept of God*, §§1.1–1.5 (pp. 1–3); 1.11–1.16 (pp. 7–10); 1.24–1.26 (pp. 15–16); §1.35–1.38 (pp. 21–23).
2. On this see Hayes, "Principled Atheism in the Buddhist Tradition"; Jackson, "Dharmakirti's Refutation of Theism."
*3. Niebuhr, *The Self and the Dramas of History*, 15ff.
*4. Richmond, *Theology and Metaphysics*, 129.
5. The Upanishads are part of the Hindu corpus of *shruti* or sacred literature. Some of them predate the Buddha, and some are also theistic and substantivist in their metaphysics.
*6. Maritain, *Redeeming the Time*, 238.
*7. Maritain, *Redeeming the Time*, 239.
*8. Maritain, *Existence and the Existent*, 81.
*9. Maritain, *The Range of Reason*, 59.
10. Dharmasiri here refers to the Buddhist analysis of the person into five

streams or "aggregates" (*skandha*) of changing but causally connected events. The point of such an analysis is to attempt a complete account of everything that makes up a given human individual's personality without resorting to the postulation of an independent eternal principle like a "soul." On this see Collins, *Selfless Persons*.

*11. Trenckner et al., eds., *Majjhima Nikaya* 3:19. [In this and the following source-notes given by Dharmasiri, I omit the Pali text that he provides – ed.]

*12. Trenckner et al., eds., *Majjhima Nikaya* 1:421.

*13. Morris et al., eds., *Anguttara Nikaya* 2:212.

*14. Trenckner et al., eds., *Majjhima Nikaya* 3:32.

*15. Feer, ed., *Samyutta Nikaya* 2:17.

*16. Feer, ed., *Samyutta Nikaya* 1:135; Trenckner, ed., *Milindapanha*, 28.

17. *Dukkha* means "suffering." Its omnipresence is the first noble truth of Buddhism.

*18. Morris et al., eds., *Anguttara Nikaya* 3:440.

*19. Trenckner et al., eds., *Majjhima Nikaya* 3:19.

20. Buddhaghosa was the most important commentator upon and systematizer of those texts that we now call the Pali canon. He was probably active in Sri Lanka in the early fifth century C.E. A good introduction to his life and work may be found in Nyanamoli, trans., *The Path of Purification* 1:xv-xxvii.

21. That is, not from an action other than that which gave rise to it. *Kamma* is the Pali form of the more familiar Sanskrit *karma*.

*22. Rhys Davids, ed., *Visuddhimagga*, 555.

*23. Rhys Davids, ed., *Visuddhimagga*, 554.

*24. Feer, ed., *Samyutta Nikaya* 2:75-76.

*25. Trenckner et al., eds., *Majjhima Nikaya* 1:258.

*26. Morris et al., eds., *Anguttara Nikaya* 2:158.

27. Gilbert Ryle (1900–1976) was a British philosopher. In his most famous work, *The Concept of Mind* (1949), he argues that traditional mind-body (or soul-body) dualism is mistaken.

28. P. F. Strawson (1919–) is a British philosopher educated at Oxford where he also teaches. In his central work *Individuals* (first published in 1959) he develops a metaphysics in which "person" (rather than "mind" or "body" or "soul") is the primitive category.

*29. Strawson, *Individuals*, 89.

*30. Strawson, *Individuals*, 104-5.

*31. "The way in which we know God who has been called 'the Soul of the World,' 'the Mind of the Universe,' might also be compared with the way one knows the soul or mind of another creature." Wisdom, *Paradox and Discovery*, 15. [John Wisdom is a British philosopher, born in 1904, educated at Cambridge, and heavily influenced by G. E. Moore and Ludwig Wittgenstein – ed.]

*32. Plantinga, *God and Other Minds*, 271. [Alvin Plantinga is an American philosopher of religion whose work has been largely devoted to defending the epistemic repectability of belief in God. He currently teaches at the University of Notre Dame – ed.]

*33. Feer, ed., *Samyutta Nikaya* 4:400–401.

*34. Tillich, *Christianity and the Encounter of the World Religions*, 75. On Tillich, see notes to Chapter 1.

35. An *imposthume* is a swollen abscess.

*36. Feer, ed., *Samyutta Nikaya* 4:202.

*37.Morris et al., eds., *Anguttara Nikaya* 1:44.
*38. Feer, ed., *Samyutta Nikaya* 4:88.
*39. Trenckner et al., eds., *Majjhima Nikaya* 1:500.
*40. Maritain, *The Range of Reason* 59.
*41. Maritain, *Existence and the Existent* 69.
*42. Barth, *Church Dogmatics*, III/2:356.
*43. Trenckner et al., eds., *Majjhima Nikaya* 3:227–28.
*44. Trenckner et al., eds., *Majjhima Nikaya* 3:30–31.
*45. Woods et al., eds., *Papancasudani* 1:38.
*46. Trenckner et al., eds., *Majjhima Nikaya* 3:237.
*47. Trenckner et al., eds., *Majjhima Nikaya* 1:37.

12. "RELIGIOUS HARMONY" AND EXTRACTS FROM
THE BODHGAYA INTERVIEWS

1. Reprinted by permission from Tenzin Gyatso, *Kindness, Clarity, and Insight*, 45–50; and from *The Bodhgaya Interviews*, 11–14; 21–23; 38–39.
2. The Dalai Lama's own autobiographical account of the events leading up to his exile may be found in *My Land and My People*. A useful brief introduction to the history and meaning of the office of Dalai Lama is Lopez, "The Dalai Lama of Tibet."
3. *Bodhisattva* means "a being who will become awakened" or "a being turned toward awakening." Most broadly, the term indicates anyone who is self-consciously engaged in Buddhist practice with the goal of becoming a Buddha. The "vehicle" of a Bodhisattva means simply his or her religious practices.
4. The Madhyamikas are the "followers of the Middle School," a Buddhist philosophical movement that looks to Nagarjuna (second century C.E.?), as its founder. The Cittamatrins are the "followers of the Mind-Only School," a Buddhist school whose two most important early figures are Asanga and Vasubandhu (fourth-fifth centuries C.E.).
5. The Vaibhashikas are those who base their philosophical thought upon a second-century text called *Mahavibhasha*. The Sautrantikas are "followers of the Sutra School."
6. The Prasangikas are the "absurd-conclusionists," thinkers who specialize in the application of the *reductio ad absurdum* to all metaphysical systems. The Svatantrikas are the "self-dependence believers" — they, unlike the Prasangikas, think that some independently valid arguments for the truth of philosophical theses can properly be offered.
7. A devotee of the Hindu deity Shiva.
8. "Shakyamuni" means "sage of the Shakyas." It is one of the titles given to the historical Buddha.
9. The Dalai Lama refers here to the theory that every Buddha has three bodies: an apparent physical body (*nirmanakaya*) in which he appears to teach beings like us in the worlds of physical form; a radiant body of enjoyment (*sambhogakaya*) in which he inhabits pure Buddha-lands and gives joy to the beings therein; and a transcendent changeless body of dharma (*dharmakaya*). On this see Nagao, "On the Theory of Buddha-Body."
10. -ji is an honorific suffix in most Indian languages.

11. *Moksha* and *nirvana* are effectively synonyms for the Buddhist religious goal.
12. The Tushita heaven is simply one among many Buddhist paradises. Buddhist cosmology is exceptionally rich in ideas about heavens and hells.

13. "SELF-AWAKENING AND FAITH – ZEN AND CHRISTIANITY"

1. Reprinted from Abe, *Zen and Western Thought*, 186–202.
2. On the Kyoto School see Kasulis, "The Kyoto School and the West."
3. The best history of Zen Buddhism in English is that by Dumoulin, *Zen Buddhism: A History*. An excellent introduction to the basic ideas of Zen is Kasulis, *Zen Action, Zen Person*.
4. Abe uses this English term to represent the Sanskrit *shunyata*, which is in turn translated into Chinese and Japanese as *mu*. Perhaps a more common English rendering is "emptiness."
*5. Tillich and Hisamatsu, "Dialogues East and West," 115. [Hisamatsu was one of Abe's teachers in Zen. On Tillich see notes to Chapter 1.]
6. That is, the Christian emphasis on theism is not just a statement about what exists (ontology), but also a statement about what is valuable (axiology).

14. "SCHOLASTIC PHILOSOPHY AND MODERN CIVILIZATION"

1. Reprinted by permission from Ikeda, *A Lasting Peace*, 59–68.
2. The Lotus Sutra was written in Sanskrit (in which language its title is *Saddharmapundarikasutra*) and translated into Chinese and Japanese. It was (and is) probably the single most influential text in the history of East Asian Buddhism. A good English translation is Hurvitz, trans., *Scripture of the Lotus Blossom of the Fine Dharma*. Nichiren's invocation to the *Lotus* (in Japanese) runs *Namu myo-ho-ren-ge-kyo* ("Salutation to the Lotus Sutra"). On Nichiren see Anesaki, *Nichiren, the Buddhist Prophet*. This is old, but still a good introduction. The literature on Nichiren in English is still not extensive, perhaps because he does not fit Western stereotypes of what Buddhist teachers ought to be like.
3. More information on Soka Gakkai may be found in Earhart, *Religion in the Japanese Experience*, 244–55; and in Kirimura, "About Daisaku Ikeda." Both these sources provide materials from within the Soka Gakkai community. An interesting counterweight may be had from Fujiwara, *I Denounce Soka Gakkai*.
4. Justin, known as the martyr, was executed at Rome probably in the year 165. He was one of the earliest of the Greek apologists. Tertullian, who died around 220, wrote in Latin; some of his thinking was later declared heretical by the church. Origen, who died around 254, was one of the church's first great systematic theologians, He was active in Alexandria. Augustine, who died in 430, was Bishop of Hippo in North Africa, the author of the *Confessions* and *The City of God*, as well as a large corpus of biblical commentary.
5. *Credo quia absurdum est.*
6. Ikeda seems to be claiming that the Roman Empire fell in the first century. It would be more accurate to point to the fifth century.
7. José Ortega y Gasset (1883–1955) was a Spanish philosopher influenced by the neo-Kantian school in Marburg. His later work is perhaps best characterized as a kind of humanism.

INTRODUCTION TO PART FOUR

1. Halbfass, *India and Europe*, 187.
2. On this see Young, *Resistant Hinduism*.
3. Quoted in Halbfass, *India and Europe*, 225.
4. *Ekam eva sad vipra bahudha vadanti*, *Ṛgveda* I:164:46.
5. I recommend here John Updike's 1987 novel *'S'* for a splendid and comic presentation of this trend. There can be little doubt that Updike based much in this novel on the doings of Bhagwan Shree Rajneesh (since 1988 known as Osho Rajneesh) in Oregon in the early and middle 1980s.
6. "Vaishnavism" refers to belief in and worship of Vishnu as supreme deity or chosen God; "Shaivism" does the same for Shiva.

15. EXTRACTS FROM *THE LIGHT OF TRUTH*

1. Reprinted by permission from Sarasvati, *The Light of Truth*, chapter 13, §60–61 (pp. 618–19); §70 (p. 622); §73–74 (pp. 624–25); §83 (p. 629); §94 (p. 636); pp. 723–24, 732.
2. The best available biography of Dayananda is Jordens, *Dayananda Sarasvati: His Life and Ideas*.
3. Dayananda begins the thirteenth chapter of *The Light of Truth* with these words. He then devotes some thirty pages to a piecemeal analysis of various stories from the Old Testament, none of which is represented here.
4. At this point Dayananda begins his critique of sections of the New Testament. He treats seventy-one episodes from the New Testament, beginning with the Gospel of Matthew and ending with the Book of Revelation. His method is usually to quote or paraphrase a verse or two from the biblical book under discussion and then to provide his own critical commentary upon these verses. I have chosen seven of these discussions for inclusion here and have provided them with my own subtitles.
5. Dayananda uses the Authorized (King James) version of the Bible for his discussion. There are occasional divergences from this version, mostly in matters of capitalization and punctuation. I have left these as they are in Dayananda's text.
6. Dayananda here refers to the first two of the *pramanas*, those means by which, according to classical Hindu philosophical thought, knowledge can be attained. On the *pramana* system see Potter, *Indian Metaphysics and Epistemology*, 147–78, and the extensive bibliography contained in that volume.
7. The *Puranas* are a body of mythic and devotional literature produced in medieval India. Selections are conveniently available in Dimmitt and Van Buitenen, eds., *Classical Hindu Mythology*.
8. This translates the Hindi *sanatan dharma*, a term expressing an idea of key significance for neo-Hinduism.
9. The Sanskrit term *shastra* refers in the narrow sense to any technical treatise on any topic—grammar, astronomy, poetics, and the like. In the broad sense it refers to any work of sacred or religious significance and may even be used to denote the Veda. This appears to be how Dayananda uses it here.
*10. The first promulgator of the Vedas.

11. The author of the *Purvamimamsasutras*. Jaimini may have composed this work at the beginning of the Christian Era. Since the Vedas are of central importance for Dayananda, he also gave a place of honor to Jaimini's work, since the *Mimamsa* school is one that (theoretically, at least) builds its system entirely upon Vedic exegesis.

12. That is, the four metrical collections of hymns: *Rgveda, Yajurveda, Samaveda* and *Atharvaveda*.

16. "CHRIST, THE MESSENGER"

1. Reprinted by permission from Vivekananda, *The Complete Works of Swami Vivekananda* 4:138–53.

2. On Vedanta see Deutsch, *Advaita Vedanta: A Philosophical Reconstruction*; Potter, ed., *Advaita Vedanta up to Shamkara and His Pupils*.

3. The *Bhagavadgita*, or "Song of God," is one of the best-known and most widely translated Hindu texts. Good English translations are: Van Buitenen, *The Bhagavadgita in the Mahabharata*. This contains a transliterated Sanskrit text as well as a translation and is especially good on placing the *Gita* in its historical and literary context. Zaehner's translation, *The Bhagavad-Gita*, also contains a transliterated text, and is especially good on the theological implications of the *Gītā*, but Zaehner has a tendency to Christianize, both in translation and interpretation. Zaehner's own commentary, though, is often very useful. Finally, Miller's translation, *The Bhagavad-Gītā: Krishna's Counsel in Time of War*, reads very well and is accurate.

4. *Gita* 4:6–8. Vivekananda's translation is free. The term *prakrti* refers in general to the material or physical cosmos, and the term *maya* to God's quasi-magical creative power. The meaning of these verses is that it is through a kind of creative illusion that God (Krishna) appears to human beings as an embodied sentient being. He does this in order to re-establish the cosmic law (*dharma*) when it appears to be in danger.

17. EXTRACTS FROM *THE STORY OF MY EXPERIMENTS WITH TRUTH*

1. Reprinted by permission from Gandhi, *The Story of My Experiments with Truth*, 28–31; 59–61; 106–8; 118–20; 139–41.

2. On this see Jordens, "Gandhi and Religious Pluralism." This contains useful bibliographical resources.

3. The tradition centering upon the God Vishnu and his incarnations (*avatara*).

4. The reference is to Vaishnava temple worship. Gandhi has a good deal to say about this elsewhere in *The Story of My Experiments with Truth*. He describes his family as especially staunch Vaishnavas and frequent attenders at temple.

5. *Ramanama* means literally "the name of Rama." Rama is an incarnation of Vishnu, and the repetition of his name acts as protective charm as well as an instrument of religious self-transformation.

6. A Hindu epic recounting the deeds of Rama. The Sanskrit version, attributed to Valmiki, is perhaps best-known in the West (there is a multivolume English translation currently being published by Princeton University Press under the general editorship of Robert Goldman), but Gandhi almost certainly has in mind a

vernacular version of the epic by Tulsidas. On this see below.

7. Literally, "protection by Rama," another set of invocations to Rama as chosen deity (*ishtadevata*).

8. "Great God," that is, Rama.

9. Tulsidas was a sixteenth-century poet and religious thinker whose *Rama-caritamanasa*, a poetic version of the life of Rama, is similar to, but not identical with, that found in the Sanskrit epic called *Ramayana*. It is Tulsidas's work that Gandhi has in mind when he speaks of the *Ramayana*. An English translation of Tulsidas's work is Hill's *Holy Lake of the Acts of Rama*.

10. Gandhi here refers to the *Bhagavatapurana*, a Sanskrit text in which the life-story of Krishna, another incarnation of Vishnu, is told in a tone and style intended to excite passionate devotion (*bhakti*) in the hearer. Selections from this text are conveniently available in Dimmitt and van Buitenen, *Classical Hindu Mythology*. There is a complete English translation by J. M. Sanyal.

*11. Eleventh day of the bright and the dark half of a lunar month.

12. That is, Muslim.

*13. Laws of Manu, a Hindu lawgiver. They have the sanction of religion. [The only complete English translation of the *Manusmriti* is that by Bühler, *The Laws of Manu* — ed.]

14. Non-violence, or, more literally, "non-harming."

15. Gandhi arrived in England in 1887.

16. For details on the *Bhagavadgita* see Chapter 16 n.3 above.

17. *Bhagavadgita* 2:61–62.

18. *The Light of Asia*, first published in England in 1879, is a poetic retelling of the life-story of the Buddha. It was very popular in both Europe and India in the last quarter of the nineteenth century, and probably did more than any other single work to introduce Buddhism to the English-speaking world.

19. Helena Petrovna Blavatsky co-founded the Theosophical Society (with Henry Steele Olcott) in New York City in 1875; Annie Besant was president of that society from 1907 onward. The society was instrumental in popularizing versions of Buddhism and Hinduism in the West. Its approach was esoteric and syncretistic.

20. Matthew 5:39–40, Authorized (King James) Version; Gandhi has made slight changes in wording and spelling.

21. Thomas Carlyle (1795–1881) published *On Heroes, Hero-Worship, and the Heroic in History* in 1841.

22. Gandhi was studying law. He was called to the bar in 1891.

23. Charles Bradlaugh (1833–91) was an atheist and freethinker, famous for being elected a Member of Parliament in 1880 and then unseated for refusing to swear on the Bible. His works were widely read by Indian intellectuals, especially in Bengal.

24. Only the last-named of these three works is still widely read. This is Joseph Butler's (1692–1752) *Analogy of Religion, Natural and Revealed, to the Constitution and Course of Nature*, first published in 1736. In this book Butler argues with considerable rhetorical power and intellectual subtlety against Deism and natural theology. I have not been able to locate a copy of or a reference to "Pearson's *Many Infallible Proofs*."

25. The Plymouth Brethren are a conservative Protestant evangelical sect, radically anti-ecclesiastical and with a tendency to millenarianism. The sect began in the late 1820s in England.

26. This antinomian tendency evident among the members of certain Protestant Christian groups, so sarcastically observed by Gandhi here, is splendidly dramatized (and satirized) in James Hogg's novel *The Confessions of a Justified Sinner* (1824).
27. That is, Muslim.
28. Raychandbhai (more fully, Fajchandra Rajivbhai Mehta) was a Jaina intellectual and Gandhi's frequent correspondent and advisor on religious matters.
29. Maitland was the founder of the Esoteric Christian Union, of which Gandhi was a strong supporter, even at times a publicist. I have not been able to trace a book by him with the title *The New Interpretation of the Bible*; Gandhi may mean *The Story of the New Gospel of Interpretation Told by its Surviving Recipient*.
30. Leo Tolstoy (1828–1910) wrote this work in the early 1890s; it was first published in English in 1894. If Gandhi's memory serves him accurately here he must have read it almost as soon as it appeared. The book expresses very clearly Tolstoy's Christian philosophy of nonviolence, a philosophy that was to have great influence on Gandhi's later thinking.
31. These are religio-philosophical Hindu works. The *Panchikaran* is, I think, the *Pancikarana*, attributed to Shankara (ca. eighth century C.E.). The *Maniratnamala* is a work, attributed to Tulsidas. The *Mumukshu Prakaran* (*Mumukshuprakarana*, "Chapter on the Desire for Liberation") is a section of the *Yogavasishtha*, a work that may have been composed in the twelfth century C.E. And the *Shaddarshana Samuchchaya* (*Shaddarshanasamuccaya*) is a doxographical compendium attributed to Haribhadra Suri (ca. eighth century C.E.).
32. Gandhi was now in South Africa (Natal), serving the Indian community there.
33. I have not been able to locate a copy of this work. The title might be translated *Investigation of Religious Duty*.
34. Friedrich [Max] Müller (1823–1900) was perhaps Europe's foremost Indologist at this time; he was responsible for the first edition of the *Rgveda* and for the editorship of the *Sacred Books of the East*. The book mentioned by Gandhi was first published in the early 1890s.
35. Washington Irving (1783–1859) published the book mentioned by Gandhi in 1850.
36. Carlyle's essay on Muhammad is to be found in his *On Heroes and Hero-Worship*.
37. Gautama is generally assumed to have been the Buddha's family name.

18. "CHRISTIANITY IN THE REFLECTION OF HINDUISM"

1. Reprinted by permission from Küng and Moltmann, eds., *Christianity Among World Religions*, 31–37.
2. On Advaita (literally, "not-twoness") Vedanta see Chapter 16 n.2.
*3. Wach, *Types of Religious Experience*, 3.
*4. Potter, "Christ's Mission and Ours in Today's World."
*5. Hacker, *Theological Foundation of Evangelization*, 83.
*6. Galloway, *The Philosophy of Religion*, 122.
7. Rahner (1904–84) was one of the most influential Roman Catholic theologians of this century. His more important works on the theory of anonymous Christianity are: "Anonymous Christianity and the Missionary Task of the Church";

"Christianity and the Non-Christian Religions"; "Observations on the Problem of the 'Anonymous Christian' "; "On the Importance of the Non-Christian Religions for Salvation."

*8. *Prashnopanishad* III.6; *Brhadaranyakopanishad* IV.4.22, etc.

*9. He who realizes Brahman attains the highest. With reference to that very fact it has been declared: "Brahman is Reality, Consciousness, Infinitude; he who realises Him treasured in the cave, in the highest space, even as Brahman the omniscient, fulfills all wants at once" (*Taittiriyopanishad* II.1.1).

10. On the Vedas see notes to Chapter 15.

11. The Sanskrit term *ishta* means "chosen, sought, desired, wished," and is often used in combination with a term meaning "deity": *ishtadevata*.

12. "What is heard." Another way of referring to the Veda.

*13. "I ask you, of that Being who is to be known only from the Upanishads, who definitely projects those (all) beings and withdraws them into Himself, and who is at the same time transcendent" (*Brhadaranyakopanishad* III.9.26).

*14. Such a way of communication has already been suggested by many eminent theologians such as Prof. R. Panikkar, Swami Abhishiktananda and Fr. Bede Griffiths to name a few only.

19. VAISHNAVISM ON HANS KÜNG

1. Reprinted by permission from Yadav, "Vaisnavism on Hans Küng," 32–44.

2. A good companion piece to that reprinted here is Yadav's "Anthropomorphism and Cosmic Confidence."

3. Küng's more recent works on religious pluralism are *Christianity and the World Religions*; and *Christianity Among World Religions* (with Jürgen Moltmann) and *Christianity and Chinese Religions* (with Julia Ching).

4. All the quotations that follow are taken from the fourth chapter of Hans Küng's book *Freedom Today* (109–61).

5. "Lord Krishna" (Sanskrit)—this is an invocation of praise and homage to the god Krishna used by his devotees in India and the West.

6. "Meditation Buddhas." (Sanskrit)

7. On Radhakrishnan see Chapter 10 n.35.

8. "Immanent in action." (Latin)

9. This is Yadav's somewhat ironic label for the Church, referring to the Church's view of itself as the inheritor of God's promises to the people of Israel.

10. Also known as Benares. The proper Sanskritic form gets anglicized in various ways.

11. "Outside the Church no salvation." (Latin)

12. A *blik* is a comprehensive but unverifiable and unfalsifiable worldview, both against which and for which no imaginable evidence could count, and with which any state of affairs is compatible. Some philosophers of religion have thought that religious beliefs are like this. See especially the thought of R. M. Hare, discussed in Flew and Macintyre, eds., *New Essays in Philosophical Theology*, 96–130.

13. Yadav cites here part of §2 of the conciliar document *Nostra Aetate*. The wording he uses differs in minor particulars from that of the authorized English version. See Abbott, ed., *Documents of Vatican II*, 662.

14. Nicholas of Cusa (1401–64) was a German philosopher and theologian much

concerned with ecclesiastical reform. Pico della Mirandola (1463–94) was an Italian philosopher and a leading Renaissance humanist most of whose philosophical conclusions were rejected by the church. Erasmus (1467–1536) was an important humanist, philosopher and man of letters, born in Holland and active all over Europe.

15. Yadav's is a somewhat free rendering that does not appear to match precisely any of the standard translations. The *RSV* reads: "'Are you not like the Ethiopians to me, O people of Israel?' says the Lord. 'Did I not bring up Israel from the land of Egypt, and the Philistines from Caphtor and the Syrians from Kir?' "

16. "Original revelation." (German)

17. "Natural knowledge of God." (Latin)

18. "By right . . . in fact" . . . "in hope . . . in actuality." (Latin)

19. "The part that represents the whole." (Latin)

20. "The sign of Levi among the nations." (Latin)

21. Friedrich Nietzsche (1844–1900) was born in Prussia, studied at Leipzig, and wrote some of the most influential philosophical works of the second half of the nineteenth centry. Yadav makes passing reference to *Thus Spake Zarathustra* (1883–91) in what follows.

22. Udayana was a late-tenth-century philosopher/theologian of the Indian Nyaya school. An excellent translation and study of two of his works may be found in Tachikawa, *The Structure of the World in Udayana's Realism*. Ramanuja, active in the early twelfth century, was one of India's most influential representatives of the modified dualistic form of Vedanta (*vishishtadvaitavedanta*). Good introductions to his work may be found in Carman, *Theology of Ramanuja*, and Lipner, *The Face of Truth*. Vallabhacharya, active in the early sixteenth century, was a devotee of Vishnu and the founder of a religious sect; he too was a sophisticated philosopher/theologian.

23. On the mythology surrounding Krishna's birth see O'Flaherty, *Hindu Myths*, 204–13.

24. This Sanskrit word means "subliminal tendency" or "impulse."

25. "Beginningless tendency." (Sanskrit)

26. Dharmakirti (ca. 600–660) and Ratnakirti (early eleventh century) were Buddhists centrally concerned with problems of epistemology and cognition. A good example of the latter's work may be found translated and studied in McDermott, *An Eleventh Century Buddhist Logic of "Exists"*. The classic work on these matters is Stcherbatsky's *Buddhist Logic*. More recently see Hayes, *Dignaga on the Interpretation of Signs*. Hayes's work deals with a period in the development of Buddhist logico-epistemological thought that provides the groundwork for the thought of Dharmakirti and Ratnakirti.

27. The Nyaya religio-philosophical school of thought within Hinduism centered its attention upon logical and epistemological questions. On it see Potter, ed., *Indian Metaphysics and Epistemology*.

28. "Sacrifice." (Sanskrit)

29. Yadav here refers to the *Bhagavata Purana*'s (Hindu) expropriation of the figure of the Buddha as one more incarnation of Vishnu. For some discussion of this and similar stories see O'Flaherty, *Hindu Myths*, 231–38, and the bibliographical notes thereto. Dimmitt and Van Buitenen's *Classical Hindu Mythology* also has some

useful material on this. There is a complete English translation of the *Bhagavata Purana* by Sanyal.

30. "The deposit of faith." (Latin)

31. John T. Pawlikowski, O.S.M., is professor of social ethics at Chicago Theological Union. He has written extensively on Jewish-Christian dialogue. Yadav does not provide a reference for this quotation, and I have not been able to trace it in those of Pawlikowski's works to which I have access.

Works Cited

'Abduh, Muhammad. *Theology of Unity*. Translated by I. Musa'ad and Kenneth Cragg. London: Allen & Unwin, 1966.

'Ali, Amir. *The Spirit of Islam*. London: Christopher's, 1935.

Abbott, Walter M., S.J., ed. *Documents of Vatican II*. New York: Herder & Herder, 1966.

Abe, Masao. *Zen and Western Thought*. Edited by William R. Lafleur. Honolulu: University of Hawaii Press, 1985.

al-Attas, Syed Muhammad Naquib. *Islam, Secularism and the Philosophy of the Future*. London and New York: Mansell Press, 1985.

al-Ghazzali. *Réfutation excellente de la divinité de Jésus-Christ d'aprés les Évangiles*. Translated by R. Chidiac. Paris: E. Leroux, 1939.

——. *Tahafut al-falasifa*. Lahore: Pakistan Philosophical Congress, 1963.

Alexander, Edward. "Stealing the Holocaust." *Midstream* 26/9 (November 1980): 46–51.

Anawati, G. C. "Vers un dialogue islamo-chrétien." *Revue Thomiste* 64 (1964): 623–42.

Andersen, Dines and Smith, Helmer, eds. *Sutta Nipata*. London: Pali Text Society, 1913.

Anesaki, Masaharu. *Nichiren, the Buddhist Prophet*. Cambridge, MA: Harvard University Press, 1916.

Ansari, Zafar Ishaq. "Some Reflections on Islamic Bases for Dialogue with Jews and Christians." *Journal of Ecumenical Studies* 14 (1977): 433–47.

Arkoun, Muhammad. *Les Musulmans*. Paris, Beauchesne, 1971.

Arnold, Edwin. *The Song Celestial*. London: Routledge and Kegan Paul, 1970. First published in 1879.

——. *The Light of Asia*. New York: A. L. Burt, 1879.

Ayoub, Mahmoud. "Muslim Views of Christianity: Some Modern Examples." *IslamoChristiana* 10 (1984): 49–70.

Barth, Karl. *Church Dogmatics*. 4 vols. Edinburgh: T. & T. Clark, 1957–60.

Bauer, Yehuda. *The Holocaust in Historical Perspective*. Seattle: University of Washington Press, 1978.

Bauminger, Arieh. *Roll of Honour*. Tel Aviv: Hamenora Publishing House, 1971.

Bechert, Heinz. *Buddhismus, Staat, und Gesellschaft in den Ländern des Theravada-Buddhismus*. 3 vols. Frankfurt and Berlin, 1966–73.

——. *Die Lebenszeit des Buddha—das älteste feststehende Datum der indischen Geschichte?* Göttingen: Vandenhoeck & Ruprecht, 1986.

Berlin, George L. *Defending the Faith: Nineteenth-Century American Jewish Writing on Christianity and Jesus*. Albany, NY: State University of New York Press, 1989.

Bierman, John. *Righteous Gentile: The Story of Raoul Wallenberg*. New York: Viking Press, 1981.

Blavatsky, Helena Petrovna. *The Key to Theosophy*. Adyar, Madras: Theosophical Publishing House, 1961.

Brooks, Roger, ed. *Unanswered Questions: Theological Views of Jewish-Christian Relations*. Notre Dame, IN: University of Notre Dame Press, 1988.

Brown, Robert McAfee, and Gustav Weigel. *An American Dialogue*. New York: Doubleday, 1960.

Butler, Alfred Joshua. *The Arab Conquest of Egypt and the Last Thirty Years of the Roman Dominion*. Oxford: Clarendon Press, 1902.

Butler, Joseph. *Analogy of Religion, Natural and Revealed, to the Constitution and Course of Nature*. New York: Harper and Brothers, 1880. First published in 1736.

Bühler, George, trans. *The Laws of Manu*. Oxford: Clarendon Press, 1884.

Carlyle, Thomas. *On Heroes, Hero-Worship, and the Heroic in History*. London: Longmans, 1905. First published in 1841.

Carman, John B. *The Theology of Ramanuja*. New Haven: Yale University Press, 1974.

Caspar, R. "La foi musulmane selon le Coran." *Proche Orient Chrétien* 19 (1969): 167–72.

———. "Le salut des non-musulmans d'aprés Ghazali." *IBLA* 31 (1968): 301–13.

Chéhata, Chafik. *Essai d'une théorie générale de l'obligation en droit musulman*. Cairo: F. E. Noury, 1936.

Christian, William A., Sr. *Doctrines of Religious Communities*. New Haven: Yale University Press, 1987.

———. *Oppositions of Religious Doctrines*. London and New York: Macmillan, 1972.

Cohen, Arthur A. *The Myth of the Judeo-Christian Tradition*. New York: Harper and Row, 1970.

Collins, Steven. *Selfless Persons: Imagery and Thought in Theravada Buddhism*. Cambridge: Cambridge University Press, 1982.

Conze, Edward, trans. *The Short Prajnaparamita Texts*. London: Luzac, 1973.

Coward, Harold, ed. *Modern Indian Responses to Religious Pluralism*. Albany, NY: State University of New York Press, 1987.

———. *Pluralism: Challenge to World Religions*. Maryknoll, NY: Orbis Books, 1985.

Cox, Harvey. *The Secular City: Secularization and Urbanization in Theological Perspective*. New York: Macmillan, 1965.

Davies, Alan T., ed. *Anti-Semitism and the Foundations of Christianity*. New York: Paulist Press, 1979.

Dawidowicz, Lucy. Letter in "Letters from Readers." *Commentary* (May 1985): 18.

Dawood, N. J., trans. *The Koran*. 4th ed. Harmondsworth, England: Penguin Books, 1974.

Deutsch, Eliot. *Advaita Vedanta: A Philosophical Reconstruction*. Honolulu: University of Hawaii Press, 1969.

Dewart, Leslie. *The Future of Belief: Theism in a World Come of Age*. New York: Herder & Herder, 1966.

Dharmapala, Anagarika. *Return to Righteousness: A Collection of Speeches, Essays, and Letters of the Anagarika Dharmapala*. Edited by Ananda Guruge. Colombo, Sri Lanka: Government Press, 1965.

Dharmasiri, Gunapala. *A Buddhist Critique of the Christian Concept of God*. 2d. ed. Antioch, CA: Golden Leaves Publishing Co., 1988.

Dimmitt, Cornelia, and J.A.B. Van Buitenen, eds. *Classical Hindu Mythology: A Reader in the Sanskrit Puranas*. Philadelphia: Temple University Press, 1978.

Draper, J. W. *History of the Conflict Between Religion and Science.* New York: Appleton, 1897. First published 1874.

Dumoulin, Heinrich. *Zen Buddhism: A History.* 2 vols. London and New York: Macmillan, 1988–90.

Earhart, Byron, ed. *Religion in the Japanese Experience: Sources and Interpretations.* Encino/Belmont, CA: Dickenson Publishing Co., 1974.

Eliach, Yaffa. *Hasidic Tales of the Holocaust.* New York: Avon Books, 1983.

Fausbøll, V., ed. *Jataka.* 7 vols. London: Pali Text Society, 1877–97.

Feer, Léon, ed. *Samyutta Nikaya.* 6 vols. London: Pali Text Society, 1884–1904.

Finkel, Joshua, trans. "A Risala of al-Jahiz." *Journal of the American Oriental Society* 47 (1927): 322–34.

Fisher, Eugene J. "Covenant Theology and Jewish-Christian Dialogue." *American Journal of Theology and Philosophy* 9/1–2 (1988): 5–40.

———, A. James Rudin, and Marc H. Tanenbaum, eds. *Twenty Years of Jewish-Catholic Relations.* New York: Paulist Press, 1986.

Flew, Antony, and Alasdair Macintyre, eds. *New Essays in Philosophical Theology.* London: S.C.M. Press, 1955.

Flusser, David. *Jesus.* Translated by Ronald Walls. New York: Herder and Herder, 1969.

Freund, Else-Rahel. *Franz Rosenzweig's Philosophy of Existence: An Analysis of "The Star of Redemption."* The Hague: Martinus Nijhoff, 1979.

Friedman, Philip. *Roads to Extinction: Essays on the Holocaust.* Edited by Ada June Friedman. Philadelphia: Jewish Publication Society, 1980.

———. *Their Brother's Keeper.* New York: Crown Publishers, 1957.

Fujiwara Hirotatsu. *I Denounce Soka Gakkai.* Tokyo: Nisshin Hodo, 1970.

Galloway, George. *The Philosophy of Religion.* New York: Scribner's, 1920. First published in 1914.

Gandhi, Mohandas K. *The Story of My Experiments with Truth.* Translated [from Gujarati] by Mahadev Desai. New York: Dover Publications, 1983.

Gaudefroy-Demombynes, Maurice. *Mahomet.* Paris: A. Michel, 1957.

Geiger, Wilhelm, trans. *The Culavamsa.* London: Pali Text Society, 1973.

Gibb, H. A. R. "Pre-Islamic Monotheism in Arabia." *Harvard Theological Review* 55 (1962): 269–80.

Glatzer, Nahum N. *Franz Rosenzweig: His Life and Thought.* 2d. ed. New York: Schocken Books, 1961.

Goldman, Robert P. et al., trans. *The Ramayana of Valmiki: An Epic of Ancient India.* Princeton: Princeton University Press, 1984.

Gombrich, Richard F. *Theravada Buddhism: A Social History from Ancient Benares to Modern Colombo.* London and New York: Routledge and Kegan Paul, 1988.

Griffiths, Paul J. "Denaturalizing Discourse: Abhidharmikas and Propositionalists." Forthcoming in Frank Reynolds and David Tracy, eds., *Myth and Philosophy* (Albany, NY: State University of New York Press, 1990).

Gyatso, Tenzin [H. H. the XIVth Dalai Lama]. *The Bodhgaya Interviews.* Edited by José Ignacio Cabezón. Ithaca, New York: Snow Lion, 1988.

———. *Kindness, Clarity, and Insight.* Translated and edited by Jeffrey Hopkins, co-edited by Elizabeth Napper. Ithaca, NY: Snow Lion, 1984.

———. *My Land and My People.* New York: Potala Corporation, 1962.

Hacker, Paul. "Aspects of Neo-Hinduism as Contrasted with Surviving Traditional

Hinduism." In Hacker, *Kleine Schriften*, edited by Lambert Schmithausen (Wiesbaden: Harrassowitz, 1978), 580–608.

———. *Theological Foundation of Evangelization*. St. Augustin: Steyler, 1980.

Halbfass, Wilhelm. *India and Europe: An Essay in Understanding*. Albany, NY: State University of New York Press, 1988.

Hallencreutz, Carl F. *New Approaches to Men of Other Faiths, 1938–1968: A Theological Discussion*. Geneva: World Council of Churches, 1970.

Hausner, Gideon. *Justice in Jerusalem*. New York: Harper and Row, 1966.

Hayes, Richard P. *Dignaga on the Interpretation of Signs*. Studies of Classical India #9. Dordrecht and Boston: Kluwer, 1988.

———. "Principled Atheism in the Buddhist Tradition." *Journal of Indian Philosophy* 16 (1988): 5–28.

Heschel, Abraham Joshua. "No Religion is an Island." *Union Seminary Quarterly Review* 21 (1966): 117–33.

Hilberg, Raul. *The Destruction of the European Jews*. Chicago: Quadrangle Press, 1961.

Hill, W. D. P., trans. *The Holy Lake of the Acts of Rama: An English Translation of Tulsi Das's Ramacaritamanasa*. Oxford: Oxford University Press, 1952.

Hinnells, John R., ed. *A Handbook of Living Religions*. Harmondsworth, England: Penguin Books, 1984.

Hogg, James. *The Confessions of a Justified Sinner*. London: J. Sheils, 1898. First published in 1824.

Horner, I. B., trans. *The Collection of the Middle Length Sayings*. 3 vols. London: Pali Text Society, 1954–59.

Hurvitz, Leon, trans. *Scripture of the Lotus Blossom of the Fine Dharma*. New York: Columbia University Press, 1976.

Ibn 'Arabi. *Bezels of Wisdom*. Translated by A. W. J. Austin. New York: Paulist Press, 1980.

———. *Tarjuman al-ashwaq*. Translated by R. A. Nicholson. London: Theosophical Publishing House, 1978.

———. *La sagesse des prophètes*. Translated by T. Burckhardt. Paris, 1955.

Ibn Gabirol [Avicebron]. *Fons vitae*. Translated by Harry E. Wedeck. New York: Philosophical Library, 1962.

Ichimura Shohei. "Shunyata and Religious Pluralism." In Paul O. Ingram and Frederick J. Streng, eds., *Buddhist-Christian Dialogue: Mutual Renewal and Transformation* (Honolulu: University of Hawaii Press, 1986), 95–114.

Ikeda Daisaku. *A Lasting Peace: Collected Addresses of Daisaku Ikeda*. New York and Tokyo: John Weatherhill, 1981.

Irving, Washington. *Lives of Mahomet and His Successors*. London: Murray, 1850.

Jackson, Roger. "Dharmakirti's Refutation of Theism." *Philosophy East and West* 36 (1986): 315–48.

Jaini, Padmanabh S. *The Jaina Path of Purification*. Berkeley: University of California Press, 1979.

Jayatilleke, K. N. *The Buddhist Attitude to Other Religions*. Wheel Publications #216. Kandy: Buddhist Publication Society, 1975.

———. *Early Buddhist Theory of Knowledge*. London: Allen & Unwin, 1963.

Jha, Ganganatha, trans. *The Tattvasangraha of Shantarakshita with the Commentary of Kamalashila*. 2 vols. Gaekwad's Oriental Series, #80, #83. Baroda: Oriental Institute, 1937, 1939. Reprinted, New Delhi: Munshiram Manoharlal, 1986.

John of Damascus. "On the Heresy of the Ishmaelites." In *St. John of Damascus*, trans. Frederick H. Chase (New York: Christian Heritage, 1958), 153–63.

Jordens, J.T.F. *Dayananda Sarasvati: His Life and Ideas*. Delhi: Oxford University Press, 1978.

———. "Gandhi and Religious Pluralism." In *Modern Indian Responses to Religious Pluralism*, ed. Harold G. Coward (Albany, NY: State University of New York Press, 1987), 3–17.

Kasulis, Thomas P. "The Kyoto School and the West: Review and Evaluation" *Eastern Buddhist* 15 (1982): 125–44.

———. *Zen Action, Zen Person*. Honolulu: University of Hawaii Press, 1981.

Kerr, David A. "The Problem of Christianity in Muslim Perspective: Implications for Christian Mission." *International Bulletin of Missionary Research* (1981): 152–62.

Kirimura Yasuji. "About Daisaku Ikeda." In *Daisaku Ikeda, A Lasting Peace: Collected Addresses of Daisaku Ikeda* (New York: John Weatherhill, 1981), 281–91.

Kiyota, Minoru et al., eds. *Japanese Buddhism: Its Tradition, New Religions and Interaction with Christianity*. Los Angeles: Buddhist Books International, 1987.

Koenig, Franz. "Le monothéisme dans le monde contemporain." *MIDEO* 8 (1964–66): 407–22.

Kroner, Helga, and Leon Klenicki, eds. *Issues in the Jewish-Christian Dialogue: Jewish Perspectives on Covenant*. New York: Seabury Press, 1983.

Küng, Hans, and Jürgen Moltmann, eds. *Christianity Among World Religions. Concilium*, #183. Edinburgh: T. & T. Clark, 1986.

Küng, Hans, ed. *Christianity and the World Religions: Paths to Dialogue with Islam, Hinduism, and Buddhism*. Garden City, NY: Doubleday, 1986.

———. *Freedom Today*. New York: Sheed and Ward, 1966.

Laqueur, Walter. *The Terrible Secret*. Boston: Little, Brown, 1981.

Lecky, W.E.H. *History of European Morals from Augustus to Charlemagne*. New York: Appleton, 1870.

Lipner, Julius. *The Face of Truth: A Study of Meaning and Metaphysics in the Vedantic Theology of Ramanuja*. Albany, NY: State University of New York Press, 1986.

Littell, Franklin H. *The Crucifixion of the Jews*. New York: Harper and Row, 1975.

———. *The German Phoenix: Men and Movements in the Church in Germany*. New York: Doubleday, 1960.

Lopez, Donald S., Jr. "The Dalai Lama of Tibet." In Donald S. Lopez, Jr.and Steven Rockefeller, eds., *The Christ and the Bodhisattva* (Albany, NY: State University of New York Press, 1987), 209–16.

Luccioni, Gennie. "Le mythe aujourd'hui." *Esprit* (New Series, April 1971): 609–12.

Maimonides, Moses. *The Guide of the Perplexed*. Translated with an introduction and notes by Shlomo Pines. With an introductory essay by Leo Strauss. Chicago: University of Chicago Press, 1963.

———. *Mishneh Torah: A New Translation with Commentaries, Notes, and Tables*. Translated by Eliyahu Touger. New York and Jerusalem: Maznaim, 1986.

Maitland, Edward [with Anna Kingsford]. *The Perfect Way; or The Finding of Christ*. New York: The Metaphysical Publishing Co., 1901.

———. *The Story of the New Gospel of Interpretation Told by Its Surviving Recipient*. London: Lumley, 1894.

Malalgoda, Kitsiri. *Buddhism in Sinhalese Society 1750–1900: A Study of Religious*

Revival and Change. Berkeley: University of California Press, 1976.

Maritain, Jacques. *Existence and the Existent*. Translated by Lewis Galantire and Gerald B. Phelan. New York: Vintage Books, 1966.

———. *Redeeming the Time*. Translated by Harry Lorin Binsse. London: Geoffrey Bles, 1946.

———. *The Range of Reason*. London: Geoffrey Bles, 1953.

McDermott, A. C. Senape, trans. *An Eleventh Century Buddhist Logic of "Exists"*. Foundations of Language, supplementary series, vol. 11. Dordrecht: Reidel, 1970.

McKain, David W. *Christianity: Some Non-Christian Appraisals*. New York: McGraw Hill, 1964.

Mendes-Flohr, Paul, ed. *The Philosophy of Franz Rosenzweig*. Hanover and London: University of New England Press, 1988.

Miller, Barbara Stoler, trans. *The Bhagavad-Gita: Krishna's Counsel in Time of War*. New York: Bantam Books, 1986.

Moliére. *Les fourberies de Scapin*. Marseille: Laffitte, 1981.

Monod, Jacques. *Le hasard et la nécessité*. Translated into English *Chance and Necessity* by Austryn Wainhouse. New York: Knopf, 1971.

Morley, John F. *Vatican Diplomacy and the Jews During the Holocaust, 1939–43*. New York: Ktav Publishing Co., 1980.

Morris, R., ed. *Puggalapannati*. London: Pali Text Society, 1883.

Morris, R., E. Hardy, M. Hunt, and C.A.F. Rhys Davids, eds. *Anguttara Nikaya*. 6 vols. London: Pali Text Society, 1885–1910.

Müller, Friedrich [Max]. *India — What Can It Teach Us?* London: Longmans, 1883.

Nagao, Gadjin. "On the Theory of Buddha-Body (Buddha-kaya)." *Eastern Buddhist* 6 (1973): 25–53.

Nasr, Seyyed Hossein. *Knowledge and the Sacred*. New York: Crossroad, 1981.

Nicholson, R. A. *Rumi: Poet and Mystic*. London: Allen & Unwin, 1950.

Niebuhr, Reinhold. *Pious and Secular America*. New York: Scribner's, 1958.

———. *The Self and the Dramas of History*. London: Faber and Faber, 1956.

Nietzsche, Friedrich. *Thus Spake Zarathustra*. London: Dent, 1958. First published 1883–91.

Nishitani Keiji. *Religion and Nothingness*. Translated by Jan Van Bragt. Berkeley: University of California Press, 1982.

Novak, David. "The Covenants We Share: A Jewish Perspective." *Face to Face: An Interreligious Bulletin* 12 (1985).

———. "The Quest for the Jewish Jesus." *Modern Judaism* 8/2 (1988): 119–38.

Nusslé, Henri. *Dialogue avec l'Islam*. Neuchatel: Delachaux et Niestlé, 1949.

Nyanamoli [Bhikkhu], trans. *The Path of Purification*. 2 vols. Berkeley and London: Shambhala Press, 1976.

Oberhammer, Gerhard, ed. *Inklusivismus: eine indische Denkform*. Vienna: De Nobili Research Library, 1983.

O'Flaherty, Wendy Doniger. *Hindu Myths: A Sourcebook Translated from the Sanskrit*. Harmondsworth, England: Penguin Books, 1975.

Peck, Abraham J. "The Very Depths of Our Pain." In Roger Brooks, ed., *Unanswered Questions: Theological Views of Jewish-Christian Relations* (Notre Dame, IN: University of Notre Dame Press, 1988), 176–88.

Pelikan, Jaroslav. *The Emergence of the Catholic Tradition (100–600)*. Chicago and London: University of Chicago Press, 1971.

Penkower, Monty. *The Jews Were Expendable*. Urbana: University of Illinois Press, 1983.

Plantinga, Alvin. *God and Other Minds*. Ithaca, NY: Cornell University Press, 1967.

Potter, Karl, ed. *Advaita Vedanta up to Shamkara and His Pupils*. Vol. 3 of *The Encyclopaedia of Indian Philosophies*. Princeton: Princeton University Press, 1981.

————. *Indian Metaphysics and Epistemology: The Tradition of Nyaya-Vaisheshika up to Gangesha*. Vol. 2 of *The Encyclopedia of Indian Philosophies*. Princeton: Princeton University Press, 1977.

Potter, Philip. "Christ's Mission and Ours in Today's World." *International Review of Mission* 62 (1973): 144–57.

Pye, Michael. *Skilful Means*. London: Duckworth, 1978.

Qur'an. See Dawood.

Qutb, Sayyid. *Islam: The Religion of the Future*. Beirut and Damascus: The Holy Koran Publishing House, 1977.

Radhakrishnan, Sarvepalli. *Eastern Religions and Western Thought*. 2d ed. Oxford: Oxford University Press, 1940.

Rahman, Fazlur. *Major Themes of the Qur'an*. 2d rev. ed. Minneapolis: Bibliotheca Islamica, 1989.

Rahner, Karl. "Anonymous Christianity and the Missionary Task of the Church." In Rahner, *Theological Investigations*, vol. 12 (New York: Seabury Press, 1974), 161–78.

————. "Christianity and the Non-Christian Religions." In Rahner, *Theological Investigations*, vol. 5 (Baltimore: Helicon, 1966), 115–34.

————. "Observations on the Problem of the 'Anonymous Christian.' " In Rahner, *Theological Investigations*, vol. 14 (New York: Seabury Press, 1976), 280–94.

————. "On the Importance of the Non-Christian Religions for Salvation." In Rahner, *Theological Investigations*, vol. 18 (New York: Crossroad, 1983), 288–95.

Ramm, Bernard L. *The Evangelical Heritage*. Waco, TX: Word Books, 1973.

Rauche, G. A. *Contemporary Philosophical Alternatives and the Crisis of Truth*. The Hague: Martinus Nijhoff, 1970.

Rhys Davids, C.A.F., ed. *Visuddhimagga*. 2 vols. London: Pali Text Society, 1920–21.

Rhys Davids, T. W., and J. Estlin Carpenter, eds. *Digha Nikaya*. 3 vols. London: Pali Text Society, 1890–1911.

Richards, Glyn, ed. *A Sourcebook of Modern Hinduism*. London: Curzon Press, 1985.

Richmond, James. *Theology and Metaphysics*. London: S.C.M. Press, 1970.

Rose, R. B. "Islam and the Development of Personal Status Laws Among Christian Dhimmis." *Muslim World* 72 (1982): 159–79.

Rosenberg, Stuart E. *The Christian Problem*. New York: Hippocrene Books, 1986.

Rosenstock-Huessy, Eugen, ed. *Judaism Despite Christianity: The "Letters on Christianity and Judaism" Between Eugen Rosenstock-Huessy and Franz Rosenzweig*. New York: Schocken Books, 1971.

Rosenzweig, Franz. *The Star of Redemption*. Translated from the second German edition by William W. Hallo. New York: Holt, Rinehart and Winston, 1970. First German edition published 1921.

Rousseau, Richard W., ed. *Christianity and Islam: The Struggling Dialogue*. Scranton, PA: Ridge Row Press, 1985.

————. *Christianity and Judaism: The Deepening Dialogue*. Scranton, PA: Ridge Row Press, 1983.

Ryle, Gilbert. *The Concept of Mind*. London: Hutchinson's University Library, 1949.

Sale, George, trans. *The Koran: Commonly Called the Alcoran of Mohammed*. Many editions throughout the nineteenth century.

Samartha, Stanley J. and John B. Taylor, eds. *Christian-Muslim Dialogue: Papers Presented at the Broumana Consultation, 12–18 July 1972*. Geneva: World Council of Churches, 1973.

Sanyal, J. M., trans. *The Shrimad-Bhagabatam of Krishna-Dwaipayana Vyasa*. 5 vols. 2d ed. Calcutta: Oriental Publishing Company, 1950.

————. *Bhagavata Purana*. Calcutta: University of Calcutta Press, 1930–34.

Sarasvati, Dayananda. *The Light of Truth*. 2d ed. New Delhi: Sarvadeshik Arya Pratinidhi Sabha, 1975.

Schuoun, Frijthof. *Christianity/Islam — Essays on Esoteric Ecumenism*. Translated by G. Polit. Bloomington, IN: Indiana University Press, 1985.

Sharma, Arvind, ed. *Neo-Hindu Views of Christianity*. Leiden: E. J. Brill, 1988.

Sheard, Robert B. *Interreligious Dialogue in the Catholic Church Since Vatican II: An Historical and Theological Study*. Toronto Studies in Theology, vol. 31. Lewiston/Queenston: Edwin Mellen Press, 1987.

Shepard, William. "A Modernist View of Islam and Other Religions." *The Muslim World* 65/2 (1975): 79–92.

Shermis, Michael. "Recent Publications in the Jewish-Christian Dialogue: An Annotated Bibliography." *American Journal of Theology and Philosophy* 9/1–2 (1988): 137–42.

————. *Jewish-Christian Relations: An Annotated Bibliography and Resource Guide*. Bloomington, IN: University Press, 1988.

Signer, Michael A. "*Speculum Concilii*: Through the Mirror Brightly," in Roger Brooks, ed., *Unanswered Questions: Theological Views of Jewish-Christian Relations* (Notre Dame, IN: University of Notre Dame Press, 1988), 105–27.

Smith, Wilfred Cantwell. *Towards a World Theology*. Maryknoll, NY: Orbis Books, 1990.

Söderblom, Nathan. *The Nature of Revelation*. New York: Oxford University Press, 1933.

Spae, Joseph J. *Buddhist-Christian Empathy*. Chicago: The Chicago Institute of Theology and Culture, 1980.

Stcherbatsky, Th. *Buddhist Logic*. 2 vols. New York: Dover Publications, 1962. First published as vol. 16 of the *Bibliotheca Buddhica*, Leningrad: Academy of Sciences of the USSR, 1930–32.

Strawson, P. F. *Individuals*. London: Methuen, 1965.

Suzuki, Daisetz Teitaro. *Mysticism: Christian and Buddhist*. London: Allen & Unwin, 1957.

————. *Outlines of Mahayana Buddhism*. New York: Schocken Books, 1963.

Swidler, Leonard, ed. *Toward a Universal Theology of Religion*. Maryknoll, NY: Orbis Books, 1987.

Tachikawa Musashi. *The Structure of the World in Udayana's Realism: A Study of the Lakshanavali and the Kiranavali*. Studies of Classical India #4. Dordrecht: Reidel, 1981.

Talbi, Mohamed. "Islam and Dialogue — Some Reflections on a Current Topic." In

Richard W. Rousseau, ed., *Christianity and Islam: The Struggling Dialogue* (Scranton, PA: Ridge Row Press, 1985), 53–73.

———. "Possibilities and Conditions for a Better Understanding Between Islam and the West." *Journal of Ecumenical Studies* 25/2 (1988): 161–93.

Talmage, Frank Ephraim, ed. *Disputation and Dialogue: Readings in the Jewish-Christian Encounter.* New York: Ktav Publishing Co., 1975.

Tanenbaum, Marc H., Marvin R. Wilson, and A. James Rudin, eds. *Evangelicals and Jews in Conversation on Scripture, Theology, and History.* Grand Rapids, MI: Baker Book House, 1978.

Tillich, Paul, and Shin'ichi Hisamatsu. "Dialogues East and West: Conversations between Dr. Paul Tillich and Dr. Shin'ichi Hisamatsu." *Eastern Buddhist* 5/2 (1972).

Tillich, Paul. *Christianity and the Encounter of the World Religions.* New York: Columbia University Press, 1963.

———. *Systematic Theology.* Chicago: University of Chicago Press, 1967.

Tolstoy, Leo. *The Gospels in Brief.* Croydon: The Brotherhood Publishing Company, 1896.

———. *The Kingdom of God Is Within You.* New York: Scribner's, 1899. First published in English in 1894.

———. *What to Do?* London: W. Scott, 1888.

Trenckner, V., R. Chalmers, and C.A.F. Rhys Davids, eds. *Majjhima Nikaya.* 3 vols. London: Pali Text Society, 1888–1925.

Trenckner, V., ed. *Milindapanha.* London: Pali Text Society, 1880.

Updike, John. *'S'.* New York: Knopf, 1987.

Vallée, Gérard. *Mouvement oécumenique et religions non-chrétiennes: un début oécumenique sur la rencontre interreligieuse de Tambaram àga Uppsala (1928–1968).* Montreal: Bellarmine, 1975.

Van Buitenen, J.A.B. *The Bhagavadgita in the Mahabharata: A Bilingual Edition.* Chicago and London: University of Chicago Press, 1981.

Van den Berg, J., and Ernestine G.E. Van der Wall, eds. *Jewish-Christian Relations in the Seventeenth Century: Studies and Documents.* International Archives of the History of Ideas #119. Dordrecht/Boston/London: Kluwer, 1988.

Vivekananda [Swami]. *The Complete Works of Swami Vivekananda.* 10th ed. Calcutta: Advaita Ashrama, 1972.

Waardenburg, Jacques. "Possibilities and Conditions for a Better Understanding Between Islam and the West." *Journal of Ecumenical Studies* 25/2 (1988): 161–93.

———. "World Religions as Seen in the Light of Islam." In *Islam: Past Influence and Present Challenge,* ed. A. Welch and P. Cachia (Edinburgh: Edinburgh University Press, 1979), 245–75.

Wach, Joachim. *Types of Religious Experience.* Chicago: University of Chicago Press, 1972.

Watt, W. Montgomery. *Islamic Revelation in the Modern World.* Edinburgh: Edinburgh University Press, 1969.

———. *Muhammad at Mecca.* Oxford: Clarendon Press, 1953.

———. *Muslim Intellectual: A Study of al-Ghazali.* Edinburgh: Edinburgh University Press, 1963.

Weber, Max. *Essays in Sociology.* Translated by H. H. Gerth and C. Wright Mills. New York: Oxford University Press, 1946.

———. *The Sociology of Religion*. Translated by Ephraim Fischoff. Boston: Beacon Press, 1963.

Wisdom, John. *Paradox and Discovery*. Oxford: Basil Blackwell, 1965.

Wojtyla, Karol [John Paul II]. "The Attitude of the Church Towards the Followers of Other Religions: Reflections and Orientations on Dialogue and Mission." *Bulletin* [of the Secretariat for Non-Christians, Vatican City] 56 (1984): 126–41.

Woods, J. H., D. Kosambi, and I. B. Horner, eds. *Papancasudani*. 5 vols. London: Pali Text Society, 1922–38.

World Council of Churches. *Christians Meeting Muslims: WCC Papers on 10 Years of Christian-Muslim Dialogue*. Geneva: World Council of Churches, 1977.

———. *Guidelines on Dialogue with People of Living Faiths and Ideologies*. Geneva: World Council of Churches, 1979.

Wyman, David S. *The Abandonment of the Jews: America and the Holocaust, 1941–45*. New York: Pantheon Books, 1984.

Yadav, Bibhuti S. "Anthropomorphism and Cosmic Confidence." In *Toward a Universal Theology of Religion*, ed. Leonard Swidler (Maryknoll, NY: Orbis Books, 1987), 175–91.

———. "Vaishnavism on Hans Küng: A Hindu Theology of Religious Pluralism." *Religion and Society* 27/2 (1980): 32–44.

Yahil, Lenny. *The Rescue of Danish Jewry*. Philadelphia: Jewish Publication Society, 1969.

Young, Richard F. *Resistant Hinduism: Sanskrit Sources on Anti-Christian Apologetics in Early Nineteenth-Century India*. Publications of the De Nobili Research Library #8. Vienna: De Nobili Research Library, 1981.

Zaehner, R. C., trans. *The Bhagavad-Gita*. Oxford: Clarendon Press, 1969.

Index